Welcome Michael Ahearne.

Dr. Michael Ahearne, currently **Associate Professor of Marketing** at the University of Houston's Bauer School of Business, joins the Manning/Reece team. Dr. Ahearne **teaches sales** and **sales management** courses in the United States, Europe, and Asia to more than **one thousand undergraduate and graduate students** each year.

Outside of the classroom, Dr. Ahearne serves as the **associate editor** and **editor elect** for the *Journal of Personal Selling and Sales Management*. Dr. Ahearne also holds the position of executive director of the **Sales Excellence Institute at the University of Houston**.

To learn more about Dr. Ahearne and the work he is currently doing, please visit the following sites: www.bauer.uh.edu/marketing, www.salesexcellenceinstitute.org, www.jpssm.org.

NEW Integrated CRM Program!

Selling Today **was the first sales text to** bring you the contact-based ACT! software. In that same tradition, the eleventh edition of *Selling Today* is the **first sales text to provide you free online access to Salesforce.com**, the easy-to-learn, account-based number-one Customer Relationship Management (CRM) product used by sales organizations throughout the world. Check out why more than 41,000 sales organizations have also switched to Salesforce.com for their sales, marketing, and customer-service functions. Access www.salesforce.com, and click on the e-learning demo video for more information.

This edition is the first and only sales text to provide you with clearly written, text based Customer Relationship Management (CRM) application exercises. Using the Salesforce.com software, these exercises will prepare the students to **master the functions and understand the reports** used by salespeople today.

Selling Today **is also the first and only sales text** to provide an actual prospect database, exclusively loaded into the Selling Today/salesforce.com software. All at various stages in the sales cycle, students will access previously recorded account information on 20 prospects with $1.2 million in forecasted sales, to **create and communicate successful sales strategies** learned in the text. See Appendix 2 for more information.

OTHER MARKETING TITLES OF INTEREST

PRINCIPLES OF MARKETING

Marketing: An Introduction and MyMarketingLab Package, 9/E
Armstrong & Kotler
ISBN-10: 0138148201 ■ ISBN-13: 9780138148201

**Marketing Plan Handbook and
Marketing Plan Pro Package, 3/E**
Wood
ISBN-10: 0135136288 ■ ISBN-13: 9780135136287

Principles of Marketing, 13/E
Kotler & Armstrong
ISBN-10: 0136079415 ■ ISBN-13: 9780136079415

Marketing: Real People, Real Choices, 6/E
Solomon, Marshall & Stuart
ISBN-10: 0136054218 ■ ISBN-13: 9780136054214

Hasselback Marketing Faculty Guide, 13e
Hasselback
ISBN-10: 0136010024 ■ ISBN-13: 9780136010029

Marketing Ethics: Cases and Readings, 1/E
Murphy & Laczniak
ISBN-10: 0131330888 ■ ISBN-13: 9780131330887

CONSUMER BEHAVIOR

Consumer Behavior, 8/E
Solomon
ISBN-10: 0136015964 ■ ISBN-13: 9780136015963

Consumer Behavior, 9/E
Schiffman & Kanuk
ISBN-10: 0131869604 ■ ISBN-13: 9780131869608

Critical Thinking in Consumer Behavior: Cases and Experiential Exercises, 1/E
Graham
ISBN-10: 0131133225 ■ ISBN-13: 9780131133228

Consumer Behavior and Managerial Decision Making, 2/E
Kardes
ISBN-10: 0130916021 ■ ISBN-13: 9780130916020

MARKETING RESEARCH

Basic Marketing Research Using Microsoft Excel Data Analysis, 2/E
Burns & Bush
ISBN-10: 0132059584 ■ ISBN-13: 9780132059589

Marketing Research: An Applied Orientation and SPSS 14.0 Student CD, 5/E
Malhotra
ISBN-10: 0132221179 ■ ISBN-13: 9780132221177

Basic Marketing Research: A Decision-Making Approach with Qualtrics Access Card, 3/E
Malhotra
ISBN-10: 013715593X ■ ISBN-13: 9780137155934

Marketing Research & SPSS 13.0 Student CD Pkg., 5/E
Burns & Bush
ISBN-10: 0132280353 ■ ISBN-13: 9780132280358

Multivariate Data Analysis, 7/E
Hair, Black, Babin & Anderson
ISBN-10: 0138132631 ■ ISBN-13: 9780138132637

INTERNATIONAL MARKETING

Global Marketing, 5/E
Keegan & Green
ISBN-10: 0131754343 ■ ISBN-13: 9780131754348

Global Marketing Management, 7/E
Keegan
ISBN-10: 0130332712 ■ ISBN-13: 9780130332714

International Marketing Research, 1/E
Kumar
ISBN-10: 0130453862 ■ ISBN-13: 9780130453860

MARKETING MANAGEMENT

Marketing Management, 13/E
Kotler & Keller
ISBN-10: 0136009980 ■ ISBN-13: 9780136009986

A Framework for Marketing Management, 4/E
Kotler & Keller
ISBN-10: 0136026605 ■ ISBN-13: 9780136026600

A Framework for Marketing Management Integrated with PharmaSim, 4/E
Kotler & Keller
ISBN-10: 0136083447 ■ ISBN-13: 9780136083443

Market-Based Management, 5/E
Best
ISBN-10: 0132336537 ■ ISBN-13: 9780132336536

Marketing Management, 3/E
Winer
ISBN-10: 0131963341 ■ ISBN-13: 9780131963344

Strategic Marketing Problems: Cases and Comments, 11/E
Kerin & Peterson
ISBN-10: 0131871528 ■ ISBN-13: 9780131871526

SELLING

Selling Today: Creating Customer Value, 11/E
Manning, Reece & Ahearne
ISBN-10: 013207995X ■ ISBN-13: 9780132079952

SALES MANAGEMENT

Sales Management: Shaping Future Sales Leaders, 1/E
Tanner, Honeycutt & Erffmeyer
ISBN-10: 0132324121 ■ ISBN-13: 9780132324120

RETAILING

Retail Management: A Strategic Approach, 10/E
Berman & Evans
ISBN-10: 0131870165 ■ ISBN-13: 9780131870161

ENTERTAINMENT AND SPORTS MARKETING

Sports Marketing: A Strategic Perspective, 4/E
Shank
ISBN-10: 0132285355 ■ ISBN-13: 9780132285353

Entertainment Marketing & Communication: Selling Branded Performance, People, and Places, 1/E
Sayre
ISBN-10: 0131986228 ■ ISBN-13: 9780131986220

SERVICES MARKETING

Services Marketing: People, Technology, Strategy, 6/E
Lovelock & Wirtz
ISBN-10: 0131875523 ■ ISBN-13: 9780131875524

Principles of Service Marketing and Management, 2/E
Lovelock & Wright
ISBN-10: 0130404675 ■ ISBN-13: 9780130404671

MARKETING CHANNELS

Marketing Channels, 7/E
Coughlan, Anderson, Stern & El-Ansary
ISBN-10: 0131913468 ■ ISBN-13: 9780131913462

LOGISTICS/SUPPLY CHAIN MANAGEMENT

Contemporary Logistics, 9/E
Murphy, Jr. & Wood
ISBN-10: 013156207X ■ ISBN-13: 9780131562073

Business Logistics/Supply Chain Management and Logware CD Package, 5/E
Ballou
ISBN-10: 0131076590 ■ ISBN-13: 9780131076594

BUSINESS TO BUSINESS MARKETING

Business Market Management: Understanding, Creating, and Delivering Value, 3/E
Anderson, Narus & Narayandas
ISBN-10: 0136000886 ■ ISBN-13: 9780136000884

NEW PRODUCT MANAGEMENT

Design and Marketing of New Products, 2/E
Urban & Hauser
ISBN-10: 0132015676 ■ ISBN-13: 9780132015677

HIGH-TECH MARKETING

Marketing of High-Technology Products and Innovations, 3/E
Mohr, Sengupta & Slater
ISBN-10: 0136049966 ■ ISBN-13: 9780136049968

BRAND MANAGEMENT, BRAND STRATEGY

Best Practice Cases in Branding, 3/E
Keller
ISBN-10: 013188865X ■ ISBN-13: 9780131888654

Strategic Brand Management, 3/E
Keller
ISBN-10: 0131888595 ■ ISBN-13: 9780131888593

PRICING

The Strategy and Tactics of Pricing: A Guide to Growing More Profitably, 4/E
Nagle & Hogan
ISBN-10: 0131856774 ■ ISBN-13: 9780131856776

DIRECT MARKETING

Contemporary Direct and Interactive Marketing, 2/E
Spiller & Baier
ISBN-10: 0136086101 ■ ISBN-13: 9780136086109

MARKETING ON THE INTERNET

E-Marketing, 5/E
Strauss & Frost
ISBN-10: 0136154409 ■ ISBN-13: 9780136154402

Digital Business: Concepts and Strategy, 2/E
Coupey
ISBN-10: 0131400975 ■ ISBN-13: 9780131400979

NONPROFIT MARKETING

Strategic Marketing for Nonprofit Organizations, 7/E
Andreasen & Kotler
ISBN-10: 013175372X ■ ISBN-13: 9780131753723

INTRO TO ADVERTISING AND IMC

Advertising: Principles and Practices, 8/E
Moriarty, Mitchell & Wells
ISBN-10: 0132224151 ■ ISBN-13: 9780132224154

Kleppner's Advertising Procedure, 17/E
Lane, King & Russell
ISBN-10: 0132308290 ■ ISBN-13: 9780132308298

Integrated Advertising, Promotion, and Marketing Communications, 4/E
Clow & Baack
ISBN-10: 0136079423 ■ ISBN-13: 9780136079422

PUBLIC RELATIONS

The Practice of Public Relations, 10/E
Seitel
ISBN-10: 0132304511 ■ ISBN-13: 9780132304511

Cutlip and Center's Effective Public Relations, 10/E
Broom
ISBN-10: 0136029698 ■ ISBN-13: 9780136029694

Public Relations Practices: Managerial Case Studies and Problems, 7/E
Center, Jackson, Smith & Stansberry
ISBN-10: 0132341360 ■ ISBN-13: 9780132341363

11th Edition

Selling Today

Creating Customer Value

Gerald L. Manning
Des Moines Area Community College

Barry L. Reece
Virginia Polytechnic Institute and State University

Michael Ahearne
University of Houston

PRENTICE HALL
Upper Saddle River, New Jersey, 07458

Library of Congress Cataloging-in-Publication Data

Manning, Gerald L.
  Selling today: creating customer value / Gerald L. Manning, Barry L. Reece,
Michael Ahearne.—11th ed.
      p.   cm.
Includes bibliographical references and index.
ISBN 978-0-13-207995-2
1. Selling. I. Reece, Barry L.   II. Ahearne, Michael.   III. Title.
HF5438.25.M35 2010
658.85—dc22

2008036662

Acquisitions Editor: James Heine
Editorial Director: Sally Yagan
Product Development Manager: Ashley Santora
Editorial Project Manager: Melissa Pellerano
Editorial Assistant: Karin Williams
Director of Marketing: Patrice Lumumba Jones
Marketing Manager: Anne Fahlgren
Marketing Assistant: Susan Osterlitz
Permissions Project Manager: Charles Morris
Senior Managing Editor: Judy Leale
Associate Managing Editor: Suzanne DeWorken
Production Project Manager: Karalyn Holland
Senior Operations Specialist: Arnold Vila
Art Director: Anthony Gemmellaro
Designer: Pronk & Associates Inc.
Cover Designer: John Christiana
Cover Illustration/Photo: Veer Inc.
Director, Image Resource Center: Melinda Patelli
Manager, Rights and Permissions: Zina Arabia
Manager, Visual Research: Beth Brenzel
Image Permission Coordinator: Joanne Dippel
Photo Researcher: Poyee Oster
Manager, Cover Visual Research & Permissions: Karen Sanatar
Composition: BookMasters, Inc.
Full-Service Project Management: Sharon Anderson/BookMasters, Inc.
Printer/Binder: Quebecor World Book Services/Taunton
Typeface: 10/12 Times

Credits and acknowledgments borrowed from other sources and reproduced, with permission, in this textbook appear on appropriate page within text (or on page 495).

Microsoft® and Windows® are registered trademarks of the Microsoft Corporation in the U.S.A. and other countries. Screen shots and icons reprinted with permission from the Microsoft Corporation. This book is not sponsored or endorsed by or affiliated with the Microsoft Corporation.

Pearson Education Ltd., London
Pearson Education Singapore, Pte. Ltd
Pearson Education, Canada, Inc.
Pearson Education–Japan
Pearson Education Australia PTY, Limited

Pearson Education North Asia, Ltd., Hong Kong
Pearson Educación de Mexico, S.A. de C.V.
Pearson Education Malaysia, Pte. Ltd
Pearson Education Upper Saddle River, New Jersey

Prentice Hall
is an imprint of

10 9 8 7 6 5 4 3 2 1
ISBN-13: 978-0-13-207995-2
ISBN-10:   0-13-207995-X

To our wives (Beth Hall Manning and Vera Marie Reece) whose patience and support make our work possible.

—Jerry and Barry

To my wife Jessica and my children Molly and Jake.

—Mike

Brief Contents

Contents

Preface

As competition intensifies and transcends national borders, professional selling as a discipline has become a core part of the curriculum of numerous business schools. As instructors ourselves, we believe it is essential to provide students in professional selling with a solid understanding of the fundamentals of selling and new selling frameworks so they can compete in the real world.

This can only be achieved with a selling text that covers up-to-date academic topics and provides rich application materials. At the same time, our goal is to present complex cutting-edge sales topics in a manner that is accessible, systematic, and easy for students to understand. With these objectives in mind, we build on and expand the theme of creating and delivering value to bring you this new edition of *Selling Today: Creating Customer Value*.

The revision process begins with a thorough review of several hundred articles, books, and research reports. The authors also study popular sales training programs such as Conceptual Selling, SPIN Selling, Integrity Selling, and Solution Selling. These training programs are used by major corporations such as Microsoft, Marriott, Principal Financial Group, Wells Fargo Bank, UPS, SAS Institute, and Xerox Corporation. The authors also invest heavily in developing new, rich supplemental materials that have always been the edge of this book. Also, an extensive and much appreciated academic review process influences and guides decisions made during the revision.

Building on Traditional Strengths

Selling Today: Creating Customer Value has been successful because the authors continue to build on strengths that have been enthusiastically praised by instructors and students. These strengths have resulted in *Selling Today* becoming the number one selling international book on personal selling. In addition to this new 11th U.S. edition, two Chinese editions, a Spanish, Croatian, Indonesian, and Canadian edition, and sales of the International Edition in 31 additional countries have proven the appeal of this book throughout the world.

Previous editions of Selling Today have chronicled the evolution of consultative selling, strategic selling, partnering, customer relationship management, and value-added selling. This edition provides new material on each of these important concepts.

1. **The four broad strategic areas of personal selling,** introduced in Chapter 1, serve as a catalyst for skill development and professional growth throughout the textbook. Success in selling depends heavily on the student's ability to develop relationship, product, customer, and presentation strategies. Salespeople who have achieved long-term success in personal selling have mastered the skills needed in each of these four strategic areas.

2. **The partnering era is described in detail.** A series of partnering principles is presented in selected chapters. Strategic alliances—the highest form of partnering—are discussed in detail.

3. **Value-added selling strategies are presented throughout the text. Salespeople today are guided by a new principle of personal selling: Partnerships are established and maintained only when the salesperson creates customer value.** Customers have fundamentally changed their expectations. They want to partner with salespeople who can create value, not just communicate it. Value creation involves a series of improvements in the sales process that enhance the customer's experience.

4. **Real-world examples,** a hallmark of our previous editions and continued in this edition, build the reader's interest and promote understanding of major topics and concepts. The new Reality Today Video Series features successful young salespeople providing real world examples of sales careers and presentations. Additional examples have been obtained from a range of progressive organizations, large and small, such as Whirlpool Corporation, UPS, Mutual of Omaha, Baxter Healthcare, Marriott Hotels, and Nordstrom.

5. **A three-dimensional approach to the study of ethical decision making.** One dimension is a chapter on ethics (Chapter 5) titled Ethics: The Foundation of Relationships in Selling, which provides a contemporary examination of ethical considerations in selling. The second dimension involves the discussion of ethical issues in selected chapters throughout the text. The authors believe that ethics in selling is so important that it cannot be covered in a single chapter. The third dimension is an exciting business game entitled **Gray Issues—Ethical Decision Making in Personal Selling.** Participation in this game provides students with an introduction to a range of real-life ethical dilemmas, and it stimulates in-depth thinking about the ethical consequences of their decisions and actions. Students play the game to learn without having to play for keeps.

6. The **Knowing-Doing Gap,** common in personal selling classes, is closed by having students participate in the comprehensive role-play/simulation featured in Appendix 3. Students assume the role of a new sales trainee employed by the Park Inn International Convention Center. Serving as an excellent capstone experience, students develop the critical skills needed to apply relationship, product, customer, and presentation strategies. New to the 11th Edition are three professionally produced videos titled **The Adaptive Selling Today Training Video Series.** These videos demonstrate important skills presented in the text.

7. Each chapter features the following boxed inserts:

   ■ **Selling Is Everyone's Business.** These real-world examples explain how selling skills affect the success of persons who do not consider themselves salespeople.

   ■ **Selling in Action.** These concise inserts feature contemporary issues in selling to keep the book users abreast of the latest developments.

   ■ **Global Business Etiquette.** These brief inserts provide practical tips on how to build global relationships. Each insert focuses on a different country.

   ■ **Customer Relationship Management with Technology.** These application exercises help the student learn how to use technology to add value to the sales process.

8. A **complete update** of key terms for selling appears in each chapter. These terms are boldfaced, defined in the text, and listed at the end of each chapter. An updated glossary appears at the end of the book for quick reference.

9. **End of chapter summaries are now organized into bullet points** corresponding to the key points that appear in the Chapter Preview of each chapter. These summaries provide students with a good review tool and the "big picture" of how the concepts and themes are related to one another.

10. In addition to role-play exercises and video case problems, we are proud to introduce the **Reality Selling Today Role-Plays,** a brand-new appendix featuring eight role-play scenarios. These role-play scenarios build on what students learned in the **Reality Selling Today Video** sales presentations and interviews. Eight detailed salesperson/customer role-play scenarios using the products and sales positions of the actual salespeople that appeared in the Reality Selling Today Videos are presented. Web sites of the companies the students will be using to role-play their sales presentations are supplied to learn appropriate amounts of product and company information. The Reality Selling Today Video interviews and sales presentations provide the necessary background and contextual information for students to use in both selecting the scenario and conducting the role-play. The Reality Selling Today Role-Plays are also specifically designed to prepare students for professional selling role-play competition at the annual college and university competitive event conventions (refer to http:// coles. kennesaw.edu/ncsc/ and http://www.deltaepsilonchi.org/compevents/SRP.html for more information).

Staying on the Cutting Edge: New to This Edition

Since our last edition, the business environment and research on professional selling have undergone significant changes. As active researchers, practitioners, and consultants in the field of selling, our primary goal is to provide an up-to-date and cutting-edge treatment of the field. At the same time, we painstakingly incorporate more "learning by doing" materials to equip students with hands-on experience that are not available—at least to our best knowledge—in any other books on the market. The 11th Edition of *Selling Today: Creating Customer Value* describes how sales professionals must cope with new forces shaping the world of sales and marketing, with a balanced blend of cutting-edge academic and practical materials. The most significant changes in the new edition include:

- The Adaptive Selling Today Model with a new professionally produced video series titled **The Adaptive Selling Today Training Video Series.**
- New Chapter Opening Vignettes and Case Problems featuring real salespeople with an extensive new video program titled **The Reality Selling Today Video Series.** Seven new 10 to 13-minute videos feature live interviews and sales presentations with young successful salespeople.
- A **New Selling in America** six-part documentary video series to help students understand the important role personal selling plays in our market oriented economy. This "first-ever sales documentary" series enhances the personal selling philosophy and career content of Chapters 1 and 2, as well as the contemporary selling concepts presented throughout the text. Stresses the importance of mock role-plays in learning how to sell.
- Replacement of the ACT! Contact Management Software with easy-to-use account-based **Salesforce.com** state-of-art CRM software—with an actual data base of 20 customers. A new unit on how to manage the complex multi-call prospecting and sale environment with account based CRM software is presented
- Eight new in-depth role-plays with **video support,** representing sales careers graduates are entering.
- New and extensive referencing of academic articles and research found in professional journals such as *Journal of Professional Selling and Sales Management, Journal of Marketing, Harvard Business Review,* etc.
- Extensive updating of all chapters with research and articles from trade journals such as *Selling Power, Value Added 21 Selling, Sales and Marketing Management,* and *The American Salesperson,* etc.

Highlights of other specific changes made to the chapters and the appendices include:

Chapter 1

- New Reality Selling Today chapter opener vignette, case problem, and video.
- New model for creating value in sales.
- New insight on challenge of aligning sales and marketing in large corporations.

Chapter 2

- Extensive revision and update of unit describing employment settings in service, business to business, and business to consumer selling.
- New material on B2B and B2C selling careers.

Chapter 3

- New Reality Selling Today chapter opener vignette, case problem, and video on relationship selling.
- New coverage of the ego/empathy theory on developing relationships in selling.

Chapter 4

- New, professionally produced video titled *Communication Styles: A Key to Adaptive Selling Today* for understanding the relationship side of Adaptive Selling. New application exercises for determining and adapting one's communication style to interact more effectively with customers and sales team members.
- New chapter title: Communication Styles, A Key to Adaptive Selling Today.
- New online Adaptive Selling Today assessment exercise and Web site for determining one's communication style—as well as the style of others.
- New information on how communication styles enhance the relationship element of Adaptive Selling.
- Introduces the Adaptive Selling "Platinum Rule."

Chapter 6

- New chapter opener vignette and case problem on product selling strategies with an **enhanced live sales presentation and video interview of featured salesperson**.
- New coverage of the Salesperson's Value Proposition (SVP).

Chapter 8

- New Reality Selling Today chapter opener vignette, case problem, and video on the customer buying process.
- New coverage of the Customer Buying Center and the roles of the user, technical influencer, financial influencer, and the gatekeeper.
- New coverage on how the salesperson's sales process must mirror the customer's buying process.

Chapter 9

- New unit on Managing the Customer Database. This unit explains how account-based CRM systems are used today to effectively sell complex product solutions in multi-call and lifetime customer settings.
- New coverage on the use of highly sophisticated computerized prospect databases such as Salesgenie and OneSource.
- New coverage on using the "Center of Influence" method of prospecting.
- Introduction of the Sales Funnel, and how the sales funnel is used in the sales process for moving prospects successfully through the steps in the sales cycle.
- New **video coverage** of how CRM software is being used to manage and enhance the prospect database throughout the sales cycle.

Chapter 10

- New Reality Selling Today chapter opener vignette, case problem, and video on delivering the sales presentation
- New coverage on the pre-approach planning needed when sales teams are used.
- New coverage on how to use adaptive selling communications styles to approach individual members of the buying group.

Chapter 11

- New coverage on the use of questions throughout the Adaptive Sales Process—**with a high-quality professionally produced video titled *Questions! Questions! Questions*!**
- New table explaining how a questioning strategy can reveal the customers' problems and pain being experienced, and the pleasure that can be expected from the salesperson's value proposition.

Chapter 12

- New coverage on using computers to enhance the product demonstration.

Chapter 13

- New Reality Selling Today chapter opener vignette, case problem, and video on negotiating methods.
- A new unit on Formal Negotiations explains the tactics used by buyers and the strategies used by salespeople to achieve win–win solutions.

Chapter 14

- **New high-quality professionally developed video titled *Ask for The Order (AFTO)* for teaching how to use Adaptive Selling closing questions to help the customer make an intelligent and informed buying decision.**

Chapter 17

- New Reality Selling Today chapter opener vignette, case problem, and video on sales management.
- New insights from the vice president of sales of a large global sales organization.
- New information on the use of personality testing for sales applicants.

New Appendix 1

- Appendix 1 is a new feature of the 11th Edition and it builds on what students learned in the **Reality Selling Today Video Series** sales presentations and interviews. Eight detailed salesperson/customer role-play scenarios using the products and sales positions of the actual salespeople that appeared in the Reality Selling Today Videos are presented. Web sites of the companies the students will be using to role-play their sales presentations are supplied to learn appropriate amounts of product and company information. The Reality Selling Today video interviews, sales presentations, chapter opening vignettes, and case problems provide the necessary background and contextual information for students to use in both selecting the scenario and conducting the role-play. Specific customer role-play instructions are supplied in the instructor's manual.

Organization of This Book

The material in *Selling Today* continues to be organized around the four pillars of personal selling: relationship strategy, product strategy, customer strategy, and presentation strategy. The first two chapters set the stage for an in-depth study of these strategies. The first chapter describes the evolution of personal selling, and the second chapter gives students the opportunity to explore career opportunities in the four major employment areas: services, retail, wholesale, and manufacturing.

Research indicates that high-performance salespeople are better able to build and maintain relationships than are moderate performers. Part 2, Developing a Relationship Strategy, focuses on several important person-to-person relationship-building practices that contribute to success in personal selling. Chapter 3 is entitled Creating Value With a Relationship Strategy, and Chapter is entitled Communication Styles: A Key to Adaptive Selling. Chapter examines the influence of ethics on relationships between customers and salespeople.

Part 3, Developing a Product Strategy, examines the importance of complete and accurate product, company, and competitive knowledge in personal selling. A well-informed salesperson is in a strong position to configure value-added product solutions for complex customer's needs.

Part 4, Developing a Customer Strategy, presents information on why and how customers buy and explains how to identify prospects. With increased knowledge of the customer, salespeople are in a better position to understand complex customer's wants and needs and create customer value in the multi-call, lifetime customer settings.

The concept of a salesperson as advisor, consultant, value creator, and partner to buyers is stressed in Part 5, Developing a Presentation Strategy. As in the 10th Edition, emphasis is placed on the need-satisfaction presentation model. Part 6 includes two chapters: Opportunity Management: The Key to Greater Sales Productivity and Management of the Sales Force.

The new edition features two new appendices. Appendix 1, The Reality Selling Today Role-Plays, includes six role-play scenarios that provide students with the opportunity to, of course, sell. Appendix 2 details how to use the CRM Software, Salesforce.com. Appendix 3, which appeared in the 10th Edition, is a simulation that allows students to integrate and apply what they have learned from this textbook in all four strategic areas of personal selling.

Selling Today Supplements

New Adaptive Selling Today Training Video Series Based on a long-standing professional relationship between the authors and award-winning training video producer Art Bauer, the11th Edition of *Selling Today* includes a breakthrough video series titled The Adaptive Selling Today Training Video Series. Applying the research that the authors have conducted for the 11th Edition, these three videos bring a new reading, viewing, experiencing dimension to the classroom. Completely aligned with concepts in the 11th Edition of *Selling Today*, students have the opportunity to travel with salespeople as they are challenged in the market place to use modern adaptive selling practices. Following each video, students apply the text/video concepts with easy to implement role-play exercises presented in the text.

The first video, "**Communication Styles: A Key to Adaptive Selling Today,** details the four communication styles and their implications for adaptive selling. Using the "Platinum Rule," students are shown how to adapt or flex their communication style to build effective relationships with customers. The second video, **Questions! Questions! Questions!**, introduces the viewer to the need for and use of questions in selling. Understanding customer needs and adapting solutions to meet these needs is the second stage of the Adaptive Selling Process. The third video, **Ask for The Order (AFTO)**, explains how to use Adaptive Selling closing questions to help the customer make an intelligent and informed buying decision.

New Reality Selling Today Video Series. Seven new 10- to 15-minute videos featuring real salespeople in live interviews and sales presentations are presented with key chapters throughout the book. The selected chapters come alive with video footage filmed in real sales settings with real salespeople. Also featured are live one-on-one interviews to provide students with up-close and personal glimpses at sales careers in a variety of industries including insurance, real estate, advertising space, financial services, construction technologies, event planning, and pharmaceutical sales. Salespeople and their companies represented include Liberty Mutual, CBRE, Hilti, Marriott, McKesson Pharmaceutical, and other companies.

Selling in America Six-Part Documentary Video. This new professionally developed series helps students understand the important role personal selling plays in our market-oriented economy. This "first-ever sales documentary" series enhances the personal selling philosophy and career content of Chapters 1 and 2, as well as the contemporary selling concepts presented throughout the text. It also stresses the importance of mock role-plays in learning how to sell.

Salesforce.com CRM Software and On-line Video New to the 11th Edition is free access to the state-of-the-art CRM software Salesforce.com and an on-line Salesforce.com training video series. The Software will include a preloaded prospect database of 20 customers who are in various stages of the buying process. Student completing these self-instructional exercises will be familiar with the functionality of the Salesforce.com Software, plus they will have "hands-on" application experience of CRM with the buying and selling process.

Instructor's Manual includes detailed presentation outlines, answers to review questions, hand-outs for the ethics game, suggested responses to learning activities, hand-outs for CRM exercises, easy-to-follow instructions on how to use the role-play/simulation included in the text, descriptions of the accompanying videos, written term projects, transparency masters, and suggestions for organizing a sales course.

The **Test Bank** for the eleventh edition has been extensively rewritten and expanded. More than 50 questions for each chapter (15 True/False, 30 Multiple Choice, 5 Completion and 2 Short Answer) provide a larger selection to choose from in constructing tests. The correct answer, textbook page reference, and level of difficulty are provided.

Companion Website (www.pearsonhighered.com/manning) offers students valuable resources including an Internet Study Guide for review purposes; an online assessment tool for better understanding one's own, as well as the adaptive selling communication style of others; sales literature and support materials for completing Appendix 3; as well as materials for use with the salesforce.com CRM Software that accompanies the textbook.

The Search for wisdom in the Age of Information

The search for the fundamental of personal selling has become more difficult in the age of information. The glut of information (information explosion) threatens our ability to identify what is true, right, or lasting. The search for knowledge begins with a review of information, and wisdom is gleaned from knowledge. Books continue to be one of the best sources of wisdom. Many new books, and several classics, were used as references for the 10th Edition of *Selling Today*. A sample of the more than 40 books used to prepare this edition follows:

A Whole New Mind by Daniel H. Pink

Business Ethics by O. C. Ferrell, John Fraedrich, and Linda Ferrell

Blur: The Speed of Change in the Connected Economy by Stan Davis and Christopher Meyer

Close the Deal by Sam Deep and Lyle Sussman

Complete Business Etiquette Handbook by Barbara Pachter and Marjorie Brody

Effective Human Relations—Personal and Organizational Applications by Barry L. Reece and Rhonda Brandt

First Impressions—What You Don't Know About How Others See You by Ann Demarais and Valerie White

Hug Your Customers by Jack Mitchell

Integrity Selling for the 21st Century by Ron Willingham

Keeping the Funnel Full by Don Thomson

Marketing Imagination by Ted Levitt

Marketing—Real People, Real Choices by Michael R. Solomon, Greg W. Marshall, and Elnora W. Stuart.

Megatrends by John Naisbitt

Personal Styles and Effective Performance by David W. Merrill and Roger H. Reid

Psycho-Cybernectics by Maxwell Maltz

Questions—The Answer to Sales by Duane Sparks

Rethinking the Sales Force by Neil Rackham and John R. DeVincentis

Re-Imagine! Business Excellence in a Disruptive Age by Tom Peters

Self Matters by Phillip C. McGraw

SPIN Selling by Neil Rackham

SPIN Selling Fieldbook by Neil Rackham

Strategic Selling by Robert B. Miller and Stephen E. Heiman

The 7 Habits of Highly Effective People by Stephen R. Covey

The Customer Revolution by Patricia Seybold

The Double Win by Denis Waitley

The New Conceptual Selling by Stephen E. Heiman and Diane Sanchez

The New Professional Image by Susan Bixler and Nancy Nix-Rice

The New Solution Selling by Keith M. Eades

The Power of 5 by Harold H. Bloomfield and Robert K. Cooper

The Sedona Method by Hale Dwoskin

The Speed of Change in the Connected Economy by Stan Davis and Christopher Meyer

The Success Principles by Jack Canfield

Value-Added Selling by Tom Reilly

Working with Emotional Intelligence by Daniel Goleman

Zero-Resistance Selling by Maxwell Maltz, Dan S. Kennedy, William T. Brooks, Matt Oechsli, Jeff Paul, and Pamela Yellen

Acknowledgments

Many people have made contributions to the **eleventh** edition of *Selling Today: Creating Customer Value.* We are very appreciative of the assistance and suggestions of our Canadian co-author Dr. Herb MacKenzie, Chair, Marketing, International Business, and Strategy, at Brock University. We also are very grateful to our CRM technology associates Carl Herman and Jack Linge who contributed significantly to the development of the CRM Insights, Application Exercises, and CRM Case Studies. We thank award-winning video producer Art Bauer for his creativity, dedication, and attention to detail in the production of the Adaptive Selling Today Training Video Series. We also thank Son Lam for his help and contributions with the Reality Selling Video Series, Cases, and Role-Play exercises. Throughout the years the text has been improved as a result of numerous helpful comments and recommendations by both students and faculty. We extend special appreciation to the following reviewers:

Kate Bailey, *South Valley Bank and Trust*

Jurgita Baltrusaitye, *University of Illinois at Chicago*

Susan Baxter, *Bethune-Cookman University*

Alex Birkholz, *Wisconsin Indianhead Technical College*

Robert Bochrath, *Gateway Technical Institute*

Jim Boespflug, *Arapahoe Community College*

Jerry Boles, *Western Kentucky University*

Jim Boles, *Georgia State University*

Jerry Bradley, *Saint Joseph's University*

Duane Brickner, *South Mountain Community College*

Don Brumlow, *St. John's College*

Jeff Bruns, *Bacone College*

Murray Brunton, *Central Ohio Technical College*

Larry P. Butts, *Southwest Tennessee Community College*

Alan Canton, *California State University, Fresno*

John J. Carlisle, *New Hampshire Community Technical College, Nashua*

Mark Chock, *Marian College*

William R. Christensen, *Community College of Denver (North Campus)*

Cindy Claycomb, *Wichita State University*

Patricia W. Clarke, *Boston College*

Gloria Cockerell, *Collin College*

Lori Connors, *Delgado Community College*

David Corbett, *Ohio Valley University*

Douglas A. Cords, *California State University, Fresno*

Robert Cosenza, *The University of Mississippi*

Larry Davis, *Youngstown State University*

Lynn Dawson, *Louisiana Technical University—Ruston*

De'Arno De'Armond, *West Texas A&M University*

Dayle Dietz, *North Dakota State School of Science*

Gary Donnelly, *Casper College*

Casey Donoho, *Northern Arizona University*

Robert Dunn, *Cuesta Community College*

Mimi Eglin, *Fulton-Montgomery Community College*

Susan Emens, *Kent State University*

Joyce Ezrow, *Anne Arundel Community College*

Wendal Ferguson, *Richland College*

Dean Flowers, *Waukesha County Technical College*

Stefanie Garcia, *University of Central Florida*

Deb Gaspard, *Southeast Community College*

Richard Geyer, *Tiffin University*

Connie Golden, *Lakeland Community College*

Victoria Griffis, *University of South Florida*

David Grypp, *Milwaukee Area Technical College*

Andrew Haaland, *Tompkins Cortland Community College*

Donald Hackett, *Wichita State University*

Robert Hausladen, *University of Louisville*

Jon Hawes, *The University of Akron*

Ken Hodge, Marketing Manager, *Nordson*

Norm Humble, *Kirkwood Community College*

Phil Hupfer, *Elmhurst College*

Kathy Illing, *Greenville Technical College*

Karen James, *Louisiana State University, Shreveport*

Mark Johlke, *Bradley University*

Michael Johnson, *Chippewa Valley Tech College*

Richard Jones, *Marshall University*

Peter Johnson, *Pace University*

Jim Kaempfer, *Century College*

Ali Kara, *Pennsylvania State University, York*

Jaciel Keltgen, *Augustana College*

Katy Kemp, *Middle Tennessee State University*

Davis King, *Pennsylvania State University, Delaware County*

Wesley Koch, *Illinois Central College*

Stephen Koernig, *University of Illinois—Chicago*

Bruce Kusch, *Brigham Young University*

Bernard Kyle, *Westchester Community College*

Wilburn Lane, *Lambuth University*

James Lawson, *Mississippi State University*

R. Dale Lounsburg, *Emporia State College*

Marvin Lovett, *University of Texas, Brownsville*

George H. Lucas, Jr., *Texas A & M University*

Alice Lupinacci, *University of Texas at Arlington*

Jennifer Malarski, *Lake Superior College*

Lynnea Mallalieu, *University of North Carolina—Wilmington*

Leslie E. Martin, *University of Wisconsin, Whitewater*

Jack Maroun, *Herkimer County Community College*

Lee McCain, *Seminole Community College*

Tammy McCullough, *Eastern Michigan University*

Norman McElvany, *Johnson State College*

Kimberly McMahill, *Carl Sandburg College*

Bob McMahon, *Appalachian State University*

Robert McMurrian, *University of Tampa*

Darrel Millard, *Kirkwood Community College*

Chip Miller, *Drake University*

Ron Milliaman, *Western Kentucky University*

Irene Mittlemark, *Kingsborough Community College*

Rita Mix, *Our Lady of the Lake University—Dallas*

Russ Movritsem, *Brigham Young University*

Mark Mulder, *Grand Rapids Junior College*

Lynn Muller, *University of South Dakota*

Gordon Myron, *Lucent Technologies*

Lewis Neisner, *University of Maryland*

John Odell, *Marketing Catalysts*

Robert Owen, *Texas A&M University, Texarkana*

Mark Pantaleo, *Pensacola Christian College*

Jim Parr, *Louisiana State University*

Nancy Patterson, *University of Arkansas Community College*

Robert Perrella, *Piedmont College*

Ron Pimentel, *California State University—Bakersfield*

Richard Plank, *University of Southern Florida*

Ray Polchow, *Zane State College*

Quenton Pullman, *Nashville Technical Community College*

Walter Purvis, *Coastal Carolina Community College*

James Randall, *Georgia Southern University*

Adam Rapp, *Kent State University*

Peter Reday, *Youngstown State University*

Judy Reinders, *Milwaukee Area Technical College*

Daniel Ricica, *Sinclair Community College*

Richard Riesbeck, *West Liberty State College*

Carol Robarge, *Chippewa Valley Technical College*

Sandra Robertson, *Thomas Nelson Community College*

Mark Ryan, *Hawkeye Community College*

Stan Salzman, *American River College*

Nicholas A. Santarone, *Penn State University, Abington*

Gary Schirr, *University of Illinois at Chicago*

Donald T. Sedik, *William Rainey Harper College*

Rick Shannon, *Western Kentucky University*

C. David Shepherd, *Kennesaw State University*

Scott Sherwood, *Metropolitan State College of Denver*

Kent Sickmeyer, *Kaskaskia College*

Robert E. Smiley, *Indiana State University, Terra Haute*

C. Phillip Smith, *John C. Calhoun, State Community College, Alabama*

Diane Smith, *Henry Ford Community College*

David Snyder, *Canisius College*

Karl Sooder, *University of Central Florida*

Forrest Stegelin, *University of Georgia*

Thomas Stevenson, *University of North Carolina, Charlotte*

Philip Stillitano, *Stark State College*
Phil Straniero, *Western Michigan University*
Carol Sullinger, *University of Toledo*
Michael Swenson, *Brigham Young University*
Leslie Thompson, *Hutchinson Community College*
Robert Thompson, *Indiana State University*
Ronald Tibbles, *University of North Florida*
Gary Tucker, *Oklahoma CIty Community College*
Sven Tuzovic, *Murray State University*
Rae Verity, *Southern Alberta Institute of Technology*
Douglas Vorhies, *University of Mississippi*
Donna Waldron, *Manchester Community College*
Jeff Walls, *Indiana Tech*
Joan Weiss, *Bucks County Community College*
Stanley "Martin" Welc, *Saddleback College*
Stacia Wert-Gray, *University of Central Oklahoma*
Scott Widmier, *University of Akron*
Jim Wilkinson, *Stark State College*
Thomas Williamson, *Ohio State ATI*
Raymond Wimer, *Syracuse University*
Susan Van Winkle, *Milwaukee Area Technical College*
Amy Wojciechowski, *West Shore Community College*
John Wolper, *The University of Findlay*
Andy Wood, *West Virginia University*
Lauren Wright, *California State University, Chico*
Curtis W. Youngman, *Salt Lake Community College*
Raymond Zagorski, *University of Alaska/Kenai Penonsula College*
Donald A. Zimmerman, *University of Akron*

Finally, we thank the book team at Prentice Hall: James Heine, Melissa Pellerano, Sally Yagan, Karalyn Holland, Sharon Anderson, Poyee Oster, Judy Leale, and Anthony Gemmellaro.

About the Authors

(in alphabetical order)

Dr. Michael Ahearne
University of Houston

Michael Ahearne is a Marketing Professor and Executive Director of the Sales Excellence Institute (SEI) at the University of Houston. The SEI is widely recognized as one of the leading university-based selling programs in the world, training more than 2,000 sales students and working with more than 200 major corporations annually. He earned his Ph.D. in Marketing from Indiana University. He has also served on the faculty at the University of Connecticut and Pennsylvania State University. In addition, he has internationally lectured about sales and sales management in such countries as Austria, Belgium, France, India, Spain, and Russia.

Dr. Ahearne has published articles in leading academic journals on factors influencing the performance of salespeople, sales teams, and sales organizations. His work has appeared in the *Journal of Marketing, Journal of Marketing Research, Management Science, Journal of Applied Psychology, International Journal of Research in Marketing,* and *Journal of the Academy of Marketing Science.* In addition to reviewing for the top marketing and management journals, he currently serves as the Associate Editor of the *Journal of Personal Selling and Sales Management*—the leading international scholarly journal in the sales field. His work has also been featured in numerous trade and popular press publications including *Business 2.0, Business Investors Daily, U.S. News & World Report,* and *INC Magazine.*

Before entering academia, Dr. Ahearne played professional baseball for the Montreal Expos Organization and worked in the healthcare industry for Eli Lilly and PCS Healthcare. He actively consults in many industries including insurance, healthcare, consumer packaged goods, technology, and transportation.

Gerald L. Manning
Des Moines Area Community College

Mr. Manning served as chair of the Marketing/Management Department for more than 30 years. In addition to his administrative duties, he has served as lead instructor in sales and sales management. The classroom has provided him with an opportunity to study the merits of various experimental learning approaches such as role-plays, simulations, games, and interactive demonstrations. *Partnership Selling: A Role-Play/Simulation for Selling Today,* included in the eleventh edition, was developed and tested in the classroom by Mr. Manning. He has also applied numerous personal selling principles and practices in the real world as owner of a real estate development and management company.

Mr. Manning has served as a sales and marketing consultant to senior management and owners of over 500 businesses, including several national companies. He appears regularly as a speaker at national sales conferences. Mr. Manning has received the "Outstanding Instructor of the Year" award given annually by his college.

Dr. Barry L. Reece
Virginia Polytechnic Institute and State University

Dr. Reece has devoted more than three decades to teaching, researching, consulting, and to the development of training programs in the areas of sales, leadership, human relations, and management. He has conducted over 600 seminars and workshops for public and private sector organizations. He has written extensively in the areas of sales, supervision, communications, and management. Dr. Reece was named "Trainer of the Year" by the

Valleys of Virginia Chapter of the American Society for Training and Development and was awarded the "Excellence in Teaching Award" by the College of Human Sciences and Education at Virginia Polytechnic Institute and State University.

Dr. Reece has contributed to numerous journals and is author or co-author of thirty books including *Business, Human Relations—Principles and Practices, Supervision and Leadership in Action,* and *Effective Human Relations—Personal and Organizational Applications.* He has served as a consultant to Lowe's Companies, Inc., Wachovia, WLR Foods, Kinney Shoe Corporation, Carilion Health System, and numerous other profit and not-for-profit organizations.

Keeping Current in a Changing World

Throughout the past decade, Professors Manning, Ahearne, and Reece have relied on three strategies to keep current in the dynamic field of personal selling. First, they are actively involved in sales training and consulting. Frequent interaction with salespeople and sales managers provides valuable insight regarding contemporary issues and developments in the field of personal selling. A second major strategy involves extensive research and development activities. The major focus of these activities has been factors that contribute to high-performance salespeople. The third major strategy involves completion of training and development programs offered by America's most respected sales training companies. Professors Manning, Ahearne, and Reece have completed seminars and workshops offered by Wilson Learning Corporation, Forum Corporation, Franklin-Covey, Sedona Training Associates, Association for Humanistic Psychology, and several other organizations.

An Investment in the Future

Charles Schwab, the great industrialist and entrepreneur, said, "We are all salespeople every day of our lives, selling our ideas and enthusiasm to those with whom we come in contact." As authors, we suggest that you retain this book for future reference. Periodic review of the ideas in this text will help you daily in areas such as:

- interacting more effectively with others
- interviewing for new jobs in the future
- understanding and training salespeople who work for you or with you
- selling new ideas to senior management, co-workers, or employees you might be supervising
- selling products or services that you represent as a salesperson

We wish you much success and happiness in applying your knowledge of personal selling.

Gerald L. Manning
Barry L. Reece
Michael Ahearne

11th Edition

Selling Today

Creating Customer Value

Developing a Personal Selling Philosophy

The two chapters that make up Part 1 establish a

foundation for the entire textbook. Chapter 1 introduces

the major themes that connect all of the chapters.

Chapter 2 describes personal selling career opportunities.

"Every employee at Federal Express must be sales oriented and each manager must be an outstanding individual salesperson."
Federal Express

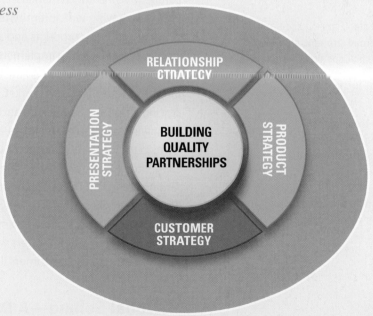

RELATIONSHIP
STRATEGY

PRESENTATION
STRATEGY

BUILDING
QUALITY
PARTNERSHIPS

PRODUCT
STRATEGY

CUSTOMER
STRATEGY

1

Personal Selling and the Marketing Concept

Chapter Preview

When you finish reading this chapter, you should be able to

1
Define personal selling and describe the three prescriptions of a personal selling philosophy

2
Describe the contributions of personal selling to the information economy

3
Discuss personal selling as an extension of the marketing concept

4
Describe the evolution of consultative selling from the marketing era to the present

5
Define strategic selling and name the four broad strategic areas in the Strategic/Consultative Selling Model

6
Describe the evolution of partnering and the nature of a strategic selling alliance

7
Explain how value-added selling strategies enhance personal selling

Reality Selling Today Video Series

Marcus Smith, pictured above, is of the most productive sales representatives of Liberty Mutual (www.libertymutual.com), uses the consultative selling approach exclusively. He believes that excellence in selling starts with an in-depth understanding of what customers value most and working closely with the customers to satisfy their needs.

Founded in 1912, Liberty Mutual is an important player in the highly competitive insurance markets. The three pillars of the company's culture include behaving with integrity, treating people with dignity and respect, and providing superior products and services. Smith is a strong believer of those corporate values. Yet to implement this relationship-oriented selling approach represents a challenge, given the constraints of resources and the competitive intensity of the insurance market. Smith's strategy is simple yet effective: placing emphasis on tracking and forecasting market information, focusing on identifying profitable customers, and directing resources to those customers.

Smith does not start his conversation with his new customers with a sales pitch. He instead spends time building rapport with the customer, say, finding some facts about life that he and his customers have in common. These ice breakers go a long way in making the customers comfortable in sharing with Smith what their actual needs are. Then he presents a balanced comparison between his offers with those of competitors. Being empathetic and honest with the customers lies at the heart of consultative selling. ■

Personal Selling—A Definition and a Philosophy

Personal selling occurs when a company representative interacts directly with a customer or prospective customer to present information about a product or service.[1] It is a process of developing relationships; discovering needs; matching the appropriate products with these needs; and communicating benefits through

FIGURE 1.1

Strategic/Consultative Selling Model	
Strategic Step	**Prescription**
Develop a Personal Selling Philosophy	☐ Adopt Marketing Concept
	☐ Value Personal Selling
	☐ Become a Problem Solver/Partner

Today, salespeople use a strategic plan based on a personal philosophy that emphasizes adopting the marketing concept, valuing personal selling, and becoming a problem solver/partner.

informing, reminding, or persuading. The term **product** should be broadly interpreted to encompass information, services, ideas, and issues. Increasingly, personal selling is viewed as a process that adds value. In an ideal situation the salesperson diagnoses the customer's needs and custom fits the product to meet these needs.

Preparation for a career in personal selling begins with the development of a personal philosophy or set of beliefs that provides guidance. To some degree this philosophy is like the rudder that steers a ship. Without a rudder the ship's direction is unpredictable. Without a personal philosophy the salesperson's behavior also is unpredictable.

The development of a **personal selling philosophy** involves three prescriptions: adopt the marketing concept, value personal selling, and assume the role of a problem solver or partner in helping customers make buying decisions (Figure 1.1). These three prescriptions for success in personal selling are presented here as part of the Strategic/Consultative Selling Model. This model is expanded in future chapters to include additional strategic steps in the selling process.

Personal Selling in the Age of Information

The restructuring of America from an industrial economy to an information economy began in the 1950s (Figure 1.2). John Naisbitt, author of the popular book *Megatrends*, noted that during this period our economy began shifting from an emphasis on industrial activity to an emphasis on information processing. He recognized that industrial America was giving way to a new society where most of us would work with information instead of producing goods.[2] We live in an age in which the effective exchange of information is the foundation of most economic transactions. Today we are in the latter stages of the age of information, and the implications for personal selling are profound. We will describe the four major developments that have shaped the information economy and discuss the implications for personal selling.

Major Advances in Information Technology

The information age has spawned the information technology revolution. Salespeople and other players in the information age use personal computers, e-mail, instant messaging,

FIGURE 1.2

Industrial Economy **1860–1960**	**Information Economy** **1960–2020**
• Major advances occur in manufacturing and transportation	
• Strategic resources are capital and natural resources	
• Business is defined by its products and factories	
• Sales success depends on meeting sales quotas	

INCREASES IN RELATIONSHIP SELLING AND RELATIONSHIP MARKETING

- • Major advances occur in information technology
- • Strategic resource is information
- • Business is defined by customer relationships
- • Sales success depends on adding value

The age of information has greatly influenced personal selling. Today, salespeople use a variety of information technology tools to gather and process information of value to the customer. They recognize that information is a strategic resource and relationship skills are needed to build a conduit of trust for information acceptance.

mobile phones, and other forms of technology to obtain and process information. The explosive growth of electronic commerce and other Internet activities has changed the way in which computers are used. Stan Davis, futurist and co-author of *Blur: The Speed of Change in the Connected Economy*, says that we now use the computer less for data crunching and more for connecting. These connections involve people to people, machine to machine, product to service, organization to organization, and all these in combination.[3] Without these connections, information age workers cannot do their jobs. People who work extensively with information, such as salespeople, need these connections to conduct their information gathering and information management responsibilities.

Strategic Resource Is Information

Advances in information technology have increased the speed at which we acquire, process, and disseminate information. David Shenk, author of *Data Smog: Surviving the Information Glut*, notes that we have moved from a state of information scarcity to one of information overload.[4] In an era of limitless data, informed salespeople can to help us decide which information has value and which information should be ignored. Salespeople are the eyes and ears in the marketplace. They can collect a wide range of competitive intelligence.[5]

Business Is Defined by Customer Relationships

Michael Hammer, consultant and author of *The Agenda*, says the *real* new economy is the customer economy. As scarcity gave way to abundance, as supply exceeded demand, and as customers became better informed, we have seen a power shift. Customers have taken more control of their own destinies.[6]

Michael Hammer is credited with popularizing the concept of reengineering the corporation. The driving factors behind reengineering are lower costs, better quality, better use of information, and improved customer satisfaction. Salespeople can play an important role in this management practice.

On the surface, the major focus of the age of information seems to be the accumulation of more and more information and the never-ending search for new forms of information technology. It's easy to overlook the importance of the human element. Humans, not computers, have the ability to think, feel, and create ideas. It is no coincidence that relationship selling and relationship marketing, which emphasize long-term, mutually satisfying buyer–seller relationships, began to gain support at the beginning of the information age. Companies such as DuPont, Kraft Foods, and General Electric have adopted a philosophy that focuses on customer satisfaction, team selling, and relationship selling.[7]

Sales Success Depends on Adding Value

Value-added selling can be defined as a series of creative improvements within the sales process that enhance the customer experience. Salespeople can create value by developing a quality relationship, carefully identifying the customer needs, and then configuring and presenting the best possible product solution. Value is also created when the salesperson provides excellent service after the sale. Neil Rackman, author of *Rethinking the Sales Force*, and other experts in sales and marketing say that success no longer depends on merely communicating the value of products and services. Success in personal selling rests on the critical ability to create value for customers.

The value added by salespeople today is increasingly derived from intangibles such as the quality of the advice offered and the level of trust that underlies the relationship between the customer and the salesperson. The value of these intangibles can erode with shocking speed when the customer feels deceived or discovers that the competition is able to add more value to the sales process.[8]

"One question: If this is the Information Age, how come nobody knows anything?"

Personal Selling as an Extension of the Marketing Concept

A careful examination of personal selling practices during the past 40 years reveals some positive developments. We have seen the evolution of personal selling through several stages. The early *persuader stage* emphasized pushing or peddling products. At this stage salespeople attempted to convince any and all market members to buy products offered. Over the years personal selling evolved to the *problem-solver stage,* obtaining the participation of buyers in identifying their problems, which can be translated into needs. At this stage the salesperson attempts to present products that correspond with customer needs.[9] Today, salespeople are no longer the flamboyant product "pitchmen" of the past. Instead they are increasingly becoming diagnosticians of customers' needs and problems. A growing number of salespeople recognize that the quality of the partnerships they create is as important as the quality of the products they sell.

Evolution of the Marketing Concept

What is the **marketing concept?** It is a principle that holds that achieving organizational goals depends on knowing the needs and wants of target markets and delivering the desired products. Under the marketing concept, customer focus and value are the paths to sales and profits.[10]

The era of marketing and the age of information began in the early 1950s (Table 1.1). A General Electric executive is credited with making one of the earliest formal statements indicating corporate interest in the marketing concept. In a paper heralding a new management philosophy, he observed that the principal marketing function of a company is to determine what the customer wants and then develop the appropriate product or service. This view contrasted with the prevailing practice of that period, which was to develop products and then build customer interest in those products.[11]

The foundation for the marketing concept is a business philosophy that leaves no doubt in the mind of every employee that customer satisfaction is of primary importance. All energies are directed toward satisfying the customer. As Peter Drucker once observed, "The customers define the business."

Although the marketing concept is a very basic business fundamental, some companies ignore it and suffer the consequences. Ford Motor Company was a leader in quality control during the 1980s and early 1990s but then seemed to shift its focus to other areas. The result was a drop in J. D. Power and Associates quality rankings and a drop in sales. Ford also failed to stay in touch with consumer tastes.[12]

TABLE 1.1   **Evolution of Personal Selling (1950 to Present)**

SALES AND MARKETING EMPHASIS	SELLING EMPHASIS
Marketing Era Begins (Early 1950s) Organizations determine needs and wants of target markets and adapt themselves to delivering desired satisfaction; product orientation is replaced by a customer orientation	• More organizations recognize that the salesperson is in a position to collect product, market, and service information concerning the buyer's needs
Consultative Selling Era (Late 1960s to early 1970s) Salespeople are becoming diagnosticians of customer's needs as well as consultants offering well-considered recommendations; mass markets are breaking into target markets	• Buyer needs are identified through two-way communication • Information giving and negotiation tactics replace manipulation
Strategic Selling Era (Early 1980s) The evolution of a more complex selling environment and greater emphasis on market niches create the need for greater structure and more emphasis on planning	• Strategy is given as much attention as selling tactics • Product positioning is given more attention • Greater emphasis on account management and team selling
Partnering Era (1990 to the present) Salespeople are encouraged to think of everything they say or do in the context of their long-term, high-quality partnership with individual customers; sales force automation provides specific customer information	• Customer supplants the product as the driving force in sales • Greater emphasis on strategies that create customer value • Adaptive selling is given greater emphasis

Sales success in the new economy requires us to think of ourselves as problem solver/partner throughout the sales process.

Business firms vary in terms of how strongly they support the marketing concept. Some firms have gone the extra mile to satisfy the needs and wants of their customers:

■ UPS founder Jim Casey adopted the marketing concept when the company was first established. He described the firm's customer focus this way: "Our real, primary objective is to serve—to render perfect service to our stores and their customers. If we keep that objective constantly in mind, our reward in money can be beyond our fondest dreams."[13]

■ Marriott Hotels uses a blend of "high tech" and "high touch" to build customer goodwill and repeat business. Each of the 8,500 sales representatives can sell the services of 10 motel brands in Marriott's portfolio. The customer with a small meeting budget might be encouraged to consider a Fairfield Inn property. The customer seeking luxury accommodations might be introduced to a Ritz-Carlton hotel (acquired a few years ago). All reservations go through the same system, so if one Marriott hotel is full, the sales representative can cross-sell rooms in another Marriott hotel in the same city.[14]

Marketing Concept Yields Marketing Mix

Once the marketing concept becomes an integral part of a firm's philosophy, its management seeks to develop a network of marketing activities that maximize customer satisfaction and ensure profitability. The combination of elements making up a program based on the marketing concept is known as the **marketing mix** (Figure 1.3). The marketing mix is a set of controllable, tactical marketing tools that consists of everything the firm can do to influence the demand for its product. The many possibilities can be organized into four groups of variables: *product, price, place,* and *promotion.*[15]

One of the four P's shown in Figure 1.3—promotion—can be further subdivided into advertising, public relations, sales promotion, and personal selling. When a company adopts the marketing concept, it must determine how some combination of these elements can result in maximum customer satisfaction.

Important Role of Personal Selling

Every marketer must decide how much time and money to invest in each of the four areas of the marketing mix. The decision must be objective; no one can afford to invest money in a marketing strategy that does not provide a good return on money invested. *Personal selling is often the major promotional method used—whether measured by people employed, by total expenditures, or by expenses as a percentage of sales.* One way to assess the magnitude of personal selling is to study employment data for the 500 largest sales forces in America. These companies employ several million salespeople and these salespeople produce over $4.5 trillion dollars in sales. Each salesperson supports, on average, 10.4 other jobs within the company.[16]

Firms make large investments in personal selling in response to several major trends: Products and services are becoming increasingly sophisticated and complex; competition has greatly increased in most product areas; and demand for quality, value, and service by customers has risen sharply. In response to these trends, personal selling has evolved to a new level of professionalism. Since the beginning of the information age, personal selling has evolved through three distinct developmental periods: the consultative selling era, the strategic selling era, and the partnering era.

FIGURE 1.3

The Marketing Mix
Each of the elements that make up the marketing mix must be executed effectively for a marketing program to achieve the desired results.

Product	Place
Price	Promotion

Evolution of Consultative Selling

Consultative selling, which emerged in the late 1960s and early 1970s, is an extension of the marketing concept (see Table 1.1). This approach emphasizes need identification, which is achieved through effective communication between the salesperson and the customer. The salesperson establishes two-way communication by asking appropriate questions and listening carefully to the customer's responses. The salesperson assumes the role of consultant and offers well-considered recommendations. Negotiation replaces manipulation as the salesperson sets the stage for a long-term partnership. Salespeople who have adopted consultative selling possess a keen ability to listen, define the customer's problems, and offer one or more solutions.

Although consultative selling is emphasized throughout this text, it is helpful to understand the role of transactional selling in our economy. **Transactional selling** is a sales process that most effectively matches the needs of the value-conscious buyer who is primarily interested in price and convenience. Many transactional buyers are well aware of their needs and may already know a great deal about the products or services they intend to purchase. Because the transaction-based buyer tends to focus primarily on low price, some marketers are adopting lower-cost selling channels. Low-cost transaction selling strategies include telesales, direct mail, and the Internet. This approach to selling is usually used by marketers who do not see the need to spend very much time on customer need assessment, problem solving, relationship building, or sales follow-up.[17]

Service, retail, manufacturing, and wholesale firms that embrace the marketing concept already have adopted or are currently adopting consultative selling practices. The major features of consultative selling are as follows:

1. The customer is seen as a *person to be served*, not a prospect to be sold. Consultative salespeople believe their function is to help the buyer make an intelligent decision. They use a four-step process that includes need discovery, selection of a solution, a need–satisfaction presentation, and servicing the sale (Figure 1.4). These customer-centered strategies are fully developed and explained in Chapters 10 to 15.

2. The consultative salesperson, unlike the peddler of an earlier era, does not try to overpower the customer with a high-pressure sales presentation. Instead the buyer's needs are identified through *two-way* communication. The salesperson conducts precall research and asks questions during the sales call in an attempt to develop a relationship and learn as much as possible about the person's needs and perceptions.

3. Consultative selling emphasizes *need identification, problem solving, and negotiation instead of manipulation*. This approach is very compatible with the *problem-solver stage* of personal selling discussed earlier in this chapter.[19] Helping the buyer make an informed and intelligent buying decision adds value to the sales process.

4. Consultative selling emphasizes *service* at every phase of the personal selling process. Several important research studies indicate the strong, positive impact of customer satisfaction on company profits.[20] The relationship between a seller and a buyer seldom ends when the sale is made. In most cases customer expectations increase after the sale.

FIGURE 1.4

The Consultative Sales Presentation Guide

This contemporary presentation guide emphasizes the customer as a person to be served.

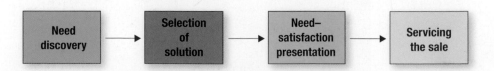

| Need discovery | → | Selection of solution | → | Need–satisfaction presentation | → | Servicing the sale |

At first glance, it may appear that consultative selling practices can be easily mastered. The truth is, consultative selling is a complex process that puts great demands on sales personnel. This approach to personal selling requires an understanding of concepts and principles borrowed from the fields of psychology, communications, and sociology. It takes a great deal of personal commitment and self-discipline to become a sales consultant/adviser.

Evolution of Strategic Selling

Strategic selling began receiving considerable attention during the 1980s (see Table 1.1). During this period we witnessed the beginning of several trends that resulted in a more complex selling environment. These trends, which include increased global competition, broader and more diverse product lines, more decision makers involved in major purchases, and greater demand for specific, custom-made solutions, continue to influence personal selling and sales training in the age of information.

As companies face increased levels of complexity in the marketplace, they must give more attention to strategic planning. The strategic planning done by salespeople is often influenced by the information included in their company's strategic market plan. **Strategic planning** is the process that matches the firm's resources to its market opportunities. It takes into consideration the various functional areas of the business that must be coordinated such as financial assets, workforce, production capabilities, and marketing.[21] Almost every aspect of strategic planning directly or indirectly influences sales and marketing.

The strategic plan should be a guide for a strategic selling plan. This plan includes strategies that you use to position yourself with the customer before the sales call even begins. The authors of *Strategic Selling* point out that there is a difference between a *tactic* and a *strategy*.[22] **Tactics** are techniques, practices, or methods you use when you are face-to-face with a customer. Examples are the use of questions to identify needs, presentation skills, and various types of closes. These and other tactics are discussed in Chapters 10 to 15.

A **strategy**, on the other hand, is a prerequisite to tactical success. If you develop the correct strategies, you are more likely to make your sales presentation to the right person, at the right time, and in a manner most likely to achieve positive results.

A selling strategy is a carefully conceived plan that is needed to accomplish a sales objective. Let's assume you are a sales representative employed by a pharmaceutical company. In an ideal situation, you want to establish a dialogue with the physician and learn

Salespeople who build partnering relationships are rewarded with repeat business and referrals. These relationships require a strategic approach to selling.

Selling in Action

THE WAR BETWEEN SALES AND MARKETING

 Within many companies there is little alignment between sales and marketing. In fact, a real turf war often exists between these two functions. One source of friction is *economic*.

Senior management must make decisions regarding budget allocation for each function. The folks in marketing may want to spend large amounts of money on advertising to generate customer awareness of a new product. The folks in sales may feel this money would be better spent by increasing the size of the sales force. The second source of conflict is *cultural*. Sales and marketing attract different types of people who spend their time in different ways. The marketing staff may be focused on program elements (product warranty, price, placement of the product, etc.). Salespeople, in contrast, want to focus their attention on existing and potential customers. One way to end the war between sales and marketing is to encourage more joint planning and information sharing. The leaders of both functions must try to achieve common ground in terms of philosophies and values.[a]

about the types of patients she sees, diseases she treats, and challenges facing her practice. However, you do not want to call on busy doctors who may have no use for the drugs offered by your company. A strategy might include a careful study of the entire physician population in your territory. This analysis will help you identify those who need information about the drugs your company offers.[23] With this information you can select the most appropriate selling tactic (method), which might be to present samples to doctors who are not currently prescribing your drug.

Strategic planning, an important element of the *problem-solver stage,* sets the groundwork for a value-added form of consultative selling that is more structured, more focused, and more efficient. The result is better time allocation, more precise problem solving, and a greater chance that there will be a good match between your product and the customer needs.

Adaptive selling is another key element of the *problem-solver stage.* **Adaptive selling** can be defined as altering sales behaviors during a customer interaction in order to improve communication. It relates to a salesperson's ability to collect information regarding the customer's needs and responding appropriately. Adaptive selling frequently requires complex behavioral adjustments.[24]

Adaptive selling requires a strategic selling plan.

Adaptive selling that can be defined as altering sales behaviors during a customer interaction in order to improve communication. It relates to a salesperson's ability to collect information regarding the customer's needs and responding appropriately. Adaptive selling frequently requires complex behavioral adjustments.

Many companies have discovered that specialized sales training is an effective strategy. When Microsoft wanted to build a stronger partnership with its customers, all of its 5,000 sales professionals completed the Solution Selling sales training course. This training, based on concepts presented in *The New Solution Selling*, by Keith Eades, helped Microsoft salespeople create greater value for its customers.[25]

Strategic/Consultative Selling Model

When you study a value-added approach to personal selling that combines strategic planning, consultative selling practices, and partnering principles, you experience a mental exercise that is similar to solving a jigsaw puzzle. You are given many pieces of information that ultimately must form a complete picture. Putting the parts together isn't nearly as difficult if you can see the total picture at the beginning. Therefore, a single model has been developed to serve as a source of reference throughout the entire text. Figure 1.5 shows this model.

The Strategic/Consultative Selling Model features five steps, and each step is based on three prescriptions. The first step involves the development of a personal selling philosophy. Each of the other four steps relates to a broad strategic area of personal selling. Each step makes an important and unique contribution to the selling/buying process.

DEVELOPING A RELATIONSHIP STRATEGY Success in selling depends heavily on the salesperson's ability to develop, manage, and enhance interpersonal relations with the customer. People seldom buy products or services from someone they dislike or distrust. Harvey B. Mackay, founder of Mackay Envelope Corporation, says, "People don't care how much you know until they know how much you care." Most customers are more apt to openly discuss their needs and wants with a salesperson with whom they feel comfortable.

A **relationship strategy** is a well-thought-out plan for establishing, building, and maintaining quality relationships. This type of plan is essential for success in today's marketplace, which is characterized by vigorous competition, look-alike products, and customer loyalty dependent on quality relationships as well as quality products. The relationship strategy must encompass every aspect of selling from the first contact with a prospect to servicing the sale once this prospect becomes an established customer. The relationship strategy is an integral dimension of **relationship selling**. Relationship selling is a form of personal selling that involves securing, developing, and maintaining long-term relationships with customers.[26] Increased support for relationship selling recognizes the growing importance of partnerships in selling. The primary goal of the relationship strategy is to create rapport, trust, and mutual respect, which ensures a long-term partnership. To establish this type of relationship, salespeople must *adopt a win-win philosophy; that is, if the customer wins, I win; project a professional image; and maintain high ethical standards* (see Figure 1.5). Chapters 3, 4 and 5 provide important information on development of the relationship strategy.

Some people think that the concept of *relationships* is too soft and too emotional for a business application; these people think that it's too difficult to think about relationships in strategic terms. In fact, this is not the case at all. Every salesperson can and should formulate a strategic plan that builds and enhances relationships.

DEVELOPING A PRODUCT STRATEGY Products and services represent problem-solving tools. The **product strategy** is a plan that helps salespeople make correct decisions concerning the selection and positioning of products to meet identified customer needs. The three prescriptions for the product strategy are *become a product expert, sell benefits*, and *configure value-added solutions*. The development of a product strategy begins with a thorough study of one's product (see Figure 1.5) using a feature–benefit analysis approach. Product features such as technical superiority, reliability, fashionableness, design integrity, or guaranteed availability should be converted to benefits that appeal to the customer. Today's high-performance salespeople strive to

STRATEGIC/CONSULTATIVE SELLING MODEL*	
Strategic step	**Prescription**
Develop a Personal Selling Philosophy	☐ Adopt Marketing Concept ☐ Value Personal Selling ☐ Become a Problem Solver/Partner
Develop a Relationship Strategy	☐ Adopt Win-Win Philosophy ☐ Project Professional Image ☐ Maintain High Ethical Standards
Develop a Product Strategy	☐ Become a Product Expert ☐ Sell Benefits ☐ Configure Value-Added Solutions
Develop a Customer Strategy	☐ Understand the Buying Process ☐ Understand Buyer Behavior ☐ Develop Prospect Base
Develop a Presentation Strategy	☐ Prepare Objectives ☐ Develop Presentation Plan ☐ Provide Outstanding Service

*Strategic/consultative selling evolved in response to increased competition, more complex products, increased emphasis on customer needs, and growing importance of long-term relationships.

Product	Place
Price	Promotion

FIGURE 1.5

The Strategic/Consultative Selling Model is an extension of the marketing concept.

become product experts. Chapter 6 focuses on company, product, and competition knowledge needed by salespeople.

Product knowledge is not the only important element of a product strategy. In fact, salespeople who are too focused on selling products often fail to identify complete solutions to the customer's problem. Stephen Covey, author of the best-selling book, *The 7 Habits of Highly Effective People*, says "Diagnose before you prescribe." If the salesperson does not deeply engage the customer and fails to diagnose the problem correctly, chances are the solution recommended may not be the best one.[27]

The development of a product strategy often requires thoughtful decision making. Today's more knowledgeable customers seek a cluster of satisfactions that arise from the product itself, from the manufacturer or distributor of the product, and from the salesperson. The "new" product that customers are buying today is the sum total of the satisfactions that emerge from all three sources. The cluster of satisfactions concept is discussed in more detail in Chapter 7.

Selling Is Everyone's Business

SALES SUCCESS PAVES THE WAY FOR HISPANIC ENTREPRENEUR

At age 19 Rosado Shaw wanted to be a salesperson, but the company she worked for wouldn't let her sell. She had recently dropped out of elite Wellesley College and took a job with a company that makes umbrellas and tote bags. One day she took a sick day and called on the marketing staff at the Museum of Natural History. The result of this impromptu sales call was a $140,000 order. She then went to the president of the company and asked him, "Are you going to let me sell now, or what?" After two years in sales, Shaw moved to a rival firm, Umbrellas Plus, and acquired more experience. Years later she purchased controlling interest in the company and turned it into a $10 million enterprise.[b]

Entrepreneur Rosado Shaw.

DEVELOPING A CUSTOMER STRATEGY Patricia Seybold, author of *The Customer Revolution,* says we are in the midst of a profound revolution—the customer revolution. And it's bigger than the Internet revolution:

> *Customers have taken control of our companies' destinies. Customers are transforming our industries. And customers' loyalty—or lack thereof—has become increasingly important. . . .*[28]

Customers have become increasingly sophisticated in their buying strategies. More and more, they have come to expect value-added products and services and long-term commitments. Selling to today's customers starts with getting on the customers' agenda and carefully identifying their needs, wants, and buying conditions.

A **customer strategy** is a carefully conceived plan that results in maximum responsiveness to the customer's needs. This strategy is based on the fact that success in personal selling depends, in no small measure, on the salesperson's ability to learn as much as possible about the prospect. It involves the collection and analysis of specific information on each customer. When developing a customer strategy, the salesperson should *develop an understanding of the customer's buying process, understand buyer behavior, and develop a prospect base.* The

Patricia Seybold, CEO and founder of the Patricia Seybold Group, and best-selling author of The Customer Revolution, says we are in the midst of a profound revolution—the customer revolution.

first two parts of the customer strategy are introduced in Chapter 8. Suggestions concerning ways to develop and manage a solid prospect base are discussed in Chapter 9.

The customer strategy is dictated by the needs of the customer. For example, its best to consider relationship formation from the customer's perspective. When a *consultative* selling approach is required, the customer strategy will usually encompass a long-term relationship and ongoing collaboration. If a *transactional* approach is required, the customer strategy would not, in most cases, emphasize need assessment, problem solving, relationship building, and sales follow-up.[29]

DEVELOPING A PRESENTATION STRATEGY Typical salespeople spend about 30 percent of their time in actual face-to-face selling situations. However, the sales presentation is a critical part of the selling process. The **presentation strategy** is a well-developed plan that includes *preparing the sales presentation objectives, preparing a presentation plan that is needed to meet these objectives, and renewing one's commitment to provide outstanding customer service* (see Figure 1.5).

The presentation strategy usually involves developing one or more objectives for each sales call. For example, a salesperson might update personal information about the customer, provide information on a new product, and close a sale during one sales call. Multiple-objective sales presentations, which are becoming more common, are discussed in Chapter 10.

Presale presentation plans give salespeople the opportunity to consider those activities that take place during the sales presentation. For example, a salesperson might preplan a demonstration of product features to use when meeting with the customer. Presale planning ensures that salespeople are well organized during the sales presentation and prepared to offer outstanding service.

INTERRELATIONSHIP OF BASIC STRATEGIES The major strategies that form the Strategic/Consultative Selling Model are by no means independent. The relationship, product, and customer strategies all influence development of the presentation strategy (Figure 1.6). For example, one relationship-building practice might be developed for use during the initial face-to-face meeting with the customer and

FIGURE 1.6

The major strategies that form the Strategic/Consultative Selling Model are by no means independent of one another. The focus of each strategy is to satisfy customer needs and build quality partnerships.

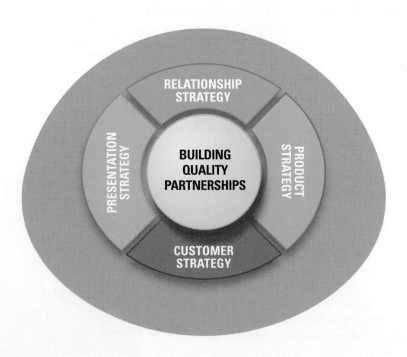

another for possible use during the negotiation of buyer resistance. Another relationship-building method might be developed for use after the sale is closed. The discovery of customer needs (part of the customer strategy) greatly influences planning for the sales presentation.

Evolution of Partnering

Partnering became a buzzword in the 1990s and in the 2000s it became a business reality.[30] Partnering has been driven by several economic forces. One is the demise of the product solution in several industries. When products of one company are nearly identical to the competition, the product strategy becomes less important than the relationship, customer, and presentation strategies. By contrast, some partnerships grow out of the need for customized products or services. Many manufacturers have formed partnerships with companies that offer flexibility in terms of product configuration, scheduling of deliveries, or some other factor.

Today's customer wants a quality product *and* a quality relationship. Salespeople willing to abandon short-term thinking and invest the time and energy needed to develop a high-quality, long-term relationship with customers are greatly rewarded. A strong partnership serves as a barrier to competing salespeople who want to sell to your accounts. Salespeople who are able to build partnerships enjoy more repeat business and referrals. Keeping existing customers happy makes a great deal of sense from an economic point of view. Experts in the field of sales and marketing know that it costs four to five times more to get a new customer than to keep an existing one. Therefore, even small increases in customer retention can result in major increases in profits.[31]

Partnering is a strategically developed, long-term relationship that solves the customer's problems. A successful long-term partnership is achieved when the salesperson is able to skillfully apply the four major strategies and, thus, add value in various ways (Figure 1.7). Successful sales professionals stay close to the customer and constantly search for new ways to add value.

The salespeople at Mackay Envelope Corporation achieve this goal by making sure they know more about their customers than the competitors know. Salespeople who work for Xerox Corporation are responding to a sales orientation that emphasizes postsale service. Bonuses are based on a formula that includes not only sales but also customer satisfaction.

Strategic Selling Alliances—The Highest Form of Partnering

Throughout the past decade we have seen the growth of a new form of partnership that often is described as a **strategic selling alliance**. The goal of strategic selling alliances is

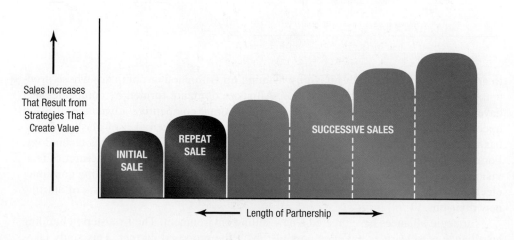

Sales Increases That Result from Strategies That Create Value

INITIAL SALE

REPEAT SALE

SUCCESSIVE SALES

← Length of Partnership →

FIGURE 1.7

Partnering is a strategically developed, long-term relationship that solves the customer's problems. A successful partnering effort results in repeat sales and referrals that expand the prospect base. The strength of the partnership increases each time the salesperson uses value-added selling strategies.

National account managers at Campbell's work closely with sales teams that call on culinary accounts. They add value by helping these customers improve their menu. These improvements add value and help build long-term partnerships.

to achieve a marketplace advantage by teaming up with another company whose products or services fit well with your own.[32] Alliances often are formed by companies that have similar business interests and, thus, gain a mutual competitive advantage. It is not uncommon for a company to form several alliances. Corning, a maker of glass products, has formed partnerships with several companies that need innovative glass technology. For example, Corning formed an alliance with Samsung, a Korean manufacturer of television screens. RadioShack has formed strategic alliances with several leading consumer electronics manufacturers. This move helped the company avoid the costs of starting new divisions.[33]

Strategic alliances have created a new selling environment. The first step in building an alliance is to learn as much as possible about the proposed partner. This study takes

Cushman & Wakefield understands that in today's global market customers want a partnership that emphasizes a quality product and a quality relationship. Trust is a key element of a strong partnership.

place long before face-to-face contact. Alliances that are formed between companies that vary greatly in such areas as customer focus, financial stability, or ethical values will likely fail.[34] The second step is to meet with the proposed partner and explore mutual benefits of the alliance. At this point the salesperson (or account manager) is selling advice, assistance, and counsel, not specific products. Building win-win alliances requires the highest form of consultative selling. Very often, the salesperson is working with a company team made up of persons from such areas as research and development (R&D), finance, and distribution. Presentations and proposals usually focus on profit impact and other strategic alliance benefits.[35]

Partnering Is Enhanced with High Ethical Standards

In the field of selling there are certain pressures that can influence the ethical conduct of salespeople, and poor ethical decisions can weaken or destroy partnerships. To illustrate, let us assume a competitor makes exaggerated claims about a product. Do you counteract by promising more than your product can deliver? What action do you take when there is a time management problem and you must choose between servicing past sales and making

Customer Relationship Management with Technology

INTRODUCING SALESFORCE.COM CRM SOFTWARE

Today, many sales professionals use computers to help them better perform the tasks associated with successful personal selling. Various software programs are used, including e-mail, electronic spreadsheets, word processors, configuration systems, presentation packages, fax managers, and customer relationship management (CRM) systems. A basic CRM system consists of a database containing information about the people with whom a company maintains relationships, such as customers, prospects, coworkers, and suppliers. For your use with the CRM studies in this text, you will be provided with access to the Salesforce.com, an Internet-based CRM system. You can learn the fundamentals of CRM with this application, including searching for customer and product-related information, managing time and priorities, communicating, and forecasting sales. (See Appendix 2 CRM Instructions for Accessing Salesforce.com. on p. 404 and the CRM Application Exercise Introducing Salesforce.com Software on p. 24. Also go to www.salesforce.com and view introductory and sales demonstration videos.)

Close more deals the easy way. The world's leading sales force automation solution makes selling easier, so sales teams actually use it from day one. The result: more leads, better forecasts, and bigger deals. From the software-as-a-service leader. **www.salesforce.com**

salesforce.com

Selling Power *magazine, www.sellingpower.com, p. 97, March 2008.*

new sales? What if a superior urges you to use a strategy that you consider unethical? These and other pressures must be dealt with everyday.

Although Chapter 5 is devoted entirely to ethical considerations in personal selling, it should be noted that ethics is a major theme of the text. The topic of ethics has been interwoven throughout several chapters. The authors believe that ethical decisions must be made everyday in the life of a salesperson, so this important topic cannot be covered in a single chapter.

Partnering Is Enhanced with Customer Relationship Management

Many companies have adopted some form of customer relationship management. **Customer relationship management (CRM)**, sometimes referred to as *sales automation*, is the process of building and maintaining strong customer relationships by providing customer value.[36] A modern CRM program relies on a variety of technologies to improve communications in a sales organization and enhance customer responsiveness. A variety of CRM applications will be discussed throughout the text.

Value Creation—The New Selling Imperative

We have defined value-added selling as a series of creative improvements within the sales process that enhance the customer experience. The **information economy** will reward those salespeople who have the skills, the knowledge, and the motivation to determine how to create value at every step of the sales process.

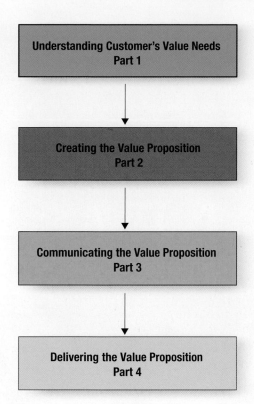

FIGURE 1.8

Creating and Delivering Customer Value Model
The salesperson's role in value creation is illustrated in this figure.*

*Adapted from Figure 1.2, Making and Delivering Value, Solomon, Marshall, and Stuart, *Marketing: Real People, Real Choices*, Prentice Hall, Upper Saddle River, NJ 2008, Page 23.

As Figure 1.8 shows, value creation begins with an understanding of the customer's value needs. Salespeople can create value in many ways: establishing a relationship based on trust, carefully identifying the customer's needs, and identifying the best possible product solution. In the case of a complex sale, understanding the customer's value needs may take a great deal of time and may involve bringing in team members who have specific technical expertise.

Creating an appealing value proposition (Part 2) requires a detailed study of the customer's value needs. If you discover that timely delivery of your product is of critical importance, you must give the client what they want. And if you promise on-time delivery, you must back up your claims.

Communicating the value proposition (Part 3) presents another major challenge. Traditional selling has too often emphasized communicating only the value that lies in the product. The focus of the sales call has too often been the product, not creating value for the customer.[37]

Delivering value (Part 4) can be very challenging. It may require coordination of credit approval, training, installation, service, and other aspects of the sale. Of course each element of the selling process provides an opportunity to add value.

Value-added selling consists of a series of creative ways to improve and enhance the customer experience. Wisconsin Cheese offers its sales organization value-adding ideas and supports them with strategic tools and programs.

WHEN YOU OFFER
MORE THAN SALES,
YOU GET MORE SALES.

With value-adding tools and programs from the Wisconsin Milk Marketing Board, you can show your operator customers how to increase their profits using REAL Wisconsin Cheese — on-trend recipes, menu enhancement programs, merchandising ideas, suggestions for pairing Wisconsin Cheese with popular beverages — all the tools you need to build profitable, long-term relationships. So give operators what they really want — ideas that build their sales and increase their profits.

For your free Why Wisconsin CD-ROM, call 1-800-383-9662, ext. 229.

WISCONSIN CHEESE

© 2002 Wisconsin Milk Marketing Board, Inc.

Chapter Learning Activities

Reviewing Key Concepts

Define personal selling and describe the three prescriptions of a personal selling philosophy

Personal selling occurs when a company representative interacts directly with a customer or prospective customer to present information about a product or service. Salespeople are encouraged to develop a personal selling philosophy based on three prescriptions: adopt the marketing concept, value personal selling, and assume the role of a problem solver or partner.

Describe the contributions of personal selling to the information economy

The restructuring of America from an industrial economy to an information economy began in 1950s. We now live in an age in which the effective exchange of information is the foundation of most economic transactions. Salespeople use a variety of information technology tools to gather and process information of value to the customer.

Discuss personal selling as an extension of the marketing concept

The *marketing concept* is the belief that a firm should dedicate all its policies, planning, and operations to the satisfaction of the customer. Salespeople today are problem solvers who obtain the participation of buyers in identifying their problems, which can be translated into needs.

Describe the evolution of consultative selling from the marketing era to the present

The *marketing era* that began in the United States in the 1950s looked first at customer needs and wants and then created goods and services to meet those needs and wants. *Consultative selling* emerged in the late 1960s and early 1970s as an approach that emphasizes the identification of customer needs through effective communication between the salesperson and customer. The evolution of selling continued with the development of *strategic selling and partnering.*

Define strategic selling and name the four broad strategic areas in the Strategic/Consultative Selling Model

Strategic selling evolved in the 1980s and involves the preparation of a carefully conceived plan to accomplish sales objectives. Strategic selling is based on a company's *strategic market plan,* which takes into consideration the coordination of all the major functional areas of the business—production, marketing, finance, and personnel. The four broad strategic areas in the Strategic/Consultative Selling Model (after development of personal selling philosophy) are developing a relationship strategy, developing a product strategy, developing a customer strategy, and developing a presentation strategy.

Describe the evolution of partnering and the nature of a strategic selling

Partnering is a strategically developed, long-term relationship that solves the customer's problems. The long-term partnership is achieved when the salesperson is able to skillfully apply the four major strategies and therefore add value in various ways. The *strategic selling alliance* is the highest form of partnering. The goal of this type of alliance is to achieve a marketplace advantage by teaming up with another company whose products fit well with your own alliance.

Explain how value-added selling strategies enhance personal selling

Value-added selling has emerged as a major response to the customer economy. This approach to personal selling is defined as a series of creative improvements that enhance the customer's experience. The information economy rewards those salespeople who have the skills, the knowledge, and the motivation to determine how to create value at every step of the sales process.

Key Terms

Personal selling	Strategic planning	Customer strategy
Product	Tactics	Presentation strategy
Personal selling philosophy	Strategy	Partnering
Value-added selling	Adaptive selling	Strategic selling alliance
Marketing concept	Relationship strategy	Customer relationship management (CRM)
Marketing mix	Relationship selling	
Consultative selling	Product strategy	Information economy
Transactional selling		

Review Questions

1. Explain how personal selling can help solve the problem of information overload.
2. According to the Strategic/Consultative Selling Model (see Figure 1.1), what are the three prescriptions for developing a successful personal selling philosophy?
3. Why is peddling or "pushing products" inconsistent with the marketing concept?
4. What is consultative selling? Give examples.
5. Diagram and label the four-step Consultative Sales Presentation Guide.
6. List and briefly explain the four broad strategic areas that make up the selling process.
7. Briefly describe the evolution of partnering. Discuss the forces that contributed to this approach to selling.
8. Provide a brief description of value-added selling. What economic forces have motivated companies to adopt value-added selling?
9. Briefly describe why some organizations are developing strategic selling alliances.
10. Explain why the ethical conduct of salespeople has become so important today.

Application Exercises

1. Assume that you are an experienced professional salesperson. A professor who teaches at a nearby university has asked you to speak to a consumer economics class about the benefits of personal selling to customers. Make an outline of what to say.
2. A friend of yours has invented a unique and useful new product. This friend, an engineer by profession, understands little about marketing and selling this new product. She does understand, however, that "nothing happens until somebody sells the product." She has asked you to describe the general factors that need to be considered when you market a product. Prepare an answer to her question.
3. Sharon Alverez has been teaching college biology courses. She is offered a position selling pharmaceutical products. This position requires that she call on doctors and pharmacists to explain her product line. Describe the similarities and the differences between personal selling and teaching.
4. To learn more about industry-based global sales training programs, access www.wilsonlearning.com. Click on the "Sales Effectiveness" link and examine the content of the various sales courses offered throughout the world by this company. From this review, describe the similarities between what this company offers and the material in this chapter.

Role-Play Exercise

The purpose of this role-play is to provide you with an opportunity to engage in a basic need identification exercise. You will be meeting with someone (a class member) who is preparing for an important job interview and needs a pen and/or pencil. Prior to the meeting, make a list of the questions you will ask. Then pair off with the class member and ask your questions. Be sure to take notes. At the end of the interview, be prepared to recommend the most appropriate pen and/or pencil.

CRM Application Exercise

Introducing Salesforce.com CRM Software

The CRM system that you will use with this book is a demonstration version of Salesforce.com, the best-selling Internet-based CRM application. See appendix 2 on p. 404 for instructions on how to log into and use the Salesforce.com CRM software. Using your Salesforce.com login, you will access a database of information about prospective customers for a company selling network systems. In the case study and exercises ahead, you assume the role of a salesperson who is selling these network systems. The emphasis in these exercises is customer relationship management. No prior experience or prior knowledge of networking systems is required to complete these exercises.

Salesforce.com is a database program, which means that it uses records and fields. Records are the screens that contain information about each person. Fields are the boxes on the records for entering and displaying data, such as the name of the person (e.g., Bradley Able). Salesforce.com also functions as a contact management program because it maintains a record for each contact (person). In Salesforce.com this contact (person) is always associated with a company or organization.

You can experiment with Salesforce.com without concern about damaging the application. To get acquainted with the Salesforce.com version of CRM, click on the various menu items and icons and observe the functions that are available to you. Experimenting with this software gives you a feel for the potential power of using technology to enhance your sales career. Test Salesforce.com's report capabilities by looking at a mailing list: Select "Reports," then "Mailing List."

As you experiment with Salesforce.com, you can obtain help at any time by pressing the Help and Training Button. (See the Learning CRM Software exercise in Chapter 2.)

Reality Selling Today Video Case Problem

At the beginning of this chapter, you were given an introduction to Marcus Smith, employed by Liberty Mutual, a successful insurance company. Smith is responsible for introducing a very large number of products and services and he must always keep one eye on the competition. He must be prepared to answer questions about his own products and services and those of the competition. He must also be prepared to discuss the intricacies of the insurance terms, and possible bundles of insurance policies to offer his customers the best value.

Marcus Smith
Liberty Mutual

Like every other professional salesperson, Smith is constantly involved in learning. We now know that the principles of selling can be learned and applied by people whose personal characteristics are quite different. Most successful salespeople spend considerable time acquiring product knowledge, keeping up to date in their industry and related industries, and learning more about their customers. Smith acquired his formal training in professional selling from the Program in Excellence in Selling at the University of Houston. In the insurance industry, salespeople often go through industry-related training and a formal exam to acquire a license to sell personal and property insurance. Smith also undergoes a rigorous Liberty Mutual training program that covers courses in four concentrations: products and services, company, competition, and quoting.

Smith realizes the importance of a relationship strategy that is built upon a win-win philosophy. In addition to building a strong relationship with the customer, he must be able to work effectively with others who directly or indirectly influence the sale. He shares market information with his peers periodically because a broad view of the market as a whole is crucial in the highly competitive insurance industry. The salesperson who is honest, accountable, and sincerely concerned about the customer's welfare brings added value to the sales. (See chapter opener on p. 4, and Reality Selling Today Role-Play 1 in Appendix 1 on p. 392 for more information.)

Questions

1. Does it appear that Smith has adopted the three prescriptions of a personal selling philosophy? (See Strategic/Consultative Selling Model.) Explain.

2. What prescriptions of the relationship strategy (see Strategic/Consultative Selling Model) have been adopted by Marcus Smith?

3. Value-added selling is defined as a series of creative improvements in the sales process that enhance the customer's experience. Describe the various ways that Marcus Smith can create value for his customers.

4. Let's assume you are considering a career in personal selling. Describe how you balance between information collection (i.e., information about the market, about the competitor, about the customers in your assigned market and in other markets) and information utilization (i.e., using the information gathered to close sales).

Partnership Selling: Role-Play/Simulation

[If your instructor has chosen to use the *Partnership Selling Role-Play/Simulation* exercise that accompanies this text, these boxes alert you to your Role-Play/ Simulation assignments. Your instructor will also provide you with needed information.]

Preview the role-play/simulation materials in Appendix 3. These materials are produced by the Park Inn International Hotel and Convention Center, and you will be using them in your role as a new salesperson (and, at times, as the customer) for the hotel and its convention services.

The role-play exercises begin in Chapter 6, as you begin to create your product strategy. However, in anticipation of the role-play, you can begin to imagine yourself in the role of an actual salesperson. Start to think about how you can develop your personal selling philosophy. What are some ethical guidelines that you may wish to adopt for yourself? (Ethics is also the subject of Chapter 5, "Ethics: The Foundation for Relationships in Selling.") What skills do you need to develop to become a partner with your prospective customers? (Refer to the position description in Part I of Appendix 3.)

The Park Inn has implemented a quality improvement process. How does this affect your role as a sales representative? (Refer to the Total Quality Customer Service Glossary in Part I of Appendix 3.)

2

Personal Selling Opportunities in the Age of Information

Chapter Preview

When you finish reading this chapter, you should be able to

1
Explain how personal selling skills have become one of the master skills needed for success in the information age and how personal selling skills contribute to the work performed by knowledge workers

2
Discuss the rewarding aspects of a career in selling today

3
Discuss the different employment settings in selling today

4
Identify the four major sources of sales training

► Introduction

Job seekers who visit Monster.com or CareerBuilder.com are usually surprised to discover that sales careers represent one of the largest job posting categories. Many thousands of entry-level sales positions are listed every day. The next big surprise comes when they discover the great variety of companies that hire salespeople. Some companies, such as Marriott and United Parcel Service (UPS), are well known throughout the nation. Other companies, such as SpeechPhone, LLC, and World Golf Hospitality, Inc., may be unfamiliar to the job seeker. SpeechPhone, LLC, founded in 2002, sells call forwarding, message retrieval, and other phone services. World Golf Hospitality, Inc., founded in 1992, plans corporate-travel events and meetings that typically involve golf. The company has created travel programs for major events including the Masters, the Ryder Cup, and the U.S. Open tournaments.[1]

In recent years, the labor market has become a place of churning dislocation caused by the heavy volume of mergers, acquisitions, business closings, bankruptcies, and downsizings. Personal selling careers have become an attractive employment option to the thousands of professionals who walk away from—or are pushed out of—corporate jobs. ■

Personal Selling in the Age of Information

The late Stanley Marcus, chairman emeritus of the prestigious Neiman Marcus retail company, said, "Sooner or later in business, everybody has to sell something to somebody." He noted that even if you are not in sales, you must know how to sell a product, a service, an idea, or yourself.[2] Marcus's views have garnered a great deal of support among observers of the information age. Today's workforce is made up of millions of knowledge workers who succeed only when they add value to information. **Knowledge workers** are individuals whose work effort is centered around creating, using, sharing, and applying knowledge. The new economy is about the growing value of knowledge, making it the most important ingredient of what people buy and sell.[3] One way to add value to information is to collect it, organize it, clarify it, and present it in a convincing manner. This skill, used every day by professional salespeople, is invaluable in a world that is overloaded with information.

As noted in Chapter 1, relationships began to become more important at the beginning of the information age. In many cases, information does not have value unless people interact effectively. A salesperson may possess information concerning an important new technology, but that information has no value until it is communicated effectively to an investor, a customer, or someone else who can benefit from knowing more about his product. A bank loan officer may have the resources needed to assist a prospective homeowner reach her dream, but in the absence of a good relationship, communications may break down.

Why Knowledge Workers Need Selling Skills

In his best-selling book *Megatrends*, John Naisbitt noted that "the game of life in the information age is people interacting with other people."[4] With its emphasis on effective and adaptive interpersonal interaction, selling has become one of the master skills. Furthermore, individuals who have developed skills associated with careers in sales are more likely to be successful when they decide to go out on their own because more often than not, those skills translate very well to other businesses.[5] Today, personal selling skills contribute in a major way to four groups of knowledge workers who usually do not consider themselves salespeople:

- Managerial personnel
- Professionals (accountants, consultants, lawyers, etc.)
- Entrepreneurs
- Customer service representatives

Managerial Personnel

People working in managerial occupations represent a large group of knowledge workers. They are given such titles as executive, manager, or administrator. Leaders are constantly involved in capturing, processing, and communicating information. Some of the most valuable information is acquired from customers. This helps explain the rapid growth in what is being described as "executive selling." Chief executive officers and other executives often accompany salespeople on sales calls to learn more about customer needs and in some cases to assist with presentations. Manny Fernandez of the Gartner Group, a technology consulting firm based in Stamford, Connecticut, spends more than half his time traveling on sales calls.[6] Leaders also must articulate their ideas in a persuasive manner and win support for their vision. Brian Tracy, author of *The 100 Absolutely Unbreakable Laws of Business Success*, says, "People who cannot present their ideas or sell themselves effectively have very little influence and are not highly respected."[7]

Professionals

Today's professional workers include lawyers, designers, programmers, engineers, consultants, dietitians, counselors, doctors, accountants, and many other specialized knowledge workers. Our labor force includes nearly 20 million professional service providers, persons who need many of the skills used by professional salespeople. Clients who purchase professional services are usually more interested in the person who delivers the service than in the firm that employs the professional. They seek expert diagnosticians who are truly interested in their needs. The professional must display good communication skills and be able to build a relationship built on trust.

Technical skills are not enough in the information age. Many employers expect the professional to bring in new business in addition to keeping current customers satisfied. Employers often screen professional applicants to determine their customer focus and ability to interact well with people.

Many firms are providing their professional staff with sales training. The accounting firm Ernst & Young sets aside several days each year to train its professional staff in personal selling. The National Law Firm Marketing Association recently featured Neil

"WILSON, WHAT EXACTLY IS A KNOWLEDGE WORKER AND DO WE HAVE ANY ON THE STAFF?"

The new economy's workforce is made up of millions of knowledge workers who succeed only when they add value to information. Today's salesperson collects information, organizes it, clarifies it, and presents it in a convincing manner, thereby adding value.

Rackham, author of *Spin Selling*, as keynote speaker at its national conference. The Wicker Corporation, a manufacturer of equipment for the plastics industry, has initiated a program designed to motivate its researchers, engineers, and manufacturing staff members to get involved in sales. Faced with increased competition and more cost-conscious customers, a growing number of law, accounting, engineering, and architectural firms are discovering the merits of personal selling as an auxiliary activity.[8]

Entrepreneurs

Thousands of new businesses are started each year in the United States. As noted previously, people who want to start a new business frequently need to sell their plan to investors and others who can help get the firm established. Once the firm is open, owners rely on personal selling to build their businesses.

James Koch, chief executive officer of the Boston Beer Company (brewer of Samuel Adams beer), makes a strong case for personal selling. Like most new companies, his started with no customers. To get the new company established, he assumed the role of salesperson and set a goal of establishing one new account each week.

Today Koch continues to spend time on the street, visiting convenience stores, supermarkets, and taverns. Competition from popular craft beers such as Fat Tire and Magic Hat, and imports such as Stella Artois and Beck, present a major challenge. He's also trying to get the attention of young men who think of Samuel Adams as their father's beer. He readily admits that selling his beer is the most rewarding part of his job. Koch could have sold his company to a megabrewer long ago, but that option is not appealing to this wealthy entrepreneur who loves to sell.[9]

Neil Rackham, author of Spin Selling, *recently addressed the National Law Firm Marketing Association at its National Conference. According to Rackham, "more than a million people across the world have been trained in the SPIN MODEL to help them sell more effectively."*

Selling Is Everyone's Business

SELLING PHILANTHROPY TO THE "CYBER-STINGY"

As president of the Community Foundation Silicon Valley, Peter Hero is selling the concept of philanthropy to high-tech millionaires. Although Silicon Valley is home to several thousand millionaires, his job is not easy. Many of the wealthy residents are very young and they don't spend much time thinking about leaving behind a lasting civic legacy. And many of those who are skilled at generating wealth don't have a clue when it comes to giving it away. Yet the foundation is growing and large grants are being given to education programs, social-service agencies, and neighborhood groups. Thanks to Peter Hero, philanthropy is becoming another growth industry in Silicon Valley.[a]

Peter Hero, president of Community Foundation Silicon Valley.

Customer Service Representatives

The assignment of selling duties to employees with customer service responsibilities has become quite common today. The term **customer service representative (CSR)** is used to describe knowledge workers who process reservations, accept orders by phone or other means, deliver products, handle customer complaints, provide technical assistance, and assist full-time sales representatives. Some companies are teaming CSRs and salespeople. After the sale is closed, the CSR helps process paperwork, check on delivery of the product, and engage in other customer follow-up duties.

Assigning sales duties to customer service representatives makes sense when you consider the number of contacts customers have with CSRs. When a customer seeks assistance with a problem or makes a reservation, the CSR learns more about the customer and often provides the customer with needed information. Customer needs often surface as both parties exchange information. It is important to keep in mind the advice offered by the authors of *Selling the Invisible*: "Every act is a marketing act. Make every employee a marketing person."[10]

Increasingly, work in the information economy is understood as an expression of thought. At a time when people change their careers eight or more times during their lives, selling skills represent important transferable employment skills.

Your Future in Personal Selling

The 500 largest sales forces in America employ 17.5 million salespeople.[11] These companies will seek to recruit 500,000 college graduates. A large number of additional salespeople are employed by smaller companies. In addition, the number of sales positions is increasing in most industrialized countries. A close examination of these positions reveals that there is no single "selling" occupation. Our labor force includes hundreds of different selling careers and chances are there are positions that match your interests, talents, and ambitions. The diversity within selling becomes apparent as you study the career options discussed in this chapter.

Although many college students ultimately become salespeople, often it's not their first career choice. Students tend to view sales as dynamic and active but believe a selling career requires them to engage in deceitful or dishonest practices. The good news is that old stereotypes about sales are gradually going by the wayside. Students who study the careers of highly successful salespeople discover that ethical sales practices represent the key to long-term success.

A professional selling position encompasses a wide range of tasks (Figure 2.1), and, therefore, salespeople must possess a variety of skills. A salesperson representing Federal Express (FedEx) makes numerous sales calls each day in an attempt to establish new accounts and provide service to established accounts. There is a wide range of potential customers who can use FedEx delivery services. A salesperson working for a Caterpillar construction equipment dealer may make only two or three sales calls per day. The products offered by the dealer are expensive and are not purchased frequently.

Just as selling occupations differ, so do the titles by which salespeople are known. Their titles reflect, in part, the variety of duties they perform. A survey of current job announcements indicates that companies are using such titles as these:

Account Executive	Sales Consultant
Account Representative	Business Development Manager
Sales Account Manager	Sales Associate
Relationship Manager	Marketing Representative
District Representative	Territory Manager

Two factors have contributed to the creation of new titles. First, we have seen a shift from "selling" to "consulting." When salespeople assume a consulting role, the value of the relationship exceeds the value of the transaction. Second, the new titles reflect a difference in education and skill sets needed for the position.[12]

Salespeople, regardless of title, play an important role in sustaining the growth and profitability of organizations of all sizes. They also support the employment of many nonselling employees.

Rewarding Aspects of Selling Careers

From a personal and economic standpoint, selling can be a rewarding career. Careers in selling offer financial rewards, recognition, security, and opportunities for advancement to a degree that is unique, when compared with other occupations.

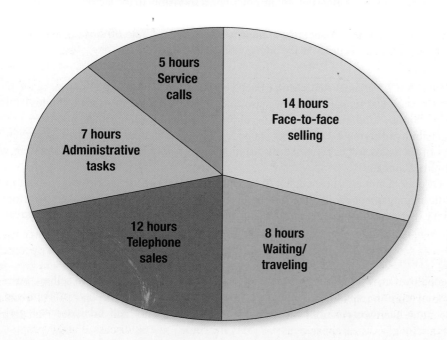

FIGURE 2.1

How salespeople spend their time during an average 46-hour workweek (approximate).

TABLE 2.1 Executive and Sales Force Compensation

	TOTAL COMPENSATION	BASE SALARY	BONUS PLUS COMMISSIONS
Executive	$147,824	$99,800	$48,440
Top Performer	$161,501	$91,452	$74,539
Mid-level Performer	$ 99,501	$62,625	$36,772
Low-level Performer	$ 70,994	$47,702	$20,835
Average for All Reps	$119,637	$75,905	$44,888

Source: Rebecca Aronauer, "The 2007 Compensation Survey," *Sales & Marketing Management*, May 2007, p. 30. Used with permission of the Nielsen Business Media, Inc.

ABOVE-AVERAGE INCOME Studies dealing with incomes in the business community indicate that salespeople earn significantly higher incomes than most other workers. Some salespeople actually earn more than their sales managers and other executives within the organization. This high level of compensation (whether from base salary, bonus, or incentives) is justified for good performance. Table 2.1 provides a summary of the 2007 compensation survey by *Sales & Marketing Management* magazine. Executive and sales force compensation continues to climb despite uncertain economic conditions.[13]

In recent years we have seen new ways to report compensation for salespeople. The Hay's Group, working with C&C Market Research Inc., developed a reporting method that tracks earnings for different types of sales approaches. Research indicates that salespeople involved in transactional sales earned the lowest compensation. Sales personnel involved in value-added sales earned the highest level of compensation. These highly paid salespeople created improvements in the sales process that enhanced the customer experience.[14]

ABOVE-AVERAGE PSYCHIC INCOME Two major psychological needs common to all people are recognition and security. **Psychic income**, which consists of factors that provide psychological rewards, helps satisfy these important needs and motivates us to achieve higher levels of performance. The need for recognition has been established in numerous studies that have examined human motivation. Workers from all employment areas indicate that recognition for work well done is an important morale-building factor.

In selling, recognition occurs more frequently and with greater intensity than it does in most other occupations. Because selling contributes so visibly to the success of most business firms, the accomplishments of sales personnel seldom go unrecognized. Most people want to achieve some measure of security in their work. Selling is one of those occupations that usually provides job security during both good and bad times.

OPPORTUNITY FOR ADVANCEMENT Each year, thousands of openings appear in the ranks of supervision and management. Because salespeople work in positions of high visibility, they are in an excellent position to be chosen for advancement to positions of greater responsibility. The top executives of many of today's companies began their careers in the ranks of the sales force. As noted by Kinni, "Today's C-suites are literally bursting with sales professionals."[15]

Of course, not all salespeople can become presidents of large corporations, but in the middle-management ranks there are numerous interesting and high-paying positions in which experience in selling is a prime requisite for advancement. Information on careers in sales management is presented in Chapter 17.

Opportunities for Women

Prodded by a growing awareness that gender is not a barrier to success in selling, business firms are recruiting qualified women in growing numbers. The percentage of women in the sales force has increased considerably. Although women are still relative newcomers to

Selling in Action

OPPORTUNITIES FOR WOMEN IN SALES

 In a world that is beginning to value diversity, we are seeing growing opportunities for women in sales. However, some misinformation concerning women in sales still exists. Four common myths follow:

Myth: *Women will not relocate or stick around long enough to repay the firm's hiring and training expenses.* Today, working women make up nearly half of the workforce and they have made significant gains in a wide range of traditionally male-dominated areas. About 50 percent of the working women contribute more than half of their family's income. Most of the women in this group need to work, want to work, and seek rewarding career opportunities.

Myth: *Women earn significantly less in sales than their male counterparts.* Although a pay gap between men and women exists in the field of sales, it is relatively small compared with the earnings gap for women who work full-time in the workforce as a whole.

Myth: *Buyers are less accepting of female salespeople.* In the field of personal selling, perceived expertise, likability, and trustworthiness can have a major influence on purchase decisions. Women who project these qualities seldom face rejection based on gender.

Myth: *Women face special problems when assigned to selling positions in foreign countries.* The truth is recent research suggests that businesswomen often enjoy a significant edge over their male counterparts when given overseas assignments.[b]

industrial sales, they have enjoyed expanded career opportunities in such areas as real estate, insurance, advertising services, investments, and travel services. A growing number of women are turning to sales employment because it offers excellent economic rewards and in many cases a flexible work schedule. Flexible schedules are very appealing to women who want to balance career and family.

At Pitney Bowes, the nation's largest provider of corporate mail services, about 24 percent of the top employees are women. Many of the top salespeople are women who were formerly teachers.[16] Nationally, about 20 percent of all financial advisers are women.[17]

Employment Settings in Selling Today

Careers in sales include both inside and outside sales positions. ***Inside* salespeople** are those who perform selling activities at the employer's location, typically using the telephone. Many manufacturers and wholesalers have developed inside sales forces to take orders, make calls on smaller customers, and provide support for field salespeople. In some cases the inside salespeople are called customer service representatives and provide a number of support services on behalf of field salespeople.

Inside sales can be either *inbound* or *outbound. Inbound* inside salespeople respond to calls initiated by the customer. Telemarketing is a common form of outbound inside sales that serves several purposes including sales and service. In some cases this includes technical support personnel who provide technical information and answer questions. Some companies utilize sales assistants to confirm appointments, conduct credit checks, and follow up on deliveries.[18] The use of telemarketing has grown rapidly as businesses use this method to contact potential new customers and to follow up on current small customers or customers in distant areas.

Unlike inside sales, **outside salespeople** travel to meet prospects and customers in their place of business or residence. Information technology companies like Hewlett-Packard employ thousands of salespeople to sell computer systems, peripherals, and integrated technology solutions to other companies, large and small. Wholesalers, like Super Value, employ outside salespeople that, in addition to selling products, offer a variety of services to its customers, such as maintaining inventories, merchandising, providing promotional support, gathering and interpreting market information, extending credit, and distributing goods. In addition, many direct to consumer salespeople, such as interior designers, engage at least partially in outside sales, e.g., financial services, life insurance, direct sales.

Inside and outside salespeople for the same company often work together and rely heavily upon each other. For example, inside salespeople often prospect, generating and qualifying leads for outside salespeople to call on personally. Also, once an initial sale is made by an outside salesperson, inside salespeople are asked to provide ongoing customer contact and service, taking responsibility for meeting customer needs while being alert for opportunities to sell additional products or services.

Selling Through Channels

Many times people mistakenly think of selling jobs as being limited to the interaction between the company and the end user of the good or service. However, goods and services flow from manufacturer to end user through a *channel of distribution*.

As can be seen in Figure 2.2, sales jobs exist throughout this supply chain.[19] In fact, many of the most promising sales careers in terms of career advancement and compensation exist in the beginning of the channel flow in the form of business-to-business, or "*B2B*," sales. **Trade selling** refers to the sale of a product or service to another member of the supply chain. For example, a manufacturer of household goods may employ sales representatives to sell its products to retailers. It may instead (or also) sell its products to wholesalers that warehouse the product and in turn the wholesaler employs sales representatives to sell these and other products to retailers that the manufacturer does not want to service directly.

Similar scenarios exist with industrial products where the end user is a business rather than an individual consumer and with services where the end user is either a consumer or business user. Another example of B2B sales is **missionary, or detail, sales**. Rather than selling directly to the end user, the detail salesperson attempts to generate goodwill and stimulate demand for the manufacturer's product among channel members.

As you can see, selling careers may be classified in several ways. One of the most useful classifications is based upon the sales channels depicted in Figure 2.2. Three major channels exist—service sales channels, business goods channels, and consumer goods channels.

Career Opportunities in the Service Channel

Sales careers in service sales include both business-to-business and business-to-consumer sales. Today approximately 80 percent of the U.S. labor force is employed in some

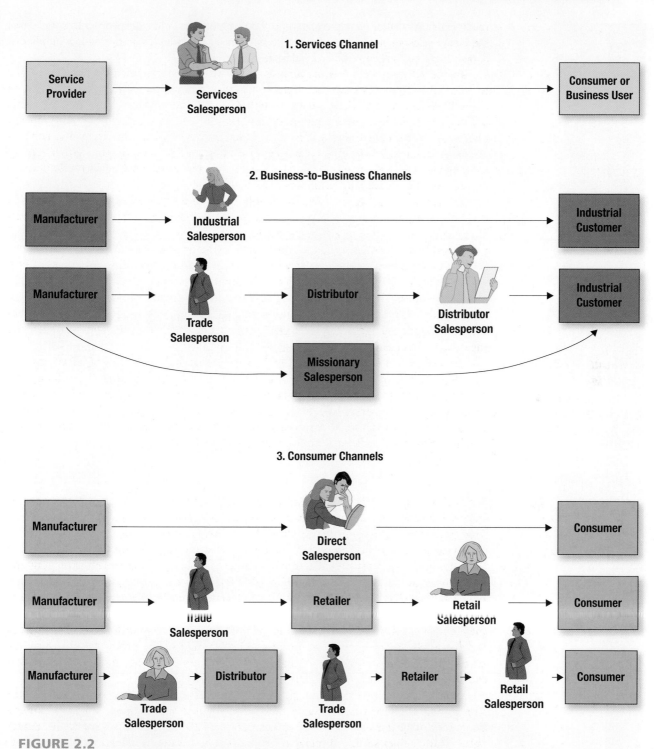

FIGURE 2.2

Shown here are salespeople in different channels.

capacity in the service sector of the economy. Table 2.2 lists the largest U.S. service companies based on total revenues.[20] The growth rate for the service industry is much higher than the growth rate for product companies. Service companies provide career opportunities in a variety of settings.

HOTEL, MOTEL, AND CONVENTION CENTER SERVICES Every year in the United States, thousands of seminars, conferences, and business meetings take place in hotels, motels, and convention centers. The salespeople employed by these companies play

TABLE 2.2 The Largest U.S. Service Companies

SERVICES	RANK IN FORTUNE 500	REVENUES $ MILLION
Hotel, Motel, and Convention Center Services		
Marrion International	203	11,500
Harrah's Entertainment	309	7,411
Telecommunications Services		
Verizon Communications	18	75,112
AT&T	39	43,862
Sprint Nextel	59	34,680
Financial Services		
Diversified Financials		
General Electric	7	157,153
American Express	69	30,080
Data Services		
First Data	224	10,490
Fiserv	488	4,086
Securities		
Morgan Stanley	30	52,498
Savings Institutions		
Washington Mutual	99	21,326
Golden West Financial	326	6,662
Banking		
Commercial Banks		
Citigroup	8	131,045
Bank of America Corp.	12	83,980
J.P. Morgan Chase & Co.	17	79,902
Wells Fargo	46	40,407
Radio, Television, and Internet		
Advertising		
Omnicom Group	225	10,481
Interpublic Group	348	6,274
Publishing Printing		
R.R. Donnelley & Sons	265	8,651
Gannett	296	7,666

SERVICES	RANK IN FORTUNE 500	REVENUES $ MILLION
Real Estate		
Cendant	114	19,471
Host Murriott	502	3,942
Insurance		
New York Life Insurance	74	28,051
MetLife	35	46,983
Business Services		
Payroll Services		
Automatic Data Proc.	271	8,499
Ceridian	986	1,459
Networking		
Motorola	54	36,843
Cisco Systems	83	24,801
Diversified Outsourcing		
Aramark	215	10,963
Brink's	395	5,488
Computer; Office Equipment		
Intnl Business Machines	10	91,134
Hewlett-Packard	11	86,696
Dell	25	55,908
Xerox	142	15,701
Apple Computer	159	13,931
Computer Software		
Microsoft	48	39,788
Oracle	196	11,799
Information Technology Services		
Electronic Data Systems	108	20,537
Computer Sciences	141	15,849
Science Applications Intnl	285	8,022
Unisys	372	5,759
Temporary Help		
Manpower	136	16,080
Kelly Services	407	5,290

Source: "The Largest U.S. Service Companies," www.Money.cnn.com/magazines/fortune/fortune500 (accessed on January 29, 2007).

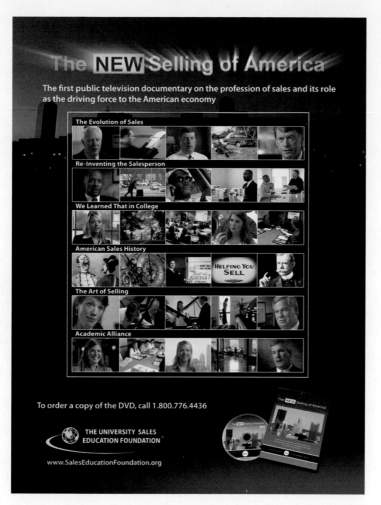

*"The NEW Selling In America"
documentary video provides
excellent insight into Personal
Selling Opportunities in The Age
of Information. This five part
program leaves no question
about "selling" being one of the
master skills for success today.*

important roles in attracting clients to utilize these facilities. Salespeople diversify
markets and upgrade services to sell room space, food, beverages, entertainment, and
other services to create an attractive atmosphere for potential clients.

Typical of the salespeople employed in this service sector is Brian Moon, sales
manager of the Renaissance Esmeralda Resort and Spa located in Indian Wells,
California. This resort is a world-class facility located in the desert. Brian Moon highlights the numerous "features of the facility including exquisite swimming pools and the
Oasis Water Park, featuring a wave machine to simulate ocean waves.[21] When client
resistance is encountered, Brian and his sales force work diligently to identify the
sources of the resistance, clarify the issues, and resolve the problems so as to consum-
mate the sale.

TELECOMMUNICATIONS SERVICES The deregulation of telephone service resulted in the
fragmentation of major telephone companies and the creation of numerous new
communications companies. This has led to an increased need for telecommunications
salespeople. These individuals must have a thorough knowledge of their system and a good
understanding of competing telecommunications systems.

FINANCIAL SERVICES Today there are more than one million sales jobs in the securities
and financial service field and employment continues to increase. Banks, credit unions,
brokerage firms, and other businesses continue to expand, branch out, and diversify,
selling a broader range of financial planning and investment services. Brad Duffy,
financial service wholesaler for Riversource Investments, educates and advises

financial advisors for American Express on new and existing products offered by his company.[22]

MEDIA SALES Revenue from advertising supports the radio, television, newspaper, and magazine industries and is also a major source of profit for the Internet. Amy Vandeveer, a sales representative featured in Chapter 6, sells advertising space for Texas Monthly. Both local and national advertising support each of these and each must sell advertising to remain in business. In fact, newspapers and magazines generate far more revenue from the sales of advertising than from subscriptions. The wide variety of client needs and the task of meeting these needs make the work of media sales representatives interesting. Additionally, the requirement for the members of the media sales staff to develop or to help the client develop commercials makes this work very interesting.

REAL ESTATE The purchase of a home is usually the single largest expenditure in the average person's lifetime. The purchase of commercial property by individual investors or business firms also represents a major economic decision. Therefore, the 800,000 people who sell real estate assume an important responsibility.

Busy real estate salespeople often hire sales associates to conduct open houses or to perform other tasks. Real estate salespeople must obtain listings, advertise the properties, conduct visits by potential clients, and sell properties. Susana Rosas, a sales representative for CBRE featured in Chapter 3, stresses the need to create relationships with her clients.[23] Honesty is essential in establishing and maintaining good relationships. Jodi believes that if the experience is good for the client, it will result in referrals to friends and members of the family, providing additional clients.

INSURANCE Selling insurance has often been a very rewarding career in sales. The types of insurance sold include fire, liability, health, automobile, casualty, homeowner, and business. There are two general types of insurance salespeople. One type consists of salespeople employed by major insurance companies such as Allstate, Farmers, Prudential, Travelers, State Farm, Geico, Hartford, and Mutual of Omaha. Salespeople like Marcus Smith, who we introduced in Chapter 1, sell various insurance products only for Liberty Mutual. The second type consists of independent insurance agents who represent a number of various companies. The typical independent agency offers a broad line of personal and business insurance services.

BUSINESS SERVICES The great expansion of new businesses and the expansion of existing businesses have resulted in an increase in the demand for business services provided by outside contractors. Some of the services provided by outside contractors include computer programming, training, printing, credit reporting, payroll and accounting, payment processing, recruiting, transportation, and security. Many other sales careers involving the sale of services exist. This field is increasing at a rapid pace and sales positions become available in service sales every day.

Career Opportunities in the Business Goods Channel

Manufacturers employ sales and sales support personnel in a variety of different positions in outside and inside sales. Outside salespeople interact with potential customers on a face-to-face basis. Some of the categories of outside salespeople include field sales-people, sales or application engineers, and detail salespeople. Inside salespeople include customer service representatives (CSRs), who rely primarily of the telephone and the Internet to communicate with customers, to identify new prospects, and to carry out other sales activities.

INDUSTRIAL SALESPEOPLE Industrial salespeople include both technical salespeople (sales engineers or application engineers) and nontechnical salespeople. Sales engineers or technical salespeople sell heavy equipment, machinery, chemical products, aircraft, complex electronic equipment, and military equipment. Such salespeople must have a good technical understanding of their products and customer needs. Nontechnical salespeople generally sell office equipment, disposable goods such as adhesives, cleaners, packaging, and office supplies.

SALES ENGINEER OR APPLICATIONS ENGINEER Sales or applications engineers must possess a detailed and thorough technical knowledge of their products as well as competing products. These salespeople must be able to identify and analyze customer problems and develop solutions to these problems that meet the customer's needs. These sales engineers must be technically proficient in all aspects of their products and in communicating the merits and advantages of their products to the customer.

Steve Tice, president of Sim Graphics Engineering Corporation, and Steve Glenn, vice president for new business development, are the primary sales engineers for the corporation.[24] Sim Graphics develops automated graphic simulation systems for use in industry, hospitals, and educational institutions. Their company utilizes customized demonstration presentations for potential customers. Many potential customers fail to understand the complexity of the systems, so demonstrations are needed to show what actually is available. On some occasions it is necessary to build and demonstrate a prototype or to make a full-blown demonstration. A customer that does not understand the product will be reluctant to purchase something they don't comprehend.

FIELD SALESPEOPLE **Field salespeople** interact with new customers and current customers. They must be able to identify customer needs and requirements and to recommend the proper product or service to meet the customer's needs. Field salespeople who provide excellent service to their customers often receive information from their satisfied customers on new leads. These customers often provide recommendations to other potential customers for the field salesperson.

Betty Robertson, president of Lyncole Industries, is also the field sales representative for her company. Lycole sells piping and associated supplies to contractors. Betty states that following up on the installation of the equipment is very important. The contractors she sells to are potential repeat customers; it is essential to follow up and make certain that the customer is satisfied.[25]

DETAIL SALESPEOPLE **Detail salespeople** serve to develop goodwill, provide information, and stimulate demand for the manufacturer's products. A detail salesperson does not sell the product but receives recognition for increasing the sale of products

Global Business Insight

WHAT MOTIVATES SALESPEOPLE?

A recent study of more than 40,000 salespeople worldwide reported that 36 percent of U.S. salespeople and 33 percent of the salespeople in the United Kingdom say they work primarily to earn substantial incomes. The same statistic for New Zealand and Norway peers was only 9 percent and 11 percent, respectively. Unlike their counterparts in other countries who considered sales a temporary step to being promoted to management, successful U.S. salespeople preferred to make more money in sales rather than be promoted into management.[c]

Well-trained retail salespeople can add value to the traditional shopping experience.

indirectly. Detail salespeople must be able to provide technical product information and offer sound advice in areas including credit policies, pricing, display, layout, and storage.

Deborah Karrish, a sales representative for Amgen, stresses relationship selling in her work with medical facilities while selling to both medical staff and physicians. She had to learn the technology of her products, how they were manufactured, and how the medicines could be utilized most effectively in treating patients. She went through a pairing program with physicians to learn how the products are used. Deborah knows it is necessary to establish good relationships with the medical staff. Failing to establish good relationships generally means that the people will not work with the salesperson.

Career Opportunities in the Consumer Goods Channel

Sales careers in the consumer goods channel include both retail selling and direct selling careers. Conventional retailers face increased competition from online retailers. Consumers spend billions of dollars on Internet purchases. Traditional retailers are forced to offer customers more than products in order to compete effectively against online sellers. Well-trained salespeople can add value to the traditional shopping experience.

RETAIL SELLING A large number of salespeople work in retail. Retail selling is probably an excellent area for gaining initial sales experience. Retail selling careers abound in a number of product areas.

Asbury Automotive Group employs 1,440 sales personnel. These salespeople take pride in their work and are rewarded with a promising career. Many of the sales personnel were recruited at college and university job fairs. Some work as management trainees, selling cars for 8 to 15 months, making $45,000 to $60,000 per year in salary plus bonus. Then they are trained and certified to work in the finance and insurance department. Next, some are promoted to new or used-car manager, earning $100,000 to $150,000 per year. The final promotion opportunity is general manager of the dealership.[26]

Mike Patterson, the owner of MP Yacht Services, provides specialized electrical repairs and installations for boats. His easy sales approach and high technical performance have attracted a large group of repeat customers to provide electrical services that competitors are unable to provide. Mike firmly believes that one should never bad-mouth a competitor, and his philosophy has resulted in competitors referring customers to MP Yacht Services.[27]

Don Huder, vice president of sales, service, and marketing for the Saturn Agency in Santa Anna, California, focuses on identifying and solving the customer's needs.[28] Relationship selling requires commitment and absolute honesty. The Saturn culture is based upon teamwork, and sales commissions are shared among the entire team. Joseph Phu, a Saturn sales representative, says that the service program is a key part of customer relationship. A computerized system is used to remind sales personnel to call the Saturn buyer three days after the purchase.

The sales staff at Julian's Men's shop in Chapel Hill, North Carolina, takes pride in their work. This family-owned business, founded in 1942, is located near the University of

Customer Relationship Management with Technology

LEARNING CRM SOFTWARE

Many salespeople are at first apprehensive about using computers; yet research shows a high degree of acceptance, with this comment often heard: "I don't know how I got along without it."

Following the instructions in this text's customer relationship management (CRM) application exercises and case study gives you a good understanding of basic CRM. This knowledge can be valuable as you enter today's selling environment. Many sales organizations are using CRM, and your understanding of the basics can help you learn more rapidly any system in use by your potential employers. Some people, after following these instructions, list their use of CRM on their résumés.

Many users of CRM enter information about friends and family into their databases and use it to enhance all their relationships. CRM helps people remember the status of relationships, steps to take, and pending events, such as anniversaries and birthdays. (See the exercise "Learning CRM Software" on p. 47 for more information.)

North Carolina. The store sells custom-order suits to UNC alumni who live all over the South. Some buy private-label suits created by the founder's son, Alexander Julian, who is a noted fashion designer.[29]

DIRECT SELLING Direct salespeople are independent contractors who represent manufacturers selling products or services directly to consumers, usually face to face but also via the telephone or Internet. In 2005, there were more than 14.1 million direct sellers in the United States, accounting for $30.5 billion in annual revenues.[30] Personal care, home/family care, wellness, and leisure/educational products, along with services like utilities, phone, and legal, are the major industries represented by this form of selling.

A rapidly growing form of direct sales is network (or multilevel) marketing. In this form of distribution, manufacturers eschew advertising and other trade/promotional spending, relying instead on a large network of independent consultants or distributors to sell the product or service directly to consumers or businesses. The independent consultant builds his or her business not only through the direct sales of the product or service to consumers, but also by sponsoring new consultants to sell the company's products or services. The sponsoring consultant then earns commissions on the product/service sales generated by the new consultant, in addition to what he or she personally sells. The number of levels that a consultant is paid on varies by company, but the benefit to the consultant is the ability to leverage both his or her own efforts plus that of other consultants in his or her "downline."

Learning to Sell

"Are salespeople made or are they born?" This classic question seems to imply that some people are born with certain qualities that give them a special advantage in the selling field. This is not true. The principles of selling can be learned and applied by people whose personal characteristics are quite different.

In the past few decades, sales training has been expanded on four fronts. These four sources of training are corporate-sponsored training, training provided by commercial vendors, certification studies, and courses provided by colleges and universities.

Corporate-Sponsored Training

Hundreds of business organizations, such as Apple Computer, IBM, Maytag, Western Electric, and Zenith, have established training programs. These large corporations spend millions of dollars each year to develop their salespeople. *Training* magazine, which conducts annual analyses of employer-provided training in U.S. organizations, indicates that salespeople are among the most intensively trained employee groups. A new salesperson preparing for a consultative selling position may spend a few months to a year or more in training. For many salespeople, the training is as close as their laptop computer. Lucent Technologies, for example, uses Web-based training for about one-third of its training courses.[31]

Training Provided by Commercial Vendors

The programs designed by firms specializing in the development of sales personnel are a second source of sales training. Some of the most popular courses are offered by Wilson Learning Corporation, Miller Heiman Inc., Dale Carnegie Training, and AchieveGlobal. (See Table 2.3.) The legendary Professional Selling Skills (PSS) course, developed in the late 1960s by Gene Keluche, is still offered by AchieveGlobal. This carefully designed course, once owned by Xerox, has been completed by millions of salespeople.[32]

Certification Programs

The trend toward increased professionalism in personal selling has been the stimulus for a third type of training and education initiative. Many salespeople are returning to the

TABLE 2.3 Sales Training Offered by Commercial Vendors

Training programs provided by commercial vendors are very popular. This table introduces a few of the well established sales training programs offered throughout America

COMPANY	TRAINING PROGRAMS	DESCRIPTION
Sales Performance International www.spisales.com	• Solution Selling • Opportunity Selling	Provides sales training based on concepts explained in *The New Solution Selling* by Keith Eades.
Integrity Systems, Inc. www.integritysystems.com	• Integrity Selling • The Customer	Provides sales training based on concepts explained in *Integrity Selling for the 21st Century* by Ron Willingham.
Huthwaite, Inc. www.huthwaite.com	• Spin Selling Certificate • Creating Client Value	Provides sales training based on concepts in *The Spin Selling Fieldbook* by Neil Rackham.
Miller Heiman, Inc. www.millerheiman.com	• Strategic Selling • Conceptual Selling	Provides sales training based on concepts presented in *Strategic Selling* and *The New Conceptual Selling*.
Achieve Global www.achieveglobal.com	• Professional Selling • Professional Sales	Provides the original Xerox Skills (PSS) *Professional Selling Skills (PSS)* sales training. *Course Content Coaching* has been updated.
Wilson Learning Worldwide www.wilsonlearning.com	• The Versatile Salesperson	Provides updated sales training based on the original Larry Wilson *Counselor Selling Training Program*.
Dale Carnegie Training, Inc. www.dalecarnegie.com	• Sales Advantage • How to Sell Like a Pro	One of the largest international training companies providing sales training using many of the concepts presented in the Dale Carnegie books, such as *How to Win Friends and Influence People*.

TABLE 2.4   **Sales Training Offered by a Sample of Universities**

A large number of two- and four-year colleges, and universities have established extensive education programs for students interested in sales. Sales programs have also recently become an important part of the MBA curriculum at several elite universities. This table from the University Sales Education Foundation provides a representative sample of universities that offer a variety of sales training program options.

University Sales Programs

| School | Location | Accreditations | | | Students | Program Type | | | | | | Internships Req'd |
		AACSB	USCA	Other		Certificate	Concentration	Emphasis	Major	Minor	Other	
Ball State University	Muncie, IN	✓	✓	✓	350	✓				✓		N
Baylor University	Waco, TX	✓	✓		115		✓	✓				Y
Bradley University	Peoria, IL	✓	A		40	✓				✓		Y
College of St. Catherine	St. Paul, MN		A	✓	180	✓				✓		Y
DePaul University	Chicago, IL	✓	A		700					✓		Y
Georgia Southern University	Statesboro, GA	✓	A		55		✓					N
Illinois State University	Normal, IL	✓	✓	✓	253	✓	✓		✓			N
Indiana University	Bloomington, IN	✓	✓		200		✓					N
Kennesaw State University	Kennesaw, GA	✓			150		✓	✓	✓	✓		N
Nicholls State University	Thibodaux, LA	✓			50		✓					N
Northern Illinois University	DeKalb, IL	✓	✓	✓	180	✓		✓				N
Ohio University	Athens, OH	✓	✓	✓	200	✓						Y
The College of New Jersey	Ewing, NJ	✓			20		✓			✓		N
University of Akron	Akron, OH	✓	✓		100	✓	✓		✓	✓		N
University of Central Florida	Orlando, FL	✓			40	✓	✓					Y
University of Connecticut	Storrs, CT	✓		✓	250		✓			✓		Y
University of Dayton	Dayton, OH	✓			200		✓					N
University of Houston	Houston, TX	✓	✓		180	✓				✓		Y
University of Louisville	Louisville, KY	✓			20		✓					N
University of Toledo	Toledo, OH	✓	✓	✓	413		✓	✓	✓			Y
University of Washington	Seattle, WA	✓		✓	379	✓		✓				Y
University of Wisconsin Eau Claire	Eau Claire, WI	✓			100		✓					N
Washington State University - Vancouver	Vancouver, WA		A		30	✓						N
Western Kentucky University	Bowling Green, KY	✓	A		105				✓	✓		N
Western Michigan University	Kalamazoo, MI	✓			350				✓			N
William Paterson University	Wayne, NJ	✓	✓	✓	85				✓	✓		N

A = Associate Member

Source: Used with permission of the HR Chally Group.

classroom to earn certification in a sales or sales-related area. In the pharmaceutical industry many salespeople earn the Certified Medical Representative (CMR) designation. The CMR curriculum includes nearly 40 courses that are delivered to more than 9,000 students. The National Automobile Dealers Association sponsors the Code of Conduct Certification program for automotive sales representatives. Both of these certification programs require extensive study of modules and the completion of rigorous examinations. Sales & Marketing Executives–International offers the Certified Sales Executive (CSE) designation to sales professionals who meet the highest standards of education, experience, and ethical conduct.

Some companies have developed their own sales training certification programs. The Pitney Bowes Certified Postal Consultant (CPC) program is designed to improve the level of assistance given to customers who want to upgrade their mail process. It is available to members of the 4,000-person Pitney Bowes sales force who sell both products (postage meters) and services. Freightliner developed a certification program for its 1,800-member sales force. The various courses include topics ranging from product knowledge to truck-selling skills.[33]

College and University Courses

The fourth source of sales training is personal selling courses offered by colleges and universities throughout the United States. A large majority of the nation's community colleges and undergraduate business schools offer this course, and it is attracting more interest among business majors. Sales training has become an important part of the MBA curriculum at several elite universities as well.[34] Although there is no formulaic answer

For over 35 years, the Certified Medical Representatives Institute has been empowering sales representatives who call on medical professionals. The CMR certification program is designed to increase sales performance.

Today's physicians look for us.

Leadership is reflected in the professionals who represent your company. The CMR Institute has been advancing the knowledge of pharmaceutical professionals for nearly 40 years. From the renowned curriculum of our CMR® Certification Program to the advanced technology of CMR InterActive™, you'll find a knowledge opportunity to help your company lead. To learn more call us at 1.800.274.2674 or visit www.cmrinstitute.org.

CMR INSTITUTE®

Advancing knowledge. Enhancing healthcare.™

that can be applicable to all selling situations,[35] these courses provide students with a repertoire of skills that help them become more effective. Some two- and four-year colleges have developed extensive education programs for students interested in a sales career. The University Sales Center Alliance (www.salescenteralliance.com) was established in 2002 to advance the sales profession through academic leadership. The University of Akron, the University of Houston, Ball State University, Baylor University, Kennesaw State University, and many other schools offer undergraduate programs for students who are preparing for a career in personal selling.

Chapter Learning Activities

Reviewing Key Concepts

Explain how personal selling skills have become one of the master skills needed for success in the information age and how personal selling skills contribute to the work performed by knowledge workers

Today's workforce is made up of millions of *knowledge workers* who succeed only when they add value to information. The new economy rewards salespeople and other knowledge workers who collect, organize, clarify, and present information in a convincing manner. Selling skills contribute in a major way to four groups of knowledge workers who usually do not consider themselves salespeople: customer service representatives, professionals (accountants, consultants, lawyers, etc.), entrepreneurs, and managerial personnel.

Discuss the rewarding aspects of a career in selling today

Selling careers offer many rewards not found in other occupations. Income, both monetary and psychic, is above average, and there are many opportunities for advancement. Salespeople enjoy job security, mobility, and independence. Opportunities in selling for members of minority groups and for women are growing. In addition, selling is very interesting work, because a salesperson is constantly in contact with people. The adage "no two people are alike" reminds us that sales work is never dull or routine.

Discuss the different employment settings in selling today

The text describes each of the three major career options and employment opportunities in the field of personal selling, namely services, business goods, and consumer goods. Keep in mind that each category features a wide range of selling positions, varying in terms of educational requirements, earning potential, and type of customer served. The discussion and examples should help you discover which kind of sales career best suits your talents and interests.

Identify the four major sources of sales training

Sales training can be acquired from four key sources: corporate-sponsored training, training provided by commercial vendors, certification programs, and courses offered by colleges and universities. Many MBA programs are now also including professional selling and sales management in the curriculum.

Key Terms

Knowledge workers	Inside salespeople	Field salespeople
Customer service representative (CSR)	Outside salespeople	Detail salespeople
	Trade selling	Direct salespeople
Psychic income	Missionary, or detail, sales	

Review Questions

1. List and describe the four employment settings for people who are considering a selling career.

2. Explain the meaning of *psychic income.*

3. Explain why personal selling is an important auxiliary skill needed by lawyers, engineers, accountants, and other professionals.

4. What future is there in selling for women?

5. Develop a list of retail products that require well-developed personal selling skills.

6. Some salespeople have an opportunity to earn certification in a sales or sales-related area. How can a salesperson benefit from certification?

7. Explain why high-performance value-added salespeople earn much more than high-performance transactional salespeople.

8. List three titles commonly used to describe manufacturing salespeople. Describe the duties of each.

9. Develop a list of eight selling career opportunities in the service field.

10. List and briefly describe the four major sources of sales training.

Application Exercises

1. Examine a magazine or newspaper ad for a new product or service that you have never seen before. Evaluate its chances for receiving wide customer acceptance. Does this product require a large amount of personal selling effort? What types of salespeople (service, manufacturing, wholesale, or retail) are involved in selling this product?

2. For each of the following job classifications, list the name of at least one person you know in that field:

   a. Full-time retail salesperson
   b. Full-time wholesale salesperson
   c. Full-time manufacturer's salesperson
   d. Full-time person who sells a service

   Interview one of the people you have listed, asking the following questions concerning their duties and responsibilities:

   a. What is your immediate supervisor's title?
   b. What would be a general description of your position?
   c. What specific duties and responsibilities do you have?
   d. What is the compensation plan and salary range for a position like yours?

   Write a job description from this information.

3. Shelly Jones, a vice president and partner in the Chicago office of the consulting firm Korn/Ferry International, has looked into the future and he sees some new challenges for salespeople. He recently shared the following predictions with *Selling* magazine:

   a. Salespeople will spend more time extending the range of applications or finding new markets for the products they sell.
   b. The selling function will be less pitching your product and more integrating your product into the business equation of your client. Understanding the business environment in which your client operates will be critical.
   c. In the future you will have to be a financial engineer for your client. You need to understand how your client makes money and be able to explain how your product or service contributes to profitable operation of the client's firm.

   Interview a salesperson who is involved in business-to-business selling, a manufacturer's representative, for example, and determine whether this person agrees with the views of Shelly Jones.

4. There are many information sources on selling careers and career opportunities on the Internet. Two examples include Monster.com and CareerBuilder.com. Search the Internet for information on selling careers.

Use your search engine to find career information on a pharmaceutical representative, a field sales engineer, and a retail salesperson.

Role-Play Exercise

This role-play will give you experience in selling your knowledge, skills, and experience to a prospective employer. You will be meeting with a class member who will assume the role of an employer who is developing a new sales team. Prior to this interview, reflect on the courses you have completed, work experience, and other life experiences that may have value in the eyes of the employer. You may also want to reflect on any volunteer work you have completed and leadership roles you have held. Be prepared to discuss the personal selling skills you are developing in this course.

CRM Application Exercise

Learning CRM Software

After using the user ID and password supplied with your book to log onto Salesforce.com, you will become acquainted with the layout and features of the Salesforce.com application. Start by pressing the Setup and Training button, and then select "Training." Finally, select "View Classes" and choose the "Sales Representative Fundamentals" class. This prerecorded online training class will introduce you to the screens and terminology you will use in the exercises in this book. Complete this prerecorded training. Make sure you finish the Completion module to record your successful training.

Case Problem

Ronald McMains is 23 years old and works for Metropolitan Financial Bank in the information services department. He was employed part-time while attending college and decided to accept a full-time position after graduation.

The position in information services offers an opportunity to learn a great deal about banking, a secure income, a good insurance and retirement program, two weeks of vacation a year, and 15 days of sick leave a year, if needed. There also will be opportunities to move into supervision within the next couple of years because the company is expanding rapidly.

Ron has been thinking about changing jobs and has been described by his friends as an opportunist—a person who seeks out opportunities and takes advantage of them. He sees himself the same way and someday hopes to earn well above the average income.

Ron has been interviewing for several positions. One company has offered him a position that involves calling on potential dealers for a new line of fiberglass powerboats. The manufacturer has a patent on an improved fiber-glassing technique that is setting new standards for boat strength. The boat has proved to be a success and has sold extraordinarily well in the five territories that the company already has opened. Letters are coming from dealers all over the country expressing an interest in taking on a dealership. The company has decided to open up new territories in the southern half of Wisconsin and northern half of Illinois. The latter is the territory they have offered to Ron.

The specific responsibilities of the position include calling on marinas and boat dealers in the territory and setting up the better ones as distributors of the new line of boats. Ron would evaluate each potential distributorship and would select and appoint the new distributors. The company's excellent training program would teach Ron how to help each new dealer set up a promotional program to sell the boats.

The company has offered Ron a commission program that includes a "draw against commission" form of compensation. In this type of program, a drawing account enables the salesperson to receive a set amount either weekly or monthly that is later subtracted from earned commissions. Ron's draw would equal his current salary, including his overtime pay. Ron's commissions would be based on the number of boats his dealers sold. The company expects this territory to be one of the best; and if Ron is successful, his income could be well into the $50,000 to $60,000 range within the second year, if not sooner.

Ron would have to relocate about 100 miles from where he now lives. The company has offered relocation expenses to cover the cost of the entire move. Ron realizes he would be away from home on an average of one night a week, and this poses no problems. The company will cover all of Ron's travel and lodging expenses and will provide him with a new car.

Questions

1. List the pros and cons of this job opportunity.

2. On the basis of the information given, should Ron accept the new job? Why or why not?

Part 1 | Role-Play Exercise

DEVELOPING A PERSONAL SELLING PHILOSOPHY

Scenario

You are currently working part-time at the Best Buy Store located in Jordan Creek Town Center Mall. You are a full-time student majoring in marketing at Vista College. The manager of your store wants you to identify potential customers on your campus and sell Dell laptop computers to those who have a need for this product.

Customer Profile

Melissa Tores is a full-time commuter student who lives with her parents and shares one computer with her mom. Each morning she drives about 20 miles to the campus (one way) and spends most of the day attending classes, working in the library, and visiting with friends. She currently spends about two hours each evening on the computer at home.

Salesperson Profile

You started working at the Best Buy Store shortly after graduating from high school. The store manager was impressed with your computer expertise and your friendly manner. Although you are able to sell any type of computer, you tend to specialize in laptop computers, which are ideal for college students who have mobile computing needs. Your personal computer is a new Dell laptop, which replaced your desktop computer.

Product

You sell several different laptop computers that vary in price from $535 to $1,299 (type "Best Buy + Dell laptops computers" into your search engine for specific Dell laptop computers carried by Best Buy) Each laptop is equipped with specific, easily accessible ports to interact with a variety of external components. All of your notebooks offer both productivity and entertainment applications. Services offered by Dell include helpful assistance via telephone or online tutorials at www.support.dell.com. Dell's warranty also provides for service and support to be handled by the Geek Squad (www.geeksquad.com), which is located in the store.

Instructions

For this role-play you will meet with Melissa Torres and determine her interest and need for a laptop computer. You will meet with Melissa Torres and determine her interest and need for a notebook computer. Prior to meeting with Ms. Torres, preplan your relationship strategy, product strategy, customer strategy, and presentation strategy. Chapter 1 provides a description of each strategic area. Be prepared to close the sale if you feel the customer will benefit from this purchase.

Developing a Relationship Strategy

High-performance salespeople are generally better able to build and maintain relationships than moderate performers. Part 2 includes three chapters that focus on person-to-person relationship-building strategies. Chapter 3 explains how to create value with a relationship strategy. Chapter 4 introduces communication style bias and explains how to build strong interpersonal relationships with style flexing. The influence of ethical decisions on relationships in selling is discussed in Chapter 5.

"All selling is ultimately relationship selling. This is especially true in complex sales where the relationship continues after the sale."

Brian Tracy, Author, *The 100 Absolutely Unbreakable Laws of Business Success*

3

Creating Value with a Relationship Strategy

Reality Selling Today Video Series

Susana Rosas, a real estate broker at CB Richard Ellis (www.cbre.com/usa/us/tx/houston+galleria), pictured above, places a great deal of emphasis on building rapport during the first contact. She, like most other real estate professionals, knows that rapport with commercial real estate clients is of critical importance. She knows that to build relationship with clients, a good knowledge of the market is necessary but not sufficient. She has to master a multitude of skills, among which keeping an open and empathetic conversation style with her clients is the key. Above all, listening closely to everything that prospects say helps a salesperson to accurately identify their wants and needs. Furthermore, she works closely with her team members in the same collaborative manner to make sure all of those identified needs are met. ■

Developing a Relationship Strategy

Developing and applying the wide range of interpersonal skills needed in today's complex sales environment can be challenging. Daniel Goleman, author of the best-selling books *Emotional Intelligence* and *Working with Emotional Intelligence*, notes that there are many forms of intelligence that influence our actions throughout life. One of these, **emotional intelligence**, refers to the capacity for monitoring our own feelings and those of others, for motivating ourselves, and for managing emotions well in ourselves and in our relationships. People with a high level of emotional intelligence display many of the qualities needed in sales work: self-confidence, trustworthiness, adaptability, initiative, optimism, empathy, and well-developed social skills.[1]

Goleman and other researchers state that there are widespread exceptions to the rule that IQ predicts success. In the field of personal selling and most other business occupations, emotional intelligence is a much greater predictor of success.[2] The good news is that emotional intelligence can be enhanced with a variety of self-development activities, many of which are discussed in this chapter.

Daniel Goleman, author of the best-selling book Working with Emotional Intelligence, *defines emotional intelligence as the capacity for monitoring our own feelings and those of others, for motivating ourselves, and for managing emotions well in ourselves and in our relationships. People with a high level of emotional intelligence, which he says can be learned and improved on, display many of the qualities needed in sales work: self-confidence, trustworthiness, adaptability, initiative, optimism, empathy, and well-developed social skills.*

Information age selling involves three major relationship challenges. The first major challenge is building new relationships. Salespeople who can quickly build rapport with new prospects have a much greater chance of achieving success in personal selling. The second major challenge is transforming relationships from the personal level to the business level. Once rapport is established, the salesperson is in a stronger position to begin the need identification process. The third major challenge is the management of relationships. To achieve a high level of success, salespeople have to manage a multitude of different relationships."[3] Salespeople must develop relationship management strategies that focus on four key groups. These groups are discussed later in this chapter.

In this chapter we introduce the win-win philosophy and discuss the importance of projecting a professional image. Chapter 4, on adaptive selling explains how an understanding of our own communication style and the communication style of the customer can help us better manage the relationship process. Chapter 5 focuses on the importance of maintaining high ethical standards to build long-term relationships with the customer (Figure 3.1).

Strategic/Consultative Selling Model	
Strategic Step	**Prescription**
Develop a Personal Selling Philosophy	☑ Adopt Marketing Concept
	☑ Value Personal Selling
	☑ Become a Problem Solver/Partner
Develop a Relationship Strategy	☐ Adopt Win-Win Philosophy
	☐ Project Professional Image
	☐ Maintain High Ethical Standards

Relationships Add Value

Ron Willingham, author of *Integrity Selling for the 21st Century*, says there is a relationship between the salesperson's achievement drive and his view of personal selling. Salespeople who feel a professional responsibility to create as much value for customers as possible exhibit more energy, a stronger work ethic, and a greater eagerness to ask customers for decisions.[4]

The manner in which salespeople establish, build, and manage relationships is not an incidental aspect of personal selling; in the information age it is the key to success. In the information economy, business is defined by customer relationships and sales success depends on adding value (see Figure 1.2). Daniel Pink, author of *A Whole New Mind,* says we are moving from the information age to the conceptual age. He predicts that one of the major players in the conceptual age will be the **empathizer**. Empathizers have the ability to imagine themselves in someone else's position and understand what that person is feeling. They are able to understand the subtleties of human interaction.[5]

We have defined value-added selling as *a series of creative improvements in the sales process that enhance the customer experience.* Customers perceive that value is added when they feel comfortable with the relationship they have with a salesperson. A good relationship causes customers to feel that, if a problem arises, they will receive a just and fair solution. A good relationship creates a clearer channel of communication about issues that might surface during each step of the sales process. Len Rodman, CEO of Black & Veatch, a large engineering and construction company, recalls a problem operation on the West Coast. Earnings were minimal and the person in charge could not sell to high-tier clients. He put a salesperson in charge whose strength was building relationships. Within an 18-month period, that region became one of the most profitable.[6]

The salesperson who is honest, accountable, and sincerely concerned about the customer's welfare brings added value to the sale. These characteristics give the salesperson a competitive advantage—an advantage that is becoming increasingly important in a world of "look-alike" products and similar prices.

Partnering—The Highest-Quality Selling Relationship

Salespeople today are encouraged to think of everything they say or do in the context of their relationship with the customer. They should constantly strive to build a long-term partnership. In a marketplace characterized by increased levels of competition and greater product complexity, we see the need to adopt a relationship strategy that emphasizes the "lifetime" customer. High-quality relationships result in repeat business and those important referrals. A growing number of salespeople recognize that the quality of partnerships they create is as important as the quality of the products they sell. Today's customer wants a quality product *and* a quality relationship. One example of this trend is the J.D. Power and Associates customer satisfaction studies. For example, the Domestic Hotel Guest Satisfaction Study measures guest satisfaction among frequent business travelers. J.D. Power conducts customer satisfaction research in several different industries.[7]

Today's customer wants a quality product and a quality relationship. This means that salespeople can create value with a well-developed relationship strategy.

In Chapter 1 we defined *partnering* as a strategically developed, high-quality, long-term relationship that focuses on solving the customer's buying problems.[8] This definition is used in the sales training video titled "Partnering—The Heart of Selling Today." Traditional industrial age sales training programs emphasized the importance of creating a good first impression and then "pushing" your product. Partnering emphasizes building a strong relationship during every aspect of the sale and working hard to maintain a quality relationship with the customer after the sale. Today, personal selling must be viewed as a process, not an event.[9]

Selling Is Everyone's Business

SELLING HIP CHAIRS

Gregg Buchbinder is chairman of Emeco Ltd., a small company in Pennsylvania that manufactures modern chairs. One of the company's newest products is a sleek, six-and-a-half-pound aluminum chair called the Superlight. This chair was created by renowned architect Frank Gehry. When Buchbinder acquired Emeco from his father in 1998, he dreamed of becoming a producer of hip home furnishings. The problem was that Emeco was unfamiliar to most of the architects and designers he wanted to do business with. So Buchbinder hit the streets of SoHo, knocking on shop doors with a copy of a magazine that showed his modern aluminum chairs. He also visited trade shows in search of new prospects. Today revenues have reached about $10 million and Buchbinder is optimistic about the future.[a]

Customer Relationship Management with Technology

COMMUNICATING THROUGH CRM

Customer relationship management (CRM) software can be used to enhance the quality of your relationships. A good example is the system's ability to improve communications between you and your contacts. With Salesforce.com., for example, you can quickly prepare and send a letter, a fax, or an e-mail to one or more people in the database. Recipients of your appointment confirmations, information verifications, company or product news, or brief personal notes recognize and appreciate your effort to keep them informed. The written word conveys consideration and helps avoid misunderstandings and miscommunications. CRM empowers you to easily use the written word to advance your relationship building. (See the exercise "Preparing Letters with CRM" on p. 71 for more information.)

Larry Wilson, noted author and founder of Wilson Learning Worldwide, identifies partnering as one of the most important strategic thought processes needed by salespeople. He points out that the salesperson who is selling a "one-shot" solution cannot compete against the one who has developed and nurtured a long-term, mutually beneficial partnership. Wilson believes there are three keys to a partnering relationship:

- The relationship is built on shared values. If your client believes that you both share the same ideas and values, it goes a long way toward creating a powerful relationship.
- Everyone needs to clearly understand the purpose of the partnership and be committed to the vision. Both the salesperson and the client must agree on what they are trying to do together.
- The role of the salesperson must move from selling to supporting. The salesperson in a partnership is actively concerned with the growth, health, and satisfaction of the company to which she is selling.[10]

Salespeople willing to abandon short-term thinking and invest the time and energy needed to develop a high-quality, long-term relationship with customers are rewarded with greater earnings and the satisfaction of working with repeat customers. Sales resulting from referrals also increase.

Relationship Strategies Focus on Four Key Groups

Establishing and maintaining a partnering-type relationship internally as well as one with the customers is a vital aspect of selling. High-performance sales personnel build strong relationships with four groups (Figure 3.2):

1. *Customers.* As noted previously, a major key to success in selling is the ability to establish working relationships with customers in which mutual support, trust, and goals are nurtured over time. Salespeople who maintain regular contact with their

FIGURE 3.2

An effective relationship strategy helps high-performing salespeople build and maintain win-win relationships with a wide range of key groups.

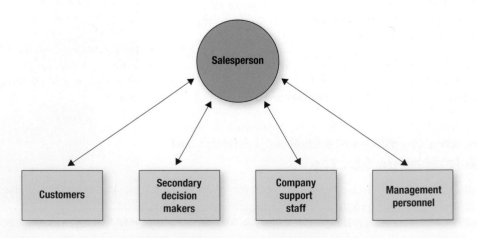

customers and develop sound business relationships based on mutual trust are able to drive up sales productivity according to research conducted by the American Productivity and Quality Center.[11]

Cisco Systems is one of many companies that now measure themselves by the quality of their relationships with their customers. Salespeople earn their bonuses in large part based on customer satisfaction instead of gross sales or profit.[12]

2. *Secondary decision makers.* High-performance salespeople understand the importance of building relationships with the people who work with customers. In many selling situations, the first person the salesperson meets is a receptionist, a secretary, or an assistant to the primary decision maker. These persons often can facilitate a meeting with the prospect. Also, the prospect may involve other people in making the buying decision. For example, the decision to buy new office furniture may be made by a team of persons including the buyer and persons who will actually use the furniture.

3. *Company support staff.* The maintenance of relationships internally is a vital aspect of selling. Support staff may include persons working in the areas of market research, product service, credit, training, or shipping. Influencing these people to change their priorities, interrupt their schedules, accept new responsibilities, or fulfill any other request for special attention is a major part of the salesperson's job. At UPS, the drivers are the eyes and ears of the sales force. The most successful UPS salespeople nurture a relationship with the drivers in their sales territory.[13]

4. *Management personnel.* Sales personnel usually work under the direct supervision of a sales manager, a department head, or some other member of the firm's management team. Maintaining a good relationship with this person is very important.

Adapting the Relationship Strategy

Ideally, the relationship strategy should be adapted to the type of customer you are working with. Chapter 1 provided a description of the three most common types of selling situations: transactional selling, consultative selling, and strategic alliance selling. Transactional buyers are usually aware of their needs and often stay focused on such issues as price, convenience, and delivery schedules. They usually know a great deal about the products or services they wish to purchase. In the transactional sale, the relationship strategy is often secondary.

In the consultative sale, however, the impact of relationships on the sale is quite important. A consultative sale emphasizes need identification, which is achieved through effective communication and a relationship built upon mutual trust and respect. The consultative salesperson must display a keen ability to listen, define the customer's problem, and offer one or more solutions. The opportunity to uncover hidden needs and create custom solutions is greatly enhanced by a well-conceived relationship strategy.[14]

In terms of relationship building, strategic alliance selling is often the most challenging. Very often the salesperson is working with a company team made up of people from such areas as research and development (R&D), finance, and distribution. The salesperson must build a good working relationship with each team member. Forming an alliance with another company involves building relationships with several representatives of that buying organization.

We will revisit these three types of selling situations later in Chapter 5 when we discuss the trust factor. In the meantime, keep in mind that customers almost never buy products from someone whom they dislike. A salesperson who is not viewed as being helpful and trustworthy will not succeed in any type of selling situation.

Thought Processes That Enhance Your Relationship Strategy

Industrial age folklore created the myth of the "born" salesperson—a dynamic, outgoing, highly assertive individual. Experience acquired during the information age has taught us that many other factors determine sales success. Key among these factors are a positive self-concept and the ability to relate to others in effective and productive ways. With the aid of knowledge drawn from the behavioral sciences, we can develop the relationship strategies needed in a wide range of selling situations.

Self-Concept—An Important Dimension of the Relationship Strategy

Your **self-concept** is the bundle of facts, opinions, beliefs, and perceptions about yourself that are present in your life every moment of every day.[15] The self-concept you have today reflects information you have received from others and life events that occurred throughout childhood, adolescence, and adulthood. You are *consciously* aware of some of the things you have been conditioned to believe about yourself. But many comments and events that have shaped your self-concept are processed at the *unconscious* level and continue to influence your judgments, feelings, and behaviors whether you are aware of them or not.[16]

Phillip McGraw, author of *Self Matters*, says we often sabotage our own success by adopting limiting beliefs. These are the specific things we think about that cause us to conclude that we are not capable of achieving success. These beliefs restrict our thinking and our actions.[17] McGraw, better known as "Dr. Phil," has developed a one-sentence guide to understanding the importance of your self-concept: *The past reaches into the present, and programs the future, by your recollections and your internal rhetoric about what you perceived to have happened in your life.*[18] Past experiences and events, which McGraw describes as "defining moments," can influence your thinking for a lifetime.

How can you develop a more positive self-concept? How can you get rid of self-destructive ways of thinking? Bringing your present self-concept out into the open is the first step in understanding who you are, what you can do, and where you are going. Improving your self-concept does not happen overnight, but it can happen. A few practical approaches are summarized as follows:

Stephen Covey, author of The Seven Habits of Highly Successful People, *says the ability to build effective, long-term relationships is based on character strength, not quick-fix techniques.*

1. *Focus on the future and stop being overly concerned with past mistakes or failures.* We should learn from past errors, but we should not be immobilized by them.
2. *Develop expertise in selected areas.* By developing "expert power" you not only improve your self-image but also increase the value of your contributions to your employer and your customers.
3. *Learn to develop a positive mental attitude.* To develop a more positive outlook, read books and listen to audiotapes that describe ways to develop a positive mental attitude.

Consider materials developed by Jack Canfield, Stephen Covey, Brian Tracy, Dale Carnegie, and Phillip McGraw.

Global Business Etiquette

PATIENCE AND SENSITIVITY HELP CLINCH THE DEAL

Going global? If so, pack plenty of sensitivity and patience. And be prepared to emphasize value-added selling. Too often Americans rely on the "time is money" belief and they take shortcuts in some key areas. For example, they do not spend enough time learning about the culture of the country they are visiting. Also, they often fail to take the time needed to build a relationship with the client. Assaf Kedem, a representative of U.S.-based Intercomp, recalls having lunch with two prospects in Germany. For three hours the German executives asked questions about America and talked about their favorite foods and interests. Business was never discussed. Kedem viewed that long lunch as an important first step in building a relationship that will last for years.[b]

Later in this chapter you will learn how to develop and initiate a plan for self-improvement. If you want to improve your self-image, consider adopting this plan.

The Win-Win Philosophy

As noted in Chapter 1, the marketing concept is a philosophy that leaves no doubt in the mind of every employee that customer satisfaction is of primary importance. Salespeople, working closely with customers, are in the best position to monitor customer satisfaction.

Adopting the win-win philosophy is the first step in developing a relationship strategy. Stephen Heiman and Diane Sanchez, authors of *The New Conceptual Selling*, describe the "win-win" approach as follows:

> *In Win-Win selling, both the buyer and seller come out of the sale understanding that their respective best interests have been served—in other words, that they've both won. It is our firm conviction, based on thousands of selling situations, that over the long run the only sellers who can count on remaining successful are the ones who are committed to this Win-Win philosophy.*[19]

The win-win strategy is based on such irrefutable logic that it is difficult to understand why any other approach would be used. The starting point to the development of a win-win philosophy is to compare the behaviors of persons who have adopted the win-lose approach with the behaviors of persons who have adopted the win-win approach (Figure 3.3).

Empathy and Ego Drive

We have described the growing importance of being able to *empathize,* the ability to imagine yourself in someone else's position, to understand what that person is feeling. A salesperson simply cannot sell well without the invaluable ability to get critical feedback from the client through empathy. When you sense what the customer is feeling, you can change pace and make whatever modifications in your sales presentation are needed.[20] Fortunately, the ability to relate and connect with customers can be learned.

Ego drive is another basic quality that is of critical importance in personal selling. **Ego drive** is an inner force that makes the salesperson want and need to make the sale. Closing the sale provides a powerful means of enhancing the salesperson's ego. Research indicates that top salespeople have the motivation to make the sale and empathy gives them the connecting tool with which to do it. Therefore, empathy and ego drive reinforce each other.[21]

Character and Integrity

Shoshana Zuboff, contributing columnist for *Fast Company* magazine, sees widespread acceptance of wrong as normal. She points to acceptance in some industries of the belief that "It's not wrong because everyone is doing it."[22] Employees working for prominent companies such as Merck, WorldCom, Putman Investments, Tyco, and Edward D. Jones & Company have been involved in ethical lapses.[23] Most white-collar crime is committed by persons who lack character and integrity.

Win-Lose People	Win-Win People
• See a problem in every solution	• Help others solve their problems
• Fix the blame	• Fix what caused the problem
• Let life happen to them	• Make life a joyous happening for others and themselves
• Live in the past	• Learn from the past, live in the present, and set goals for the future
• Make promises they never keep	• Make commitments to themselves and to others and keep them both

FIGURE 3.3

The starting point to developing a win-win relationship strategy is to compare behaviors of win-lose salespeople with those of salespeople who have adopted the win-win approach.

(Adapted from a list of losers, winners, and double winners in *The Double Win* by Denis Waitley.)

Character is composed of personal standards, including honesty, integrity, and moral strength. It is a quality that is highly respected in the field of personal selling. **Integrity** is the basic ingredient of character that is exhibited when you achieve congruence between what you know, what you say, and what you do.[24] In a world of uncertainty and rapid change, integrity has become a valuable character trait. Salespeople with integrity can be trusted to do what they say they will do. One way to achieve trustworthiness in personal selling is to avoid deceiving or misleading the customer. More is said about this topic in Chapter 5, which examines the ethical conduct of salespeople.

Verbal and Nonverbal Strategies That Add Value to Your Relationships

The first contact between a salesperson and a prospect is very important. During the first few minutes—or seconds, in most cases—the prospect and the salesperson form impressions of each other that either facilitate or distract from the sales call. Malcolm Gladwell, author of the best-selling book *Blink*, says that when two people meet for the first time, both will make very superficial, rapid judgments about the other person. This decision-making process, he argues, usually happens subconsciously in a split second (in the blink of an eye).[25]

Every salesperson projects an image to prospective customers, and this image influences how a customer feels about the sales representative. The image you project is the sum total of many verbal and nonverbal factors. The quality of your voice, the clothing you wear, your posture, your manners, and your communication style represent some of the factors that contribute to the formation of your image. We discuss several forms of verbal and nonverbal communication in this chapter. Communication style is examined in Chapter 4.

Nonverbal Messages

When we attempt to communicate with another person, we use both verbal and nonverbal communications. **Nonverbal messages** are "messages without words" or "silent messages." These are the messages (other than spoken or written words) that we communicate through facial expressions, voice tone, gestures, appearance, posture, and other nonverbal means.[26]

Nonverbal communication, such as facial expression, voice tone, handshakes, gestures, appearance, and posture, are all important aspects of the relationship strategy. Research indicates these nonverbal messages convey much more than verbal messages.

Research indicates that when two people communicate, *nonverbal messages convey much more impact than verbal messages*. Words play a surprisingly small part in the communication process. Every spoken message has a vocal element, coming not from *what* we say but from *how* we say it. The voice communicates in many ways: through tone, volume, and speed of delivery. A salesperson wishing to communicate enthusiasm needs to use a voice that is charged with energy.

As we attempt to read nonverbal communication, it is important to remember that no *one* signal carries much meaning. If the person you meet for the first time displays a weak grip during the handshake, don't let this one signal shape your first impression. Such factors as posture, eye contact, gestures, clothing, and facial expression must all be regarded together.[27]

Nonverbal messages can reinforce or contradict the spoken word. When your verbal message and body language are consistent, they tend to give others the impression that you can be trusted and that what you say reflects what you truly believe. When there is a discrepancy between your verbal and nonverbal messages, you are less apt to be trusted."[28]

ENTRANCE AND CARRIAGE As noted earlier, the first impression we make is very important. The moment a salesperson walks into a client's office, the client begins making judgments. Susan Bixler, author of *The Professional Image* and *Professional Presence*, makes this comment:

> All of us make entrances throughout our business day as we enter offices, conference rooms, or meeting halls. And every time we do, someone is watching us, appraising us, sizing us up, and gauging our appearance, even our intelligence, often within the space of a few seconds.[29]

Bixler says that the key to making a successful entrance is simply believing—and projecting—that you have a reason to be there and have something important to offer the client. You can communicate confidence with a strong stride, a good posture, and a friendly smile. A confident manner communicates to the client the message, "This meeting will be beneficial to you."

SHAKING HANDS An inadequate handshake is like dandruff: No one mentions it, but everyone notices it. Today, the handshake is an important symbol of respect and in most business settings it is the proper greeting.[30]

In the field of selling, the handshake is usually the *first* and frequently the *only* physical contact one makes during a sales call. The handshake can communicate warmth, genuine concern for the prospect, and an image of strength. It also can communicate aloofness, indifference, and weakness to the customer. The message we communicate with a handshake is determined by a combination of five factors:

1. *Eye contact during handshake.* Eyes transmit more information than any other part of the body, so maintain eye contact throughout the handshaking process and display a pleasant smile.
2. *Degree of firmness.* Generally speaking, a firm handshake communicates a caring attitude, while a weak grip (the dead-fish handshake) communicates indifference.
3. *Depth of interlock.* A full, deep grip communicates friendship to the other person.
4. *Duration of grip.* There are no specific guidelines to tell us what the ideal duration of a grip should be. However, by extending the duration of the handshake we can often communicate a greater degree of interest and concern for the other person. Do not pump up and down more than once or twice.
5. *Degree of dryness of hands.* A moist palm not only is uncomfortable to handle but also can communicate the impression that you are quite nervous. Some people have a physiological problem that causes clammy hands and should keep a handkerchief within reach to remove excess moisture.[31]

The best time to present your name is when you extend your hand. When you introduce yourself, state your name clearly and then listen carefully to be certain you hear the

Selling in Action

REMEMBERING NAMES

In the field of personal selling, remembering a person's name is very important. To improve your ability to recall names, use one or more of these memory aids.

- *Verify the spelling.* After hearing the name ask, "Is that Reece with a 'c' or 's'?" Repetition helps you remember the name.

- *Ask how the person wants to be addressed.* Ask, "Should I call you Thomas or Tom?" This presents another opportunity for repetition.

- *Relate the name to something easy to remember.* If the person's last name is Park, connect this name with "Yosemite" in your mind. Some aspect of appearance (hairstyle, eyeglasses, etc) might serve as a connecting reference.

- *Use the name quickly.* Work the person's name into the conversation right away: "Mary, can I ask you a few questions?"

- *Use the name frequently.* During and at the end of the meeting, work the name into the conversation: "Eric, thank you for meeting with me."

Source: Adapted from "Secrets of Power Persuasion for Salespeople," by Roger Dawson. See Roger Dawson, "And Your Name Was Again?" *Value-Added Selling* 21, July 16, 2007, p. 2. Used with permission.

customer's name. To ensure that you remember the customer's name, repeat it. In some cases you need to check to be sure you are pronouncing it properly.

FACIAL EXPRESSIONS If you want to identify the inner feelings of another person, watch facial expressions closely. The face is a remarkable communicator, capable of accurately signaling emotion in a split second and capable of concealing emotion equally well. We can often determine if the customer's face is registering surprise, pleasure, or skepticism (see Figure 3.4). Facial expressions are largely universal, so people around the world tend to "read" faces in a similar way. It is worth noting that the smile is the most recognized facial signal in the world and it can have a great deal of influence on others. George Rotter, professor of psychology at Montclair University, says, "Smiles are an enormous controller of how people perceive you." People tend to trust a smiling face.[32] Get in the habit of offering a sincere smile each time you meet with a prospect.

EYE CONTACT When the customer is talking, eye contact is one of the best ways to say, "I'm listening." If you are looking across the room or at papers in your briefcase, the customer will assume you are not listening. However, prolonged eye contact can send the wrong message. A prolonged, direct stare can be threatening. To avoid the prolonged stare, take fleeting glances at your notes. As the customer speaks, nod occasionally to indicate agreement or interest.[33]

FIGURE 3.4

Our subtle facial gestures are continuously sending messages to others.

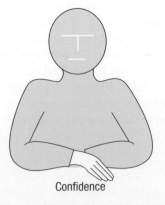

Confidence

Boredom

Evaluation

Spending an afternoon with a customer on the golf course is part of the relationship strategy of this salesperson. Many companies support this approach to building and maintaining relationships.

Effect of Appearance on Relationships

We form opinions about people based on a pattern of immediate impressions conveyed by appearance. The clothing we wear, the length and style of our hair, the fragrances we use, and the jewelry we display all combine to make a statement about us to others—a statement of primary importance to anyone involved in selling.

We all have certain views, or **unconscious expectations**, concerning appropriate dress. In sales work we should try to anticipate the expectations of our clientele. The clothing worn by salespeople does make a difference in terms of customer acceptance because it communicates powerful messages. The clothing we wear can influence our credibility and likability.

Most image consultants agree that there is no single "dress for success" look. The appropriate wardrobe varies from one city or region to another and from company to company. However, there are some general guidelines that we should follow in selecting clothing for sales work. Three key words should govern our decisions: simplicity, appropriateness, and quality.[34]

SIMPLICITY The color of clothing, as well as design, communicates a message to the customer. Some colors are showy and convey an air of casualness. In a business setting we want to be taken seriously, so flashy colors should usually be avoided.

APPROPRIATENESS Selecting appropriate clothing for sales work can be a challenge. We must carefully consider the clients we serve and decide what may be acceptable to them. Many salespeople are guided by the type of products they sell and the desired image projected by their employers. Deciding what constitutes appropriate attire in today's business casual world begins with an understanding of what it means to "dress down." **Business casual** is clothing that allows you to feel comfortable but looks neat and professional. Pay close attention to the clothing your clients wear.[35] If a client is wearing a nice sport coat, a collared long-sleeved shirt, and dress slacks, don't wear khaki trousers and a short-sleeve polo shirt. In recent years, the casual dress trend has reversed at many companies, and workplace dress codes have become more formal.[36]

QUALITY The quality of our wardrobe also influences the image we project to customers. A salesperson's wardrobe should be regarded as an investment, with each item carefully selected to look and fit well. Susan Bixler says, "If you want respect, you have to dress as well as or better than your industry standards."[37]

VISUAL INTEGRITY Visual presence must have a certain amount of integrity and consistency. The images you project are made up of many factors, and lack of attention to important details can negate your effort to create a good impression. Too much jewelry, a shirt that does not fit well, or unshined shoes can detract from the professional look you want to project. People often are extra alert when meeting someone new and this heightened consciousness makes every detail count.[38]

Keep in mind that customer contact often takes place in several settings. The first meeting with a customer may take place in her office, but the second meeting may be on the golf course. And the third meeting may take place at a nice restaurant. The clothing you wear in each of these settings is important.

Effect of Voice Quality on Relationships

As noted previously, every spoken message has a vocal element. What we hear is greatly influenced by the speaker's tone of voice, vocal clarity, and verbal expressiveness. On the telephone, voice quality is even more important because the other person cannot see your facial expressions, hand gestures, and other body movements. You cannot trade in your current voice for a new one. However, you can make your voice more pleasing to others. How? Consider these suggestions:

1. *Do not talk too fast or too slowly.* Rapid speech often causes customers to become defensive. They raise psychological barriers because a "rapid-fire monologue" is associated with high-pressure sales methods. Many salespeople could improve their verbal presentation by talking more slowly. The slower presentation allows others to follow, and it allows the speaker time to think ahead—to consider the situation and make judgments. Another good tip is to vary the speed of your speech, leaving spaces between thoughts. Crowding too many thoughts together may confuse the listener.[39]

2. *Avoid a speech pattern that is dull and colorless.* The worst kind of voice has no color and no feeling. Enthusiasm is a critical element of an effective sales presentation. It also is contagious. Your enthusiasm for the product is transmitted to the customer.

3. *Avoid bad speech habits.* Kristy Pinand, a youthful-looking 23-year-old, routinely used "teen speak." For example, she described a recent promotion as "so cool." Her supervisor felt she not only looked young, but she also sounded very young, and this image could potentially hurt her ability to win the respect of clients. She urged Ms. Pinand to select her words more carefully. Ms. Pinand heeded the constructive advice and now rehearses her remarks aloud before she calls a client.[40]

Some speech habits can make us sound poorly educated and inarticulate. At age 22, Mike White learned that his east Tennessee accent and colorful backwoods speech patterns created problems at work. He recognized that his southern drawl was a "turnoff" to some of the image-conscious people he worked with. One day his sales manager asked him if he had his racquetball equipment with him, and White replied, "Yeah, I brung it." Fortunately, White's supervisor was willing to tactfully correct his grammatical problems and help him communicate with greater clarity. Today, Mike White is CEO of a successful company and a frequent speaker at trade shows.[41]

Effect of Etiquette on Your Relationships

The study of etiquette (sometimes called *manner* or *protocol*) reveals a number of ways to enhance your relationship strategy. Salespeople who possess knowledge of the rules of etiquette can perform their daily work with greater poise and confidence. Think of etiquette as a universal passport to positive relationships and respect.

With practice, anyone can develop good etiquette without appearing to be "stiff" and at the same time win the respect and admiration of others. Space does not permit a complete review of this topic, but we cover some of the rules of etiquette that are especially important to salespeople.

1. *Avoid the temptation to address a new prospect by first name.* In a business setting, too much familiarity too quickly can cause irritation.

2. *Avoid offensive comments or stories.* Never assume that the customer's value system is the same as your own. Rough language, off-color stories, or personal views on political issues can do irreparable damage to your image.

3. *Recognize the importance of punctuality.* Ann Marie Sabath, owner of a firm that provides etiquette training for business employees, says " . . . we teach people that if you're early, you're on time, and if you're on time, in reality, you're late." Showing up late for an appointment will be viewed as rudeness by most clients.[42]

4. *When you invite a customer to lunch, do not discuss business before the meal is ordered unless the client initiates the subject.* Also, avoid ordering food that is not easily controlled, such as ribs, chicken, or lobster.

5. *When you use voice mail, leave a clear, concise message.* Do not speak too fast or mumble your name and number.

6. *Avoid cell phone contempt.* Turn off the cell phone ringer anytime you are with a client. Never put your phone on the table during a meal.

It has been said that good manners make other people feel better. This is true because good etiquette requires that we place the other person's comfort ahead of our own. One of the best ways to develop rapport with a customer is to avoid behavior that might be offensive to that person.

Conversational Strategies That Enhance Relationships

The foundation for a long-term relationship with the customer is frequently a "get acquainted" type of conversation that takes place before any discussion of business matters. Within a few minutes it is possible to reduce the relationship tension that is so common when two people meet for the first time. This informal visit with the customer provides the salesperson with an opportunity to apply three guidelines for building strong relationships featured in *How to Win Friends and Influence People*, the classic book written by Dale Carnegie.

- *Become genuinely interested in other people.* Tim Sanders, chief solutions officer at Yahoo!, says, "How we are perceived as human beings is becoming increasingly important in the new economy."[43] When you become genuinely interested in the customer, you create an experience that is long remembered.

- *Be a good listener; encourage others to talk about themselves.* Stephen Covey, the noted author and consultant, recommends empathic listening. This requires listening with your ears, your eyes, and your heart.[44] We live in a culture where empathic listening is quite rare. Interrupting has become all too common as people rush to fill every gap in the conversation.

■ *Talk in terms of the other person's interest.*[45] When you are initiating a conversation with a customer, don't hesitate to use small talk to get the conversation started. This may involve current events, business, or sports. Be sure to focus on topics that the customer is interested in.

The length of this conversation depends on your sense of the prospect's reaction to your greeting, how busy the prospect appears to be, and your awareness of topics of mutual interest. In developing this conversation the following three areas should be considered.

Comments on Here and Now Observations

Observant salespeople are aware of the things going on around them. These observations can be as general as unusual developments in the weather or as specific as noticing unique artifacts in the prospect's office. These observations often provide the basis for *small talk,* which can break the ice and speed up the building of a relationship.

Compliments

When you offer a *sincere* compliment to your prospect, you are saying, "Something about you is special." Most people react positively to compliments because they appeal to the need for self-esteem. Your admiration should not be expressed, however, in phony superlatives that seem transparent. Jack Canfield, author of *The Success Principles*, reminds us that everything we say to a customer produces an effect: "Know that you are constantly creating something—either positive of negative—with your words."[46]

Search for Mutual Acquaintances or Interests

A frequent mode for establishing rapport with a new prospect is to find friends or interests you have in common. If you know someone with the same last name as your prospect, it may be appropriate to ask whether your friend is any relation. Anything you observe in the prospect's office or home might suggest an interest that you and your prospect share. A strong bond often develops between two persons who share the same interest or hobby. Frances Carlisle, an estate planner in New York, says her love of animals lands her many clients. Some of these clients wish to include provisions for the care of pets in their estate plans. Sometimes an unusual hobby (such as sky diving, mountain climbing, or auto racing) is the perfect way to stand out and cultivate relationships with clients.[47]

Ken Viselman, chairman of Itsy Bitsy Entertainment in New York, provides salespeople with many artifacts to talk about in his office. He states that "behind every object in [my] office is a story and a bit of my life." These items include an 18th century armoire, a crowded shelf of toys, and a Picasso lithograph, to name only a few.

Strategies for Self-Improvement

Orson Welles, one of the most highly respected actors in this country, once said, "Every actor is very busy getting better or getting worse." To a large extent, salespeople are also "very busy getting better or getting worse." To improve, salespeople must develop an ongoing program for self-improvement (see Chapter 16). It is important to keep in mind that all improvement is self-initiated. Each of us controls the switch that allows personal growth and development to take place.

At the beginning of this chapter, we introduced the concept of emotional intelligence. We noted that this form of intelligence can be increased with the aid of self-development activities. Would you like to develop a more positive self-image? Improve your ability to develop win-win relationships? Develop effective nonverbal communication skills? Improve your speaking voice? These relationship-building strategies can be achieved if you are willing to follow these steps:

Step one: Set goals. The goal-setting process begins with a clear, written statement that describes what you want to accomplish. If your goal is too general or vague, progress toward achieving that goal is difficult to observe. Next, you must identify the steps you will take to achieve your goal. Perseverance is the key to goal achievement.

Step two: Use visualization. To **visualize** means to form a mental image of something. The power to visualize (sometimes called *guided imagery*) is in a very real sense the power to create. If you really want to succeed at something, picture yourself doing it successfully. For example, spend time developing mental pictures of successful sales presentations or visualize yourself as one of the top salespeople in your organization. Once you have formed a clear mental picture of what you want to accomplish, identify the steps needed to get there and then mentally rehearse them. The visualization process needs to be repeated over and over again.[48]

Step three: Use positive self-talk. People with a strong inner critic will receive frequent negative messages that can erode their self-esteem. It helps to refute and reject those negative messages with positive self-talk. **Self-talk** takes place silently in the privacy of your mind. It is the series of personal conversations you have with yourself almost continually throughout the day. Just like statements from other people, your self-talk can dramatically affect your behavior and self-esteem.[49]

Step four: Reward your progress. When you see yourself making progress toward a goal, or achieving a goal, reward yourself. This type of reinforcement is vital when you are trying to change a behavior. There is nothing wrong with taking pride in your accomplishments.

Self-improvement efforts can result in new abilities or powers, and they give us the motivation to utilize more fully the talents we already have. As a result, our potential for success is greater.

Chapter Learning Activities

Reviewing Key Concepts

Explain the importance of developing a relationship strategy

The manner in which salespeople establish, build, and maintain relationships is a major key to success in personal selling. The key relationships in selling include management personnel, company support staff, secondary decision makers, and customers.

The concept of *partnering* is revisited and discussed in detail. Partnering emphasizes building a strong relationship during every aspect of the sale and working hard to maintain a quality relationship with the customer after the sale. Partnerships can be strengthened when salespeople use value-added relationship strategies.

Discuss how thought processes can enhance your relationship strategy

An understanding of the psychology of human behavior provides a foundation for developing relationship strategies. In this chapter we discuss the link between self-concept and success in selling. Self-imposed fears can prevent salespeople from achieving success. The relationship strategy is built on the win-win philosophy, empathy and ego drive, and character and integrity.

Identify and describe the major nonverbal factors that shape our sales image

We describe several factors that influence the image we project to customers. The image others have of us is shaped to a great extent by nonverbal communication. We may choose the right words to persuade a customer to place an order, but aversive factors communicated by our clothing, handshake, facial expression, voice quality, and etiquette miscues may prejudice the customer against us and our product or service.

Describe conversational strategies that help us establish relationships

The various conversational strategies that enhance relationships are reviewed. These include comments on here and now observations, compliments, and the search for mutual acquaintances. Dale Carnegie's guidelines for building strong relationships are discussed.

Explain how to establish a self-improvement plan based on personal development strategies

We discussed the importance of adopting strategies for self-improvement. A four-step, self-improvement plan is the key to relationship building.

Key Terms

Emotional intelligence	Character	Business casual
Empathizer	Integrity	Visualize
Self-concept	Nonverbal messages	Self-talk
Ego drive	Unconscious expectations	

Review Questions

1. List the three prescriptions that serve as the foundation for development of a relationship strategy.
2. How important are establishing, building, and maintaining relationships in the selling process? List the four groups of people with whom sales personnel must be able to work effectively.
3. Why is partnering described as the highest-quality selling relationship? Why has the building of partnerships become more important today?
4. Defend the statement, "Successful relationships depend on a positive self-image."
5. Describe the win-win approach to selling.
6. How is our self-image formed? Why is a positive self-image so important in personal selling?
7. Describe the meaning of the term *emotional intelligence.*
8. Identify three conversational methods that can be used to establish relationships.
9. Describe the meaning of nonverbal messages. Why should salespeople be concerned about these messages?
10. List and describe each step in the four-step self-improvement plan.

Application Exercises

1. Select four salespeople you know and ask them if they have a relationship strategy for working with customers, management personnel, secondary decision makers, and company support staff. Ask each salesperson to give you two or three specific examples of steps they have taken to build and maintain a positive relationship with their customers.

2. The partnering style of selling is emphasized throughout the book. To gain more insight into the popularity of this concept, use one of your Internet search engines to key in the words "partnering + selling." Notice the large number of documents related to this query. Click on and examine several of these documents to learn more about this approach to selling.

3. Complete the following etiquette quiz. Your instructor will provide you with answers so you can check your responses.

   a. On what side should you wear your name tag?

   b. Is it appropriate to drink beer from a bottle at a reception?

   c. When introducing a female salesperson to a male prospect, whose name should be spoken first?

   d. At the table, when should you place your napkin in your lap?

   e. Is it ever proper to comb, smooth, or touch your hair while seated at a restaurant table?

4. In October, people of the Hindu religion celebrate Diwali, the festival of lights. The festival of lights is one of the most important and most beautiful Indian festivals. Rick Saulle, a pharmaceutical sales representative employed by Pifzer, knew that one of the most important physicians he called on was Indian and would celebrate Diwali. He also knew that it is commonplace to provide sweets to Indians who celebrate Diwali. Saulle visited an Indian grocery store and purchased a plate of Indian sweets to celebrate Diwali. When he presented the sweets to the physician, the response was very positive. The doctor grabbed Saulle's hand, shook it forcefully, and sincerely thanked him for honoring this important holiday.[50]

   As a nation, we serve as host to a kaleidoscope of the world's cultures, and the trend toward greater diversity will accelerate in the years ahead. Reflect on the gift given by Mr. Saulle and then answer these questions.

   a. Is it appropriate for a salesperson to give a gift to someone who is celebrating a religious holiday?

   b. In addition to giving a gift, what are some other ways to recognize a religious festival or holiday?

   c. List and describe three religious holidays or festivals celebrated by denominations other than Christian.

5. Move quickly through the following list of traits. Use a check mark beside those that fit your self-image. Use an *X* to mark those that do not fit. If you are unsure, indicate with a question mark.

_____	I like myself.	_____	I trust myself.
_____	People trust me.	_____	I often do the wrong thing.
_____	I usually say the right thing.	_____	People avoid me.
_____	I dislike myself.	_____	I enjoy work.
_____	I waste time.	_____	I control myself.
_____	I put up a good front.	_____	I enjoy nature.
_____	I use my talents.	_____	I am dependent on others for ideas.

	I feel hemmed in.		I am involved in solving community problems.
_____	I use time well.	_____	I do not use my talents fully.
_____	I enjoy people.	_____	I do not like myself.
_____	I usually say the wrong thing.	_____	I do not like to be around people.
_____	I am discouraged about life.	_____	People like to be around me.
_____	I have not developed my talents.		

Now look at the pattern of your self-assessment.

   a. Is there a pattern?

   b. Is there a winner or loser pattern?

   c. What traits would you like to change? (List them.)

   d. Pick the trait you would like to change the most and prepare a plan to achieve this change. Your plan should include specific goal statements.

6. It is pointed out in this chapter that clothing communicates strong messages. In this exercise you become more aware of whether or not your clothes communicate the messages you want them to communicate.

   a. Make a chart like the one that follows:

ITEM OF CLOTHING BEING ANALYZED	WHAT I WANT MY CLOTHES TO SAY ABOUT ME TO OTHERS	WHAT OTHERS THINK MY CLOTHING SAYS

   b. In the first column, list the clothing you are now wearing, for example, dress slacks, dress shoes, and sweater; athletic shoes, jeans, and t-shirt; or suit, tie, and dress shoes.

   c. In the middle column, describe the message you would like the clothes you have chosen to say. For example, "I want to be comfortable," "I want people to trust me," or "I want people to take me seriously."

   d. Have somebody else fill in the third column by describing what your clothes do say about you.

   e. Compare the two columns. Do your clothes communicate what you want them to? Do the same exercise for social dress, casual dress, business attire, and hairstyle.

Note: If you are currently employed, analyze the clothing you wear at work.

Role-Play Exercise

This is a two-part role-play exercise. Part one involves preparation for a sales call on a new prospect whom you have not met previously. The primary objective of this meeting is to get acquainted with the prospect and begin the process of building a long-term relationship. You anticipate that this prospect will become a very good customer. Review the text material on thought processes that will enhance your relationship strategy, nonverbal strategies that add value to your relationships, and conversational strategies that enhance relationships. Prepare a written outline of what you plan to say and do during the first 5 to 10 minutes of the meeting.

Think of this outline as your "strategic plan." Part two involves a role-play with a class member who will play the role of the prospect. Throughout the role-play, try to say and do everything that was part of your plan. At the end of the role-play, give your strategic plan outline to the prospect and request feedback on your performance.

CRM Application Exercise

Preparing Letters with CRM

The Salesforce.com application demonstrates how customer relationship management (CRM) programs are designed to be used by people in a hurry or without extensive typing skills. Menu choices can be made with the mouse, by typing simple key combinations, or by selecting an icon. This means that a procedure such as sending an e-mail to a contact (Dottie Smith) can be started by (1) searching for the Dottie Smith contact record; (2) clicking the Send Email button in "Activity History"; (3) clicking the Select Template button and selecting the "Park Inn New Contact" template. A professional e-mail with contact and customer names in the appropriate places appears. The e-mail already has the date, salutation, closing line, your name, and your title on your screen. All you need to do is type the body of the e-mail and press send. Note that after you send the e-mail, it is part of Dottie Smith's permanent activity history.

Search for the Brad Able contact record. With Brad Able's record on the screen, click the Mail Merge button and select the "Confirm Appointment" template. Make the necessary changes to the letter to confirm an appointment to meet at Brad Able's office next Thursday at 9:00 A.M. to discuss his training needs. Your letter should feature the win-win approach discussed in the chapter.

Reality Selling Today Video Case Problem

Susanna Rosa
CB Richard Ellis

The commercial real estate services industry is highly competitive. CBRE, the firm featured at the beginning of this chapter, offers a wide variety of services such as industrial and logistical services, real estate consulting, investment properties services, and global corporate services. When clients want to find an office space, they hold their realtor to high standards. After all, the term of a lease contract is a long-term one, and the stakes are high. CBRE salespeople understand the magnitude and trend of the commercial real estate market. They know that the customers are eager to partner with someone who can be trusted to look after their best interests.

When new salespeople join the CBRE sales force, they usually work under a senior broker. The mentor helps these recruits form a professional image that appeals to the type of clientele served by the company. In the end, there is a direct link between the image projected by the salespeople and the success of the company. CBRE also adopts a team-based selling approach to ensure that the client is in good hands as the relationship between CBRE and the client develops. Susana Rosas, an experienced broker in CBRE's Houston office, believes that working under a mentor to learn how to process a deal with a relationship orientation is invaluable. That mentality is part of CBRE's culture and success. Susana works closely with her team members through several stages of the relationship with CBRE clients, from prospecting to postsales follow-up. When working with new recruits and her team members, she emphasizes the following points:

- Customers notice even the little details, such as the firmness of a handshake or a proper introduction.
- Salespeople at CBRE must be able to build rapport with a variety of personality types. Some customers are quiet, reserved, and somewhat guarded when expressing their views. Others are more impulsive and express their views openly. Salespeople are encouraged to alter their communication style to increase the comfort level of

the customer. Susana believes that it is always important for a salesperson to gauge how his or her communication style impacts the prospect. A positive attitude is another important aspect of the relationship-building process at CBRE.

■ Susana is a strong believer that salespeople should find out what customers value. Most of the time, a salesperson must come up with innovative solutions to seemingly irreconcilable needs, such as the need to have a large space to accommodate cyclical ups and downs of the customer's industry and the need for efficiency. What is the most important aspect of commercial real estate sales? Most customers do not open up and share important information until they trust the salesperson. (See chapter opener on p. 51, and Reality Selling Today Video Role-Play 2 in Appendix 1 on p. 394 for more information.)

Questions

1. Does it appear that the CBRE salesperson supports the three prescriptions that serve as a foundation of the relationship strategy? (See the Strategic/Consultative Selling Model in Figure 3.1.) Explain your answer.

2. Why should real estate salespeople spend time developing a relationship strategy? What might be some long-term benefits of this strategy?

3. Is it ever appropriate to touch your client other than with a handshake? Explain your answer.

4. How differently would you behave when dealing with a return client versus a new client?

5. What are some precautions to take when preparing a meeting with a foreign-born prospect?

4

Communication Styles: A Key to Adaptive Selling Today

Chapter Preview

When you finish reading this chapter, you should be able to

1
Discuss how communication style influences the relationship process in sales

2
Identify the two major dimensions of the communication-style model

3
Explain the four communication styles in the communication-style model

4
Learn how to identify your preferred communication style and that of your customer

5
Learn to achieve interpersonal versatility and build strong selling relationships with style flexing

▶ Adaptive Selling Today Training Video Series

COMMUNICATION STYLES—A KEY TO ADAPTIVE SELLING

Communication—or behavior—styles, as they are sometimes called, have been described as one of the most popular training programs in sales and management.

In this two-part Adaptive Selling Today Training Video, you'll meet Lana, a senior salesperson. While working with Ron, one of her top customers, Sandra, her sales team member (all featured in the photo above); and Raymond, her marketing manager, she shares what she has learned about building selling relationships with communication styles. We will learn how Lana and her team take a "No, this won't work" response from Ron and, with the adaptive selling "Platinum Rule," attempt to build a mutually rewarding relationship.

Every year publications such as *Business Week, Fortune*, and *Fast Company* feature profiles of well-known business leaders. These articles often focus on the communication styles of the executives who provide leadership in companies across America. Who can forget Al "Chainsaw" Dunlap, who was described as aggressive, frank, opinionated, and impatient? He earned his nickname by ordering huge layoffs when he was the CEO responsible for restructuring companies such as Scott Paper and Sunbeam Corporation. Deborah Hopkins earned the nickname "Hurricane Debby" for the way she conducted business while holding leadership positions at Unisys, GM Europe, Boeing, and Lucent Technologies. Her demanding, ambitious, and sometimes emotional style occasionally created personality clashes. By contrast, Bill Gates is described as a quiet, reflective person who often seems preoccupied with other matters. And then there is Jeff Bezos, the founder and CEO of Amazon.com, who is often described as the happy extrovert.

He seems to enjoy being with other people and often displays spontaneous, uninhibited behavior.[1]

We form impressions of people by observing their behavior. The thoughts, feelings, and actions that characterize someone are generally viewed as their **personality**.[2] Communication style is an important aspect of our personality. ∎

Communication Styles—An Introduction to Adaptive Selling

Almost everyone has had the pleasant experience of meeting someone for the first time and developing an instant mutual rapport. There seems to be a quality about some people that makes you like them instantaneously—a basis for a mutual understanding that is difficult to explain. On the other hand, we can all recall meeting people who "turn us off" almost immediately. Why does this happen during the initial contact?

The impressions that others form about us are based on what they observe us saying and doing. They have no way of knowing our innermost thoughts and feelings, so they make decisions about us based on what they see and hear.[3] The patterns of behavior that others observe can be called **communication style**. *Behavior styles* and *social styles* are additional terms frequently used to describe these patterns of behavior.

Adaptive selling, introduced in chapter one, is defined as altering sales behaviors in order to improve communication with the customer. It relates to a salesperson's ability to collect information regarding the customer's needs and responding appropriately. Adaptive selling frequently requires complex behavioral adjustments.[4] Adjusting one's communication style in order to fit individual customer needs and preferences is an important element of adaptive selling.

Communication-Style Bias

Bias in various forms is quite common in our society. In fact, local, state, and national governments have passed many laws to curb blatant forms of racial, age, and sex bias. We also observe some degree of regional bias when people from various parts of the country meet.

The most frequently occurring form of bias is not commonly understood in our society. What has been labeled **communication-style bias** is a state of mind that almost every one of us experiences from time to time, but we usually find it difficult to explain the symptoms. Communication-style bias can develop when we have contact with another person whose communication style is different from our own. For example, a purchasing agent was overheard

We form impressions of others by observing their behavior. Jeff Bezos, founder of Amazon.com, is often described as the happy extrovert who frequently displays spontaneous, uninhibited laughter. By contrast, Microsoft's Bill Gates is described as a quiet, reflective person who often seems preoccupied with other matters.

saying, "I do not know what it is, but I just do not like that sales representative." The agent was no doubt experiencing communication-style bias but could not easily describe the feeling.

Your communication style is the "you" that is on display every day—the outer pattern of behavior that others see. If your style is very different from the other person's, it may be difficult for the two of you to develop a rapport. All of us have had the experience of saying or doing something that was perfectly acceptable to a friend or coworker and being surprised when the same behavior irritated someone else. However, aside from admitting that this happens, most of us are unable to draw meaningful conclusions from these experiences to help us perform more effectively with people in the future.[5]

In recent years, thousands of sales professionals have learned to manage their selling relationships more effectively through the study of communication styles. Books, such as *I'm Stuck, Your Stuck* by Tom Ritchey, *People Styles at Work* by Robert Bolton and Dorothy Grover Bolton, and *The Versatile Salesperson* by Roger Wenschlag, serve as good references. Many training companies offer seminars that provide enrollees with a practical understanding of communication-style theory and practice. Wilson Learning (www.wilsonlearning.com) offers a program titled *The Versatile Salesperson.* This program helps salespeople develop the interpersonal skills necessary to work effectively with customers whose communication style is different from their own. More than seven million people worldwide have completed Wilson Learning programs that focus on communication styles.[6]

Communication-Style Principles

The theory of behavioral- or communication-style bias is based on a number of underlying principles. A review of these principles can be beneficial before we examine specific styles.

1. *Individual differences exist and are important.* It is quite obvious that we all differ in terms of physical characteristics such as height, shoe size, facial features, and body build, but the most interesting differences are those patterns of behavior that are unique to each of us. Voice patterns, eye movement, facial expression, and posture are some of the components of our communication style. Additional characteristics are discussed later in this chapter. Research by the Swiss psychoanalyst Carl Jung and others has helped us understand the importance of individual differences.

2. *A communication style is a way of thinking and behaving.* It is not an ability but, instead, a preferred way of using abilities one has. This distinction is very important. An ability refers to how well someone can do something. A style refers to how someone likes to do something.[7]

3. *Individual style differences tend to be stable.* Our communication style is based on a combination of hereditary and environmental factors. Our style is somewhat original at the time of birth; it takes on additional individuality during the first three to five years of life. By the time we enter elementary school, the teacher should be able to identify our preferred communication style. While an individual's communication style tends to remain fairly constant throughout life, adapting to different communication counterparts or the ability to "flex" can be enhanced.

4. *There is a finite number of styles.* Most people display one of several clusters of similar behaviors, and this allows us to identify a small number of behavioral

Group sales presentations can be very challenging because in most cases you are attempting to adapt to several different communication styles.

categories. By combining a series of descriptors, we can develop a single "label" that describes a person's most preferred communication style.

5. *To create the most productive relationships, it is necessary to get in sync with the communication style of the people you work with.*[8] Differences between people can be a source of friction unless you develop the ability to recognize and respond to the other person's style.

The ability to identify another person's communication style, and to know how and when to adapt your own preferred style to it, can afford you a crucial advantage in dealing with people. Differences between people can be a source of friction. The ability to "speak the other person's language" is an important relationship-management skill.[9]

Improving Your Relationship Selling Skills

Anyone who is considering a career in selling can benefit greatly from the study of communication styles. These concepts provide a practical method of classifying people according to communication styles and give the salesperson a distinct advantage in the marketplace. A salesperson who understands communication-style classification methods and learns how to adapt them can avoid common mistakes that threaten interpersonal relations with customers. Awareness of these methods greatly reduces the possibility of tension arising during the sales call.

The first major goal of this chapter is to help you better understand your own most preferred communication style. The second goal is to help you develop greater understanding and appreciation for styles that are different from your own. The third goal is to help you manage your selling relationships more effectively by learning to adapt your style to fit the communication style of the customer. This practice is called "style flexing."

Communication-Style Model

This section introduces you to the four basic communication styles. One of these will surface as your most preferred style. The communication-style model that defines these styles

---

Selling Is Everyone's Business

PERSONAL SELLING FILLS THE SEATS

Mark Cuban, owner of the NBA Dallas Mavericks, has been described as "probably the most involved owner in day-to-day activities that the pro basketball league has ever seen." When he bought the team, it had not been in the playoffs for 10 years. His mission, of course, was not only to improve the team's on-court performance but also to dramatically increase its revenue from season ticket sales and sponsorships. Within one week, he added 30 new salespeople to the team's 5-member sales force. Cuban says, "I think the key to any business is to be able to connect with customers and prove to them that you can give better value than the next guy. We take things into our own hands by selling and talking directly to customers." In one year, paid attendance increased 60 percent, season ticket sales increased 25 percent, sponsorship revenue increased 30 percent, and the Mavericks made the playoffs.[a] Mark Cuban put his emotive communication style "on stage" with his recent appearance on the "Dancing with the Stars" television program.

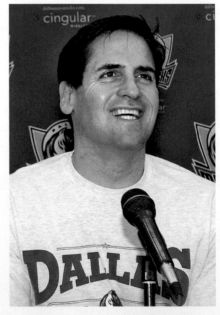

Mark Cuban, owner of the NBA Dallas Mavericks.

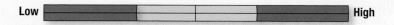

Low ────────────────────────── High

FIGURE 4.1

The first step in determining your most preferred communication style is to identify where you are on the dominance continuum.

is based on two important dimensions of human behavior: dominance and sociability. We look at the dominance continuum first.

Dominance Continuum

Dominance can be defined as the tendency to control or prevail over others.[10] Dominant people tend to be quite competitive. They also tend to offer opinions readily and to be decisive, opinioned, self-assertive, and vocal. Each of us falls somewhere on the dominance continuum, illustrated by Figure 4.1.

A person classified as being high in dominance is generally a "take charge" type of person who makes a position clear to others. A person classified as being low in dominance is usually more reserved, unassertive, and easygoing. Dominance has been recognized as a universal behavioral characteristic. David W. Johnson developed the Interpersonal Pattern Exercise to help people achieve greater interpersonal effectiveness. He believes that people fall into two dominance categories:

1. *Lower dominance.* These people have a tendency to be quite cooperative and let others control things. They tend to be lower in assertiveness.
2. *Higher dominance.* These people tend to like to control things and frequently initiate demands. They are more aggressive in dealing with others.[11]

The first step in determining your most preferred communication style is to identify where you fall on the dominance continuum. Do you tend to rank low or high on this scale? To answer this question, complete the Dominance Indicator form in Table 4.1. Rate yourself on each scale by placing a check mark on the continuum at the point that represents how you perceive yourself. If most of your check marks fall to the right of center, you are someone who is higher in dominance. If most of your check marks fall to the left of center, you are someone who is lower in dominance. Is there any best place to be on the dominance continuum? The answer is no. Successful salespeople can be found at all points along the continuum.

TABLE 4.1   Dominance Indicator

Rate yourself on each scale by placing a check mark on the continuum at the point that represents how you perceive yourself.

I PERCEIVE MYSELF AS SOMEWHAT	
Cooperative —+———————+————————+————————+————————+—	Competitive
Submissive —+———————+————————+————————+————————+—	Authoritarian
Accommodating —+———————+————————+————————+————————+—	Domineering
Hesitant —+———————+————————+————————+————————+—	Decisive
Reserved —+———————+————————+————————+————————+—	Outgoing
Compromising —+———————+————————+————————+————————+—	Insistent
Cautious —+———————+————————+————————+————————+—	Risk taking
Patient —+———————+————————+————————+————————+—	Hurried
Complacent —+———————+————————+————————+————————+—	Influential
Quiet —+———————+————————+————————+————————+—	Talkative
Shy —+———————+————————+————————+————————+—	Bold
Supportive —+———————+————————+————————+————————+—	Demanding
Relaxed —+———————+————————+————————+————————+—	Tense
Restrained —+———————+————————+————————+————————+—	Assertive

FIGURE 4.2

The second step in determining your most preferred communication style is to identify where you are on the sociability continuum.

High

Low

Sociability Continuum

Sociability reflects the amount of control we exert over our emotional expressiveness.[12] Individuals who are higher in sociability tend to express their feelings freely, while people who are low in this dimension tend to control their feelings. Each of us falls somewhere on the sociability continuum, illustrated in Figure 4.2.

Sociability is also a universal behavioral characteristic. It can be defined as the tendency to seek and enjoy interaction with others. Therefore, high sociability is an indication of a person's preference to interact with other people. Lower sociability is an indicator of a person's desire to work in an environment where the person has more time alone instead of having to make conversation with others. The person who is classified as being lower in the area of sociability is more reserved and formal in social relationships.

The second step in determining your most preferred communication style is to identify where you fall on the sociability continuum. To answer this question, complete the Sociability Indicator form shown in Table 4.2. Rate yourself on each scale by placing a check mark on the continuum at the point that represents how you perceive yourself. If most of your check marks fall to the right of center, you are someone who is higher in sociability. If most of your check marks fall to the left of center, you are someone who is lower in sociability. Keep in mind that there is no best place to be. Successful salespeople can be found at all points along this continuum.

As you reflect on your dominance and sociability ratings, keep in mind that self-ratings can be misleading. Many people do not see themselves in the same way that others see them. Friends and coworkers who frequently observe your behaviors may be in a better position to identify your communication style.

With the aid of the dominance and sociability continuums, we are now prepared to discuss a relatively simple communication-style classification plan that has practical application in the field of selling. We describe the four basic styles: Emotive, Directive, Reflective, and Supportive.

Four Styles of Communication

By combining these two dimensions of human behavior, dominance and sociability, we can form a partial outline of the communication-style model (Figure 4.3). Dominance is represented by the horizontal axis, and sociability is represented by the vertical axis. Once the two dimensions of human behavior are combined, the framework for communication-style classification is established.

TABLE 4.2   Sociability Indicator

Rate yourself on each scale by placing a check mark on the continuum at the point that represents how you perceive yourself.

I PERCEIVE MYSELF AS SOMEWHAT		
Disciplined	—/————/————/————/————/—	Easygoing
Controlled	—/————/————/————/————/—	Expressive
Serious	—/————/————/————/————/—	Lighthearted
Methodical	—/————/————/————/————/—	Unstructured
Calculating	—/————/————/————/————/—	Spontaneous
Guarded	—/————/————/————/————/—	Open
Stalwart	—/————/————/————/————/—	Humorous
Aloof	—/————/————/————/————/—	Friendly
Formal	—/————/————/————/————/—	Casual
Reserved	—/————/————/————/————/—	Attention seeking
Cautious	—/————/————/————/————/—	Carefree
Conforming	—/————/————/————/————/—	Unconventional
Reticent	—/————/————/————/————/—	Dramatic
Restrained	—/————/————/————/————/—	Impulsive

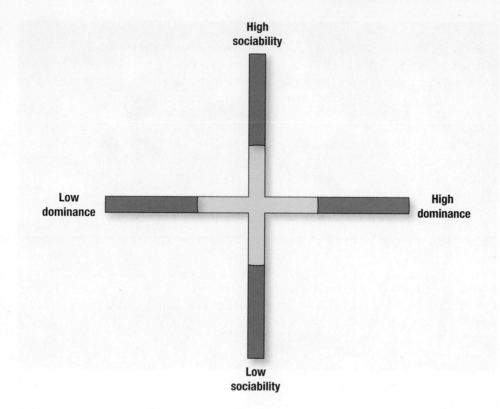

FIGURE 4.3

When the dominance and sociability dimensions of human behavior are combined, the framework for communication-style classification is established.

EMOTIVE STYLE The upper right-hand quadrant of Figure 4.4 defines a style that combines higher sociability and higher dominance. We call this the **Emotive style**. Emotive people like Al Roker and Jay Leno usually stand out in a crowd. They are expressive and willing to spend time maintaining and enjoying a large number of relationships.[13] Oprah Winfrey, the well-known television personality, and talk show host David Letterman provide excellent models of the Emotive communication style. Rosie O'Donnell provides still another example. They are

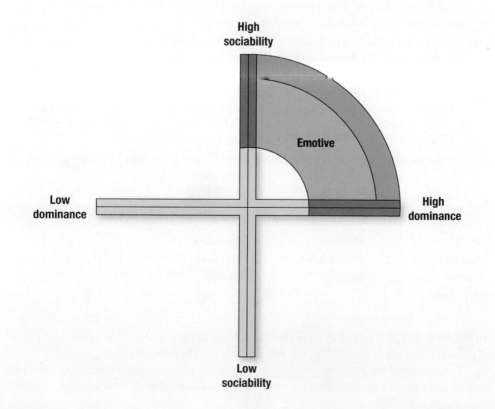

FIGURE 4.4

The Emotive style combines high sociability and high dominance.

Emotive people like Oprah Winfrey are enthusiastic, outspoken, and stimulating. By contrast, persons who display the Reflective style like Tiger Woods are more reserved and tend not to express dramatic opinions.

outspoken, enthusiastic, and stimulating. Robin Williams, the popular actor, and Richard Branson, the founder of Virgin Atlantic Airways, also project the Emotive communication style. The Emotive person wants to create a social relationship quickly and usually feels more comfortable in an informal atmosphere. Some of the verbal and nonverbal clues that identify the Emotive person follow:

1. *Appears quite active.* This person gives the appearance of being busy. A person who combines higher dominance and higher sociability often displays spontaneous, uninhibited behavior. The Emotive person is likely to express feelings with vigorous movements of the hands and a rapid speech pattern.

2. *Takes the social initiative in most cases.* Emotives tend to be extroverts. When two people meet for the first time, the Emotive person is more apt to initiate and maintain the conversation as well as to initiate the handshake. Emotives rate higher in both directness and openness.

3. *Likes to encourage informality.* The Emotive person moves to a "first name" basis as soon as possible (too soon, in some cases). Even the way this person sits in a chair communicates a preference for a relaxed, informal social setting.

4. *Expresses emotional opinions.* Emotive people generally do not hide their feelings. They often express opinions dramatically and impulsively.

Key Words for the Emotive Style		
Sociable	Emotional	Personable
Spontaneous	Unstructured	Persuasive
Zestful	Excitable	Dynamic
Stimulating		

DIRECTIVE STYLE The lower right-hand quadrant defines a style that combines higher dominance and lower sociability. We will call this the **Directive style** (Figure 4.5).

To understand the nature of people who display the Directive communication style, picture in your mind's eye the director of a Hollywood film. The person you see is giving orders in a firm voice and is generally in charge of every facet of the operation. Everyone on the set knows this person is in charge. Although the common stereotyped image of the Hollywood film director is probably exaggerated, this example is helpful as you attempt to become familiar with the Directive style.

Martha Stewart (television personality), Senator and Republican Presidential Nominee John McCain, and Vice President Dick Cheney project the Directive style. These people have been described as frank, demanding, assertive, and determined.

In the field of selling you will encounter a number of customers who are Directives. How can you identify these people? What verbal and nonverbal clues can we observe? A few of the behaviors displayed by Directives follow:

People who display the Directive style, such as John McCain and Hillary Clinton, like to take charge and maintain control. People who display the Directive style are generally viewed as determined, bold, and serious.

1. *Appears to be quite busy.* The Directive generally does not like to waste time and wants to get right to the point. Judy Sheindl of the *Judge Judy* television show displays this behavior.
2. *May give the impression of not listening.* In most cases the Directive feels more comfortable talking than listening.
3. *Displays a serious attitude.* A person who is lower in sociability usually communicates a lack of warmth and is apt to be quite businesslike and impersonal. Mike Wallace, former star of the popular *60 Minutes* television show, seldom smiles or displays warmth.
4. *Likes to maintain control.* The person who is higher on the Dominance continuum likes to maintain control. During meetings the Directive often seeks to control the agenda.[14]

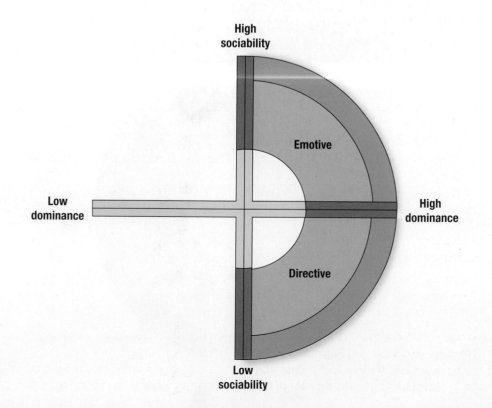

FIGURE 4.5

The Directive style combines high dominance and low sociability.

Business Week *identifies Steven Reinemund, CEO, and Indra Nooyi, president of PepsiCo, as the "odd couple." Indra (born and raised in India) is a free-spirited strategist while Steven is a spit-and-polish detail man. Individuals with different communication styles can work well together if they possess communication-style flexibility.*

John Abbott Photography

Key Words for the Directive Style		
Aggressive	Serious	Opinionated
Intense	Determined	Impatient
Demanding	Frank	Bold
Pushy		

REFLECTIVE STYLE The lower left-hand quadrant of the communication-style model features a combination of lower dominance and lower sociability (Figure 4.6). People who regularly display this behavior are classified as having the **Reflective style**.

FIGURE 4.6

The Reflective style combines low dominance and low sociability.

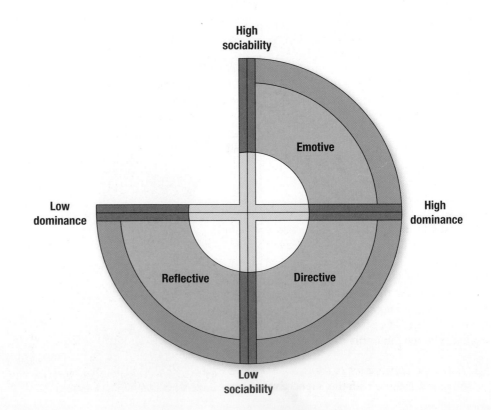

The Reflective person tends to examine all the facts carefully before arriving at a decision. Like a cautious scientist, this individual wants to gather all available information and weigh it carefully before taking a position. The reflective type is usually a stickler for detail.[15] The late physicist Albert Einstein fits the description. Dr. Joyce Brothers (psychologist), former U.S. President Jimmy Carter, and Federal Reserve Board Chairman Ben Bernanke also display the characteristics of the Reflective type.

Federal Reserve Board Chairman Ben Bernanke and former U.S. President Jimmy Carter display the Reflective style. Persons with the Reflective style are often observed as precise, industrious, and deliberate.

The Reflective communication style combines lower dominance and lower sociability; therefore, people with this classification tend to be reserved and cautious. Some additional behaviors that characterize this style follow:

1. *Controls emotional expression.* Reflective people tend to curb emotional expression and are less likely to display warmth openly. Bill Gates displays this personality trait.

2. *Displays a preference for orderliness.* The Reflective person enjoys a highly structured environment and generally feels frustration when confronted with unexpected events.

3. *Tends to express measured opinions.* The Reflective individual usually does not express dramatic opinions. This communication style is characterized by disciplined, businesslike actions.

4. *Seems difficult to get to know.* The Reflective person tends to be somewhat formal in social relationships and therefore can be viewed as aloof by many people.

In a selling situation, the Reflective customer does not want to move too fast. This person wants the facts presented in an orderly and unemotional manner and does not want to waste a lot of time socializing.

Key Words for the Reflective Style

Precise	Aloof	Serious
Deliberate	Scientific	Industrious
Questioning	Preoccupied	Stuffy
Disciplined		

SUPPORTIVE STYLE The upper left-hand quadrant shows a combination of lower dominance and higher sociability (Figure 4.7). This communication style is called the **Supportive style** because these people find it easy to listen and usually do not express their views in a forceful manner. Former U.S. President Gerald Ford and the late Princess Diana, and entertainers Meryl Streep, Kevin Costner, Paul Simon, and Julia Roberts display the characteristics of the Supportive style.

Low visibility generally characterizes the lifestyle of Supportive people. They complete their tasks in a quiet, unassuming manner and seldom draw attention to what they have accomplished. In terms of assertiveness, persons with the Supportive style rank quite low. Someone who ranks higher on the dominance continuum might view the Supportive individual as being too easygoing. Other behaviors that commonly characterize the Supportive person follow:

1. *Gives the appearance of being quiet and reserved.* People with the Supportive

Julia Roberts and the late Princess Diana display the Supportive style. Persons with the Supportive style are generally observed as warm, patient, and easygoing.

FIGURE 4.7

The Supportive style combines
low dominance and high
sociability.

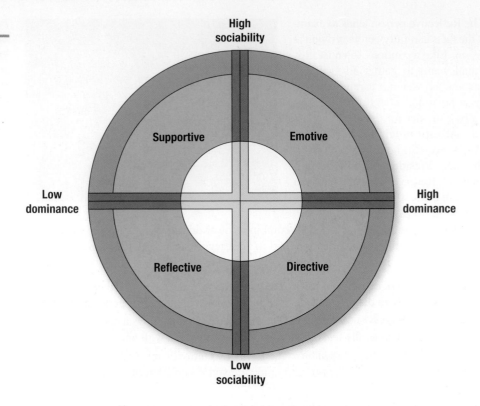

communication style can easily display their feelings, but not in the assertive manner
common to the Emotive individual.

  2. *Listens attentively to other people.* In selling, good listening skills can be a real asset.
     This talent comes naturally to the Supportive person.
  3. *Tends to avoid the use of power.* Whereas the Directive person may rely on power to
     accomplish tasks, the Supportive person is more likely to rely on friendly persuasion.
  4. *Makes decisions in a thoughtful and deliberate manner.* The Supportive person
     usually takes longer to make a decision.

Key Words for the Supportive Style		
Lighthearted	Docile	Relaxed
Reserved	Patient	Compliant
Passive	Sensitive	Softhearted
Warm		

Popularity of the Four-Style Model

We are endlessly fascinated by ourselves, and this helps explain the growing popularity of
the four-style model presented in this chapter. To satisfy this insatiable appetite for information, many training and development companies offer training programs that present
the four social or communication styles. Figure 4.8 features the approximate equivalents
of the four styles presented in this chapter. Although four-style programs were initially
created and marketed in the United States, they have become a global phenomenon
according to the staff at Wilson Learning Corporation.[16] Inscape Publishing, the company
that developed the DiSC learning instrument over three decades ago, reports that more
that 40 million people worldwide have completed DiSC workshops.[17]

Determining Your Communication Style

You now have enough information to identify your own communication style. If your location
on the dominance continuum is right of center and your position on the sociability continuum
is below the center mark, you fall into the Directive quadrant. If your location on the

Supportive (Manning/Reece)	Emotive (Manning/Reece)
Amiable (Wilson Learning)	Expressive (Wilson Learning)
Supportive-Giving (Stuart Atkins Inc.)	Adapting-Dealing (Stuart Atkins Inc.)
Relater (People Smarts)	Socializer (People Smarts)
Steadiness (Personal Profile System)	Influencing (Personal Profile System)
Supportive (DiSC Behavioral Style)	Influencing (DiSC Behavioral Style)
Reflective (Manning/Reece)	Directive (Manning/Reece)
Analytical (Wilson Learning)	Driver (Wilson Learning)
Conserving-Holding (Stuart Atkins Inc.)	Controlling-Taking (Stuart Atkins Inc.)
Thinker (People Smarts)	Directive (People Smarts)
Cautiousness/Compliance (Personal Profile System)	Dominance (Personal Profile System)
Conscientious (DiSC Behavioral Style)	Dominance (DiSC Behavioral Style)

FIGURE 4.8

The four basic communication styles have been used in a wide range of training programs. For comparison purposes the approximate equivalents to the four communication styles discussed in this chapters are listed.

dominance continuum is left of center and your position on the sociability continuum is above the center mark, then your most preferred style is Supportive. Likewise, lower dominance matched with lower sociability forms the Reflective communication style, and higher dominance matched with higher sociability forms the Emotive style.

AN ON-LINE ASSESSMENT OF YOUR COMMUNICATION STYLE You can gain further insight into your communication style by accessing the www.pearsonhighered.com/manning Web site and clicking on the On-Line Assessment of Your Communication Style link. After completing the assessment, you will be supplied with a profile indicating your most preferred communication style. You will also be presented with a profile of your secondary style. **See On-Line application Exercises 1, 2, 3, and 4 on p. 93 for more details on using this on-line assessment tool.**

Of course, all of us display some characteristics of the Emotive, Directive, Reflective, and Supportive styles. However, one of the four styles is usually predominant and readily detectable.[18] This, is your preferred style.

Some people who study the communication-style model for the first time may initially experience feelings of frustration. They find it hard to believe that one's behavioral style tends to remain quite uniform throughout life. People often say, "I am a different person each day!" It is certainly true that we sometimes feel different from day to day, but our most preferred style tends to remain stable.

Tom Ritchey's book I'm Stuck, You're Stuck *presents the theory behind the popular DiSC Behavioral Style Model. The DiSC model was first introduced under the name Performax by Carlson Learning.*

Tom Ritchey is also president of Inscape Publishing. Inscape now owns the rights to the DiSC Model. DiSC training products are marketed worldwide, through approved distributors like Training Solutions. Over 40 million people have participated in DiSC behavioral style training.

The Supportive person might say, "I sometimes get very upset and tell people what I am thinking. I can be a Directive when I want to be!" There is no argument here. Just because you have a preferred communication style does not mean you never display the behavioral characteristics of another style. Some people use different styles in different contexts and in different relationships.[19] Reflective people sometimes display Emotive behavior, and Emotive people sometimes display Reflective behavior. We are saying that each person has one most preferred and habitually used communication style.

Minimizing Communication-Style Bias

Salespeople often make the mistake of focusing too much on the content of their sales presentation and not enough on how they deliver their message.[20] Communication-style bias is a barrier to success in selling. This form of bias is a common problem in sales

Selling in Action

CLOSING THE SALE WITH ADAPTIVE SELLING

Rich Goldberg, CEO of Warm Thoughts Communications, a New Jersey–based marketing communications company, sensed he was about to lose an important client. He met with his staff, and together they created a profile based on their knowledge of the client's communication style. It soon became apparent that there was a mismatch between the client and the salesperson who called on that person. The customer was low in sociability but high in dominance. The customer was also described as someone who needed facts and figures. The salesperson was working on relationship building, and this approach was agitating the client. Goldberg counseled his staff to keep conversations with this customer brief, use facts and figures frequently, and clearly spell out the company's commitment to the client.[b]

work simply because salespeople deal with people from all four quadrants. You cannot select potential customers on the basis of their communication style. You must be able to develop a rapport with people from each of the four quadrants. When people of different styles work together but don't adapt to one another, serious problems can develop.[21]

How Communication-Style Bias Develops

To illustrate how communication-style bias develops in a sales situation, let us observe a sales call involving two people with different communication styles. Lana Wheeler entered the office of Ron Harrington, one of her large accounts, with a feeling of optimism. She was sure that her proposal would save Ron's company several thousand dollars a month. She was 99 percent certain that, this being her third call on Ron, the sale would be closed. Ten minutes after meeting Ron, she was walking out of his office without the order. What went wrong?

Lana Wheeler is an "engaging" type who is an Emotive in terms of communication style. Her sales calls are typically fast paced. She entered Ron's office and immediately began to close the sale. Ron interrupted and told Lana he couldn't commit to her proposal. Lana appeared to ignore Ron's response, told him she could put some more figures together on pricing, and then used another trial close. Ron finally told Lana, "Look, you don't understand the way I do business. We have bigger issues than additional figures. As I said, this is a 'no go' project."

Ron's communication style is Directive. He feels uncomfortable when someone is making a decision for him. He wants to maintain control and be in charge of making his own decisions.

In the training video, "Communication Styles, A Key to Adaptive Selling" Lana, Ron, Raymond and Sandra all moved into their excess zones, before learning about the platinum rule, and developed communication style bias. After learning flex-ability and versatility salespeople can adapt to the style of others, and then build the kind of rapport that adds value to the sale.

He felt tension when Lana tried to get him to make a decision on her terms. If Lana had spent more time asking questions, listening more closely, and allowing Ron to feel like the decision was his, she may have found out what the "bigger issues" were. The approach she used would be more appropriate for the Supportive or the Emotive communication style.

A salesperson who is highly adaptable can usually build a rapport with customers regardless of their communication style. Style flexibility is a sales strategy that can be learned.

Adaptive Selling Requires Versatility

Personal selling has become more customer-focused than ever before, so every effort should be made to reduce the tension between the salesperson and customer. Dr. David Merrill, one of the early pioneers in the development of communication style instruments and training programs, uses the term **versatility** to describe our ability to minimize communication-style bias.[22] Roger Wenschlag, author of *The Versatile Salesperson*, describes versatility as "the degree to which a salesperson is perceived as developing and maintaining buyer comfort throughout the sales process." *Adapting* to the customer's preferred communication style can enhance sales performance.[23]

Adaptive selling is another term used to describe how salespeople use communication styles and versatility to manage their selling relationships. Roger Wenschlag, author of The Versatile Salesperson, describes versatility as "the degree to which a salesperson is perceived as developing and maintaining buyer comfort throughout the sales process." He goes on to state that "adapting to the customer's preferred communication style can enhance sales performance."

MATURE AND IMMATURE BEHAVIOR There is a mature and an immature side to each behavioral style. Let us examine the Emotive style to illustrate this point. People with this style are open, personable individuals who seem genuinely friendly. The natural enthusiasm displayed by the mature Emotive is refreshing. On the other hand, an Emotive person who is too talkative and too emotional may have difficulty building rapport with some customers; this is the immature side of the Emotive communication style.

You recall that we use the words *industrious* and *precise* to describe the Reflective style. These are words that apply to the mature side of the Reflective person. We also use the words *aloof* and *stuffy*. These words describe the immature side of the Reflective. The good news is that we all have the potential for developing the mature side of our communication style.

STRENGTH–WEAKNESS PARADOX It is a fact of life that your greatest strength can become your greatest weakness. If your most preferred style is Reflective, people are likely to respect your well-disciplined approach to life as one of your strengths. However, this strength can become a weakness if it is exaggerated. The Reflective person can be too serious, too questioning, and too inflexible. Robert Haas, former CEO of Levi Strauss & Company, is known for extraordinary (some say obsessive) attention to detail. Those who work with him say an offhand conversation can sound like a lecture. This Reflective, however, has the ability to flex his style. Levi's employees were fiercely loyal to Haas and describe him as compassionate to a fault.[24]

Customer Relationship Management with Technology

BEING PREPARED

Customer relationship management (CRM) software empowers a salesperson with information essential to continue a relationship. The software can be used to record, retain, and produce personal information including such factors as marital status, names and ages of children, and individual preferences.

Before placing a call, the salesperson might review the database information to refresh her memory about the prospect. This can be especially helpful when preparing to talk with someone with a specific communication style. (See the exercise "Identifying Communication Styles" on p. 94 for more information.)

FIGURE 4.9

The completed communication-style model provides important insights needed to manage the relationship process in selling.

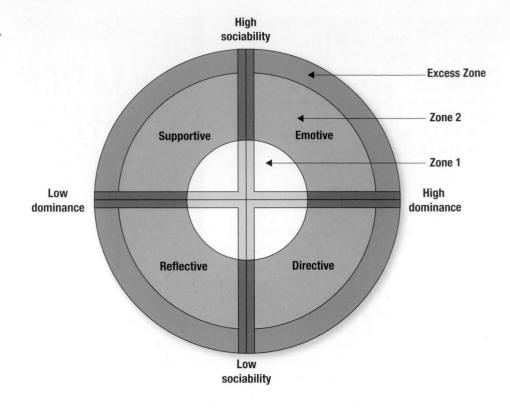

People with the Directive style are open and frank. They express their true feelings in a direct manner. In most cases we appreciate candor, but we do not like to be around people who are too straightforward or too blunt in expressing their views. Steven Ballmer, CEO of Microsoft, was known as a very demanding executive during his early years with the company. His explosive temper was legendary and he often put the fear of God into his staff members. He once needed throat surgery because he yelled so much. Later he became more diplomatic and less domineering.[25] When people come across as *opinionated*, they tend to antagonize others. We should avoid pushing our strengths to the point of unproductive excess.[26]

To illustrate how strengths become weaknesses in excess, let us add more detail to our communication-style model. Note that it now features three zones that radiate out from the center (Figure 4.9). These dimensions might be thought of as intensity zones.

In his early years Steve Ballmer, CEO of Microsoft, pushed his Directive strengths to the point of excess. His explosive temper was legendary. In recent years, he has displayed greater adaptability and versatility, and is now observed as being more diplomatic and less domineering.

Zone one People who fall within this zone display their unique behavioral characteristics with less intensity than those in zone two. The Emotive person, for example, is moderately high on the dominance continuum and moderately high on the sociability continuum. As you might expect, zone one communication styles are more difficult to identify because there is less intensity in both dimensions (dominance and sociability).

Zone two Persons who fall within this zone display their unique behavioral characteristics

The excess zone is characterized by a high degree of intensity and rigidity. We are more apt to move into the excess zone under very stressful conditions.

with greater intensity than persons in zone one. The zone two Reflective, for example, falls within the lowest quartile of the dominance continuum and the lowest quartile of the sociability continuum.

The boundary line that separates zone one and zone two should not be seen as a permanent barrier restricting change in intensity. Under certain circumstances we should abandon our most preferred style temporarily. A deliberate move from zone one to zone two, or vice versa, is called *style flexing*.

Excess zone The excess zone is characterized by a high degree of intensity and rigidity. When people allow themselves to drift into this zone, they become very inflexible, which is often interpreted by others as a form of bias toward their style. In addition, the strengths of the inflexible person become weaknesses. Extreme intensity in any quadrant is bound to threaten interpersonal relations.

We are apt to move into the excess zone and exaggerate our style characteristics under stressful conditions. Stress tends to bring out the worst in many people. Some of the behaviors that salespeople and customers may display when they are in the excess zone follow:

Emotive style	Expresses highly emotional opinions
	Stops listening to the other person
	Tries too hard to promote own point of view
	Becomes outspoken to the point of being offensive
Directive style	Gets impatient with the other person
	Becomes dictatorial and bossy
	Does not admit being wrong
	Becomes extremely competitive
Reflective style	Becomes stiff and formal
	Is unwilling to make a decision
	Avoids displaying any type of emotion
	Is overly interested in detail
Supportive style	Agrees with everyone
	Is unable to take a strong stand
	Becomes overly anxious to win approval of others
	Tries to comfort everyone

Achieving Versatility Through Style Flexing

Style flexing is the deliberate attempt to adapt one's communication style to accommodate the needs of the other person. You are attempting to communicate with the other person on his or her own "channel." Ron Willingham, in his book *Integrity Selling*, reminds us: "People are more apt to buy from you when they perceive you view the world as they view the world."[27] In a selling situation you should try to determine the customer's most preferred style and flex your own accordingly. If your preferred communication style is Directive, and your customer is a Supportive, try to be more personal and warmer in your presentation. Once you know the customer's style, flexing your style can make the difference between a presentation that falters and one that exceeds your expectations.[28] Style sensitivity and flexing add value to the sales process.

Throughout the preapproach, you should learn as much as possible about the customer and try to determine her style. Once you are in the presence of the customer, do not become preoccupied analyzing the person's style. If you are trying hard to analyze the person's style, you may not listen closely enough to what she is trying to tell you. If you are truly tuned into the customer, you can absorb many clues that help you determine her style. After the sales call, analyze the communication and record your findings. Use this information to plan your next contact with the customer.[29] Listen closely to the customer's tone of voice. A Supportive person sounds warm and friendly. The Reflective customer's voice is more likely to be controlled and deliberate. Pay particular attention to gestures. The Emotive individual uses his hands to communicate thoughts and ideas. The Directive also uses gestures to communicate but is more controlled and less spontaneous. The Reflective person appears more relaxed, less intense. The Emotive individual is an open, impulsive communicator, while the Reflective person is quite cautious. The Supportive type is personal and friendly, while the Reflective person may seem difficult to get to know. To avoid relationship tension, consider the following suggestions for each of the four styles.

Selling to Emotives

If you are attempting to sell products to an Emotive person, keep in mind the need to move at a pace that holds the attention of the prospect. Be enthusiastic and avoid an approach that is too stiff and formal. Take time to establish goodwill and build relationships. Do not place too much emphasis on the facts and details. To deal effectively with Emotive people, plan actions that provide support for their opinions, ideas, and dreams.[30] Plan to ask questions concerning their opinions and ideas, but be prepared to help them get "back on track" if they move too far away from the topic. Maintain good eye contact and, above all, be a good listener.

Selling to Directives

The key to relating to Directives is to keep the relationship as businesslike as possible. Developing a strong personal relationship is not a high priority for Directives. In other words, friendship is not usually a condition for a good working relationship. Your goal is to be as efficient, time disciplined, and well organized as possible and to provide appropriate facts, figures, and success probabilities. Most Directives are goal-oriented people, so try to identify their primary objectives and then determine ways to support and help with these objectives. Early in the sales presentation, ask specific questions and carefully note responses. Look for specific points you can respond to when it is time to present your proposals.

Selling to Reflectives

The Reflective person responds in a positive way to a thoughtful, well-organized approach. Arrive at meetings on time and be well prepared. In most cases it is not necessary to spend a great deal of time building a social relationship. Reflective people appreciate a no-nonsense, businesslike approach to personal selling. Use specific questions that show clear direction. Once you have information concerning the prospect's needs, present your proposal in a slow, deliberate way. Provide as much documentation as possible. Do not be in too big a hurry to close the sale. Never pressure the Reflective person to make quick decisions.

Selling to Supportives

Take time to build a social relationship with the Supportive person. Spend time learning about the matters that are important in this individual's life—family, hobbies, and major interests. Listen carefully to personal opinions and feelings. Supportive individuals like to conduct business with sales personnel who are professional but friendly. Therefore, study their feelings and emotional needs as well as their technical and business needs. Throughout the presentation, provide personal assurances and support for their views. If you disagree with a Supportive person, curb the desire to disagree too assertively; Supportive people tend to dislike interpersonal conflict. Give them the time to comprehend your proposal. Patience is important.

As you develop your communication-style identification skills and become more adept at style flexing, you are better able to manage the relationship process. With these skills you should be able to open more accounts, sell more to established customers, and more effectively meet the pressures of competition. Most important, your customers will view you as a person better able to understand and meet their needs.

Word of Caution

It is tempting to put a label on someone and then assume the label tells you everything you need to know about that person. If you want to build an effective partnering type of relationship with a prospect, you must acquire additional information about that person. Stuart Atkins, a respected authority on communication styles and author of *The Name of Your Game*, says we should be careful not to use labels that make people feel boxed in, typecast, or judged. He believes we should not classify *people*; we should classify their *strengths* and *preferences* to act one way or another under certain circumstances.[31] You also must be careful not to let the label you place on yourself become the justification for your own inflexible behavior. Try not to let the label justify or reinforce why you are unable or unwilling to communicate effectively with others.

Chapter Learning Activities

Reviewing Key Concepts

Discuss how communication style influences the relationship process in sales

Many sales are lost because salespeople fail to communicate effectively with the prospect. Communication-style bias contributes to this problem. Every salesperson who is willing to develop style sensitivity and engage in appropriate style flexing can minimize one of the most common barriers to success in selling.

Identify the two major dimensions of the communication-style model

The communication-style model is based on two continuums that assess two major aspects of human behavior: dominance and sociability. By combining them as horizontal and vertical continuums, we create quadrants that define four styles of communication. We have called these the Emotive, Directive, Reflective, and Supportive styles.

Explain the four communications styles in communication-style model

The Emotive style combines high sociability and high dominance, whereas the Directive style combines high dominance and low sociability. The Reflective style combines low dominance and low sociability, whereas the Supportive style combines low dominance and high sociability.

Learn how to identify your preferred communication style and that of your customer

With practice you can learn to identify your preferred communication style. The starting point is to rate yourself on each scale (dominance and sociability) by placing a check mark at a point along the continuum that represents how you perceive yourself. Completion of the dominance and sociability indicator forms will help you achieve greater awareness of your communication style. This same approach can be used to identify the customer's preferred style.

Learn to achieve interpersonal versatility and build strong selling relationships with style flexing

A third dimension of human behavior—versatility—is important in dealing with communication styles that are different from your own. You can adjust your own style to meet the needs of others—a process called *style flexing*. Style flexing is an attempt to change or alter your style to meet the needs of the customer.

Key Terms

Personality	Sociability	Versatility
Communication style	Emotive style	Style flexing
Adaptive selling	Directive style	Platinum Rule
Communication-style bias	Reflective style	
Dominance	Supportive style	

Review Questions

1. What is the meaning of the term *communication style?*
2. Describe the five major principles that support communication-style theory.
3. What are the benefits to the salesperson who understands communication style?

4. What two dimensions of human behavior are used to identify communication style?

5. Describe the person who tends to be high in sociability.

6. What are the four communication styles? Develop a brief description of each of the styles.

7. What is the reaction of most people who study communication styles for the first time? Why does this reaction surface?

8. Define style flexing. How can style flexing improve sales productivity?

9. Explain the statement, "Your greatest strength can become your greatest weakness."

10. What suggestions would you give a salesperson who is planning to meet with a new prospect who displays the reflective communication style?

On-Line Communication/Adaptive Style Assessment Application Exercises

1. Communication or Behavior Styles is one of the most popular training programs. Worldwide, forty seven million people have participated in the Wilson and DiSC programs. An understanding of communication styles assists us in building better personal and business relationships As indicated in this chapter, the first step in applying what you have learned about communication styles is to identify and understand your own style. Using the On-Line Communication Style Assessment at the www.pearsonhighered.com/manning <http://www.pearsonhighered.com/manning> website, assess your communication style.

   a. Do you agree with your assessment of your most preferred style? How about your results on your secondary style?

   b. Referring back to the material presented in the chapter, identify the strengths and weaknesses of your style.

   c. Identify the styles you enjoy working with best. Identify the styles you enjoy working with least.

   d. Referring to the table on p. 89 can you identify those behaviors you tend to exhibit when you feel stressed?

   e. Explain why you think so many individuals and companies have participated in this program. From Figure 4.8 on p. 85 list the names other training programs have used to identify your most preferred style.

2. Self-awareness is important in personal selling. As we get to know ourselves, we can identify barriers to acceptance by others. Once you have identified your most preferred communication style, you have taken a big step in the direction of self-awareness. We have noted that self-ratings can sometimes be misleading because some people lack a high degree of self-awareness. They do not see themselves as others see them. Consider asking four or five people (coworkers, for example) to assess and print the profile of your communication style using the on-line assessment. Then compare these ratings with your self-rating.

3. Many salespeople, after being introduced to communication-style concepts, attempt to categorize each of their customers. They report that their relationships become mutually more enjoyable and productive. Select four people whom you know quite well (supervisor, subordinate, customer, teacher, friend, or members of your sports team). Using the On-Line Communication Style Assessment at the www.pearsonhighered.com/manning Web site, assess the communication style of each of these people. Explain how this information can improve your relationship with each of these people.

4. To assess your ability to style flex, assume you are going to make four sales calls on customers displaying each of the four communication styles. For purposes of illustration, consider your first call is on an emotive customer with a communication

style like Jay Leno. The second call is on a supportive customer with a communication style like Julia Roberts, the third is on a reflective customer with a communication style like Tiger Woods, and the last is on a directive customer like Martha Stewart. For each of these customers refer to the on-line Communication Style assessment and assess the behaviors you would demonstrate as you established your relationship with them. Print each of the profiles and compare them to one another. Did you flex your style of communication to better interact with the customer representing Jay Leno's style versus the customer representing Julia Roberts' style? Did you flex differently for the customer representing Tiger Woods, and Martha Stewart?

5. Myers-Briggs Personality Types and Jungian Personality Types are two very popular descriptions of the concepts in this chapter. Using your search engine, access the Internet sites that refer to these concepts. Type in "Jungian" + personality profiles to access the Jungian personality types. To access the Myers-Briggs types, type in "Myers-Briggs" + personality profiles. Does the number of queries indicate anything about the validity and popularity of these theories? Examine specific queries about both of these theories. Do you see the relationship between these two theories and the material in this chapter? Each year about two and a half million Americans complete the Myers-Briggs Type Indicator (M.B.T.I.). Why is this psychological-assessment instrument so popular?

Role-Play Exercise

For the purpose of this role-play, assume the role of Ray Perkins, who is described in the case problem below. Ray is described as a quiet, amiable person who displays the Supportive communication style. You will meet with Ms. Maynard, who is also described in the case problem. For the purpose of this role-play, assume that Ms. Maynard displays the characteristics of the Directive communication style. Prior to the role-play, study the chapter material on style flexing and information on how to sell to persons with the Directive communication style.

CRM Application Exercise

Identifying Communication Styles

The previous salesperson carefully recorded the communication styles of most of the people in the Salesforce.com CRM database and identified the prospects as Emotive, Directive, Reflective, or Supportive. If you feel like talking to an Emotive, you can find them by running the report "Contacts by Communication Style" in the Reports tab of the Salesforce.com system. Using the information you have used in this chapter, explain how you would use style flexing when working with these four contacts.

Case Problem

Ray Perkins has been employed at Grant Real Estate for almost two years. Prior to receiving his real estate license, he was a property manager with a large real estate agency in another community. During his first year with Grant, he was assigned to the residential property division and sold properties totaling $825,000. He then requested and received a transfer to the commercial division.

Three months ago, Ray obtained a commercial listing that consisted of 26 acres of land near a growing residential neighborhood. The land is zoned commercial and appears to be ideally suited for a medium-sized shopping center. Ray prepared a detailed prospectus and sent it to Vera Maynard, president of Mondale Growth Corporation, a firm specializing in development of shopping centers. One week later he received a letter from Ms. Maynard requesting more information. Shortly after receiving Ray's response, Ms. Maynard called to set up an appointment to inspect the property. A time and date were finalized, and Ray agreed to meet her plane and conduct a tour of the property.

Ray is a quiet, amiable person who displays the Supportive communication style. Friends say that they like to spend time with him because he is a good listener.

Questions

1. If Ms. Maynard displays the characteristics of the Directive communication style, how should Ray conduct himself during the meeting? Be specific as you describe those behaviors that would be admired by Ms. Maynard.

2. If Ms. Maynard wants to build a rapport with Ray Perkins, what behavior should she display?

3. It is not a good idea to put a label on someone and then assume the label tells us everything about the person. As Ray attempts to build a rapport with Ms. Maynard, what other personal characteristics should he try to identify?

5

Ethics: The Foundation for Relationships in Selling

Chapter Preview

When you finish reading this chapter, you should be able to

1
Describe how ethical decisions influence relationships in selling

2
Discuss factors that influence character development

3
Describe the factors that influence the ethical conduct of sales personnel

4
Discuss guidelines for developing a personal code of ethics

5
Describe ethical and legal issues in international business

▶ Introduction

A few years ago Student Loan Xpress, a San Diego–based education finance lender, adopted aggressive sales tactics designed to build a strong working relationship with company clients. It offered some university financial aid administrators stock options and consulting opportunities to solidify working relationships. This plan generated a great deal of negative publicity once attorneys general in several states began investigating whether the company's tactics were legal. The parent company of Student Loan Xpress, CIT Group, placed three Student Loan Xpress executives on leave amidst a widening investigation of conflicts of interest among universities and lenders.[1]

Unethical sales practices encouraged by management personnel pose a major dilemma for salespeople. In some cases the motivation to engage in unethical sales practices may increase when companies provide incentive structures that entice salespeople to go over the line.[2]

Making Ethical Decisions

Business ethics comprise principles and standards that guide behavior in the world of business. They help translate your values into appropriate and effective behaviors in your day-to-day life. Whether a specific behavior is right or wrong, ethical or unethical, is often determined by company leaders, customers, investors, the legal system, and the community.[3] Of course, the views of various stakeholders may be in conflict. Kickbacks and secret payoffs may be acceptable practices to the vice president of sales and marketing, yet may be viewed as unethical by members of the sales force, the board of directors, investors, and the general public.

There is no one uniform code of ethics for all salespeople. However, a large number of business organizations, professional associations, and certification agencies have established written codes. For example, the National Association

NASP Standards of Professional Conduct
1. **Ethics and Professionalism:** I will act with the highest degree of professionalism, ethics, and integrity.
2. **Representation of Facts:** I will fairly represent the benefits of my products and services.
3. **Confidentiality:** I will keep information about my customers confidential.
4. **Conflicts of Interest:** I will disclose potential conflicts of interest to all relevant parties and, whenever possible, resolve conflicts before they become a problem.
5. **Responsibility to Clients:** I will act in the best interest of my clients, striving to present products and services that satisfy my customers' needs.
6. **Responsibility to Employer:** I will represent my employer in a professional manner and respect my employer's proprietary information.
7. **Responsibility to NASP Members:** I will share my lessons of experience with fellow NASP members and promote the interests of NASP.
8. **Responsibility to the Community:** I will serve as a model of good citizenship and be vigilant to the effects of my products and services on my community.
9. **Continuing Education:** I will maintain an ongoing program of professional development.
10. **Laws:** I will observe and obey all laws that affect my products, services, and profession.

FIGURE 5.1

This code of ethics serves as a foundation for a relationship strategy by members of the National Association of Sales Professionals (NASP).

Source: National Association of Sales Professionals. nasp.com/pr/aboutus/standardsofconduct.asp. Used with permission.

of Sales Professionals (NASP) states that members must abide by its Standards of Professional Conduct[4] (Figure 5.1).

Today, we recognize that character and integrity strongly influence relationships in personal selling. As noted in the previous chapter, character is composed of your personal standards of behavior, including your honesty and integrity. Your character is based on your internal values and the resulting judgments you make about what is right and what is wrong. The ethical decisions you make reflect your character strength.

We are indebted to Stephen Covey, author of *The Seven Habits of Highly Effective People*, for helping us better understand the relationship between character strength and success in personal selling. In his best-selling book, Covey says that there are basic principles that must be integrated into our character. One example is to always do what you say you are going to do. "As we make and keep commitments, even small commitments, we begin to establish an inner integrity that gives us the awareness of self-control and courage and strength to accept more of the responsibility for our own lives."[5] Fulfilling your commitments builds trust, and trust is the most important precondition of partnering.

Character Development

Colleges and universities are beginning to play a more active role in character development. Courses that focus on ethics are becoming quite common. When a new ethics course was developed at the University of Virginia, the faculty indicated that the purpose of the course is not to point out what is right and what is wrong. The course is designed to help students understand the consequences of their actions when they face an ethical dilemma.[6]

Despite a growing interest in business ethics, unethical behavior has become all too common. A survey conducted by *Newsweek* suggests that the current generation of workers may be more tolerant of deception. Many of those involved in the survey did not view lying and cheating as unacceptable.[7] Employees who are involved in unethical behavior often report that they were under pressure to act unethically or illegally on the job.

The Erosion of Character

As the past decade unfolded, many large, inflexible corporations were transformed into smaller, more nimble competitors. New economy thinking prevailed as business firms, large and small, worked hard to become lean, innovative, and profitable. We witnessed an almost unrelenting emphasis on earnings that was driven, in some cases, by executive greed. It was during this period that some of America's most respected companies began to cross the ethical divide.[8]

A company cannot enjoy long-term success unless its employees are honest, ethical, and uncompromising about values and principles. Yet many employees engage in dishonest practices that erode character. The collapse of Lehman Bros., one the largest U.S. corporation ever to file for bankruptcy, can be traced to a culture that emphasized risk taking, personal ambition over teamwork, and earnings growth at any cost. The new economy depends on innovation and aggressive development of markets, but actions that weaken the moral contract with employees, customers, and shareholders can bring serious consequences. Let's examine some "half-truths" that have influenced the erosion of character in a business setting.

■ *We are only in it for ourselves.* Some critics of today's moral climate feel that the current moral decline began when society's focus shifted from "what is right" to "what is right for me." In personal selling, this point of view can quickly subtract rather than add value to a relationship with the customer. Fortunately, there are many salespeople for whom integrity and self-respect are basic values. Darryl Ashley, a pharmaceutical representative for Eli Lilly Company, suspected that a pharmacist (a customer) was diluting chemotherapy drugs in order to increase profit margins. Ashley shared his suspicions with one of the cancer doctors who were purchasing the drug from the pharmacist. Tests indicated that the drug had been diluted.[9]

■ *Corporations exist to maximize shareholder value.* In the past, corporations were more often viewed as *economic* and *social* institutions—organizations that served a balanced group of stakeholders. In recent years analysts, stock traders, CEOs, and the media have too often focused on a single standard of performance—share price.[10] Marjorie Kelly, former editor of *Business Ethics*, says, "Managing a company solely for maximum share price can destroy both share price and the entire company."[11]

    Pressure to increase "numbers" led to sales abuses at WorldCom Incorporated. Some salespeople double-booked accounts in order to make their quota and collect increased commissions. The false reporting was identified by an internal company probe and the guilty sales representatives were fired.[12]

■ *Companies need to be lean and mean.*[13] Downsizing has become a common practice even when the economy is strong. After the layoffs, companies must deal with serious problems of low morale and mistrust of management. Those employees who remain after a company reduces its ranks often feel demoralized, overworked, and fearful. The stress of long hours and a faster pace can result in quality losses and bad

Character strength builds as we display loyalty, mutual commitment, and the pursuit of long-term goals. These are the qualities needed to build strong buyer–seller relationships.

Selling Is Everyone's Business

LIFE AFTER ENRON

Cary and Rachel Bryant, husband and wife, believed they had a bright future at Enron Corporation. Then the company filed for bankruptcy and they were terminated on the same day. Cary and Rachel immediately started sending out résumés and making phone calls. However, no one returned their calls. Finally, they decided to stop and reevaluate their careers. They decided that returning to the high-pressure corporate world was not a good idea. Cary decided to start a contracting company. In order to build his business, he started making cold calls on people in the neighborhood. He often called on homeowners whose homes looked like they needed repair. His business began to grow and today Bryant Contractors (www.bryantcontractors.com) is doing well. Meanwhile, Rachel decided to begin selling a line of skin-care products she had developed prior to working for Enron. In the years ahead, Cary and Rachel will rely on their personal selling skills to grow their businesses.[a]

service that alienate customers. Richard Sennett, author of *The Corrosion of Character*, says that the decline of character strength can be traced to conditions that have grown out of our fast-paced, high-stress, information-driven economy. He states that character strength builds in a climate that encourages loyalty, mutual commitment, and the pursuit of long-term goals.[14] These are the qualities needed to build strong buyer–seller relationships.

Today, many business firms are struggling to align their values, ethics, and principles with the expectations of their salespeople and their customers. The process of negotiating ethical standards and practices must be ongoing. Citigroup Incorporated, the world's largest financial services firm, is working hard to move beyond regulatory scandals. Charles Prince, Citigroup CEO, wants the company to better balance its "delivering-the-numbers" culture with a long-term attention to reputation. He readily admits that " . . . at times, our actions have put at risk our most precious commodity—the trust of our clients, the patience of our employees, and the faith of our shareholders."[15]

Can moral behavior be taught? The National Business Ethics Survey, conducted annually by the Ethics Resource Center (www.ethics.org), found that 90 percent of employees said that ethics training is useful or somewhat useful to them. A growing number of students are completing business ethics courses as part of their undergraduate or graduate programs.[16]

Factors Influencing the Ethics of Salespeople

In the field of personal selling, the temptation to maximize short-term gains by some type of unethical conduct is always present. Salespeople are especially vulnerable to moral corruption because they are subject to many temptations. A few examples follow:

The competition is using exaggerated claims to increase the sale of its product. Should you counteract this action by using exaggerated claims of your own to build a stronger case for your product?

You have visited the buyer twice, and each time the person displayed a great deal of interest in your product. During the last visit the buyer hinted that the order might be signed if you could provide a small gift. Your company has a long-standing policy that gifts are not to be given under any circumstances. What do you do?

Your sales manager is under great pressure to increase sales. At a recent meeting of the entire sales staff, this person said, "We have to hit our numbers no matter what it takes!" Does this emotional appeal change your way of dealing with customers?

During a recent business trip you met an old friend and decided to have dinner together. At the end of the meal you paid for the entire bill and left a generous tip. Do you now put these non-business-related expenses on your expense account?

FIGURE 5.2

Factors Influencing the Ethical Behavior of Salespeople

In personal selling the temptation to maximize short-term gains by some type of unethical conduct is always present. The forces in this figure can help salespeople deal honestly and openly with prospects at all times.

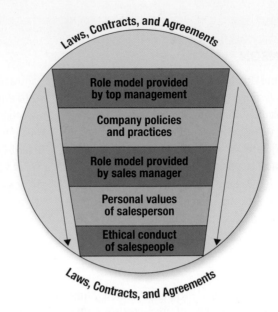

These ethical dilemmas arise frequently in the field of selling. How do salespeople respond? Some ignore company policy, cast aside personal standards of conduct, and yield to the pressure. However, a surprising number of salespeople are able to resist. They are aided by a series of factors that help them distinguish right from wrong. Figure 5.2 outlines the forces that can help them deal honestly and openly with prospects at all times. Next we discuss each of these factors.

Top Management as Role Model

Ethical standards tend to filter down from the top of an organization. Employees look to company leaders for guidance. The organization's moral tone, as established by management personnel, is the most important single determinant of employee ethics. At Best Buy, Richard Schulze, founder and chairman, is the person who must put ethics concerns on the front burner and make sure that employees stay focused on that priority. The most influential ethics spokesman at Timberland is CEO Jeffrey Swartz, a third-generation CEO whose grandfather founded the company. With pride, he points out Timberland's slogan: "Boots, Brand, Belief."[17]

In recent years, top management has often been guided by advice from professional service firms such as McKinsey & Company, Arthur Andersen, and Merrill Lynch and Company. Too often these firms are recommending strategies that result in quick, short-term gains. Alan M. Webber, who has been studying professional service firms for 20 years, notes, "They want the money right now." He says, " . . . to make the most money, you actually have to believe in the product or service you offer and care for the customers or clients whom you serve."[18]

Minnesota Life Insurance Company has been able to steer clear of scandal for more than 100 years by adopting a values-based management philosophy that rewards integrity and honesty. Success at the management level requires commitment to the company's core values. Managers must demonstrate their ability to infuse ethical values in their subordinates. The Minnesota Life Insurance Company mission and values statement includes the following statement on integrity: "We keep our promises. In all our activities, we adhere to the highest standards of ethical conduct."[19]

Company Policies and Practices

Company policies and practices can have a major impact on the ethical conduct of salespeople. Many employees do not have well-developed moral sensitivity and, therefore, need the guidance of ethics policies. These policies should cover distributor relations, customer service, pricing, product development, and related areas.[20]

Global Business Etiquette

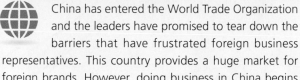

DOING BUSINESS IN CHINA

China has entered the World Trade Organization and the leaders have promised to tear down the barriers that have frustrated foreign business representatives. This country provides a huge market for foreign brands. However, doing business in China begins with a careful study of Chinese business customs.

- Patience is critical when doing business in China. Avoid taking the initiative until you fully understand the rules.

- Business entertaining is frequently done banquet style. If you host a banquet, plan your menu carefully because foods have different meanings. You will be in complete control and no one will eat or drink until you give the signal. Toasting is a ritual in China.

- Chinese businesspeople do not make deals quickly. They prefer to spend time building relationships that will last for years. Harmony is important.

- When making introductions, the oldest and highest-ranking person is introduced first. Chinese bow slightly when greeting another person and the handshake follows.

- Gift giving is a complex process in China. Gifts should be given after all business transactions have been completed. Avoid gifts that suggest death in the Chinese culture: clocks, knife openers, and handkerchiefs, for example.[b]

Developing policy statements forces a firm to "take a stand" on various business practices. Distinguishing right from wrong can be a healthy activity for any organization. The outcome is a more clear-cut philosophy of how to conduct business transactions. Furthermore, the efforts of salespeople can be compromised by the unethical actions of their companies. Selling products for a company that condones unethical practices is very difficult for the salesperson who maintains high ethical standards.[21]

Mutual of Omaha Executives provides its employees with a carefully worded document titled "Values for Success." Several of these values form the foundation for a corporate culture that encourages ethical behavior:[22]

- **Openness and Trust** We encourage an open sharing of ideas and information, displaying a fundamental respect for each other as well as our cultural diversity.

- **Honesty and Integrity** We are honest and ethical with others, maintaining the highest standards of personal and professional conduct.

- **Customer-Focus** We never lose sight of our customers, and constantly challenge ourselves to meet their requirements even better.

Most marketing companies provide salespeople with guidelines in such areas as sharing confidential information, reciprocity, bribery, gift giving, entertainment, and business defamation.

SHARING CONFIDENTIAL INFORMATION Personal selling, by its very nature, promotes close working relationships. Customers often turn to salespeople for advice. They disclose confidential information freely to someone they trust. It is important that salespeople preserve the confidentiality of the information they receive.

It is not unusual for a customer to disclose information that may be of great value to a competitor. This might include the development of new products, plans to expand into new markets, or anticipated changes in personnel. A salesperson may be tempted to share confidential information with a representative of a competing firm. This breach of confidence might be seen as a means of gaining favor. In most cases this action backfires. The person who receives the confidential information quickly loses respect for the salesperson. A gossipy salesperson seldom develops a trusting relationship with a customer.

RECIPROCITY **Reciprocity** is a mutual exchange of benefits, as when a firm buys products from its own customers. Some business firms actually maintain a policy of reciprocity. For example, the manufacturer of commercial sheets and blankets may purchase hotel services from firms that use its products.

Is there anything wrong with the "you scratch my back and I'll scratch yours" approach to doing business? The answer is sometimes yes. In some cases, the use of reciprocity borders on commercial blackmail. Salespeople have been known to approach firms that supply their company and encourage them to buy out of obligation. Reciprocity agreements are illegal when one company pressures another company to join in the agreement.

A business relationship based on reciprocity has other drawbacks. There is the ever-present temptation to take such customers for granted. A customer who buys out of obligation may take a backseat to customers who were won in the open market.

BRIBERY The book *Arrogance and Accords: The Inside Story of the Honda Scandal* describes one of the largest commercial corruption cases in U.S. history. Over a 15-year period, Honda officials received more than $50 million in cash and gifts from dealers eager to obtain fast-selling Honda cars and profitable franchises. Eighteen former Honda executives were convicted of obtaining kickbacks; most went to prison.[23]

In some cases, a bribe is wrong from a legal standpoint. In almost all cases, the bribe is wrong from an ethical point of view. However, bribery does exist, and a salesperson must be prepared to cope with it. It helps to have a well-established company policy to use as a reference point.

Salespeople who sell products in foreign markets need to know that giving bribes is viewed as an acceptable business practice in some cultures. However, bribes or payoffs may violate the U.S. Foreign Corrupt Practices Act (FCPA). Lucent Technologies Incorporated dismissed two high-ranking executives in China after it found potential violations of the FCPA.[24]

GIFT GIVING Gift giving is a common practice in America. However, some companies do maintain a "no gift" policy. Many companies report that their policy is either no gifts or nothing of real value. Some gifts, such as advertising novelties, planning calendars, or a meal, are of limited value and cannot be construed as a bribe or payoff.

There are some gray areas that separate a gift from a bribe. Most people agree that a token of insignificant price, such as a pen imprinted with a company logo or a desk calendar, is appropriate. These types of gifts are meant to foster goodwill. A bribe, on the other hand, is an attempt to influence the person receiving the gift.

Are there right and wrong ways to handle gift giving? The answer is yes. The following guidelines are helpful to any salesperson who is considering giving gifts to customers:

1. Do not give gifts before doing business with a customer. Do not use the gift as a substitute for effective selling methods.
2. Never convey the impression you are "buying" the customer's business with gifts. When this happens, the gift becomes nothing more than a bribe.
3. When gift giving is done correctly, the customer clearly views it as symbolic of your appreciation—a "no strings attached" goodwill gesture.
4. Be sure the gift is not a violation of the policies of your firm or of your customer's firm. Some firms do not allow employees to accept gifts at all. Other firms place a dollar limit on a gift's value.

In summary, if you have second thoughts about giving a gift, do not do it. When you are sure some token is appropriate, keep it simple and thoughtful.

ENTERTAINMENT Entertainment is a widespread practice in the field of selling and may be viewed as a bribe by some people. The line dividing gifts, bribes, and entertainment is often quite arbitrary.

Salespeople must frequently decide how to handle entertaining. A few industries see entertainment as part of the approach used to obtain new accounts. This is especially true when competing products are nearly identical. A good example is the cardboard box industry. These products vary little in price and quality. To win an account may involve knowing whom to entertain and how to entertain.

Entertainment is a highly individualized process. One prospect might enjoy a professional football game, while another would be impressed most by a quiet meal at a good restaurant. The key is to get to know your prospect's preferences. How does the person

Personal selling, by its nature, promotes close working relationships. It is important that salespeople preserve the confidentiality of information they receive. Violation of this ethical responsibility will quickly erode a relationship with the customer.

spend leisure time? How much time can the person spare for entertainment? You need to answer these and other questions before you invest time and money in entertainment.

BUSINESS DEFAMATION Salespeople frequently compare their product's qualities and characteristics with those of a competitor during the sales presentation. If such comparisons are inaccurate, are misleading, or slander a company's business reputation, such conduct is illegal. Competitors have sued hundreds of companies and manufacturer's representatives for making slanderous statements while selling.

What constitutes business defamation? Steven M. Sack, coauthor of *The Salesperson's Legal Guide*, provides the following examples:

1. *Business slander.* This arises when an unfair and untrue oral statement is made about a competitor. The statement becomes actionable when it is communicated to a third party and can be interpreted as damaging the competitor's business reputation or the personal reputation of an individual in that business.
2. *Business libel.* This may be incurred when an unfair and untrue statement is made about a competitor in writing. The statement becomes actionable when it is communicated to a third party and can be interpreted as damaging the company.
3. *Product disparagement.* This occurs when false or deceptive comparisons or distorted claims are made concerning a competitor's product, services, or property.[25]

Selling in Action

WHEN THE COMPETITION USES NEGATIVE PRACTICES

Negative selling practices create two problems for companies with integrity. First, the salesperson must use valuable time correcting misinformation presented by the competition. Second, a sale may be delayed until the customer rejects the untruth. Jim Galtan, director of sales for Schick Technologies, Inc., the leading manufacturer of digital dental X-ray technology, often learns that the competition has said something negative about his product. When this happens, he looks the customer in the eye and says, "Having the best product often frustrates our competition." He also tells customers that if the competition is honest in their assessment, they should be willing to prepare a letter outlining their concerns. Galtan says documentation is the easiest way to cope with negative selling because no one's going to document untruth.[c]

USE OF THE INTERNET Use of the Internet offers salespeople many advantages, but it can also create a number of ethical dilemmas. For example, e-mail abuse has become a modern-day problem because some employees forget that their employer owns the e-mail system. E-mail messages that contain inflammatory or abusive content, embarrassing gossip, or breaches of confidentiality can lead to legal liabilities. A growing number of companies are developing policies that define permissible uses of their e-mail system.[26]

Some resourceful salespeople have created their own Web sites to alert, attract, or support clients. The rise of these "extranets" has created some problems because they often function outside of the company's jurisdiction. What should top management do if a top salesperson encourages her customers to participate in a special Web auction for a backlogged product? What if the salesperson makes exaggerated claims about a new product? Every marketing firm needs to carefully monitor the development and use of extranets.[27]

The effectiveness of company policies as a deterrent to unethical behavior depends on two factors. The first is the firm's attitude toward employees who violate these policies. If violations are routinely ignored, the policy's effect soon erodes. Second, policies that influence personal selling need the support of the entire sales staff. Salespeople should have some voice in policy decisions; they are more apt to support policies they have helped develop.

Sales Manager as Role Model

The salesperson's actions often mirror the sales manager's behavior and expectations. This is not surprising when you consider the relationship between salespeople and their supervisors. They look to their supervisors for guidance and direction. The sales manager is generally the company's closest point of contact with the sales staff. This person is usually viewed as the chief spokesperson for top management.

Sales managers generally provide new salespeople with their first orientation to company operations. They are responsible for interpreting company policy. On a continuing basis, the sales manager monitors the salesperson's work and provides important feedback concerning conduct. If a salesperson violates company policy, it is usually the sales manager who is responsible for administering reprimands. If the moral fiber of a sales force begins to break down, the sales manager must shoulder a great deal of responsibility.

Sales managers influence the ethical behavior of salespeople by virtue of what they say and what they do. From time to time, managers must review their expectations of ethical behavior. Salespeople are under continuous pressure to abandon their personal

Sales managers influence the ethical behavior of salespeople by virtue of what they say and what they do.

ethical standards to achieve sales goals. Values such as integrity and honesty must receive ongoing support from the sales manager. The role of the sales manager will be discussed in more detail in Chapter 17.

Salesperson's Personal Values

Ann Kilpatrick, a sales representative in the transportation industry, encountered an unexpected experience when entertaining a potential client. The client said, "Let's go to Johnny's." She was not familiar with Johnny's, but on arrival discovered it was a raunchy bar. Kilpatrick related that she sat there for five minutes and then said, "This is not what I was expecting. This is a sleazy place. Let's go somewhere else where we can talk." She was not willing to compromise her personal values to win a new account.[28]

Values represent the ultimate reasons people have for acting as they do. Values are your deep personal beliefs and preferences that influence your behavior. To discover what really motivates you, carefully examine what you value.[29] Values serve as a foundation for our attitudes, and our attitudes serve as a foundation for our behavior (Figure 5.3). We do not adopt or discard values quickly. In fact, the development and refinement of values is a lifelong process.

Customers have a very negative view of salespeople who lack integrity. Yet, the temptation to lie about a product's features or benefits grows when you are trying to meet sales quotas. John Craig, a pharmacist at Hancock Drugs in Scottsburg, Indiana, describes a meeting with a pushy sales representative employed by a pharmaceutical company. The salesperson emphasized the wonders of a powerful, expensive painkiller but failed to describe its side effects. Craig said, "He was very pushy at the beginning," and this behavior revealed a character flaw.[30]

VALUES CONFLICT Values help us establish our own personal standards concerning what is right and what is wrong. Ron Willingham, author of *Integrity Selling for the 21st Century*, says, "Selling success is more an issue of who you are than what you know."[31] A salesperson's ethics and values contribute more to sales success than do techniques or strategies. Some salespeople discover a values conflict between themselves and their employer. If you view your employer's instructions or influence as improper, you have three choices:

1. Ignore the influence of your values and engage in the unethical behavior. The end result is likely to be a loss of self-respect and a feeling of guilt. When salespeople experience conflicts between their actions and values, they also feel a loss of confidence and energy.[32] Positive energy is the result of creating value for the customer. Negative energy is experienced when salespeople fail to honor and embrace their ethical values.

2. Voice strong opposition to the practice that is in conflict with your value system. Take a stand and state your beliefs. When ethical infractions occur, it's best to bring them up internally and try to influence decisions made by your peers or superiors. In some cases, doing the right thing may not be popular with others. Price Pritchett, the author of *The Ethics of Excellence*, says, "Not everybody will be on your side in your struggle to do the right thing."[33]

3. Refuse to compromise your values and be prepared to deal with the consequences. This may mean leaving the job. It also may mean that you will be fired.

Salespeople face ethical problems and decisions every day. In this respect they are no different from the doctor, the lawyer, the teacher, or any other professional. Ideally, they make decisions on the basis of the values they hold.[34]

FIGURE 5.3

Values represent the ultimate reasons salespeople have for acting as they do. Values serve as a foundation for our attitudes, and our attitudes serve as a foundation for our behavior.

Laws, Contracts, and Agreements

Take another look at Figure 5.2 (page 100) and you will notice that all of the key elements, personnel, and policies are influenced by laws, contracts, and agreements. Everyone involved in sales and marketing is guided by legal as well as ethical standards. We live in a society in which the legal system plays a key role in preventing people from engaging in unethical behavior.

LAWS The specific obligations imposed by government on the way business operates take the form of *statutes*, laws passed by Congress or state legislatures. Some of the most common laws deal with price competition, credit reporting, debt collection practices, contract enforcement, and land sales disclosure. The Uniform Commercial Code (UCC) is a major law influencing sales throughout the United States (see Table 5.1). The UCC is a legal guide to a wide range of transactions between the seller and the buyer. This law has been adopted throughout the United States and, therefore, has implications for most salespeople.

"A WINNING PHILOSOPHY BASED ON STRONG ETHICS AND VALUES AND HOW THEY CONTRIBUTE TO SUCCESS IN SALES...AND LIFE." —ZIG ZIGLAR

INTEGRITY SELLING FOR THE 21ST CENTURY

How to Sell the Way People Want to Buy

RON WILLINGHAM

Ron Willingham says a salesperson's ethics and values contribute more to sales success than do techniques and strategies.

A majority of the states have passed legislation that establishes a cooling-off period during which the consumer may void a contract to purchase goods or services. Although the provisions of **cooling-off laws** vary from state to state, their primary purpose is to give customers an opportunity to reconsider a buying decision made under a salesperson's

---

TABLE 5.1 • Uniform Commercial Code Defines Legal Side of Selling

Any list of the major developments in American law would have near its top the adoption of the Uniform Commercial Code (UCC), a body of statutes that replaces several areas of business law formerly covered individually by each state's common law of contracts.

The Uniform Commercial Code (UCC) is the source of the major laws influencing sales throughout the United States. Several areas featured in the UCC focus directly on the seller–buyer relationship. Some of the primary areas follow:

1. *Definition of a sale.* The code defines the legal dimensions of a sale. It clearly states that salespeople have the authority to legally obligate the company they represent.
2. *Warranties and guarantees.* The code distinguishes between express warranties and implied warranties. Express warranties are those that are described by the express language of the seller. Implied warranties are the obligations imposed by law on the seller that are not assumed in express language.
3. *Salesperson and reseller.* In many cases, the salesperson has resellers as customers or prospects. Salespeople must be aware of their employer's obligations to the reseller.
4. *Financing of sales.* Often salespeople work for firms that are directly involved in financing products or services or in arranging such financing from outside sources. A salesperson needs to be familiar with the legal aspects of these credit arrangements.
5. *Product consignment.* In some cases, goods are delivered to the buyer, but the title remains with the seller. This type of transaction can become complicated if the goods have a limited life span. Depreciation may occur with the passing of time. Salespeople should be familiar with the company's rights in cases in which goods are sold on consignment.

persuasive influence. Many laws are designed to deal specifically with sales made in the consumer's home. For example, the Federal Trade Commission (FTC) established the National Do Not Call Registry in an attempt to reduce the number of telemarketing calls.

CONTRACTS AND AGREEMENTS The word *contract* may bring to mind the familiar multipage, single-spaced documents that no ordinary person seems able to understand. In fact, contracts can be oral or written. A **contract** is simply a promise or promises that the courts will enforce. Oral contracts are enforceable, but written contracts are preferable. They reduce the possibility of disagreement and the courts give them great weight in a lawsuit. A written contract can consist of a sales slip, a notation on a check, or any other writing that evidences the promises that the parties made.[35]

Salespeople are sometimes the legal representatives of their company and, therefore, must be careful when signing written contracts. They often oversee contracts with customers, suppliers, and resellers. Salespeople also frequently sign employment contracts at the time they are hired. Most of these agreements include a noncompete clause. One of the most common clauses, a noncompete clause prohibits salespeople from joining a competing firm for a year after they leave. Most clauses are legally binding even when an employee's position is cut. Employers see employment contracts as an effective way to protect intellectual property, customer lists, and other resources an employee might take to a competing firm.[36]

Many companies are learning that resolving legal disputes can be very costly and time-consuming. Resolving a dispute in the courts can sometimes take several years. A serious effort to prevent unethical activities can prevent costly litigation.

ETHICS BEYOND THE LETTER OF THE LAW Too often people confuse ethical standards with legal standards. They believe that if you are not breaking the law, then you are acting in an ethical manner.[37] A salesperson's ethical sense must extend beyond the legal definition of what is right and wrong. To view ethics only in terms of what is legally proper encourages the question, "What can I get by with?" A salesperson must develop a personal code of ethics that extends beyond the letter of the law.

Bruce Weinstein, a professional ethicist who is often introduced as "The Ethics Guy," offers sound advice on living an ethical life. He says we should do the right thing simply because it's the right thing to do. The only way you can build a loyal and growing client base is to demonstrate that you have the customers own best interests at heart. You are trying to make things better for them. "Here is where ethics differs from the law. It demands more of us," says Weinstein.[38]

A Personal Code of Ethics That Adds Value

Many people considering a career in selling are troubled by the thought that they may be pressured into compromising their personal standards of right and wrong. These fears may be justified. The authors of *The Ethical Edge*, a book that examines organizations that have faced moral crises, contend that business firms have given too little thought to the issue of helping employees to function ethically within organizations.[39] Many salespeople wonder whether their own ethical philosophy can survive in the business world. These are some of their questions:

"Can a profitable business and good ethics coexist?"

"Are there still business firms that value adherence to high ethical standards?"

"Is honesty still a valued personal trait in the business community?"

In the field of athletic competition, the participants rely heavily on a written set of rules. The referee or umpire is ever present to detect rule violations and assess a penalty. In the field of personal selling, there is no universal code of ethics. However, some general guidelines can serve as a foundation for a personal code of business ethics.

1. *Personal selling must be viewed as an exchange of value.* Salespeople who maintain a value focus are searching for ways to create value for their prospects or customers. This value may take the form of increased productivity, greater profit, enjoyment, or security. The value focus motivates the salesperson to carefully identify the

Customer Relationship Management with Technology

EXERCISING CARE WITH CRM DATA

Customer relationship management systems enable you to collect information about people with whom you maintain relationships, including the taking of notes. It is a good practice to record more than basic transaction information, such as personal details about your customers. Reviewing your observations about the customers' behavior and your recording of their statements can help you understand them and their needs. Rereading their comments about ethical issues can assist you in assessing the value of maintaining a business relationship with them.

To be fair, it is important to record only the facts concerning your observations, not necessarily your conclusions. Information in an electronic database can last a long time and, for reasons such as litigation or company acquisitions, can be "mobile." This means that others may form an opinion about your customer, based on your recorded observations, with potential detrimental consequences for your customer. Because the customer may not be aware of the existence of the information in your database, that person does not have a fair opportunity to correct any erroneous conclusions. Another reason to carefully record only the facts is the possibility that the information may be read by the customer. For example, there are instances in which a customer later joined the sales organization and gained access to the customer relationship management (CRM) system.

Most CRM systems contain scheduling functions, which means that you can set aside time on your calendar to attend meetings, make phone calls, and perform tasks. The scheduling tools usually include alarms, which remind you that a deadline is approaching. The disciplined use of these features can help you get tasks done on time. Taking advantage of the system's reminder tools can be especially important when it involves fulfilling your commitments. The system can help you build trust by reminding you to always do what you said you would do. (See the exercise "Preparing Mailing Lists with CRM" on p. 113 for more information.)

prospects' wants and needs.[40] Salespeople who accept this ethical guideline view personal selling as something you do *for* customers, not something you do *to* customers. The role of the salesperson is to diagnose buyer needs and determine whether value can be created. Always be prepared to add value.

2. *Relationship comes first, task second.* Sharon Drew Morgan, author of *Selling with Integrity*, says that you can't sell a product unless there is a level of comfort between you and the prospect. She encourages salespeople to take the time to create a level of comfort, rapport, and collaboration that encourages open communication.[41] Placing task before relationship is based on the belief that the salesperson knows more than the customer. Morgan reminds us, "The buyer has the answers, and the seller has the questions."[42] These answers surface only when the buyer–seller relationship is characterized by rapport and trust.

3. *Be honest with yourself and with others.* To achieve excellence in terms of ethical practices, you have to believe that everything you do counts. Tom Peters in *Thriving on Chaos* said, "Integrity may be about little things as much as or more than big ones."[43] Integrity is about accuracy in completing your expense account. There is always the temptation to inflate the expense report for personal gain. Integrity is also about avoiding the temptation to stretch the truth, to exaggerate, or to withhold information. Paul Ekman, author of *Telling Lies*, says that withholding important information is one of the primary ways of lying.[44] A complete and informative sales presentation may include information concerning the product's limitations. If you let your character and integrity be revealed in the little things, others can see you as one who acts ethically in all things. Any violation of honesty, however small, dilutes your ethical strength, leaving you weaker for the big challenges you will face sooner or later.[45]

The Trust Factor

Everyone involved in personal selling must work hard to build relationships based on trust. When the customer and the salesperson trust each other, they will usually find ways to

Personal selling must be viewed as an exchange of value. Salespeople who accept this ethical guideline view personal selling as something you do for customers, not something you do to customers.

form a productive partnership. Although trust is an essential element of every sale, the meaning of trust changes with the type of sale.[46]

■ *Trust in Transactional Sales.* The primary customer focus in this type of sale is trust in the product. Is the product reliable? Is the product priced as low as possible? Can the product be delivered in a timely fashion? The transactional buyer may purchase a product from a salesperson they do not feel totally comfortable with if it meets their purchase criteria.

■ *Trust in Consultative Sales.* In a consultative sale, the customer focus shifts from the product to the person who sells the product. The consultative buyer is thinking, "Can I trust this salesperson to identify my problem and offer me one or more solutions?" Customers involved in a consultative sale usually do not separate the product from the person selling it. They want to do business with a salesperson who displays such positive qualities as warmth, empathy, genuineness, competence, and integrity.

■ *Trust in Strategic Alliance Sales.* The strategic alliance buyer wants to do business with an institution that can be trusted. This buyer looks beyond the well-qualified salesperson and assesses the entire organization. A strategic alliance customer will not feel comfortable partnering with a company whose values differ greatly from their own. Ethical accountability will greatly influence the way an alliance partner is judged and valued.

Trust exists when we strongly believe in the integrity, ability, and character of a person or an organization. Although trust is an intangible, it is at the very core of all meaningful relationships. Trust is quickly lost and slowly won.[47]

Ethical and Legal Issues in International Business

Ethical and legal issues that are quite complex on the domestic scene become even more complicated at the international level. International business is growing, and the United States is deeply involved in the global marketplace. Thomas Friedman, author of the best-selling book *The World Is Flat: A Brief History of the Twenty-First Century*, says today's highly competitive and global marketplace is flattening the world of international business. In order to compete with China, India, and other dynamic economics, U.S.-based companies must adopt a more aggressive global focus.[48]

Culture Issues

Today's global marketplace reflects a kaleidoscope of cultures, each with its own unique qualities. **Culture** is the sum total of beliefs, values, knowledge, ethnic customs, and objects that people use to adapt to their environment. Cultural barriers can impede acceptance of products in foreign countries and weaken interpersonal relationships. When the salesperson understands the cultural background of the foreign customer, communication problems are less likely. Many people from Asia, Arab countries, and much of Africa prefer a more indirect style of communication and therefore value harmony, subtlety, sensitivity, and tact more than brevity.[49] The customer who seems to be agreeing with everything you say may have no intention of buying your product. This person may simply be displaying polite and tactful behaviors.

Perceptions of time differ from country to country. Americans value promptness, but businesspeople from other countries often approach meetings in a more relaxed manner. Arriving late for a meeting may not be viewed as a problem. Many companies are spending thousands of dollars to make sure that employees sent abroad are culturally prepared. Eastman Chemical Company, for example, has developed a highly successful orientation program for employees who have accepted overseas assignments.[50]

Legal Issues

Doing business in the global marketplace continues to be an ethical minefield. Illegal demands for bribes, kickbacks, or special fees may stand in the way of successful transactions. The Foreign Corrupt Practices Act prohibits U.S. companies from using bribes or kickbacks to influence foreign officials. But monitoring illegal activities throughout the world is a very difficult task.[51] Motorola and some other U.S. businesses are using software to analyze invoices and payments in order to uncover possible payoffs. Gifts from suppliers to U.S. companies can also be a problem. Each year United Technologies sends a letter to foreign suppliers saying "we don't want gifts."[52]

American businesses acknowledge that it is difficult to compete with organizations from other countries that are not bound by U.S. laws. However, the International Business Ethics Institute (www.business-ethics.org) believes U.S. companies have been a very positive role model for rest of the business world. As noted previously in this chapter, high ethical standards depend on strong leadership provided by management personnel at all levels of the organization. Integrity starts at the top.

Chapter Learning Activities

Reviewing Key Concepts

Describe how ethical decisions influence relationships in selling

Character and integrity strongly influence relationships in personal selling. Unethical sales practices will ultimately destroy relationships with customers. These practices undermine trust, which is at the very core of all meaningful relationships.

Discuss factors that influence character development

Many colleges and universities are playing a more active role in character development. Character education is often integrated into courses that focus on ethics. Character is composed of personal standards of behavior, so all of us can do things that build character. Keeping our commitments to others provides just one example of how character is built.

Describe the factors that influence the ethical conduct of sales personnel

Salespeople can benefit from the stabilizing influence of good role models. Although top management personnel are usually far removed from day-to-day selling activities, they can have a major impact on salespeople's conduct. Dishonesty at the top of an organization can cause an erosion of ethical standards at the lower echelons. Sales managers provide another important role model. They interpret company policies and help establish guidelines for acceptable and unacceptable selling practices.

Discuss guidelines for developing a personal code of ethics

Salespeople must establish their own standards of personal conduct. They must decide how best to serve their company and build strong partnerships with their customers. The pressure to compromise one's ethical standards surfaces almost daily. The primary deterrent is a strong sense of right and wrong. Three general guidelines can serve as a foundation for a personal code of ethics:

a. Personal selling must be viewed as an exchange of value.

b. Relationship comes first, task second.

c. Be honest with yourself and with others.

Describe ethical and legal issues in international business

At the international level, ethical and legal issues can be very complex. The global marketplace reflects a great number of cultures, each with its unique qualities. Coping with illegal activities throughout the world is also very challenging. Illegal demands for bribes, kickbacks, or special fees can serve as a barrier to business transactions.

Key Terms

Business ethics	Values	Contract
Reciprocity	Cooling-off laws	Culture

Review Questions

1. What is the definition of *business ethics*? Why is this topic receiving so much attention today?
2. Carefully review the Standards of Professional Conduct developed by the National Association of Sales Professionals (NASP). Select the three standards you feel would present the greatest challenge to salespeople. Explain your answer.
3. How does business slander differ from business libel?
4. What major factors help influence salespeople's ethical conduct?
5. What is the Uniform Commercial Code? Why is it needed?
6. Why must a salesperson's ethical sense extend beyond the legal definition of what is right and wrong?
7. Explain why the sales manager plays such an important role in influencing the ethical behavior of salespeople.
8. A company policy on ethics should cover several major areas. What are they?
9. Is it ever appropriate to give gifts to customers? Explain.
10. List and describe three guidelines used as a foundation of a self-imposed code of business ethics.

Application Exercises

1. You find that you have significantly overcharged one of your clients. The error was discovered when you received payment. It is unlikely that the customer or your company will become aware of the overcharge. Because of this error, the company realized a higher net profit on the sale. Your commissions are based on this profit. What, if anything, will you do about the overcharge?
2. Access the National Association of Sales Professionals Web site at www.nasp.com. Click on the sales certification link and examine the steps to becoming a certified sales professional. Also click "Registry of Accredited Salespeople" and the "Directory of Members." Examine the backgrounds of several members of the NASP.

Reviewing the Standards of Professional Conduct printed in this chapter, discuss your views on the impact professional certification has on the ethical behavior of salespeople. Do you think the designation CPSP would affect the impression a customer might have of a salesperson?

3. You work for a supplier of medical equipment. Your sales manager informs you that he wants you to capture a certain hospital account. He also tells you to put on your expense account anything it costs to secure the firm as a client. When you ask him to be more specific, he tells you to use your own judgment. Up to this time you have never questioned your sales manager's personal code of ethics. Make a list of the items you believe can be legitimately charged to the company on your expense account.

4. For some time your strongest competitor has been making untrue derogatory statements about your product and about your company. You know for a fact that her product is not as good as yours, yet hers has a higher price. Several of your best customers have confronted you with these charges. Describe how you plan to answer them.

5. Sales managers must approve expense reports turned in by members of the sales force. Assume the role of sales manager for a sales force that includes twelve salespeople who travel frequently and average about two overnight trips each week. Recently you noticed that the expense reports turned in by two of your salespeople seem quite high. You suspect that these salespeople are padding their expense reports. What steps should you take to determine if cheating is occurring? How can a sales manager prevent the padding of expense reports?

Role-Play Exercise

This morning you met with a customer who has purchased office supplies from you for almost three years. You are quite surprised when she says, "I am prepared to place a $10,500 order, but you must match an offer I received from a competitor." She then explains that the competitor is offering *new* customers a seven-day trip to Disney World in Orlando if they place an order over $10,000. All expenses will be paid. What would you do?

Prepare to role-play your response with another student. Review the material in this chapter, paying special attention to ways you can add value and build long-term relationships with ethical decision making.

CRM Application Exercise

Preparing Mailing Lists with CRM

Log onto the Salesforce.com system. Go to the Reports tab and select the "Park Inn Mailing List" report. Choose the printable view. The mailing information for each contact will be displayed on the screen. Select "Eile," "Print," and print this list.

A friend of yours is a salesperson with a firm that installs the cables used to connect network components, a service that your company does not offer. Your friend wants to know if you will share the customer list that you printed. What should be your response?

Case Problem

Dana Davis dropped into the store's receiving department of Regina Steel Fabricators, one of the company's oldest and best accounts. Dana had been called by Tyler Hensman, their senior purchasing person, to inspect the last shipment of structural tubing sold them. According to Tyler, when the tubing was sheared to the lengths required, the shear had dimpled the ends of the tubes, and the dimples had not been removed as requested. The tubes were, therefore, not perfectly round, and the casters that were to fit into the ends would not do so without considerable effort. Davis was puzzled by the quality control problem. The company has a long-standing policy of not shipping a product to a customer unless it has passed inspection by the quality control staff.

Dana arrived just after lunch, and while waiting for Gary Anderson, the store's supervisor, noticed that there was a large shipment of stainless steel bolts and nuts sitting in the store's receiving area. They were marked type 304 stainless steel, one of the cheaper grades. Dana was curious because a price quotation had been given to Tyler Hensman the previous week on the same material in type 316 stainless steel, a much more expensive grade.

Dana Davis approached a young clerk who was working in the receiving area. "Where did that shipment come from?"

"Quality Distribution," the young man replied, without looking directly at Dana.

"What was the cost of the material?" Dana inquired.

"Don't know. My copy of the order doesn't show a cost, nor does the packing slip that came in the shipment," the young man said as he shrugged his shoulders.

"Is it supposed to be type 304 or type 316?" Dana persisted.

"It just says stainless steel bolts and nuts on my copy of the purchase order," replied the clerk. "And the packing slip just says stainless steel as well. There's no mention of type of stainless. If you want to find out more, you'll have to contact Tyler Hensman in our purchasing department. This order was placed by him."

Dana Davis was getting more curious about the shipment from Quality Distribution. Upon returning to the office, Dana decided to call Tyler Hensman and ask for the order. A decision was made not to mention what was seen in the store's receiving area. "Tyler, I'm calling about that price quotation I gave you last week for 316 stainless steel bolts and nuts. Will you give us an order?"

"Sorry. I placed the order with Quality Distribution last week because their price was better," Tyler replied. "You'll have to sharpen your pencil if you want our business."

Dana Davis knew there was no way Quality Distribution could compete on price because it was basically a small jobber firm that really wasn't in the stainless steel business. But Dana didn't want to say that to Tyler Hensman.

"How much sharper?"

"Just a bit, but you know it wouldn't be honest for me to tell you," Tyler laughed.

After they talked for a few more minutes, Dana Davis promised to check pricing options and determine if the next price could be more competitive. After hanging up the phone, Dana sat at his desk, staring at the wall. Davis realized a careful approach was needed. There was something wrong and the issue needed to be resolved quickly. This was an important long-term account for American Steel, and the company couldn't afford to lose it.

Questions

1. Has Dana Davis's behavior been ethical? Why or why not?

2. Has Tyler Hensman's behavior been ethical? Why or why not?

3. What should Dana Davis do?

Part 2 | Role-Play Exercise

DEVELOPING A RELATIONSHIP STRATEGY

Scenario

You are an experienced sales representative employed by American Steel Processing, a company that has been in business for over 25 years. American is an ISO 9002–certified manufacturing company that has earned many accolades, including three consecutive J. D. Power and Associates awards for customer satisfaction. Over the years the company has invested heavily in automation technology as a means of ensuring consistent manufacturing quality. The American Steel processing sales force understands that the company will not be the lowest bidder in most sales situations because the highest quality can never be obtained at the lowest price.

Customer Profile

Tyler Hensman has held the position of senior purchasing agent at Regina Steel Fabricators for several years. Throughout this period of time, Tyler has negotiated over a dozen purchase agreements with Dana Davis, senior account representative with American Steel Processing. Tyler takes pride in purchasing quality steel products at the best price.

Salesperson Profile

Dana Davis began working for American Steel Processing Company about four years ago. After completion of an extensive sales training program, Dana was assigned to a territory in central Ohio. After three successful years, Dana Davis was promoted to senior account representative.

Product

American Steel Processing sells a wide range of steel products. Many of the orders filled are for high-stress steel beams, stainless steel bolts and nuts, and structural tubing used in commercial building construction. Most orders specify a certain quality of steel.

Instructions

For this role play you will assume the role of Dana Davis, senior account representative employed by American Steel Processing. To prepare for the role-play, you should carefully read the case problem at the end of Chapter 5. This information will help you understand the issues that need to be addressed during the role-play. During the early stages of the role-play, you will want to obtain more information from the customer and resolve any misunderstandings. You want to obtain the order for type 316 stainless steel bolts and nuts, and maintain a good relationship with this important customer. Keep in mind that ethical decisions can greatly influence the relationship between a salesperson and the customer. Reflect on the important information covered in Chapter 5 prior to meeting with Tyler Hensman.

Part

3

Developing a Product Strategy

Part 3 examines the important role of complete and accurate product, company, and competitive knowledge in personal selling. Lack of knowledge in these areas impairs the salesperson's ability to configure value-added solutions. Part 3 also describes several value-added selling strategies.

"Service is not a competitive edge, it is THE competitive edge. People do not buy just products; they also buy expectations. One expectation is that the item they buy will produce the benefits the seller promised. Another is that if it doesn't, the seller will make good on the promise."

Karl Albrecht and Ron Zemke, *Service America: Doing Business in the New Economy*

6

Creating Product Solutions

▶ Reality Selling Today Video Series

For the last ten years, Amy Vandaveer, in the photo above, has had a highly successful sales career. She has a bachelor's degree in marketing from the University of Texas and has sold sales technology software, sales training programs, and media services. Currently, Amy is a sales representative for *Texas Monthly* (www.texasmonthly.com), a magazine that focuses largely on leisure activities and events in Texas. *Texas Monthly's* sales staff is responsible for selling the large amount of advertising space available in the magazine. It may sound like a relatively easy job; after all, *Texas Monthly* has a large, loyal reader base and would be an attractive advertising outlet for many businesses. Remember, though, that *Texas Monthly* has many direct and indirect competitors, all of whom are trying to sell their services to the same group of businesses that Amy works with.

Because of the many options available to a prospective advertiser, Amy must become an expert on what her customers want, what *Texas Monthly* can offer them, and what *Texas Monthly's* competitors can offer. By doing so, she can improve her ability to answer customers' questions and emphasize the benefits, in the context of her customers' needs, of choosing *Texas Monthly* over other advertising outlets. She is no longer just selling advertising space; instead, she can offer her customers her own knowledge and experience at creating solutions that address their needs.[1] ■

Developing a Product Solution That Adds Value

As noted in Chapter 1, a product strategy helps salespeople make correct decisions concerning the selection and positioning of products to meet identified customer needs. The **product strategy** is a well-conceived plan that emphasizes becoming a product expert, selling specific benefits, and configuring value-added solutions (Figure 6.1). Configuring value-added solutions is discussed in detail in Chapter 7.

Strategic/Consultative Selling Model	
Strategic Step	**Prescription**
Develop a Personal Selling Philosophy	☑ Adopt Marketing Concept
	☑ Value Personal Selling
	☑ Become a Problem Solver/Partner
Develop a Relationship Strategy	☑ Adopt Win-Win Philosophy
	☑ Project Professional Image
	☑ Maintain High Ethical Standards
Develop a Product Strategy	☐ Become a Product Expert
	☐ Sell Specific Benefits
	☐ Configure Value-Added Solutions

FIGURE 6.1

Developing a product strategy enables the salesperson to custom fit products or services to the customer's needs.

Selling Solutions

A **solution** is a mutually shared answer to a recognized customer problem. In many selling situations, a solution is more encompassing than a specific product. It often provides measurable results such as greater productivity, increased profits, or less employee turnover. Selling a solution, versus selling a specific product, usually requires a greater effort to define and diagnose the customer's problem.[2] Think of **solution selling** as a process by which the salesperson uncovers and clarifies a customer's problem, works with the customer to create a vision of how things could be better, and then develops a plan for implementing the vision.[3]

Most salespeople have adopted a broad definition of the term *product*. It is broadly interpreted to encompass infor-

According to Keith Eades, author of The New Solution Selling, *a solution is a mutually shared answer to a recognized customer problem. It is more encompassing than a specific product, and it provides measurable results. Eades states that more than 500,000 individuals worldwide have been trained in solution selling. Solution selling forms the core of Microsoft's selling processes.*

mation, services, ideas, tangible products, or some combination of these that satisfy the customer's needs with the right solution.[4] Let's look at the sales process at two firms:

- Trilogy, an Austin, Texas–based company, creates configuration software for large manufacturers such as Boeing and Hewlett-Packard. These two companies sell products with a great many variants. Boeing, for example, can use a wide range of components to assemble a plane that matches the customer's highly specific preferences. With the aid of Trilogy software, Boeing sales representatives, using a laptop computer, can translate a customer's specific needs into a workable specification.[5]

- Sunflower Travel Corporation, based in Wichita, Kansas, creates specialized vacation packages for individuals and groups. A package might include airline tickets, hotel reservations, and accommodations on a cruise line. The sales staff at Sunflower have the knowledge to plan a highly customized trip.[6]

From the customer's point of view, salespeople employed by Trilogy and Sunflower are selling primarily information and expertise. The problem-solving ability these salespeople provide the customer is viewed as the product. When you sell a complex product, it is knowledge and expertise that create value.

TAILORING THE PRODUCT STRATEGY A product strategy should be tailored to the customer's buying needs. Transactional buyers are usually well aware of their needs. Most of these customers have conducted their own research and have a good understanding of the product that will meet their needs. The office manager who frequently buys a large amount of copy paper knows that this standard item can be purchased from several vendors. The quality of the paper usually does not vary from one vendor to another.

The consultative buyer may lack needs awareness and will usually welcome need clarification. This customer will want help evaluating possible solutions and usually needs a customized product solution. The customized solution appeals to the customer's desire for choices that are tailored to their needs. Developing a product strategy for the strategic alliance customer usually offers the greatest challenge. Study of the proposed alliance partner can be very time-consuming, but the rewards of a successful alliance may be substantial. In some cases, the company that wishes to form an alliance with a new customer must be prepared to make a large investment in capital-intensive technology and additional personnel.[7]

Explosion of Product Options

The domestic and global markets are overflowing with a vast array of goods and services. In some industries, the number of new products introduced each year is mind-boggling. Consumer-product makers, for example, churn out more than 30,000 new products each year. Want to buy a product in the securities and financial services field? In the segment of mutual funds alone, you can choose from more than 7,000 products.[8]

For the customer, this much variety creates a "good news–bad news" situation. The good news is that almost all buyers have a choice when it comes to purchasing a product or service. People like to compare various options. The bad news is that so many choices

often complicate the buying process. One of the most important roles of the salesperson is to simplify the customer's study of the product choices. Later in this chapter we discuss how product features (information) can add value when converted into specific benefits (knowledge) that can help the buyer make an intelligent buying decision.

Creating Solutions with Product Configuration

The challenge facing both customers and salespeople in this era of information overload is deciding which product applications, or combination of applications, can solve the buying problem. If the customer has complex buying needs, then the salesperson may have to bring together many parts of the company's product mix to develop a custom-fitted solution. The product selection process is often referred to as **product configuration**. Salespeople representing Cisco Systems are often involved in the sale of new products to new and established customers. They use Cybrant Solutions Architect software to quickly identify solutions. The software helps salespeople ask prospects the right questions to discover their needs and then configures a solution that best meets those needs.[9]

Amy Vandaveer takes pride in her ability to create solutions based on product configuration. In fact, every proposal she prepares is customized to fit the needs of a *Texas Monthly* customer.

Many companies use product configuration software because it develops customized product solutions quickly and accurately. It incorporates product selection criteria and associates them directly with customer requirements. Members of the sales force can use the sales configurator to identify product options, prices, delivery schedules, and other parts of the product mix while working interactively with the customer. Most of today's product configuration software can be integrated with contact management software programs such as Salesforce, ACT!, and NetSuite. In addition to improving the quality of the sales proposal, this software reduces the time-consuming process of manually preparing written proposals.

A major element of product configuration is *quotation management*. Quick and accurate pricing is critical in today's fast-paced sales environment. Leading companies are aggressively automating their quotation management process.[10]

Selling Is Everyone's Business

SELLING MOTHERHOOD

Cynthia Cunningham and Shelley Murray worked 60-hour workweeks to achieve success as BankBoston branch managers. They wanted more time with their children, but the long hours created a major barrier to motherhood. Then they came up with a novel plan: package themselves and share one job. Once the plan was developed, the selling began. They wrote a letter that described their accomplishments, attached a résumé, and delivered the package to several senior executives. Eventually they met with more than a dozen executives and finally hit pay dirt. They began sharing a vice president–level job that involved teaching branch personnel and small businesses how to sell their services to customers. Cynthia and Shelley now work 20 to 25 hours each week at what has since become Fleet Bank.[a]

Cynthia Cunningham and Shelley Murray.

Preparing Written Proposals

Written proposals are frequently part of the salesperson's product strategy. It is only natural that some buyers want the proposed solution put in writing. *Written proposals* can be defined as a specific plan of action based on the facts, assumptions, and supporting documentation included in the sales presentation.[11] A well-written proposal adds value to the product solution and can set you apart from the competition. It offers the buyer reassurance that you will deliver what has been promised. Written proposals, which are often accompanied by a sales letter, vary in terms of format and content. Many government agencies, and some large companies, issue a request for proposal (RFP) that specifies the format of the proposal. Most proposals include the following parts:

Budget and overview. Tell the prospect the cost of the solution you have prescribed. Be specific as you describe the product or service features to be provided and specify the price. When you confirm pricing with a proposal, misunderstandings and mistakes can be avoided.

Objective. The objective should be expressed in terms of benefits. A tangible objective might be to "reduce payroll expense by 10 percent." An intangible objective might be stated as "increased business security offered by a company with a reputation for dependability." Focus on specific benefits that relate directly to the customer's needs.

Strategy. Briefly describe how you will meet your objective. How will you fulfill the obligations you have described in your proposal? In some cases this section of your proposal includes specific language: "Your account will be assigned to Susan Murray, our senior lease representative."

Schedule. Establish a time frame for meeting your objective. This might involve the confirmation of dates with regard to acquisition, shipping, or installation.

Rationale. With a mixture of logic and emotion, present your rationale for taking action now. Once again, the emphasis should be on benefits, not features.[12]

Selling in Action

WRITING EFFECTIVE SALES LETTERS

 Sales letters are increasingly being used by salespeople to describe features and benefits, position products, build relationships, and provide assurances to customers. Sales letters also are used in conjunction with prospecting plans. There are several standard rules that apply to all written sales letters. These include the following:

1. Sales letters should follow the standard visual format of a business letter. They should contain (in the following order) either a letterhead or the sender's address, date, inside address (the same as on the outside of the envelope), salutation, body of letter, complimentary close, typed name and handwritten signature of sender, and a notation of enclosures (if there are any).

2. Placement of the letter on paper should provide a balanced white-space border area surrounding the entire letter. Three to five blank lines should separate the date and inside address; a single blank line should separate the inside address and the salutation, salutation and opening paragraph of the letter, and each paragraph. A single blank line should separate the last paragraph and the complimentary close. Single spacing should generally be used within the paragraphs.

3. Proper business punctuation includes a colon after the salutation and comma after the complimentary close.

4. Most sales letters include at least three paragraphs. The first paragraph should indicate the objective of your letter; the second should be a summary of the benefits proposed; and the third paragraph should state what the next action step will be for the salesperson, the customer, or both.

5. Proper grammar and spelling must be used throughout the entire letter. Business letters provide an opportunity to build a stronger relationship with the customer and close the sale. Improper placement, punctuation, spelling errors, or weak content convey a negative impression to the reader and may result in a lost sale.

6. The use of the personal pronoun "I" should be minimized in a sales letter. To keep the letter focused on the customer's needs, the pronouns "you" and "your" should appear throughout the body of the letter.

Some written proposals follow a specific format developed by the company. The length of a proposal can vary from a single page to dozens of pages for a complex product.

The proposal should be printed on quality paper and free of any errors in spelling, grammar, or punctuation. Before completing the proposal, review the content one more time to be sure you have addressed all the customer's concerns. Bob Kantin, author of *Sales Proposals Kit for Dummies*, says the proposal is really the first "product" that the customer receives from you, so be sure it is perfect.[13] Neil Rackham, noted author and sales consultant, says to address your proposal to the "invisible" customer. Very often the proposal will be reviewed by individuals the salesperson has never met. And these are often the people who will make or break the deal.[14]

The remainder of this chapter is divided into five major sections. The first two sections examine the kinds of product information and company information required by the salesperson. The third section describes the type of information about the competition that is helpful to salespeople. Sources of information are covered in the fourth section, and the fifth section describes how product features can be translated into buyer benefits.

Becoming a Product Expert

One of the major challenges facing salespeople is winning the customer's trust. A survey reported in *Sales & Marketing Management* ranked product knowledge as the number-one characteristic of salespeople who are able to build trust.[15] Ideally, a salesperson possesses product knowledge that meets and exceeds customer expectations. Tom Peters says that when it comes to product knowledge, remember: "More, more, more. And, more important: Deeper, deeper, deeper." In summary: "He or she who has the largest appetite for Deep Knowledge wins."[16] This section reviews some of the most common product information categories: (1) product development and quality improvement processes, (2) performance data and specifications, (3) maintenance and service contracts, and (4) price and delivery. Each is important as a potential source of knowledge concerning the product or service.

Product Development and Quality Improvement Processes

Companies spend large amounts of money in the development of their products. In **product development**, the original idea for a product or service is tested, modified, and retested several times before it is offered to the customer. Each of the modifications is made with the thought of improving the product. Salespeople should be familiar with product development history. Often this information sets the stage for stronger sales appeals.

Patagonia, a company that makes high-quality sports and outdoor equipment and clothing, uses a unique product development process. Patagonia hires many expert kayakers, skiers, climbers, and fishermen who under actual conditions help develop and test the company's products. In the outdoor recreation market, Patagonia wins high praise for its many product innovations.[17]

Quality improvement continues to be an important long-term business strategy for most successful companies. Salespeople need to identify quality improvement processes that provide a competitive advantage and to be prepared to discuss this information during the sales presentation. Gulfstream Aircraft Company, Ritz-Carlton Hotels, Toyota, and Sea Ray Boats provide examples of companies that have implemented important quality controls. **Quality control**, which involves measuring products and services against established standards, is one dimension of the typical quality improvement process.

Sea Ray Boats, a quality leader in the pleasure boat industry, worked hard to become an ISO 9002 certified builder. This certification, from the International Organization for Standardization (ISO), assures a high level of quality in the manufacturing process. The company is the industry leader in robotic applications, a means of ensuring consistent quality from boat to boat. Sea Ray Boats has also earned two consecutive J.D. Power and Associates awards for customer satisfaction.[18]

Sea Ray Boats, a quality leader in the pleasure boat industry, worked hard to become an ISO 9002 certified builder. Sea Ray has also earned two consecutive J.D. Power and Associates awards for customer satisfaction. High-performing salespeople are familiar with these important product knowledge achievements and able to communicate the benefits to prospective boat buyers.

Performance Data and Specifications

Most potential buyers are interested in performance data and specifications. Some typical questions that might be raised by prospects are:

"What is the frequency response for this stereo loudspeaker?"
"What is the anticipated rate of return on this mutual fund?"
"What is the energy consumption rating for this appliance?"
"Are all your hotel and conference center rooms accessible to persons with physical disabilities?"

A salesperson must be prepared to address these types of questions in the written sales proposal and the sales presentation. Performance data are especially critical in cases in which the customer is attempting to compare the merits of one product with another.

To become familiar with the performance of Whirlpool appliances, salespeople literally "live" the brand. The company rented and redesigned an eight-bedroom farmhouse near corporate headquarters and outfitted it with Whirlpool dishwashers, refrigerators, washers, dryers, and microwaves. Salespeople, in groups of eight, live at the house for two months and use all of the appliances. Whirlpool engineers visit the home and present information on design, performance data, and specifications. A recent graduate of the training program says, "I have a confidence level that's making a difference in my client contacts."[19]

Maintenance and Service Contracts

Prospects often want information concerning maintenance and care requirements for the products they purchase. The salesperson who can quickly and accurately provide this information has the edge. Proper maintenance usually extends the life of the product, so this information should be provided at the time of the sale.

Today, many salespeople are developing customized service agreements that incorporate the customer's special priorities, feelings, and needs. They work hard to acquire a real understanding of the customer's specific service criteria. If call return expectations are very important to the customer, the frequency and quantity of product-related visits per week or month can be included in the service contract. Customized service agreements add value to the sale and help protect your business from the competition.[20]

Pricing and Delivery

Potential buyers expect salespeople to be well versed in price and delivery policies and be in a position to set prices and plan deliveries. If a salesperson has pricing authority, buyers perceive the person as someone with whom they can really talk business. The ability to set prices puts the salesperson in a stronger position.[21]

Decision-making authority in the area of pricing gives the salesperson *more power and responsibility.* If the salesperson negotiates a price that is too low, the company may lose money on the sale. Price objections represent one of the most common barriers to closing a sale, so salespeople need to be well prepared in this area.

In most situations, the price quotation should be accompanied by information that creates value in the mind of the customer. The process of determining whether or not the proposal adds value is often called **quantifying the solution**. When the purchase represents a major buying decision, such as the purchase of a new computer system, quantifying the solution is important. One way to quantify the solution is to conduct a cost–benefit analysis to determine the actual cost of the purchase and savings the buyer can anticipate from the investment (Table 6.1).

TABLE 6.1 Quantifying the Solution with Cost–Benefit Analysis

Quantifying the solution often involves a carefully prepared cost–benefit analysis. This example compares the higher-priced Phoenix semitruck trailer with the lower-priced FB model, which is a competing product.

COST SAVINGS OF THE PHOENIX VERSUS FB MODEL FOR A 10-YEAR PERIOD (ALL PRICES ARE APPROXIMATE)	
	Cost Savings
• Stainless steel bulkhead (savings on sandblasting and painting)	$ 425.00
• Stainless steel rear door frame (savings on painting)	425.00
• Air ride suspension (better fuel mileage, longer tire life, longer brake life)	3,750.00
• Hardwood or aluminum scuff (savings from freight damages and replacement of scuff)	1,000.00
• LED lights (last longer; approximate savings: $50 per year × 10 years)	500.00
• Light protectors (save $50 per year on replacement × 10 years)	500.00
• Threshold plate (saves damage to entry of trailer)	200.00
• Internal rail reinforcement (saves damage to lower rail and back panels)	500.00
• Stainless steel screws for light attachment (savings on replacement cost)	200.00
• Domestic oak premium floor—$1\frac{3}{8}$ (should last 10 years under normal conditions)	1,000.00
• Doors—aluminum inner and outer skin, outside white finish, inside mill finish, fastened by five aluminum hinges (savings over life of trailer)	750.00
• Five-year warranty in addition to standard warranty covers bulkhead rust, LED lights, floor, scuff liner, glad hands, rear frame, mudflap assembly, and threshold plate (Phoenix provides a higher trade-in value)	1,500.00
Total approximate savings of Phoenix over 10-year period (all the preceding is standard equipment on a Phoenix; this trailer will sell for $23,500; an FB standard trailer would sell for $19,500)	$10,750.00
Less additional initial cost of Phoenix over FB standard	4,000.00
Overall cost savings of Phoenix over FB trailer	$ 6,750.00

Another way to quantify the solution is to calculate return on investment (ROI). As products and services become more complex and more expensive, customers are more likely to look at the financial reasons for buying. This is especially true in business-to-business selling. Salespeople who can develop a sales proposal that contains specific information on return on investment are more likely to get a favorable response from key decision makers. Chief financial officers, for example, are more inclined to approve an expensive purchase if it results in a good return on investment.[22]

Performing accurate ROI calculations often requires the collection of detailed financial information. You may need to help the prospect collect information within the company to build a case for the purchase. BAX Global offers customers multi-modal shipping solutions. It has the capabilities to employ more than one mode of transportation for a customer. In order to develop a customized solution for the customer, the sales representative must collect a great deal of financial and nonfinancial data from the prospect. Transportation modes (trucks, airplanes, railroads, etc.) vary in terms of cost, speed, dependability, frequency, and other criteria, so preparation of the sales proposal can be a complicated process.[23]

The use of ROI selling appeals requires more work upfront, but it often leads to shorter sales cycles. The salesperson who is not well schooled in financial issues, and cannot compute and supply price information accurately, may be at a serious disadvantage. In Chapter 7, we discuss how to position products according to price.

Know Your Company

We should never underestimate information about the company itself as a strong appeal that can be used during the sales presentation. This is especially true when the customer is considering a strategic alliance. Before teaming up with another company, the strategic alliance buyer will want to learn a great deal about the firm the salesperson represents. In many cases, you are selling your company as much or more as you are selling a product.

Some companies such as Microsoft, Four Seasons Hotels, and American Express have what might be called "brand power." These companies, and the products offered to consumers, are quite well known. However, if you are selling loudspeakers made by Klipsch or financial services offered by Van Kampen Equity, you may find it necessary to spend considerable time providing information about the company. In this section we examine the types of information needed in most selling situations.

A quick response to a customer's questions about product configurations or pricing can serve as a product strategy improvement within the sales process. This salesperson is adding value by using his notebook computer and cell phone to access and quickly communicate information.

Company Culture and Organization

Many salespeople take special pride in the company they work for. Salespeople employed by Cisco Systems feel good about the company's high ranking on *Fortune* magazine's list of the 100 best companies to work for. This network-equipment provider survived the dot-com bubble burst and has recorded record sales in recent years.[24]

As noted in Chapter 5, character and integrity are the hallmark of a successful sales organization. Michael L. Eskew, chairman and CEO, UPS Incorporated, says, "The strategies change and the purpose changes, but the values never change."[25]

Every organization has its own unique culture. **Organizational culture** is a collection of beliefs, behaviors, and work patterns held in common by people employed by a specific firm. Most organizations over a period of time tend to take on distinct norms and practices. At GEAR for Sports, employees are guided by a statement of values that communicates what is held important by the company (Figure 6.2). Research indicates that the customer orientation of a firm's salespeople is influenced by the organization's culture. A supportive culture that encourages salespeople to offer tailor-made solutions to buyer problems sets the stage for long-term partnerships.[26]

Many prospects use the past performance of a company to evaluate the quality of the current product offering. If the company has enjoyed success in the past, there is good reason to believe that the future will be bright.

Company Support for Product

Progressive marketers support the products they sell. In some cases, product support takes the form of sales tools that can be used in preparation for a sales call or during a sales call. Hunter Douglas, a manufacturer of window fashions, has developed a Dealer Merchandising Portfolio. A dealer sales representative can select and order sample books, brochures, videos, in-store display material, and many other items.[27]

Company support after the sale is also very important. Olin Mathieson, a major chemical corporation, regularly checks with customers to get their reaction to services and keep real needs in perspective. Jagemann Stamping Company, a tool-and-die firm in Manitowoc, Wisconsin, often uses a sales team made up of a salesperson, an engineer, and line workers.

FIGURE 6.2

GEAR For Sports® Vision

Guided by our GEAR values, we strive to be the leader in quality and delivery of our customer's image through marketing innovative sportswear, accessories and services.

GEAR Values

GEAR For Sports' business is predicated on respect for, and attention to, all of our customers, business partners, employees, government and community. We value:

Customers
by exceeding their expectations.

Excellence
by taking pride and responsibility in everything we do.

Employees
by demonstrating respect and consideration for each other.

Teamwork
by fostering trust and recognition among all stakeholders.

Professionalism
by exhibiting integrity and proficiency.

Innovation
by embracing creativity and change.

Social Responsibility
by caring for and sharing with each other and our community.

At GEAR for Sports, the employees are guided by a statement of values that communicates what is held important by the company. Shared values are especially important when the sales process involves development of strategic partnerships.

Source: Courtesy of GEAR for Sports.

Line workers can often answer the technical questions raised by a customer. Whenever there is a problem or defect, a small group of line workers is sent out with either a salesperson or an engineer to investigate. This involvement raises the worker's commitment to the customer.[28]

Know Your Competition

Acquiring knowledge of your competition is another important step toward developing complete product knowledge. Salespeople who have knowledge of their competitor's strengths and weaknesses are better able to emphasize the benefits they offer and add value. Prospects often raise specific questions concerning competing firms. If you cannot provide answers or if your answers are vague, the sale may be lost.

Your Attitude Toward Your Competition

Regardless of how impressive your product is, the customer naturally seeks information about similar products sold by other companies. Therefore, you must acquire facts about competing products before the sales presentation. It has never been easier to obtain information about competing products. Check the competitor's Web site, annual reports, press releases, and marketing material. Once armed with this information, you are more confident in your ability to handle questions about the competition.

The attitude you display toward your competition is of the utmost importance. Every salesperson should develop a set of basic beliefs about the best way of dealing with competing products. A few helpful guidelines follow:

1. *In most cases, do not refer to the competition during the sales presentation.* This shifts the focus of attention to competing products, which is usually not desirable.

2. *Never discuss the competition unless you have all your facts straight.* Your credibility suffers if you make inaccurate statements. If you do not know the answer to a specific question, simply say, "I do not know."

3. *Never criticize the competition.* You may be called on to make direct comparisons between your product and competing products. In these situations, stick to the facts and avoid emotional comments about apparent or real weaknesses.

4. *Be prepared to add value.* The competition may come to your prospect with a comparative advantage in price, delivery, or some other area. Be prepared to neutralize the competitor's proposal with a value-added approach. If your competitor has slow delivery, encourage the customer to talk about why prompt delivery is important.[29]

Customers appreciate an accurate, fair, and honest presentation of the facts. They generally resent highly critical remarks about the competition. Avoid mudslinging at all costs. Fairness is a virtue that people greatly admire.

Become an Industry Expert

Salespeople need to become experts in the industry they represent. In many cases this means moving beyond the role of product specialist and becoming a business analyst. Staying current and developing an understanding of business processes takes time and may require additional education.[30] If your clients work in the banking industry, read the appropriate trade journals and become active in professional associations that serve bankers' needs.

Sources of Product Information

There are several sources of product information available to salespeople. Some of the most common include (1) product literature developed by the company, (2) sales training programs, (3) plant tours, (4) internal sales and sales support team members, (5) customers, (6) product, and (7) publications.

Product Literature, Catalogs, and Web-Based Sources

Most companies prepare materials that provide a detailed description of their product. This information is usually quite instructional, and salespeople should review it carefully. If the company markets a number of products, a sales catalog is usually developed. To save salespeople time, many companies give them computer software that provides a constantly updated, online product catalog. Advertisements, promotional brochures, and audio-cassettes also can be a valuable source of product information.

Mitsubishi Caterpillar Forklift America presents its basic product information online, so it's available to dealer representatives in the privacy of their homes, hotel rooms, or wherever else they bring their laptops. Each of the seven product information courses takes about an hour. To reinforce basic product knowledge, the company offers advanced instructor-led courses.[31] Some companies are using interactive distance learning (delivered via satellite) to present different types of sales training.

Plant Tours

Many companies believe that salespeople should visit the manufacturing plant and see the production process firsthand. Such tours not only provide valuable product information but also increase the salesperson's enthusiasm for the product. A new salesperson may spend

Knowing, understanding, and being able to clarify information in product literature adds value within the sales process. Customers seek out the "product experts" who can assist them in making intelligent buying decisions.

Customer Relationship Management with Technology

STARTING FAST WITH CRM

New salespeople can be overwhelmed by the amount of information they need to master. This includes information about the company and its processes, products, and customers. Companies can now make learning easier with information technology. Information about the company and its processes can be stored on the company's network, on its virtual private network (VPN), or on CD-ROM disks. Computer-based training (CBT) permits new employees to learn at their own pace about products—specifications, features, benefits, uses, and selling points.

Companies can now provide salespeople with software that they can use accurately and effectively to create product solutions. Electronic configuration software allows salespeople to select the components necessary to assemble a custom-tailored solution to meet their prospects' needs. This software guides users through the product selection process while assuring that the components are compatible with one another.

Companies can deliver a rich body of customer information to new salespeople through the strong commitment to the use of customer relationship management software. The salesperson who carefully records her business and relationship contacts with customers and prospects over time accumulates a valuable store of information. A new salesperson taking over these accounts can quickly "come up to speed" with these people and their needs. (See the exercise "Finding Product Information in CRM" on p. 136 for more information.)

several days at the plant getting acquainted with the production process. Experienced personnel within the organization also can benefit from plant tours.

Internal Sales and Sales Support Team Members

Team selling has become popular, in part, because many complex sales require the expertise of several sales and sales support personnel. Expertise in the areas of product design, finance, or transportation may be needed to develop an effective sales proposal. Pooled commissions are sometimes used to encourage team members to share information and work as a team.

Customers

Persons who actually use the product can be an important source of information. They have observed its performance under actual working conditions and can provide an objective assessment of the product's strengths and weaknesses. Some companies collect testimonials from satisfied customers and make this persuasive information available to the sales staff. Patagonia customers include mountain bikers, backcountry skiers, sailors, paddlers, and fly fisherman. The company's success lies in maintaining a close connection to persons who actually use their products.[32]

Salespeople employed by semiconductor manufacturer Intel Corporation are expected to take the company's business customers from the conceptual stage of their purchase all the way to delivery of the finished product. The dialogue with the customer begins very early in the sales cycle when the customer needs help designing their end product.[33] This approach requires the empowerment of the sales force with greater depth and breath of product information.

Product

The product itself should not be overlooked as a source of valuable information. Salespeople should closely examine and, if possible, use each item they sell to become familiar with its features. Investigation, use, and careful evaluation of the product provide a salesperson with additional confidence.

Publications

Trade and technical publications such as *Supermarket Business* and *Advertising Age* provide valuable product information. Popular magazines and the business section of the

E-learning has become popular because it is inexpensive and fast, and it can be geared to the flexible schedules of salespeople. This regional sales team is receiving sales training from the company's home office.

newspaper also offer salespeople considerable information about their products and their competition. A number of publications such as *Consumer Reports* test products extensively and report the findings in nontechnical language for the benefit of consumers. These reports are a valuable source of information.

Word of Caution

Is it possible to be overly prepared? Can salespeople know too much about the products and services they sell? The answer to both questions is generally no. Communication problems can arise, however, if the salesperson does not accurately gauge the prospect's level of understanding. There is always the danger that a knowledgeable salesperson can overwhelm the potential buyer with facts and figures. This problem can be avoided when salespeople adopt the feature–benefit strategy.

Adding Value with a Feature–Benefit Strategy

Frederick W. Smith, founder of Federal Express, first proposed the concept of overnight delivery in a paper that he wrote as an undergraduate at Yale University. The now-famous paper was given a C by his professor. Many years later, Smith said, "I don't think that we understood our real goal when we first started Federal Express. We thought that we were selling the transportation of goods; in fact, we were selling peace of mind."[34]

Throughout this chapter, we emphasize the importance of acquiring information on the features of your product, company, and competition. Now it is important to point out that successful sales presentations translate product features into benefits that meet a specific need expressed by the customer. The "peace of mind" that Frederick W. Smith mentioned is a good example of a buyer benefit. Only when a product feature is converted to a buyer benefit does it make an impact on the customer.

Distinguish Between Features and Benefits

To be sure we understand the difference between a product feature and a benefit, let us define these two terms.

A **feature** is data, facts, or characteristics of your product or service. Features often relate to craftsmanship, design, durability, and economy of operation. They may reveal how the product was developed, processed, or manufactured. Product features often are described in the technical section of the written sales proposal and in the literature provided by the manufacturer.

A **benefit** is whatever provides the customer with a personal advantage or gain. It answers the question, "How will I benefit from owning or using the product?" If you mention to a prospect that a certain tire has a four-ply rating, you are talking about a product feature. If you go on to point out that this tire provides greater safety, lasts longer, and improves gas mileage, you are pointing out benefits.

GENERAL VERSUS SPECIFIC BENEFITS Neil Rackham, author of *The SPIN Selling Fieldbook*, says that a statement can only be a benefit if it meets a specific need expressed by the buyer. When you link a benefit to a buyer's expressed need, you demonstrate that you can help solve a problem that has been described by the customer. A general benefit shows how a feature can be helpful to a buyer, but it does not relate to a specific need expressed by the buyer. Here are two examples of specific benefits:

> "Our water purification system meets the exact specifications you have given us for EPA compliance."
>
> "Our XP400 model meets the safety criteria you've spelled out."

Rackham says that benefit statements linked to the customer's expressed need (key benefits) are especially effective in large or complex sales.[35]

Some sales training programs suggest that salespeople need to include advantages in the sales presentation. Advantages are characteristics of the product (features) that can be used or will help the buyer. Consider the following statement:

> *"Prior to shipping, all of our containers are double wrapped. This means that our product is completely free of contamination when it arrives at your hospital."*

Some salespeople develop an advantage statement for each important product feature. Unfortunately, these advantages are often included in the sales presentation even when the buyer has not expressed a need for this information. When this happens, the advantage can be described as a general benefit.

Successful salespeople focus on specific benefits that relate to an explicit need expressed by the customer. Less successful salespeople take the position that the best way to create value is to present as many benefits as possible. Today's customer measures value by how well your product benefits fit their specific needs. They use a "shotgun" approach to benefits, assuming that more benefits create higher volume. High-performance salespeople work hard to discover which benefits the customer really cares about.[36]

Use Bridge Statements

We know that people buy benefits, not features. One of the best ways to present benefits is to use a bridge statement. A **bridge statement** is a transitional phrase that connects a statement of features with a statement of benefits. This method permits customers to connect the features of your product to the benefits they receive. A sales representative of Fleming Companies, Inc., might use bridge statements to introduce a new snack food.

> "This product is nationally advertised, *which means* you will benefit from more presold customers."
>
> "You will experience faster turnover and increased profits *because* the first order includes point-of-purchase advertising materials that focus on the Valentine's Day promotion you have planned."

Some companies prefer to state the benefit first and the feature second. When this occurs, the bridge statement may be a word such as "because."

TABLE 6.2   Selling Product Benefits with a Feature–Benefit Worksheet

Salespeople employed by a hotel can enhance the sales presentation by converting features to benefits.

FEATURE	BENEFIT
Facilities	
The hotel conference rooms were recently redecorated.	This means all your meetings will be held in rooms that are attractive as well as comfortable.
All our guest rooms were completely redecorated during the past six months and most were designated as nonsmoking rooms.	This means your people will find the rooms clean and attractive. In addition, they can easily select a nonsmoking room.
Food Services	
We offer four different banquet entrees prepared by Ricardo Guido, who was recently selected Executive Chef of the Year by the National Restaurant Association.	This means your conference will be enhanced by delicious meals served by a well-trained staff.
Our hotel offers 24-hour room service.	This means your people can order food or beverage at their convenience.

Identify Features and Benefits

A careful analysis of the product helps identify both product features and buyer benefits. Once all the important features are identified, arrange them in logical order. Then write beside each feature the most important benefit the customer can derive from that feature. Finally, prepare a series of bridge statements to connect the appropriate features and benefits. By using this three-step approach, a hotel selling conference and convention services and a manufacturer selling electric motors used to power mining equipment developed feature–benefit worksheets (Tables 6.2 and 6.3). Notice how each feature is translated into a benefit that would be important to someone purchasing these products and services. Table 6.3 reminds us that company features can be converted to benefits.

Avoiding Information Overload

Knowing your product has always been essential to good selling, but concentrating on product alone can be a serious mistake. Salespeople who love their products, and possess vast product knowledge, sometimes overload their customers with product data they neither need nor want. This practice is often described as a "data dump." With the aid of specific types of questions (see Chapter 11), the customer's needs can be identified. Once the customer's needs are known, the salesperson can develop a customized sales presentation that includes selected features that can be converted to specific benefits.

TABLE 6.3   Selling Company Benefits with a Feature–Benefit Worksheet

Here we see company features translated into customer benefits.

FEATURE	BENEFIT
Our company has . . .	This means for you . . .
1. The best selection of motors in the area	• Choice of the best models to interface with your current equipment • Equipment operates more efficiently
2. Certified service technicians	• Well-qualified service personnel keep your equipment in top running condition • Less downtime and higher profits

Chapter Learning Activities

Reviewing Key Concepts

Explain the importance of developing a product strategy

A product strategy helps salespeople make the right decisions concerning the selection and positioning of products to meet specific customer needs. It is a carefully conceived plan that emphasizes becoming a product expert, selling specific benefits, and configuring value-added solutions.

Describe product configuration

Product configuration involves decisions regarding which product applications or combination of applications can solve the buying problem. In the era of information overload, product selection has become more challenging. In some cases product configuration software is used to develop customized product solutions.

Identify reasons why salespeople and customers benefit from thorough product knowledge

A salesperson whose product knowledge is complete and accurate is better able to identify and satisfy customer needs. Additional advantages to be gained from thorough product knowledge include greater self-confidence, increased enthusiasm, improved ability to develop stronger selling appeals, and improved ability to overcome objections.

Discuss the most important kinds of product and company information needed to create product solutions

Salespeople should possess product knowledge that meets or exceeds customer expectations. Some important product information categories include product development and quality improvement processes, performance data and specifications, maintenance and service contracts, and price and delivery.

Information about the company can be used to develop strong appeals that can enhance the sales presentation. This is especially true when the customer is considering a strategic alliance. Important company information includes an understanding of the firm's culture and organization, and company support for products offered.

Describe how knowledge of competition improves personal selling

Prospects often raise specific questions concerning competing firms. Salespeople who have knowledge of their competitors' strengths and weaknesses are better able to emphasize the benefits they offer and add value. The attitude you display toward your competition is of the utmost importance.

List major sources of product information

Salespeople gather information from many sources. Company literature and sales training programs are among the most important. Other sources include factory tours, customers, competition, publications, the Internet, and actual experience with the product itself.

Explain how to add value with a feature–benefit strategy

In the sales presentation and in preparing the written sales proposal, your knowledge of the product's features and your company's strengths must be presented in terms of the resulting benefits to the buyer. We distinguished between general and specific benefits. Specific benefits, linked to a customer's expressed need, are very effective.

Key Terms

Product strategy	Written proposals	Organizational culture
Solution	Product development	Feature
Solution selling	Quality control	Benefit
Product configuration	Quantifying the solution	Bridge statement

Review Questions

1. Provide a brief description of the term *product strategy*.

2. Distinguish between *product features* and *buyer benefits*.

3. What is *product configuration*? Provide an example of how this practice is used in the sale of commercial stereo equipment.

4. Review the GEAR for Sports' statement of values and then identify the two items that you believe contribute the most to a salesperson's career success.

5. Define the term *organizational culture*. How might this company information enhance a sales presentation?

6. Basic beliefs underlie the salesperson's method of handling competition. What are four guidelines a salesperson should follow in developing basic beliefs in this area?

7. Explain what the customer's expectations are concerning the salesperson's attitude toward competition.

8. List and briefly describe the five parts included in most written sales proposals.

9. What are the most common sources of product information?

10. Distinguish between a general benefit and a specific benefit. Why do customers respond positively to specific benefits?

Application Exercises

1. Secure, if possible, a copy of a customer-oriented product sales brochure or news release that has been prepared by a marketer. Many salespeople receive such selling tools. Study this information carefully; then develop a feature–benefit analysis sheet.

2. Today many companies are automating their product configuration and proposal writing activities. Go to the Internet and find these providers of the following software: www.bigmachines.com/salesforece.php and www.results-online.com. Click on each company's demonstration software and study the design of each product.

3. Select a product you are familiar with and know a great deal about. (This may be an item you have shopped for and purchased, such as a compact disc player, laptop computer, or an automobile.) Under each of the categories listed, fill in the required information about the product.

   a. Where did you buy the product? Why?

   b. Did product design influence your decision?

   c. How and where was the product manufactured?

   d. What different applications or uses are there for the product?

   e. How does the product perform? Are there any data on the product's performance? What are they?

   f. What kinds of maintenance and care does the product require? How often?

   g. Could you sell the product you have written about in categories (a) through (f)? Why or why not?

Role-Play Exercise

Study the convention center information in Part 1, Developing a Sales-Oriented Product Strategy, in Appendix 3, paying special attention to pricing on the meals and meeting rooms. Access the www.prenhal.com/manning Web site. Click on the sales proposal link and configure a sales proposal for your instructor (using your school name and address), who is responsible for setting up a student awards meeting. The meeting includes a banquet-style meal of Chicken Wellington for 26 attendees from 5:30 P.M. to 8:00 P.M. on the last Wednesday of next month. The meal will be served at 5:45 P.M., and the awards session is scheduled from 6:45 to 8:00 P.M. in the same room. The seating should be banquet style. Present the completed proposal to another student (acting as your customer) and communicate the features and benefits of your proposal.

CRM Application Exercise

Finding Product Information in CRM

Providing immediate access to product information can increase a salesperson's efficiency and responsiveness to customer requests. Computers excel at the task of quickly providing information. An example can be found in the Salesforce.com CRM case study software. Basic information about networks is available in the Documents section. After logging on the Salesforce.com, select the Documents tab, and then select the Product Information folder. Choose any of the available documents by clicking on "View," then "Open." Print the document. Using the same e-mail procedure in the CRM Application Exercise "Preparing Letters with CRM" from Chapter 3, page 71, attach this document to a new e-mail. After revising the e-mail template, click the Attach File button. In the drop-down list, select the Product Information folder; then choose the document you want to send. Click "Attach," then "Done." After reviewing your e-mail, press "Send."

Reality Selling Today Video Case Problem

Amy Vandaveer
Texas Monthly

Texas Monthly is a regional magazine covering politics, business, and culture, but focusing largely on leisure activities and events in Texas. The magazine has a large real estate advertising section, as well as classified sections in which nearly all advertisers are Texas-based businesses appealing to a prospective buyer who is interested in connecting with Texas history and culture. It also has a large, loyal reader base all over Texas, mostly urban, well educated, and affluent; and the magazine's salespeople pride themselves on their ability to find creative solutions for their customers.

Today, Amy Vandaveer, a sales representative for *Texas Monthly*, is meeting with the marketing director for the Woodlands Town Center, a major community development organization. The Woodlands is a planned community outside of Houston, and the recently added Woodlands Town Center includes restaurants, shops, and a hotel and convention center.

The marketing director's goal is to make the Woodlands Town Center a destination for Houston residents, rather than another area serving people who already live in the Woodlands. Up to this point, the Woodlands Town Center has mostly relied on word of mouth and the positive publicity that it received after winning awards to attract visitors; now, the marketing director is interested in using more print advertising and has scheduled this meeting with Amy to learn more about the possibilities of advertising with *Texas Monthly.*

As a rule, Amy uses relatively informal presentations on her sales calls. The most significant part of her presentation is a copy of *Texas Monthly*; showing potential customers a recent issue gives them the opportunity to see the magazine's overall look and feel, as well as giving them a good look at the context in which their ads would appear. Over the course of the informal presentation, Amy also shows the customer statistics on the reader base of *Texas Monthly* and the ways in which they respond to ads in the magazine, as well as a price sheet for various types of ads.

After listening to what the Woodlands Town Center needs, Amy proposes a four-page color ad, which can also be printed separately from the magazine for use as a brochure. Although the price depends on the number of stand-alone brochures that are ordered, she estimates that the cost of the ad would be about $50,000. The marketing director and Amy agree on a timeline for a more formal proposal that can be shared with the rest of the Woodlands Town Center board, and Amy moves on to the rest of her day. (See chapter opener on p. 118 and Reality Selling Today Video Role-Play 3 in Appendix 1 on p. 396 for more information.).

Questions

1. Explain how Amy Vandaveer can use the three prescriptions for a product selling strategy in preparing and presenting product solutions.

2. What are the major benefits that Amy incorporates into her presentation?

3. What are the most likely objections that the marketing director might raise?

4. In addition to the actual product strategy, how important will information about *Texas Monthly* (its history, mission, past performance, etc.) be in closing the sale?

Partnership Selling: A Role-Play/Simulation

Developing a Product Strategy

Read Employment Memorandum 1 in Appendix 3, which introduces you to your new training position with the Hotel Convention Center. You also should study the product strategy materials that follow the memo to become familiar with the company, product, and competitive knowledge you need in your new position.

Read the Customer Service/Sales Memorandum in Part I of Appendix 3 and complete the two-part customer/service assignment provided by your sales manager. In item 1, you are to configure a price/product sales proposal; in item 2 you are to write a sales cover letter for the sales proposal. Note that the information presented in the price/product sales proposal consists of product facts/features, and the information presented in your sales cover letter should present specific benefit statements. These forms should be custom-fitted to meet the specific needs of your customer, B. H. Rivera. All the product information you need is in the product strategy materials provided as enclosures and attachments to Employment Memorandum 1.

7

Product-Selling Strategies That Add Value

Chapter Preview

When you finish reading this chapter, you should be able to

1
Describe positioning as a product-selling strategy

2
Explain the cluster of satisfactions concept

3
Discuss product-positioning options

4
Explain how to sell your product with a price strategy

5
Explain how to sell your product with a value-added strategy

▶ Introduction

You have just finished paying off your college loans and it's time to replace that old rust bucket with a new car. You have looked at the sport-compact cars available, but they all seem so small. Now you are eagerly looking at cars in the sports-sedan category. The cars in this niche offer a good blend of comfort, design, and performance. However, there are almost too many choices. *Road & Track* says there are 11 different automobiles in this group. The list price for these cars ranges from $29,000 to $40,000. The Audi A4 and Saab 9-3 offer all-wheel drive; all the rest offer front- or rear-wheel drive. As you learn more about the choices available, it becomes clear that each manufacturer has taken steps to differentiate its product.[1]

Several years ago, automobile manufacturers from around the world began to develop and position cars for the sports-sedan segment. Research indicated that demand for these cars would increase. The result was the introduction of 11 different marques, each with its own unique characteristics. At the dealer level, the process of product differentiation continues. If you want something more than standard equipment, the salesperson can describe a variety of options that can add $7,000 to $10,000 to the price. Each car can be accessorized to meet your personal needs. The dealer can also help position this product with modern facilities, customer-friendly service policies, and a reputation for honesty and integrity.

Some automobile manufacturers see the sports-sedan category as critical to their success. At BMW, the 3 Series sports sedan accounts for nearly half of the company's sales worldwide. Sports sedans can be very profitable because many buyers purchase expensive options such as special wheel and tire packages, anti-skid electronics, ground-effects trim, and top-of-the line audio systems.

Salespeople at the dealer in the crowded sports sedan market, play an important role in positioning their brand for competitive advantage. Adding value depends on the salesperson's ability to provide a competitive analysis using knowledge of the manufacturer, the automobile, and the dealership.

Design can play a major role in the sports-sedan market segment. BMW and Audi recently unveiled completely redesigned cars. These new cars will face off against the Infinite G37 and the Cadillac CTS, two cars noted for advanced design.[2]

Salespeople at the dealer level can play an important role in positioning the automobile for competitive advantage. They can describe the quality control process that ensures the build quality of the BMW 330i or demonstrate the sports car driving characteristics of the Lexus IS 350. Adding value depends on the salesperson's ability to provide a competitive analysis using knowledge of the manufacturer, the automobile, and the dealership. ■

Product Positioning—A Product-Selling Strategy

Long-term success in today's dynamic global economy requires the continuous positioning and repositioning of products. **Positioning** involves those decisions and activities intended to create and maintain a certain concept of the firm's product in the customer's mind. It requires developing a marketing strategy aimed at influencing how a particular market segment perceives a product in comparison to the competition.[3] In a market that has been flooded with various types of sport-utility vehicles (SUVs), Land Rover has been positioned as a dependable vehicle that can climb a steep, rock-covered hillside with ease. Every effort has been made to create the perception of safety, durability, and security. To give sales representatives increased confidence in the Land Rover, the company has

Selling Is Everyone's Business

MICHAEL DELL'S EARLY YEARS

At the age of 12, Michael Dell, CEO of Dell Computer Corporation, was displaying the characteristics of an opportunistic entrepreneur. He turned his stamp-collecting hobby into a mail-order business that netted $2,000. This money was used to purchase his first computer. He also developed his personal selling skills at an early age. At age 16, he was selling subscriptions to his hometown paper, the *Houston Post.* Later he enrolled in college but had difficulty focusing on his course work. He often cut classes in order to spend more time assembling and selling computers. When Dell's parents discovered his newest enterprise, they pressured him to stay focused on completing his degree. Dell completed the spring semester and then spent the summer expanding his business. In the month prior to the fall semester, he sold $180,000 worth of computers. He did not return to college.[a]

Michael Dell, CEO of Dell Corporation.

arranged plant tours and the opportunity to observe actual testing of the Land Rover vehicles under extremely demanding conditions.

Good positioning means that the product's name, reputation, and niche are well recognized. However, a good positioning strategy does not last forever. The positioning process must be continually modified to match the customer's changing wants and needs.[4]

Essentials of Product Positioning

Most companies use a combination of marketing and sales strategies to give their products a unique position in the marketplace. Every salesperson needs a good understanding of the fundamental practices that contribute to product positioning. The chapter begins with a brief introduction to the concept of product differentiation. This is followed by an explanation of how products have been redefined in the age of information. The remainder of the chapter is devoted to three product-selling strategies that can be used to position a product. Emphasis is placed on positioning your product with a value-added strategy. In the age of information, salespeople who cannot add value to the products they sell will diminish in number and influence.

Achieving Product Differentiation in Personal Selling

One of the basic tenets of sales and marketing is the principle of product differentiation. **Differentiation** refers to your ability to separate yourself and your product from that of your competitors. It is the key to building and maintaining a competitive advantage.[5] The competitors in virtually all industries are moving toward differentiating themselves on the basis of quality, price, convenience, economy, or some other factor. Salespeople, who are on the front line of many marketing efforts, assume an important role in the product differentiation process.

Differentiating your product helps you stand out from the crowd. It often allows you to distance yourself from the competition. In many cases, the process of differentiation creates barriers that make it difficult for the buyer to choose a competing product simply on the basis of price.[6]

Creating a Value Proposition

A well-informed customer will usually choose the product that offers the most value. Therefore, salespeople need to position their product with a value proposition. A **value**

proposition is the set of benefits and values the company promises to deliver to customers to satisfy their needs. The value proposition presented by Porsche promises driving performance and excitement.[7] Kinko's, which is now part of FedEx, is attempting to differentiate itself from Sir Speedy, AlphaGraphics, and print shops found at Office Depot, OfficeMax, and Staples. The new value proposition promises that 1,200 FedEx Kinko's locations offer a breadth of services unparalleled in the industry. These new centers leverage the traditional strengths and brand awareness of FedEx and Kinko's.[8]

In many situations salespeople must quantify the value proposition. This is especially true when the customer is a business buyer. (Business buyer behavior will be discussed in Chapter 8.) The value quantification process raises customers' comprehension levels as they discover the merits of buying your product or service.[9] Let's assume you are selling Kenworth trucks and one of your customers is Contract Freighters, Inc., based in Joplin, Missouri. This large company is planning to purchase 700 new trucks. Your Kenworth diesel trucks cost 10 percent more than rivals' trucks. Within your proposal you should try to quantify the benefits of buying Kenworth trucks, which may include greater reliability, higher trade-in value, and the plush interiors that will help the buyer attract better drivers.[10]

The Cluster of Satisfactions Concept

Ted Levitt, former editor of the *Harvard Business Review*, says that products are problem-solving tools. People buy products if they fulfill a problem-solving need. Today's better-educated and more demanding customers are seeking a *cluster of satisfactions*. **Satisfactions** arise from the product itself, from the company that makes or distributes the product, and from the salesperson who sells and services the product.[11] Figure 7.1 provides a description of a three-dimensional *Product-Selling Model*. As noted in Chapter 6, many companies are attempting to transform themselves from *product selling* to *solution selling*. To develop and sell solutions, salespeople must be familiar with the satisfactions that meet the needs of each customer.

To illustrate how the cluster of satisfactions concept works in a business setting, let us examine a complex buying decision. Elaine Parker, a sales representative for Elmore Industries Incorporated, sells metals for manufacturing operations. Over a period of six months, she frequently called on a prospect that had the potential to become a valued customer. During every call, the buyer's receptionist told her they were happy with their current supplier. She refused to give up and finally the buyer agreed to see her. At first she was greeted with cool silence, so she decided to ask him some questions about his

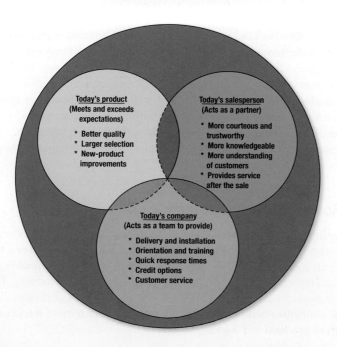

FIGURE 7.1

Product-Selling Model

The product strategy should include a cluster of satisfactions that meets the needs of today's better-educated and more demanding customers. Drawing from this cluster, the salesperson can configure value-added solutions that meet individual customer's needs.

business: "How's the slow economy affecting your sales?" The buyer's answers focused on materials costs. He said his company could not raise prices or cut quality. He wanted to lower costs, but was unsure how it could be done. Parker suggested he consider trying some new alloys that were less expensive than the standard metals he had been purchasing. As she described the new alloys, the buyer's interest began to build. She offered to make a full presentation to the buyer and his engineers at a follow-up meeting. The second meeting was a success. Soon after that meeting, Parker received her first order from the customer. Within a year, she had become the customer's most trusted advisor on technological developments in the industry and his exclusive supplier.[12]

Elaine Parker used questions to engage the customer and identify his problem. She also provided satisfactory answers to questions raised by the customers:

Questions Related to the Product

What product is best for our type of operation?

Does the product meet our quality standards?

Given the cost of this product, will we maintain our competitive position in the marketplace?

Questions Related to the Company

Does this company provide the most advanced technology?

What is the company's reputation for quality products?

What is the company's reputation for standing behind the products it sells?

Questions Related to the Salesperson

Does this salesperson possess the knowledge and experience needed to recommend the right product?

Can the salesperson clearly communicate specific buyer benefits?

Can this salesperson serve as a trusted advisor?

Will this salesperson provide support services after the sale?

Salespeople who are knowledgeable in all areas of the Product-Selling Model are better able to position a product. Knowledge helps you achieve product differentiation, understand the competition, and prepare an effective value proposition. The competitive analysis worksheet (Table 7.1) can help you discover ways to position your product as the superior choice over your competition.

A WORD OF CAUTION Because many of today's information age products are very complex, product differentiation must be handled with care. Salespeople are sometimes tempted to use technical lingo, real and invented, to impress the buyer. This problem often surfaces in a situation in which the salesperson is not sure how to describe the value-added features of the product. Robert Notte, technology chief for travel outfitter Backroads, says that during the telecom boom salespeople representing WorldCom (now MCI) and other firms babbled endlessly, using industry jargon that was often unintelligible. "They wanted you to be impressed," Mr. Notte says. Some customers were so intimidated they were afraid to ask questions . . . or make a buying decision.[13]

Product-Positioning Options

Product positioning is a concept that applies to both new and existing products. Given the dynamics of most markets, it may be necessary to reposition products several times in their lives because even solid, popular products can lose market position quickly. Salespeople have assumed an important and expanding role in differentiating products. To succeed in our overcommunicated society, marketers must use a direct and personalized form of communication with customers. Advertising directed toward a mass market often fails to position a complex product.

TABLE 7.1 **Competitive Analysis Worksheet**

A value-added product selling strategy is enhanced when salespeople analyze product, company, and salesperson attributes of the competition in relation to the benefits they offer. This information helps the salesperson create value within the sales process.

	MY COMPANY	COMPETITOR A	COMPETITOR B
Product Attributes			
Quality			
Durability			
Reliability			
Performance			
Packaging flexibility			
Warranty			
Brand			
Company Attributes			
Reputation			
Industry leadership			
Facilities			
Ease of doing business			
Distribution channels			
Ordering convenience			
Returns, credits, etc.			
Salesperson Attributes			
Knowledge/expertise			
Responsiveness			
Pricing authority			
Customer orientation			
Honesty/Integrity			
Follow-through			
Presentation skills			

Throughout the remainder of this chapter, we discuss specific ways to use various product-positioning strategies. We explain how salespeople can (1) position new and emerging products versus well-established products, (2) position products with price strategies, and (3) position products with value-added strategies.

Selling New and Emerging Products Versus Mature and Well-Established Products

In many ways, products are like human beings. They are born, grow up, mature, and grow old. In marketing, this process is known as the **product life cycle**. The product life cycle includes the stages a product goes through from the time it is first introduced to the market until it is discontinued. As the product moves through its cycle, the strategies relating to competition, promotion, pricing, and other factors must be evaluated and possibly changed. The nature and extent of each stage in the product life cycle are determined by several factors, including:

1. The product's perceived advantage over available substitutes
2. The product's benefits and the importance of the needs it fulfills
3. Competitive activity, including pricing, substitute product development and improvement, and effectiveness of competing advertising and promotion
4. Changes in technology, fashion, or demographics[14]

As we attempt to develop a product-selling strategy, we must consider where the product is positioned in terms of the life cycle. The sales strategy used to sell a new and emerging product is much different from the strategy used to sell a mature, well-established product (Figure 7.2).

Customer Relationship Management with Technology

Today salespeople are challenged to manage a steady stream of information about customers (needs) and products (solutions). From this stream of information, the sale professional must select product information that is relevant to a specific customer and deliver the information in a manner that can be understood by the customer. Customer relationship management (CRM) assists the busy salesperson by providing tools that can collect information and link it to those who need it. Most CRM systems can receive and organize information from e-mail, Web sites, and the files of reference material kept within the company's information system. Sales professionals can add value to this information by summarizing, combining, and tailoring the information to meet a customer's needs.

When new-product information is received, databases of customer data can be quickly searched to find those customers who might have an interest. The new-product information can be merged into an e-mail, fax, or letter to that customer, along with other information (benefits) that can help the customer assess its value. Later, the CRM system can display a follow-up alert, reminding the sales professional of the information that was shared with the customer. (See the exercise Informing Customers with CRM on page 155 for more information).

SELLING NEW AND EMERGING PRODUCTS Selling strategies used during the new and emerging stage (see Figure 7.2) are designed to develop a new level of expectation, change habits, and in some cases establish a new standard of quality. The goal is to build desire for the product. Highly talented and resourceful salespeople are needed during the product initiation phase. Salespeople must be resourceful, possess information regarding every aspect of the product, and be able to present a convincing value proposition.[15]

When Brother International Corporation introduced its line of Multi-Function Center (MFC) machines, the goal was to convince buyers that one machine could replace five separate machines. However, before buyers would give up their copy machine, fax machine, laser printer, and other machines, they asked some hard questions. Is a multifunction machine reliable? Does the quality match that of the current machines? Finding the best machine for each customer is challenging because Brother offers more than 10 different MFC models to choose from.

FIGURE 7.2

Product-Selling Strategies for Positioning New and Emerging Products Versus Mature and Well-Established Products

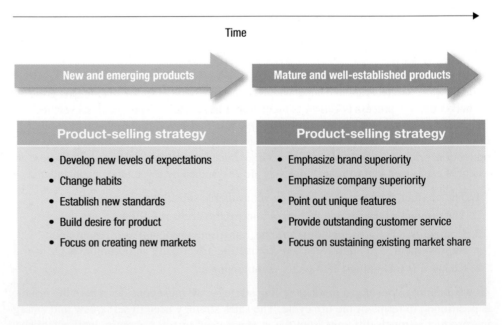

In some cases the new product is not a tangible item. Several years ago IntraLinks closed its first big sale, a $50,000 contract, with J. P. Morgan. The company got its start providing the financial services industry with the secure transmission of highly confidential information across the Internet. Patrick Wack and his business partners convinced J. P. Morgan and other financial firms that they did not need to rely on an army of foot messengers and FedEx trucks to deliver sensitive documents. They were not only selling a new product; they were selling a vision that included new levels of expectations. The value proposition focused on faster, more secure document transfer, which, in the customer's mind, translated into improved customer service and cost savings. Today Patrick Wack is selling this document transfer concept to customers in a variety of business communities.[16]

SELLING MATURE AND WELL-ESTABLISHED PRODUCTS Mature and well-established products are usually characterized by intense competition as new brands enter the market. Customers who currently buy your product will become aware of competing products. With new and emerging products, salespeople may initially have little or no competition and may dominate the market; however, this condition may not last long.

New York Life Insurance Company provides its sales agents with new products almost every year. The product portfolio was recently expanded to include the Asset Preserver, which allows the policy death benefit to be accelerated, on an income tax-free basis, to pay for long-term care services. The company also developed the Universal Life Protector, which offers long-term protection at lower prices. New products offered by a market leader are quickly copied by competing insurance companies. When competing products enter the market, New York Life agents must adopt new strategies. One positioning strategy is to emphasize the company's 150 years of outstanding service to policyholders. They can also note that New York Life is a "mutual" company; it is owned by policyholders, not corporate shareholders. The objective is to create in the customer's mind the perception that New York Life is a solid company that will be strong and solvent when it's time to pay premiums.[17]

The relationship strategy is often critical in selling mature and well-established products. To maintain market share and ward off competitors, many salespeople work hard to maintain a strong relationship with the customer. At New York Life, salespeople have found that good service after the sale is one of the best selling strategies because it builds customer loyalty.

Selling Products with a Price Strategy

Price, promotion, product, and place are the four elements that make up the marketing mix. Pricing decisions must be made at each stage of the product life cycle. Therefore, setting the price can be a complex process. The first step in establishing price is to determine the firm's pricing objectives. Some firms set their prices to maximize their profits. They aim for a price as high as possible without causing a disproportionate reduction in unit sales. Other firms set a market share objective. Management may decide that the strategic advantage of an increased market share outweighs a temporary reduction in profits. Many of the new companies doing business on the Internet adopt this approach.

Pricing strategies often reflect the product's position in the product life cycle. When large, high-definition flat-screen TVs were in the new and emerging stage, customers who wanted this innovative product were willing to pay $5,000 or more for a unit.

TRANSACTIONAL SELLING TACTICS THAT EMPHASIZE LOW PRICE Some marketers have established a positioning plan that emphasizes low price and the use of transactional selling tactics. These companies maintain a basic strategy that focuses on meeting competition. If the firm has meeting competition as its pricing goal, it makes every effort to charge prices that are identical or close to those of the competition.

Once this positioning strategy has been adopted, the sales force is given several price tactics to use. Salespeople can alter (lower) the base price through the use of discounts and allowances. Discounts and allowances can take a variety of forms. A few of the more common ones follow:

Quantity discount. The quantity discount allows the buyer a lower price for purchasing in multiple units or above a specified dollar amount.

Seasonal discount. With seasonal pricing, the salesperson adjusts the price up or down during specific times to spur or acknowledge changes in demand. Off-season travel and lodging prices provide examples.

Promotional allowance. A promotional allowance is a price reduction given to a customer who participates in an advertising or a sales support program. Many salespeople give supermarkets promotional allowances for advertising or displaying a manufacturer's products.

Trade or functional discounts. Channel intermediaries, such as wholesalers, often perform credit, storage, or transportation services. Trade or functional discounts cover the cost of these services.[18]

Another option available to salespeople facing a buyer with a low-price buying strategy is to "unbundle" product features. Let's assume that a price-conscious customer wants to schedule a conference that will be accompanied by a banquet-style meal. To achieve a lower price, the salesperson might suggest a cafeteria-style meal, thereby eliminating the need for servers. This product configuration involves less cost to the seller, and cost savings can be passed on to the buyer. Timken Company, a century-old bearing maker, has adopted bundling as a way to compete with other manufacturers around the world. The company now surrounds its basic products with additional components in order to provide customers with exactly what they need. These components can take the form of electronic sensors, lubrication systems, castings, or installation and maintenance. Giving customers bundling options has given Timken a big advantage over foreign competitors who often focus on the basic product. Salespeople who represent Timken have flexible pricing options.[19]

Selling in Action

HOW DO CUSTOMERS JUDGE SERVICE QUALITY?

In the growing service industry, there is intense price competition. From a distance, one gets the impression that every buyer decision hinges on price alone. However, a closer examination of service purchases indicates that service quality is an important factor when it comes to developing a long-term relationship with customers.

How do customers judge service quality? Researchers at Texas A&M University have discovered valuable insights about customer perceptions of service quality. They surveyed hundreds of customers in a variety of service industries and discovered that five service-quality dimensions emerged:

1. *Tangibles*: Details the customers can see, such as the appearance of personnel and equipment.

2. *Reliability*: The ability to perform the desired service dependably, accurately, and consistently.

3. *Responsiveness*: The willingness of sales and customer service personnel to provide prompt service and help customers.

4. *Assurance*: The employees' knowledge, courtesy, and ability to convey trust and confidence.

5. *Empathy*: The provision of caring, individualized attention to customers.

Customers apparently judge the quality of each service transaction in terms of these five quality dimensions. Companies need to review these service-quality dimensions and make sure that each area measures up to customers' expectations. Salespeople should recognize that these dimensions have the potential to add value to the services they sell.[b]

Source: Agency Sales Magazine from the Manufacturing Agent National Association (MANA). Used with permission..

"WE HAVE QUALITY AND WE HAVE LOW PRICES... WHICH DO YOU WANT?"

These examples represent only a small sample of the many discounts and allowances salespeople use to compete on the basis of price. Price discounting is a competitive tool available to large numbers of salespeople. Excessive focus on low prices and generous discounts, however, can have a negative impact on profits and sales commissions.

CONSEQUENCES OF USING LOW-PRICE TACTICS Pricing is a critical factor in the sale of many products and services. In markets where competition is extremely strong, setting a product's price may be a firm's most complicated and important decision.

The authors of *The Discipline of Market Leaders* encourage business firms to pick one of three disciplines—best price, best product, or best service—and then do whatever is necessary to outdistance the competition. However, the authors caution us not to ignore the other two disciplines: "You design your business to excel in one direction, but you also have to strive to hit the minimum in the others."[20] Prior to using low-price tactics, everyone involved in sales and marketing should answer these questions.

- *Are you selling to high- or low-involvement buyers?* Some people are emotionally involved with respected brands such as BMW, Sony, and Macintosh computers. A part of their identity depends on buying the product they consider the best. Low-involvement buyers care mostly about price.[21]

- *How important is quality in the minds of buyers?* If buyers do not fully understand the price–quality relationship, they may judge the product by its price. For a growing number of customers, long-term value is more important than short-term savings that result from low prices.

- *How important is service?* For many buyers, service is a critical factor. Even online customers, thought to be very interested in price, rate quality of service very highly. This is especially true in business-to-business sales. A survey conducted by Accenture reports that 80 percent of nearly 1,000 corporate buyers rate a strong brand and reliable customer service ahead of low prices when deciding which companies to do business with online.[22]

INFLUENCE OF ELECTRONIC COMMERCE ON PRICING Companies large and small are racing to discover new sales and marketing opportunities on the Internet. Products ranging from personal computers to term insurance can be purchased from various Web sites. Salespeople who are involved primarily in transactional selling and add little or no value to the sales transaction often are not able to compete with online vendors. To illustrate, consider the purchase of insurance. At the present time it is possible to purchase basic term insurance online from InsureMarket.com, AccuQuote.com, and other Web sites. A well-informed buyer, willing to visit several Web sites, can select a policy with a minimum amount of risk. In the case of long-term care insurance, which can pay for health care at home or in a nursing home, the buyer needs the help of a well-trained agent. These policies are complex and the premiums are high.

Investors now have more choices than they have had in the past. Persons who need little or no assistance buying stocks can visit the E*Trade Web site or a similar online discount vendor. The person who wants help selecting a stock can turn to a broker, such as Merrill Lynch or UBS Paine Webber, that offers both full-service and online options. Full-service brokers can survive and may prosper as long as they can add value to the sales transaction. The new economy is reshaping the world of commerce and every buyer has more choices.

Selling Your Product with a Value-Added Strategy

Many progressive marketers have adopted a market plan that emphasizes *value-added strategies.* Companies can add value to their product with one or more intangibles such as better-trained salespeople, increased levels of courtesy, more dependable product deliveries, better service after the sale, and innovations that truly improve the product's value in the eyes of the customer. In today's highly competitive marketplace, these value-added benefits give the company a unique niche and a competitive edge. Companies that don't make selling and delivering high-value solutions a high priority will consistently lose sales to competitors.[23]

To understand fully the importance of the value-added concept in selling, and how to apply it in a variety of selling situations, it helps to visualize every product as being four dimensional. The *total product* is made up of four "possible" products: the generic product, the expected product, the value-added product, and the potential product[24] (Figure 7.3).

GENERIC PRODUCT The **generic product** is the basic, substantive product you are selling. Generic product describes only the product category, for example, life

FIGURE 7.3

The Total Product Concept

An understanding of the four "possible" products is helpful when the salesperson develops a presentation for specific types of customers.

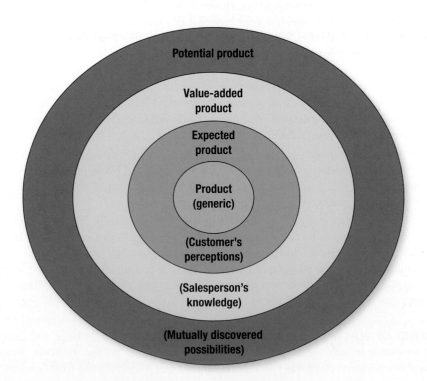

Potential product

Value-added product

Expected product

Product (generic)

(Customer's perceptions)

(Salesperson's knowledge)

(Mutually discovered possibilities)

insurance, rental cars, or personal computers. Every Ritz-Carlton hotel offers guest rooms, one or more full-service restaurants, meeting rooms, guest parking, and other basic services. For Yellow Freight System, a company that provides shipping services, the generic product is the truck and trailer that moves the customer's freight. At the generic level, Nordstrom provides categories of goods traditional to an upscale specialty-clothing retailer. The generic products at a bank are money that can be loaned to customers and basic checking account services.

The capability of delivering a generic product simply gives the marketer the right to play in the game, to compete in the marketplace.[25] Generic products, even the lowest-priced ones, often cannot compete with products that are "expected" by the customer.

EXPECTED PRODUCT Every customer has minimal purchase expectations that exceed the generic product itself.[26] Ritz-Carlton must offer not only a comfortable guest room but also a clean one. Some customers expect a "super" clean room. Yellow Freight System must provide clean, well-maintained trucks *and* well-trained drivers. The **expected product** is everything that represents the customer's minimal expectations. The customer at a Nordstrom store *expects* current fashions and well-informed salespeople.

The minimal purchase conditions vary among customers, so the salesperson must acquire information concerning the expected product that exists in the customer's mind. When the customer expects more than the generic product, the product can be sold *only* if those expectations are met. Every customer perceives the product in individualized terms, which a salesperson cannot anticipate.

Determining each customer's expectations requires the salesperson to make observations, conduct background checks, ask questions, and listen to what the customer is saying. You are attempting to discover both feelings and facts. Top salespeople encourage customers to think more deeply about the problems they face and discover for themselves the value of a solution. They *avoid* offering solutions until the needs are clearly spelled out. If the buyer says, "The average gas mileage for our fleet of delivery trucks is only 17 miles per gallon," the salesperson might respond with this question: "How does this low mileage rate affect your profitability?" To move the customer's attention from the expected product to a value-added product, you need to keep the customer focused on solutions.[27]

Research reported in the *Harvard Business Review* indicates that it is very difficult to build customer loyalty if you are selling only the expected product. Customer satisfaction and loyalty do not always move in tandem. The customer who purchases the services of Ernst & Young Consulting may feel satisfied after the project is completed but never do business with the company again. Customer loyalty is more likely to increase when the purchase involves a value-added product.[28]

Global Business Etiquette

DOING BUSINESS IN INDIA

India is a very large country that is growing in importance in terms of international trade. Indians' customs are often dictated by their religious beliefs. In addition to Hindus and Muslims, there are dozens of other religious groups. Study the Indian culture carefully before your first business trip to this country.

- Customs of food and drink are an important consideration when you do business in India. Avoid eating meat in the presence of Hindus because they are vegetarians and consider the cow a sacred animal. Muslims will not eat pork or drink alcoholic beverages.

- There is a very strict caste system in India so be aware of the caste of the clients with whom you are dealing and any restrictions that may apply to that caste.

- Most members of the Indian business community speak English.

- Indians tend to be careful buyers who seek quality and durability. They respect a salesperson who is caring and well informed. Personal relationships in business transactions are very important.[c]

VALUE-ADDED PRODUCT The **value-added product** exists when salespeople offer customers more than they expect. When you make a reservation at one of the Ritz-Carlton hotels and request a special amenity such as a tennis lesson, a record of this request is maintained in the computer system. If you make a reservation at another Ritz-Carlton at some future date, the agent informs you of the availability of a tennis court. The guest who buys chocolate chip cookies in the lobby gift shop in New Orleans may find a basket of them waiting in his room in Boston two weeks later. The hotel company uses modern technology to surprise and delight guests.[29]

In the mid-1990s, Yellow Freight System was a troubled long-haul carrier offering customers a generic product. Bill Zollars was hired to transform the company by adding a variety of services built around unprecedented customer service. The new services positioned the company to satisfy a broader range of transportation needs. For example, the company launched Yellow's Exact Express, its first time-definite, guaranteed service. Exact Express is now Yellow's most expensive and most profitable service. Today, Yellow Freight System salespeople are able to offer its 300,000 customers a value-added product.[30]

Among the most important factors that contribute to the value-added product is the overall quality of employees the customer has contact with. Sales and sales support staff who display enthusiasm and commitment to the customer add a great deal of value to the product.[31]

POTENTIAL PRODUCT After the value-added product has been developed, the salesperson should begin to conceptualize the **potential product**. The potential product refers to what may remain to be done, that is, what is possible.[32] As the level of competition increases, especially in the case of mature products, salespeople must look to the future and explore new possibilities.

In his book Value-Added Selling, *Tom Reilly states that "Value-added selling is a business philosophy. It's proactively looking for ways to enhance, augment, or enlarge your bundled package for the customer. Value-added salespeople sell a three-dimensional bundle of values: the product, the company, and themselves."*

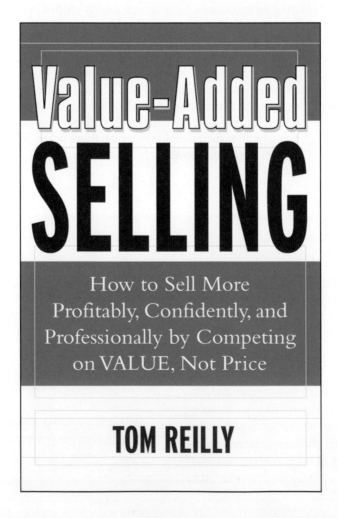

Value-Added SELLING

How to Sell More Profitably, Confidently, and Professionally by Competing on VALUE, Not Price

TOM REILLY

In the highly competitive food services industry, restaurant owners like to do business with a distribution sales representative (DSR) who wants to help make the business profitable. The DSR who assumes this role becomes a true partner and looks beyond the customer's immediate and basic needs. The potential product might be identified after a careful study of the restaurant's current menu and customer base. To deliver the potential product, a salesperson must discover and satisfy new customer needs, which requires imagination and creativity.

Steelcase Incorporated, a leading manufacturer of office furniture, has developed the "Think" chair, which is 99 percent recyclable and can be disassembled with basic hand tools in about five minutes. This $900 chair meets a growing demand for products made of parts that can be recycled several times and manufactured in ways least harmful to the environment. Steelcase developed this "potential product" after learning that customers are increasingly seeking environmentally safe products and are sometimes willing to pay a premium for them.[33]

The potential product is more likely to be developed by salespeople who are close to their customers. Many high-performing salespeople explore product possibilities with their customers on a regular basis. Potential products are often mutually discovered during these exchanges.

Every indication points toward product-selling strategies that add value becoming more important in the future. New product life cycles are shrinking, so more companies are searching for ways to add value during the new and emerging stage. Some companies that have experienced low profits selling low-priced products are reinventing those products. They search for product features that provide benefits customers think are worth paying for. Maytag Corporation developed the expensive environment-friendly Neptune washing machine for customers who will pay more for a washer that uses less water. Yellow Freight

Herman Miller salespeople can assure customers of a custom solution with their CEO's commitment.

Selling in Action

PRICING YOUR PROFESSIONAL FEES

 The age of information has created many career opportunities for people who want to sell professional services. Strong demand for professional services has surfaced in such diverse fields as telecommunications, banking, computer technology, training, and health care. Dana Martin spent 18 years working in the human resources division of Allstate Insurance Company. His specialty was the design and delivery of training programs. He decided to leave the corporate environment and start his own training firm. Martin, like thousands of other professional service providers, had to decide how much to charge for his service. Before he could sell the first training program, he had to decide how much to charge. Should he price his service on an hourly basis or on a project basis? Here are some points to consider when determining fees:

■ *Experience:* In the case of Dana Martin, new clients benefit from what he has learned during many years at Allstate.

■ *Exclusivity:* If you are one of only a small number of people with a particular capability, you may be able to charge more. Specialists often charge higher fees than generalists.

■ *Target Market:* Some markets are very price sensitive. If you are selling your services to large corporations that are used to paying high fees, you may be able to set your fees higher. If you are providing your services to small business clients, expect resistance to high fees.

■ *Value:* How important is your service to the client? In the late 1990s, many companies needed help preparing their computers for transition to the year 2000. This was known as the "Y2K" problem. These firms were willing to pay high fees for this assistance. Some service providers charge higher fees because they add value in one form or another.[d]

System created value for customers with the addition of Yellow's Exact Express and other service options.

Value Creation Investments for Transactional, Consultative, and Strategic Alliance Buyers

In most cases, value creation investments during the transactional sale are minimal. Emphasis is usually placed on finding ways to eliminate any unnecessary costs associated with the sale and avoiding delays in processing the order. Technology investments can sometimes play a big role in improving efficiencies.[34] For example, customers may be encouraged to order products online.

A considerable amount of value creation takes place in consultative sales. Higher investments in value creation are permitted because companies need to invest in developing a good understanding of the customer's needs and problems. This is especially true in large, complex sales. The opportunity to create custom-tailored solutions and deliver more real benefits to the customer provides the opportunity for high margins. If your company is selling mobile autonomous robots, for example, the sales cycle will be quite long and investments will be quite high. It may take several weeks to study the applications of this product in a hospital, a manufacturing plant, or a large warehouse facility. The use of these robots may ultimately result in significant cost savings for the customer.[35]

Value creation investments in strategic alliance sales are the highest. As noted in Chapter 1, strategic alliances represent the highest form of partnering. Building an alliance is always preceded by a careful study of the proposed partner. Creating value often requires leveraging the full assets of the company, so investments go well beyond the sales force. Alliances are often developed by a team of specialists from such areas as finance, engineering, and marketing. A proposed alliance may require investments in new technology, manufacturing facilities, and warehouses.[36]

WHAT IS LEXUS?

Lexus is... Engineering sophistication and manufacturing quality.

Lexus is... Luxury and performance.

Lexus is... An image and an expectation of excellence.

Lexus is... Valuing the customer as an important individual.

Lexus is... Treating customers the way THEY want to be treated.

Lexus is... A total experience that reflects professionalism and a sincere commitment to satisfaction.

Lexus is... "Doing it right the first time".

Lexus is... Caring on a personal level.

Lexus is... Exceeding customer expectations.

And... In the eyes of the customer I AM LEXUS !!!

LEXUS

00-LTT-034

Lexus, a major success story in the automobile industry, offers the customer a value-added strategy that encompasses the product, the company, and the salesperson.

Chapter Learning Activities

Reviewing Key Concepts

Describe positioning as a product-selling strategy

Success in today's dynamic global economy requires the continuous positioning and repositioning of products. Product positioning involves those decisions and activities intended to create and maintain a certain concept of the firm's product in the customer's mind. Salespeople can make an important contribution to the process of product positioning.

Discuss product-positioning options

We described the major product-positioning strategies available to salespeople: positioning new and emerging products versus mature and well-established products; positioning with a price strategy; and positioning with a value-added strategy.

Explain the cluster of satisfactions concept

Today's better-educated customers are often seeking a cluster of satisfactions. They seek satisfactions that arise from the product itself, from the company that makes or distributes the product, and from the salesperson who sells and services the product.

Explain how to sell your product with a price strategy

Pricing decisions must be made at each stage of the product life cycle. Some companies use transactional selling tactics that emphasize low price. Salespeople are often given permission to alter (lower) the base price through the use of discounts and allowances. Consequences of using low-price tactics are discussed in this chapter.

Explain how to sell your product with a value-added strategy
To understand fully the importance of the value-added concept in selling, it helps to visualize every product as being four dimensional. This range of possibilities includes the generic product, the expected product, the value-added product, and the potential product.

Key Terms

Positioning	Quantity discount	Expected product
Differentiation	Seasonal discount	Value-added product
Value proposition	Promotional allowance	Potential product
Satisfactions	Trade or functional discount	
Product life cycle	Generic product	

Review Questions

1. Why has product differentiation become so important in sales and marketing?
2. According to Ted Levitt, what is the definition of a product? What satisfactions do customers want?
3. Explain what is meant by *positioning* as a product-selling strategy. What is a value proposition?
4. Why have salespeople assumed an important role in positioning products?
5. Briefly describe the influence of electronic commerce on pricing. What types of products are likely to be sold on the Internet?
6. What are the possible consequences a salesperson might experience when using low-price tactics?
7. Read the Selling in Action insight titled "How Do Customers Judge Service Quality?" on page 146. How might this information help a salesperson who wants to adopt the value-added-selling strategy?
8. What are some of the common ways salespeople add value to the products they sell?
9. What are the four possible products that make up the *total product* concept?
10. Describe the difference between a generic product and a value-added product.
11. What is the relationship between value-added selling strategies and the cluster of satisfactions?
12. Is it true that selling products with a price strategy largely ignores customer satisfaction? Discuss.

Application Exercises

1. Study catalogs from two competing industrial supply firms or two competing direct-mail catalog companies. Assume one of the represented businesses is your employer. After studying the catalogs, make a comparative analysis of your company's competitive advantages.
2. Several weeks ago Erin Neff fell in love with the Scion tC coupe. After reading about the car in a magazine, she decided to visit a local Scion dealer. A test drive convinced her to place an order. What happened next was very frustrating. The salesperson, Tim Downey, immediately started recommending options she should add to the basic car: sporting wheel and tire package ($1,565), ground-effects trim ($995), performance exhaust system ($525), and a satellite radio tuner and antenna ($449). Suddenly the price of $15,950 jumped to nearly $19,000, way more than she had planned to spend. Erin returned home without placing an order. Assume the role of sales trainer and suggest ways that Tim can improve his ability to position this product so it meets the customer's needs.

3. The Ritz-Carlton hotel chain illustrates the total product concept discussed in this chapter. Research value-added information on the Ritz-Carlton chain by accessing www.ritzcarlton.com. Choose a location and click "Meetings." Click "Quick Facts" and print the information presented. Circle at least five features you consider to be value-added features. Examine the room rates by clicking "Accommodations." On the fact sheet you printed, record the room rate for single- and double-occupancy rooms.

4. Call a local financial services representative specializing in stock, bond, or equity fund transactions. Ask what percentage of clients rely on the information given to make complex decisions on their investments. Also ask this person if customers believe that advice on custom-fitting investment programs adds value to their decision making. Find out whether financial products are getting more or less complex and what effect this will have on providing value-added service in the future.

Role-Play Exercise

Study the Convention Center information in Part 1 of Appendix 3. Analyze this information and determine the value-added product that would appeal to a meeting planner (customer). Prepare a value proposition that summarizes the mix of key benefits on which your product is positioned. The proposition might include, for example, the free limousine service to and from the airport. Present your value proposition to another class member who will assume the role of the customer. Consider using information sheets, pictures, and other materials that will enhance your presentation.

CRM Application Exercise

Informing Customers with CRM

The notes in the Salesforce.com database software contain two references to Extranets, another system offered by SimNet Systems. One account is a prospective buyer of an Extranet who needs more information. The other account has an Extranet and is willing to show it to others. The Reference Library also contains information about private virtual networks, including Extranets. Find the two accounts by selecting the Reports tab and choosing the Opportunity Product Report. With the report on the screen, check the box next to Extranet and click the Drill Down button. Then, press "Show Details." Salesforce.com displays two records. An examination of the notes shows the account that has already bought the SimNet Extranet and the one with an interest. Make a note of the name of the organization now using an Extranet. Click "Opportunity" to display the prospect that needs information. Select the Documents tab and navigate to the SimNet folder. View the Extranet document. Page down to the last paragraph of that document, titled VPN. Highlight the paragraph with your mouse and select "Edit," "Copy." Close the document window. Using the Recent Items menu on the left, select the Opportunity interested in Extranets. In the Contact Roles section, click on the name of the primary contact. Click the Send an Email button in the Activity History section. Click "Select Template" and choose the Product Inquiry template. In the subject line, enter "SimNet Extranet Information." Navigate to the e-mail body and enter the following: "You might find this of interest." Press tab twice to begin a new paragraph. Paste the information from the Reference Library. Press tab twice again for a new paragraph. Type "If you wish, I can arrange for you to look at the Extranet in use at," and then enter the name of the person and organization using the Extranet. Review your e-mail and press "Send."

Case Problem

Many of the most profitable companies have discovered that there are "riches in market niches." They have developed products and services that meet the needs of a well-defined or newly created market. Steelcase Incorporated, a leading source of information and expertise on work effectiveness, has been working hard to develop products that meet the needs of people who do most of their work in an office environment. The company's motto is "the office environment company." One of its newest products is the "Think" chair. Steelcase also developed the Personal Harbor Workspaces, a self-contained, fully equipped, and totally private podlike workstation. Steelcase sales literature describes the product as ideal for companies that are tired of waiting for the future:

> *They were developed to support the individual within a highly collaborative team environment, and they work best when clustered around common work areas equipped with mobile tables, carts, benches, screens, and other Steelcase Activity Products. These "commons" are meant to be flexible spaces that enhance communication and facilitate interaction.*

Steelcase realized that selling this advanced product would not be easy, so a decision was made to develop an advanced sales team to presell the Personal Harbor before its major introduction. Once the team started making sales calls, it became evident that a traditional product-oriented sales presentation would not work. The Personal Harbor was a departure from conventional office design, so many customers were perplexed. Sue Sacks, a team member, said, "People acted like we had fallen from Mars." Team members soon realized that to explain the features and benefits of the product they had to begin studying new organizational developments such as team-oriented workforces and corporate reengineering. The advanced sales team was renamed the advanced solutions team. Sales calls put more emphasis on learning about the customers' problems and identification of possible solutions. Members of the team viewed themselves as consultants who were in a position to discuss solutions to complex business problems.

The consultative approach soon began to pay off in sales. One customer, a hospital, was preparing to build a new office building and needed workstations for 400 employees. The hospital had formed a committee to make decisions concerning the purchase of office equipment. After an initial meeting between the Steelcase sales team and the hospital committee, a visit to Steelcase headquarters in Grand Rapids, Michigan, was arranged. The hospital committee members were able to tour the plant and meet with selected Steelcase experts. With knowledge of the hospital's goals and directions, Sue Sacks was able to arrange meetings with Steelcase technical personnel who could answer specific questions. The hospital ultimately placed an order worth more than a million dollars.

Questions

1. To fulfill a problem-solving need, salespeople must often be prepared to communicate effectively with customers who are seeking a cluster of satisfactions (see Figure 7.1). Is it likely that a customer who is considering the Personal Harbor Workspaces will seek information concerning all three dimensions of the Product-Selling Model? Explain your answer.

2. What product-selling strategies are most effective when selling a new and emerging product such as the Personal Harbor Workspaces?

3. Sue Sacks and other members of her sales team discovered that a traditional product-oriented presentation would not work when selling the Personal Harbor Workspaces. Success came only after the team adopted the consultative style of selling. Why was the product-oriented presentation ineffective?

4. Sue Sacks and other members of the advanced solutions team found that the consultative approach resulted in meetings with people higher in the customer's organization. "We get to call on a higher level of buyer," she said. Also, the team was more likely to position the product with a value-added strategy instead of a price strategy. In what ways did the advanced solutions team members add value to their product? Why was less emphasis placed on price during meetings with the customer?

Part 3 | Role-Play Exercise

DEVELOPING A PRODUCT STRATEGY

Scenario

First National Bank is a full-service bank with a reputation for excellent customer service. Personal selling efforts by tellers, loan officers, and financial consultants are considered an integral part of the bank's customer service program.

Customer Profile

At age 45, Gianni Diaz is looking forward to early retirement. To supplement a company-sponsored retirement program a certificate of deposit (CD) in the amount of $4,000 is purchased each year. The annual percentage yield earned on CDs is currently in the range of 3.75 to 4.00 percent. Diaz is not interested in stocks and bonds because these products represent high-risk investments.

Salesperson Profile

Deaven Ray is a senior investment officer with First National Bank. Ray represents a wide range of financial products such as stock and bond mutual funds, blue chip stocks, diversified mutual funds, fixed annuities, money market funds, and certificates of deposit. Ray feels that Gianni Diaz may be a good candidate for an investment in fixed annuities. Diaz has agreed to meet and discuss investment options.

Product

A guaranteed-growth annuity at an annual percentage yield of 5.0 percent for a term of five years. This product, offered by General Electric Capital Assurance Company, gives the customer a guaranteed principal and a fixed rate of return. At the contract maturity date, the customer can select several payout options. This is a tax-deferred annuity, which means you won't pay income taxes on earnings until you choose to withdraw the funds. You can add funds to your account throughout the contract period. You need not close the account at the end of the contract period. You can allow your money to continue to grow at the same interest rate. If funds are withdrawn prior to the end of the contract, a withdrawal charge will be assessed. The minimum single premium purchase is $5,000.

Instructions

For this role-play activity, you will meet with Gianni Diaz and discuss current and future financial plans. You will determine whether Diaz might benefit by investing in a guaranteed-growth annuity. Prior to meeting with the customer, review the following material in Chapter 6:

- Adding value with a feature–benefit strategy
- Use of bridge statements
- General versus specific benefits

Also, think about the implications of the Product-Selling Model (Figure 7.1) introduced in Chapter 7. At the beginning of the role-play, use appropriate questions to acquire information regarding the customer's needs. Be prepared to recommend this product and close the sale if you feel the customer will benefit from this purchase.

8

The Buying Process and Buyer Behavior

Chapter Preview

When you finish reading this chapter, you should be able to

1
Discuss the meaning of a customer strategy

2
Explain the difference between consumer and business buyers

3
Understand the importance of alignment between the selling process and the customer's buying process

4
Understand the buying process of the transactional, consultative, and strategic alliance buyer

5
Discuss the various influences that shape customer buying decisions

The past decade has witnessed a major power shift in the direction of the customer. Today's customers have greater access to information that lets them make more informed decisions. They are more demanding, and salespeople must work harder to meet their needs. Every sales call must begin with the customer as the central focus of attention. Tom Peters, noted author and consultant, says, we must "become one with the customer."[1] The customer focus must encompass the buying process (how people buy) and buyer behavior (why people buy).

We know that products and services must satisfy the customer's needs, but identifying these needs can be very challenging. No one understands this challenge better than Justin Bremer, a financial advisor at Wealth Design (pictured above). Group (www.wealthdesigngroup.net). An integral part of Bremer's job is to work closely with his clients to custom design comprehensive and innovative financial plans to help them achieve and sustain long-term success. Since financial services of this nature are intangible yet highly personal, Justin Bremer must understand each customer's complex buying process. Prior to making a sales call, for example, he must perform precall planning and research. Is the client a business or an individual? What type of information will the client need to make a decision? What will make the client be open with Bremer about his or her financial situation? Understanding buyer behavior and the buying process helps create effective selling strategies. ■

Developing a Customer Strategy

The greatest challenge to salespeople in the age of information is to improve responsiveness to customers. In fact, a growing number of sales professionals believe the customer has supplanted the product as the driving force in sales today. This is especially true in those situations in which the products of one company in an industry are becoming more and more similar to those of the competition. Jerry Acuff, author of *Stop Acting Like a Seller and Start Thinking Like a Buyer*, encourages salespeople to think like buyers. In order to think like a buyer, salespeople must understand the buying process and focus on what the customer is looking for.[2]

Adding Value with a Customer Strategy

A **customer strategy** is a carefully conceived plan that results in maximum customer responsiveness. One major dimension of this strategy is to achieve a better understanding of the customer's buying needs and motives. As noted in Chapter 1, information has become a strategic resource (Figure 1.2). When salespeople take time to discover needs and motives, they are in a much better position to offer customers a value-added solution to their buying problem.

Every salesperson who wants to develop repeat business should figure out a way to collect and systematize customer information. The authors of *Reengineering the Corporation* discuss the importance of collecting information about the unique and particular needs of each customer:

> *Customers—consumers and corporations alike—demand products and services designed for their unique and particular needs. There is no longer any such notion as* the customer; there is only *this* customer, *the one with whom a seller is dealing at the moment and who now has the capacity to indulge his or her own personal tastes.*[3]

The first prescription for developing a customer strategy focuses on the customer's buying process (see Figure 8.1). Buying procedures and policies can vary greatly from one buyer to another. This is especially true in business-to-business selling. If a salesperson fails to learn how the buyer plans to make the purchase, then there is the danger that the selling process will be out of alignment with the customer's buying process. Keith Eades, author of *The New Solution Selling*, says:

> *If we haven't defined how our buyers buy, then we make assumptions that throw us out of alignment with our buyers. Misalignment with buyers is one of selling's most critical mistakes.*[4]

Strategic/Consultative Selling Model	
Strategic Step	**Prescription**
Develop a Personal Selling Philosophy	☑ Adopt Marketing Concept ☑ Value Personal Selling ☑ Become a Problem Solver/Partner
Develop a Relationship Strategy	☑ Adopt Win-Win Philosophy ☑ Project Professional Image ☑ Maintain High Ethical Standards
Develop a Product Strategy	☑ Become a Product Expert ☑ Sell Benefits ☑ Configure Value-Added Solutions
Develop a Customer Strategy	☐ Understand the Buying Process ☐ Understand Buyer Behavior ☐ Develop Prospect Base

FIGURE 8.1

Today, one of the greatest challenges to salespeople is to improve responsiveness to customers. A well-developed customer strategy is designed to meet this challenge.

Global Business Etiquette

DOING BUSINESS IN FRANCE

The French people are very proud of their history, language, social systems, and customs. They expect visitors to respect the many things that make their country unique. Preparation for a business trip to France may take a little extra time.

■ Learn basic French and use it often. Although most French businesspeople speak English, some will not admit it.

■ Introductions should be made by someone (attorney, banker, or a friend) known to the person with whom

you want to do business. French people tend to be cautious when meeting someone new.

■ Be prepared to conduct business over meals at nice restaurants. A business lunch might last for two hours. The French rarely invite business guests to their homes.

■ French businesspeople are reluctant to take risks, so negotiations may take a long time. Be well prepared to discuss the merits of your product but avoid the hard sell.[c]

To fully understand the customer's buying strategy the salesperson must conduct a careful needs discovery or assessment. This is done by asking appropriate questions, listening to the customers responses, and making careful observations. Chapter 11 provides in-depth coverage of these important adaptive selling skills.

Chapter Learning Activities

Reviewing Key Concepts

Discuss the meaning of a customer strategy

The importance of developing a *customer strategy* was introduced in this chapter. This type of planning is necessary to ensure maximum customer responsiveness. Buying procedures and policies can vary greatly from one buyer to another. If a salesperson does not learn how the buyer plans to make the purchase, then there is the strong possibility that the selling process will be out of alignment with the customer's buying process.

Explain the difference between consumer and business buyers

Business buyer behavior was compared to consumer buyer behavior. Three types of business buying situations were described: straight rebuy, new-task buy, and the modified rebuy. Systems selling, a common business buying strategy, was also described. Three types of consumer buying situations were defined: habitual buying decisions, variety-seeking buying decisions, and complex buying decisions.

Understand the importance of alignment between the selling process and the customer's buying process

Customers make buying decisions in many ways, so it would be inappropriate to view the buying process as a uniform pattern of decision making. However, there is a common decision-making model that most buyers apply to their unique circumstances. The typical stages in the buying decision process are needs awareness, evaluation of solutions, resolution of problems, purchase, and implementation.

Understand the buying process of the transactional, consultative, and strategic alliance buyer

Three value creation selling approaches that appeal to certain types of customers were discussed: the transactional process buyer, the consultative process buyer, and the strategic alliance process buyer. The consultative process buyer offers the greatest challenge to most salespeople.

Discuss the various influences that shape customer buying decisions

We noted that buyer behavior is influenced in part by individual (physical and psychological) needs. Maslow's popular model ranks these needs. There are also a number of group influences that shape our psychological needs to various degrees. Buyer behavior is influenced by the roles we assume, reference groups, social class, and culture. *Perception* was defined as the process of selecting, organizing, and interpreting information inputs to produce meaning. We discussed *emotional* and *rational buying motives* and compared patronage and product motives.

Key Terms

Customer strategy	Complex buying decision	Reference group
Consumer buyer behavior	Buying process	Social classes
Business buyer behavior	Buyer resolution theory	Culture
Buying center	Physiological needs	Subculture
New-task buy	Security needs	Buying motive
Straight rebuy	Social needs	Emotional buying motive
Modified rebuy	Esteem needs	Rational buying motive
Systems selling	Self-actualization	Patronage buying motive
Habitual buying decisions	Group influences	Product buying motive
Variety-seeking buying decisions	Role	

Review Questions

1. According to the Strategic/Consultative Selling Model, what are the three prescriptions for the development of a successful customer strategy?

2. List and describe the three most common types of organizational buying situations.

3. Describe the five major stages in the typical buying process.

4. List and describe three value creation selling approaches that appeal to various types of customers.

5. According to the buyer resolution theory, a purchase is made only after the prospect has made five buying decisions. What are they?

6. Explain how Maslow's hierarchy of needs affects buyer behavior.

7. Describe the four group influences that affect buyer behavior.

8. What is meant by the term *perception*?

9. Distinguish between emotional and rational buying motives.

10. J.D. Power, founder of J.D. Power and Associates, says, "We define quality as what the customer wants." Do you agree or disagree with his observations? Explain your answer.

Application Exercises

1. Select several advertisements from a trade magazine. Analyze each one and determine what rational buying motives the advertiser is appealing to. Do any of these advertisements appeal to emotional buying motives? Then select a magazine that is aimed at a particular consumer group, for example, *Architectural Digest*, *Redbook*, or *Better Homes and Gardens*. Study the advertisements and determine what buying motives they appeal to.

2. The $40,000 Hyundai Genesis V8, which entered the U.S. market as a 2009 model is a far cry from the popular Elantra. Hyundai's new flagship model was designed to compete with Lexus, Mercedes Benz, Cadillac and BMW. The Genesis is positioned as another choice in the luxury-car market. Will potential customers accept the Genesis as a true luxury car? Will customer perceptions play a role in acceptance of this new model?

3. J.D. Power and Associates is a global marketing information services firm that helps businesses and consumers make better decisions through credible customer-based information. The company provides an unbiased source of marketing information based on opinions of consumers. Visit www.jdpower.com and become familiar with the type of information services offered.

Role-Play Exercise

In this role-play, you will assume the role of a salesperson working at a Brook's Brothers clothing store. The inventory includes a wide range of business professional clothing such as suits, sport coats, dress shirts, and accessories; the store also offers a full range of business casual clothing. A member of your class will assume the role of a customer who visits your store for the purpose of buying clothing for work. He recently graduated from college and will start work at a new job in about two weeks. In addition to clothing, your store offers complete alteration services and credit plans. During the role-play, you should develop a relationship with the customer using strategies discussed in previous chapters and determine the customer's needs with questions, attentive listening, and observation.

CRM Application Exercise

Managing Multiple Contacts with CRM

The Salesforce.com database identifies four architectural firms. You can look up these firms and arrange to make contact with them. Start by selecting the Accounts tab. In the Accounts list, click the "Industry" field to sort the list by industry. Select the first architecture firm. Then, on the Account Detail screen, select any one of the contacts for that firm. Using the same procedure as the exercise in Chapter 3, page 71, send an e-mail to this contact. Use the Architecture Calls template. After sending the e-mail and returning to the Contact screen, select the e-mail just sent from the Activity History section. Click "Create Follow Up Task." On the Task screen, select "Phone Call" as the type and enter "Architecture Calls" as the subject. Enter "next Monday" as the date. Change the reminder time to 9:00 A.M., the time you want to schedule these calls. Click "Save." Repeat this process for all four architecture accounts.

Verify that these architecture calls have been scheduled for next Monday by returning to your home screen. The calls will be in the My Tasks section.

Reality Selling Today Video Case Problem

 Justin Bremer, the financial advisor featured at the beginning of this chapter, is continually developing new accounts, servicing existing accounts, and introducing new products and services. The major challenge of selling financial advice is undoubtedly clients' information privacy. Referrals from existing customers, therefore, are important. This positive word of mouth can only come naturally from satisfied customers. Even so, Justin understands that creating a good impression when he meets a potential client for the first time is a job half done.

Justin Bremer
Wealth Design

Individuals and businesses do not want to talk about the details of their existing financial plans to strangers, much less to new financial advisors. In addition, switching from one financial services company to another creates exorbitant costs, both in terms of time and money. Consequently, clients want to buy financial products and services from companies that not only help them balance risks and gains but also provide outstanding services over the long run. Finally, the market for financial services is quite competitive.

Wealth Design Group's competitive advantage is its ability to offer comprehensive yet innovative financial solutions to its clients. When Justin meets with a prospect, he asks several questions to determine the client's needs and buying motives. He realizes that in some cases several motives may influence the purchase decision. He also knows that buying behavior is influenced by perception, so he must probe to find out what prospects are really thinking by asking clarifying questions at the right time. He proactively goes after information that is relevant to making the sales without appearing intrusive. In short, he always makes sure that he spends enough time with his clients in the very first encounter to understand their needs and concerns. Then, he works closely with his team to come up with solutions that are customized to those specific needs. At the same time, he must make it clear to the clients about how his company stands out in the highly competitive market and provide them with in-depth analysis of their current financial health to speed up buyers' decision-making processes.

Questions

1. Does it appear that Justin Bremer has built his customer strategy on the three prescriptions featured in the Strategic/Consultative Selling Model? Explain.

2. What aspects of the need–satisfaction theory has Justin Bremer incorporated into his approach to customers? Explain.

3. As an individual looking for long-term financial solutions, would you be more influenced by rational or emotional buying motives? Explain.

4. What steps has Justin Bremer taken to initiate a long-term partnership with his customers?

Developing and Qualifying a Prospect Base

► Introduction

Andy Weight, client services manager at TotalJobs.com in the United Kingdom, uses Salesforce.com to effectively and efficiently maintain complete and accurate prospect information. "We send a personalized e-mail out to prospects and there are fields in there for them to fill in. When they submit the form back to us, the Salesforce system is automatically populated. Right now, we're creating up to 5,000 leads every month for our sales teams to follow up."

Account-based software vendors such as Salesforce, NetSuite, and Oracle Siebel are helping companies develop effective customer relationship management (CRM) systems. These systems are at the heart of every successful one-to-one marketing initiative. Success in selling depends on one's ability to identify prospects, gain insight into the prospect's needs, and develop an accurate picture of the prospect's value.[1] ∎

Prospecting—An Introduction

Gerhard Gschwandtner, publisher of *Selling Power*, says, "The main purpose of a salesperson is not to make sales, but to create customers."[2] Identifying potential customers is an important aspect of the customer strategy. In the terminology of personal selling, this process is called **prospecting**. A potential customer, or **prospect**, is someone who meets the qualification criteria established by you or your company.

Finding prospects who can make the purchase is not as easy as it sounds. This is especially true in business-to-business sales. In many situations the salesperson must make the sales presentation to multiple decision makers. One of these decision makers might be the technical expert who wants an answer to the question: "Does the product meet the company's specifications?" Another decision maker may be the person who will actually use the product. The employee who will use the forklift truck you are selling may be involved in the purchase decision. Of course, there is often a "purse-string" decision maker who has the ultimate authority to release funds for the purchase. During periods of economic uncertainty, the decision-making process often moves upward. It is sometimes difficult to make connections with upper-level executives. One solution is to plan a joint sales call involving a higher-level executive from your company.[3]

The goal of prospecting is to build a qualified **prospect base** made up of current customers and potential customers. Building a prospect base involves the use of CRM software to monitor movement of the customer through the sales process. Many successful companies find that current customers account for a large percentage of their sales. Every effort is made to devise and implement a customer strategy that builds, fosters, nurtures, and extends relationships with established customers.[4]

Importance of Prospecting

Every salesperson must cope with customer attrition, that is, the inevitable loss of customers over a period of time, which can be attributed to a variety of causes. Unless new prospects are found to replace lost customers, a salesperson eventually faces a reduction in income and possible loss of employment.

To better understand the significance of prospecting, let us examine a few common causes of customer attrition.

The customer may have a one-time need or there is an extended period of time between purchases. New prospects must be added to the prospect base.

The customer may move to a new location outside the salesperson's territory. The American population is very mobile. This cause of attrition is especially common in the retail and service areas.

A firm may go out of business or merge with another company. In some areas of business the failure rate is quite high. In recent years, we have witnessed a record number of mergers that have caused massive changes in purchasing plans.

A loyal buyer or purchasing agent may leave the position because of promotion, retirement, resignation, or serious illness. The replacement may prefer to buy from someone else.

Sales are lost to the competition. In some cases, the competition offers more value. The added value may take the form of better quality, a better price, a stronger relationship, better service, or some combination of these factors.

Some studies reveal that the average company loses 15 to 20 percent of its customers every year. Depending on the type of selling, this figure might be higher or lower. It becomes clear that many customers are lost for reasons beyond the salesperson's control. If salespeople want to keep their earnings at a stable level, they need to develop new customers.

Joe Girard, once recognized by the *Guinness Book of Records* as the world's greatest salesperson, used the "Ferris wheel" concept to illustrate the relationship between prospecting and loss of customers due to the attrition.[5] As people get off the Ferris wheel, the operator fills their seats one at a time, moves the wheel a little, and continues this process until all the original riders have left the wheel and new ones come aboard (Figure 9.1). In reality, of course, established customers do not come and go this fast. With the passing of time, however, many customers must be replaced.

Prospecting Requires Planning

Prospecting should be viewed as a systematic process of locating potential customers. Some prospecting efforts can be integrated easily into a regular sales call. Progressive marketers are doing three things to improve the quality of the prospecting effort:

1. *Increase the number of people who board the Ferris wheel.* You want to see a continuous number of potential prospects board the Ferris wheel because they are the source of sales opportunities. If the number of potential prospects declines sharply, the number of sales closed also declines.

FIGURE 9.1

The "Ferris wheel" concept, which is aimed at supplying an ongoing list of prospects, is part of world sales record holder Joe Girard's customer strategy.

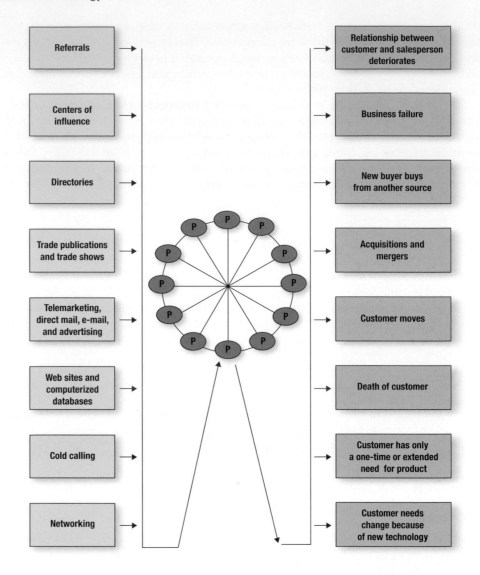

2. *Improve the quality of the prospects who board the Ferris wheel.* Companies often establish quality standards that ensure a steady supply of prospects with high profit potential. For example, some companies focus their prospecting efforts on consultative process buyers. These are prospects who often lack need awareness and need help evaluating possible solutions.

3. *Shorten the sales cycle by quickly determining which of the new prospects are qualified prospects—qualified as to need, authority to buy, ability to pay, and authority to purchase the product.* Gerhard Gschwandtner says, "Time is the ultimate scorekeeper in the game of selling." He points out that many salespeople do not meet their sales goals because they do not quickly qualify new prospects.[6] Later in this chapter we examine qualifying practices and discuss how to shorten the sales cycle with sales automation methods.

Prospecting Plans Must Be Assessed Often

In today's dynamic, ever-changing marketplace, prospecting plans must be monitored continuously. Some prospecting techniques that worked well in the past may become ineffective because of changing market conditions. Midwest Training Institute, a firm that helps companies to improve their production and sales efficiency, experienced a dramatic sales decline during the first quarter of the year. This decline came after years of steady sales increases. Joel Pecoraro, president of the company, initiated a thorough investigation and discovered that his sales staff were relying primarily on one prospecting approach that

Customer Relationship Management with Technology

USING THE SAME CRM SOFTWARE AS CISCO SYSTEMS

Cisco has deployed the Salesforce.com CRM solution to 15,000 users from Indiana to India and Dubai to Dublin. Ultimately, there will be 25,000 users. Salesforce.com provides Cisco with effective prospect management tools, namely dashboards, account planning, and partner/distributor reports.

- Dashboards track metrics such as opportunities, lead conversion rates, number of account plans, and top accounts for sales reps and managers. Individual salespeople create their own reports to help chart their progress.

- Account planning, which had previously been difficult to institute, is increasingly leveraged with Salesforce.

- Partners are part of Cisco's customer "eco-system." Overall productivity and effectiveness are improved by

extending leads to partners and tracking the conversion to opportunity and ultimately to a sale.

You have the opportunity to use a demonstration version of the same solution, Salesforce.com, used by Cisco. Just as a Cisco salesperson, you are assigned a number of prospect accounts and given individual and company information about each account's contact person in Salesforce. Your participation in the CRM case study and exercises will give you hands-on experience with the strategic development of a prospect base, using modern sales technology. You not only will be using the same software being used by thousands of salespeople but also will be working with data that are derived from authentic selling challenges. (See the exercise, "Reviewing the Prospect Database," on p. 204 for more information).

was no longer successful: The salespeople were calling established customers. Pecoraro designed an incentive program that rewarded salespeople who adopted new prospecting techniques such as attending an association meeting where the salesperson could meet potential prospects or speaking at a meeting attended by persons who might need the services offered by Midwest Training Institute.[7]

Sources of Prospects

Every salesperson must develop a prospecting system suited to a particular selling situation. Some of the many sources of prospects follow, and each should be carefully examined:

Referrals
Centers of influence, friends, and family members
Directories
Trade publications
Trade shows and special events
Telemarketing and e-mail
Direct-response advertising and sales letters
Web site
Computerized database
Cold calling
Networking
Educational seminars
Prospecting by nonsales employees

Referrals

The use of referrals as a prospecting approach has been used successfully in a wide range of selling situations. In most cases, referral leads result in higher close rates, larger sales, and shorter sales cycles. A **referral** is a prospect who has been recommended by a current customer or by someone who is familiar with the product. Satisfied customers, business

Your request for referrals are more likely to receive a positive response, if made after you have built a strong trusting relationship. In most cases referral leads result in higher close rates, larger sales and shorter sales cycles.

acquaintances, and even prospects who do not buy often can recommend the names of persons who might benefit from purchasing the product.

Customers are more likely to give a referral if they perceive value in the solution you offer. When you build value into your sales process, you increase the odds that the customer will give you a referral. Steve Lewis, managing partner of New England Financial, says, "Our attitude is that we can't ask for referrals until clients have perceived value in the process."[8]

ENDLESS CHAIN REFERRALS The endless chain approach to obtaining referrals is easy to use because it fits naturally into most sales presentations. A salesperson selling long-term health care insurance might say, "Miss Remano, whom do you know who might be interested in our insurance plan?" This open-ended question gives the person the freedom to recommend several prospects and is less likely to be answered with a no response. Be sure to use your reference's name when you contact the new prospect—"Mary Remano suggested that I call you. . . . "

REFERRAL LETTERS AND CARDS The referral letter method is a variation of the endless chain technique. In addition to requesting the names of prospects, the salesperson asks the customer to prepare a note or letter of introduction that can be delivered to the potential customer. The correspondence is an actual testimonial prepared by a satisfied customer. Some companies use a referral card to introduce the salesperson. The preprinted card features a place for your customer to sign the new prospect's name and his own name, and can be used as part of the sales presentation.

Within the field of personal selling, there is no complete agreement regarding the timing of the referral request. Some sales training programs encourage salespeople to request the referral immediately after closing the sale. Others point out that if you are working with a new customer, it takes time to earn the customer's trust. The customer may feel there is a risk involved in giving you referrals. Once you have built a strong, trusting relationship with the customer, referral requests are more likely to receive a positive response.[9]

REFERRAL ORGANIZATIONS Some salespeople have found that membership in a referral organization is an effective way to obtain good leads. BNI (Business Network International) is one of the largest business networking organizations with over 3,600 chapters worldwide (www.bni.com). BNI offers members the opportunity to share ideas, contacts, and referrals.[10] In addition, some local clubs offer referrals as a member benefit.

Centers of Influence, Friends, and Family Members

The center-of-influence method involves establishing a relationship with a well-connected, influential person who is willing to provide prospecting information. This person may not make buying decisions but has influence with other people who do. To illustrate, consider the challenge facing Gary Schneider, creator of a powerful software product that would help small farmers optimize their crop selection. After spending several years developing the product, Schneider and his wife began selling the product one copy at a time. During one cold call on a major crop insurer, American Agrisurance, he met a senior researcher who immediately saw the benefits of the software product. This respected researcher is in a position to influence buying decisions at his company and to provide prospect information for other crop insurers.[11]

A person who is new in the field of selling often uses friends and family members as sources of information about potential customers. It is only natural to contact people we know. In many cases these people have contacts with a wide range of potential buyers.

Directories

Directories can help salespeople search out new prospects and determine their buying potential. A list of some of the more popular national directories is provided next:

Middle Market Directory lists 14,000 firms worth between $500,000 and $1 million (available from Dun & Bradstreet, www.dnb.com).

TrackAmerica is a database management company that offers online information on millions of U.S. businesses and consumers (www.trackamerica.com).

Standard & Poor's Corporation Records Service provides details on more than 11,000 companies (www.spglobal.com).

Thomas Register of American Manufacturers provides a listing of 60,000 manufacturers by product classifications, addresses, and capital ratings (www.thomasregister.com).

Polk City Directory provides detailed information on the citizens of a specific community. Polk, in business for over 125 years, publishes about 1,100 directories covering 6,500 communities in the United States and Canada (www.citydirectory.com).

The Encyclopedia of Associations lists more than 23,000 U.S. associations and more than 20,000 international organizations with details on membership, publications, and conferences (www.gale.com).

These are just a few of the better-known directories. There are hundreds of additional directories covering business and industrial firms on the regional, state, and local levels. Some directories are free, whereas others must be purchased at a nominal fee. One of the most useful free sources of information is the telephone directory. Most telephone directories have a classified (yellow pages) section that groups businesses and professions by category. Web Yellow Pages (www.bigyellow.com) provides more than 11 million U.S. business listings.

Trade Publications

Trade publications provide a status report on every major industry. If you are a sales representative employed by Super Valu Stores, Fleming Companies Inc., Sysco Corporation, or one of the other huge food wholesaling houses that supplies supermarkets, then you can benefit from a monthly review of *Progressive Grocer* magazine. Each month this trade publication reports on trends in the retail food industry, new products,

Selling in Action

PROSPECTING WITH YOUR PARTNERS

When Megan Michael sees a new office building going up, she stops her car and makes inquiries about who is to occupy the building. As a sales representative for BKM Total Office, an office furniture supplier in San Diego, she needs to be aware of new office space. However, this approach is not her most important prospecting method. She has found the telephone to be her most effective prospecting tool.

Michael speaks regularly with her customers to find out if they know companies that might need BKM's products. Architects, designers, and builders who have previously worked with Michael have proved to be good sources of referrals. The key to her prospecting success is maintaining a strong relationship with her customers. She realizes that you must be an effective partner before you can ask for help.[a]

problems, innovations, and related information. Trade journals such as *Institutional Distribution, Home Furnishings, Hardware Retailer, Modern Tire Dealer*, and *Progressive Architecture* are examples of publications that might help salespeople identify prospects.

Trade Shows and Special Events

A trade show is a large exhibit of products that are, in most cases, common to one industry, such as electronics or office equipment. The prospects walk into the booth or exhibit and talk with those who represent the exhibitor. In some cases, sales personnel invite existing customers and prospects to attend trade shows so they can have an opportunity to demonstrate their newest products.

Research studies indicate that it is much easier to identify good prospects and actually close sales at a trade show. In most cases, fewer sales calls are needed to close a sale if the prospect was qualified at a trade show. Once a trade show contact is identified and judged to be a qualified lead, information regarding the lead should be carefully recorded. When a prospect enters a Xerox Corporation booth, a salesperson uses a few questions to qualify the lead and types the answers into an on-screen form. Xerox uses software developed by NewLeads on record and process data obtained from prospects who have been qualified by a salesperson working in the booth.[12]

A special event can be a baseball game, golf tournament, reception for a dignitary, or charity event. Bentley Motor Cars invited a number of potential clients to the famous Le Mans 24-hour endurance race. Prospects watched the Bentley racecar compete while sipping champagne. Back in America, charity events serve as a venue for cultivating wealthy clientele who can afford a Bentley automobile.[13]

Telemarketing and E-Mail

Telemarketing is the practice of marketing goods and services through telephone contact. It is an integral part of many modern sales and marketing campaigns. One use of telemarketing is to identify prospects. A financial services company used telemarketing to identify prospects for its customized equipment leasing packages. Leads were given to salespeople for consideration. Telemarketing also can be used to quickly and inexpensively qualify prospects for follow-up. Some marketers use the telephone to verify sales leads generated by direct mail, advertisements, or some other method.

Although the response rate for sales e-mails is quite low, they have proven to be a source of leads for many salespeople. Ideally sales e-mails should be sent only to existing

Bentley Motor Cars invited a number of potential clients to the famous LeMans 24-hour endurance race. This special event helped the company develop its prospect base.

The Thomas Register of American Manufacturers *(www.thomas register.com) is one source of prospects for salespeople. Thomas Register products are available on CD, DVD, and in a print edition.*

customers or others who have "opted in" to receive them. When you use *broadcast* e-mails, there is the risk that you will be blocked and end up on a spammer blacklist. Online sales specialist Mac MacIntosh says those who use broadcast e-mails should stay within anti-spam laws by giving recipients the right to opt out of future e-mails.[14]

Putting your company name in the subject line can help get e-mails opened by prospects who are familiar with it. Some salespeople send newsletters to current and prospective customers. Lee Levitt, director of sales for software consultant IDC, sends a monthly newsletter to current IDC clients and professionals at large technology companies. He wants to expose them to services his company can provide. Levitt says, "The key is to offer something of value they can quickly digest and use in day-to-day work."[15]

Direct-Response Advertising and Sales Letters

Many advertisements invite the reader to send for a free booklet or brochure that provides detailed information about the product or service. In the category of business-to-business marketing, advertising has strong inquiry-generating power. Some firms distribute postage-free response cards (also known as *bingo cards*) to potential buyers. Recipients are encouraged to complete and mail the cards if they desire additional information. In some cases the name of the person making the inquiry is given to a local sales representative for further action.

Sales letters, sent via e-mail or the U.S. postal service, can be incorporated easily into a prospecting plan. The prospecting sales letter is sent to persons who are in a position to make a buying decision. Shortly after mailing the letter (three or four days), the prospect is called and asked for an appointment. The call begins with a reference to the sales letter. To

Research shows that it is much easier to identify good prospects and actually close sales at a trade show.

make the letter stand out, some salespeople include product information. As noted in Chapter 6, all sales letters must be written with care. To get results, sales letters must quickly get the reader's attention.

Web Site

Thousands of companies and businesspeople have established Web sites on the World Wide Web. A **Web site** is a collection of Web pages maintained by a single person or organization. It is accessible to anyone with a computer and a modem. Large firms, such as Century 21, maintain Web sites that feature 20 to 30 Web pages. Web sites frequently offer prospects the opportunity to acquire product information that can help them make a buying decision. Financial services companies describe home financing and refinancing options. The Sun Microsystems Web site provides detailed descriptions of Sun's products and

Selling Is Everyone's Business

WINEMAKER APPLIES HER SALES SKILLS

Gina Gallo is a third-generation family winemaker who knows a thing or two about personal selling. She not only knows how to make the wines offered by E.&J. Gallo Winery, but she also knows how to sell them. The year she spent as a member of the sales force helped her learn about consumer's buying habits and the needs of retailers who sell Gallo wines. Gina Gallo sees some similarities between winemaking and sales. The better you understand your vineyards, the soil, and the grapes, the greater the chance you have of creating an excellent wine. The better you understand your customer's needs, the better you can relate to and fulfill those needs.[b]

Gina Gallo

With Salesgenie salespeople find it is easy to obtain lead generation and prospect selection information for different market segments. Through analyzing the current customer base, Salesgenie will create a list of similarly qualified prospects to call on.

solutions. When someone clicks on a Web page and requests information, they will likely become a prospect. Some Web sites offer an incentive to leave contact information.

Many working professionals are using LinkedIn to build a network of business contacts. This networking Web site is similar to MySpace and Facebook, popular social networking Web sites. LinkedIn can be a valuable prospecting tool for salespeople. There are currently 11 million LinkedIn users and membership is growing at a rate of 15 percent a month. To sign up, visit www.linkedin.com and click "Join Now" to open an account. Once you have signed up, the next step is to create a profile that will get the attention of those you wish to network with.[16]

Computerized Database

With the aid of electronic data processing, it is often possible to match product features with the needs of potential customers quickly and accurately. In many situations, a firm can develop its own computerized database. In other cases it is more economical to purchase the database from a company that specializes in the collection of such information. One example, Salesgenie, is offered by infoUSA. With the aid of this software, you can easily obtain lead generation and prospect selection information for different market segments. Gary Hand, president of Alliance Security Systems, needs to keep his sales team supplied with plenty of leads. Salesgenie provides him with a list of prospects by geographical location and by the value of each house. Salesgenie handles these two classifications easily and has therefore become a major time saver.[17] Salesgenie can provide salespeople with leads in such diverse market segments as medical services, engineering, architecture, agriculture, and education.

Another product available from infoUSA, OneSource, provides in-depth prospect information needed by sales personnel involved in complex, long-cycle sales. Let's assume you are part of a sales team that wants to do business with a group of companies that appear to be highly qualified. OneSource will provide data needed to make sales projections for a specific geographic area and industry type. The real strength of OneSource comes in high-value sales where a thorough understanding of prospects is needed for the first sales call.[18]

With the aid of a personal computer (PC), salespeople can develop their own detailed customer files. The newer PCs provide expanded storage capacity at a lower price than in the past. This means that salespeople can accumulate a great deal of information about individual customers and use this information to personalize the selling process. For example, a PC can help an independent insurance agent maintain a comprehensive record of each policyholder. As the status of each client changes (marriage, birth of children, etc.), the record can be easily updated. With the aid of an up-to-date database, the agent can quickly identify prospects for the various existing and new policy options.

Cold Calling

With some products, cold call prospecting is an effective approach to prospect identification. In **cold calling**, the salesperson selects a group of people who may or may not be actual prospects and then calls (by phone or personal visit) on each one. For example, the sales representative for a wholesale medical supply firm might call on every hospital in a given community, assuming that each one is a potential customer. Many new salespeople must rely on the cold call method because they are less likely to get appointments through referrals.

Edward Jones Corporation, a financial services company, is a strong supporter of cold calling. Sales representatives knock on doors and introduce themselves with a friendly, professional message:

> *"Hi, my name is Brad Ledwith. I represent the Edward Jones Corporation, and we sell financial services. We're a unique firm because we try to do all of our business face-to-face. I just wanted to stop by and let you know that I've opened up a Jones office in the area and to find out if it's OK to contact you when I have an investment idea."*[19]

Sales representatives such as Brad Ledwith connect personally with members of their communities.

Successful cold calls do not happen spontaneously. Some strategic thinking and planning must precede personal visits and telephone calls. Whom do you contact? What do you say during the first few seconds?

With computers, salespeople can accumulate a great deal of information about individual customers and use this information to add value during the selling process.

In order to appear confident and competent, carefully develop your opening remarks. If you appear to be nervous or unprepared, the prospect will assume you lack experience. Many salespeople who make cold call phone calls prepare a well-polished script. The script helps keep you on message and guarantees you will not leave out important information.[20]

Samantha Ettus, CEO of Ettus Media Management, a New York City public relations agency, says cold calls helped her firm land some of its biggest clients. Ettus does plenty of research before she reaches for the phone. She collects all the pertinent information she can find—memberships and professional affiliations, career history, awards received, and of course information regarding the prospect's business. Then she makes the call, which is as brief and precise as possible. Immediately after the call, she sends the prospect a personalized e-mail that summarizes what her firm has to offer. Ettus views the cold call as nothing more than a way to introduce herself and her company to a prospect.[21]

Networking

One of the most complete books on networking is *Dig Your Well Before You're Thirsty* by Harvey Mackay. He says, "If I had to name the single characteristic shared by all the truly successful people I've met over a lifetime, I'd say it's the ability to create and nurture a network of contacts."[22] Networking skills are of special importance to new salespeople who cannot turn to a large group of satisfied customers for referrals and leads. Professionals (accountants, lawyers, consultants, etc.), entrepreneurs, managerial personnel, and customer service representatives also must develop networking skills. Networking skills are also of critical importance to job seekers because at any given time about 80 percent of all available jobs are not posted in the classifieds or on Internet job boards.[23]

In simple terms, **networking** is the art of making and using contacts, or people meeting people and profiting from the connections. Although networking is one of the premier prospecting methods, some salespeople are reluctant to seek referrals in this manner. In addition, many salespeople do not use effective networking practices. Skilled networkers suggest the following guidelines for identifying good referrals:

1. *Meet as many people as you can.* Networking can take place on an airplane, at a Rotary Club meeting, at a trade show, or at a professional association meeting. Don't make the mistake of limiting your networking activities to business contacts. The term **social network** refers to your set of *direct and indirect contacts.* An indirect contact might be the brother of a close friend. The brother works for a large company and can help you see more clearly into the operation of this firm.[24]

2. *When you meet someone, tell the person what you do.* Give your name and describe your position in a way that explains what you do and invites conversations. Instead of saying, "I am in stocks and bonds," say, "I am a financial counselor who helps people make investment decisions." Listen more than you talk.

3. *Do not do business while networking.* It usually is not practical to conduct business while networking. Make a date to call or meet with the new contact later.

4. *Offer your business card.* The business card is especially useful when the contact attempts to tell others about your products or services.

5. *Edit your contacts and follow-up.* You cannot be involved with all your contacts, so separate the productive from the nonproductive. Send a short e-mail message to contacts you deem productive and include business information, brochures— anything that increases visibility.[25] Make sure your materials are professional. Use inexpensive contact management software, such as Salesforce.com, to organize your contact information.

There are three types of networks salespeople should grow and nurture (Figure 9.2). Every salesperson can be well served by networking within their own organization. You never know when someone in finance, technical support, or shipping may be needed to help solve a problem or provide you with important information. A second form of networking involves establishing contacts inside your industry. Make contact with experts in your field, top performers, leaders, successful company representatives, and even competitors. The third form of networking involves business contacts with people outside

FIGURE 9.2

Three Types of Networks
Top-performing salespeople
recognize that networking can
take place in three areas.

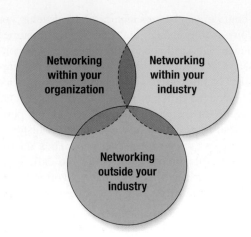

of your industry such as bankers, government officials, developers, and other people in
your community. The local golf course is frequently a good place to make these contacts.[26]

Educational Seminars

Many salespeople are using educational seminars as a method of identifying prospects.
Seminars provide an opportunity to showcase your product without pressuring prospects to
buy. Many banks, accounting firms, wine merchants, and consulting companies use seminars
to generate new prospects. Previously we mentioned that Edward Jones's sales representatives often make cold calls on prospects. They also schedule seminars that provide prospects
with an opportunity to acquire information regarding the potential benefits of investing in
a mutual fund. Another popular seminar topic is the benefits of tax-free investing. A
complimentary lunch is usually served before the informative presentation. When inviting
prospects, be clear about the seminar's content and always deliver what you promise.

Prospecting by Nonsales Employees

Should service technicians, receptionists, bank tellers, and other nonsales personnel be
involved in prospecting? In a growing number of organizations the answer is yes. Prospecting

Selling in Action

DEVELOP YOUR PROSPECT BASE WITH SEMINARS

 The use of educational seminars has become an
important prospecting method. You can educate
prospective customers with brochures, news
releases, catalogs, or your Web site, but educational seminars
offer the advantage of face-to-face contact. Barbara Siskind,
in her book *Seminars to Build Your Business*, identifies
15 objectives for hosting seminars. A few of the most important ones follow:

Obtain sales leads. This is one of the most common
objectives for seminars. You can obtain the names of
attendees and arrange appointments for future sales
calls. Seminars also may help identify actual product
users, technical support people, or engineers who,
although they may not be the decision maker, may
influence the purchase decision.

Promote your place of business. Your place of business can become a destination for people who might

otherwise not consider visiting it. You have an opportunity to create awareness of your company and
develop a positive image for your entire operation
and its capabilities.

Showcase and demonstrate your expertise. Seminars
allow you to show a carefully targeted group of people
that you really know your stuff. Salespeople can be
supported by technical experts and others in the organization who can address clients' specific concerns.

Polaroid Canada advertised educational seminars
across Canada where imaging specialists assisted prospective clients in exploring imaging solutions. Toronto-based
Charon Systems, Incorporated, a systems integrator that
deploys networks for organizations, regularly organizes
seminars for 80 to 100 technology people from midsized
firms. President David Fung estimates that 25 percent of
prospects become clients.[c]

does not need to be the exclusive responsibility of the sales force. Janet Dixon, a UPS sales representative, needed help making contact with an important prospect. This person wouldn't take her calls. She talked to the UPS service provider (driver) who called on this account and requested his help. He had serviced this company for years and was like part of the family. He knew the prospect personally and persuaded her to accept a call from the salesperson.[27]

Combination Approaches

In recent years, we have seen an increase in the number of prospecting approaches used by salespeople. In many cases, success in selling depends on your ability to use a combination of the methods described in this chapter. For example, the large number of prospects identified at a trade show might be used to develop an effective telemarketing program. Prospects are called and an effort is made to set up a personal call. Prospects identified at a trade show or educational seminar might be sent a sales-oriented newsletter, a sales letter, or an e-mail message inviting prospects to visit your Web page.

Qualifying the Prospect

One of the most important keys to success in personal selling is the ability to qualify prospects. **Qualifying** is the process of identifying prospects who appear to have a need for your product and should be contacted. Top salespeople use good research and analysis skills to qualify leads effectively.[28]

The qualifying process is also the first opportunity to consider what the needs of the buyer might be, and how those needs match with the product characteristics being sold.[29] Some sales organizations link the qualifying process with the need discovery step in the consultative sales process. In most cases, this linkage will depend on the nature and complexity of prospect's buying process. The more complex the buying process, the more likely these two sales functions will be separate steps in the sales process. We will explore fully the need discovery step in Chapter 11.

Every salesperson needs to establish qualifying criteria. The process involves finding answers to several basic questions.

1. *Does the prospect have a need for my product?* If you sell copy machines, it might appear that every business firm is a prospect. However, a firm that is outsourcing its copy work to FedEx Kinko's may not be a legitimate prospect.

    Qualifying involves probing for real needs. Let's assume you sell real estate for a large agency. You receive a call from someone who believes that owning a home is a good tax benefit. At this point it's important to find out what else makes owning a home important for that person. Get permission to ask questions and then determine the person's real needs. In the final analysis you may decide it would be a waste of your time and the prospect's time to visit several homes that are on the market.[30]

2. *Does the prospect have the authority to buy my product?* Ideally you should talk to a person who has the authority to buy or can influence the buying decision. Talking to the right person within a large organization may involve collecting information from several sources. Some buying decisions are made by individuals and others are made by a committee. Expensive products often require the approval of a decision maker higher up in the organization.

3. *Does the prospect have the financial resources to buy my product?* It is usually not difficult to obtain credit information for consumer and business buyers. If you are selling products to a business, the *Dun & Bradstreet Reference Book* is an excellent source of credit information. A local credit bureau can provide credit information for a consumer buyer.

    Although the collection of credit information is not difficult, detecting financial instability can be much more complicated. In recent years we have seen a steady stream of corporate scandals involving accounting irregularities, inflated balance sheets, and outright fraud.[31] Salespeople must be aware of the possibility that a customer may provide incorrect or misleading information.

4. *Does the prospect have the willingness to buy my product?* Rick Page, author of *Hope Is Not a Strategy*, reminds us that many prospects evaluate products but do not buy. When an evaluation stalls, the prospect may have determined that the problem is not of great enough magnitude or urgency to make the purchase. Also, in some cases there is not enough support within the company to reach closure. Rather than walk away from this situation, some salespeople move higher in the organization to determine the level of support for the purchase.[32]

A large number of senior executives say they get involved in the sale early in the decision process, yet salespeople have difficulty meeting with high-level decision makers. Most senior executives will not meet with salespeople who are making cold calls. When appointments are granted, the time allocated may be very short; 5 to 10 minutes is not uncommon. How do you establish credibility for yourself and your company in a short time period? Be sure you know a great deal about the company before the appointment and be prepared to demonstrate your knowledge of the company and the industry it serves. Do not propose solutions until you fully understand the buyer's problems. Be sure to communicate value.[33]

This list of questions can be revised to meet the needs of many different types of salespeople. A sales representative for an industrial equipment dealer may see the qualifying process differently from the person who sells commercial real estate. The main consideration is providing accurate answers to each question.

Collecting and Organizing Prospect Information

The Internet and information revolution continues to make acquiring and managing sales leads much easier.[34] When it comes to collecting and organizing prospect information, salespeople have a large assortment of computer-based systems available. Companies such as Salesforce.com, Oracle, NetSuite, Sage, and Microsoft all offer software applications designed to collect and organize prospect information. Most of these Sales Force Automation (SFA) Systems or Customer Relationship Management (CRM) Systems as they are now known have preset categories or fields that contain sales data on the prospect. This **sales data** is the information seen in most CRM systems including the contact name, title, address, phone number, e-mail, etc. It also may include information about what products have been purchased, what sales opportunities exist in the future, who the various members or influencers are in the buying center, what their preferred communication styles are, past sales and forecasted sales, volume, and percentage change and date of closing the sale. All of the sales data information about a prospect in a CRM system is presented in the account screen report. Figure 9.3 shows an account screen report for Able Profit Machines. The information in this report, including any notes about previous sales calls is accessed and studied before the salesperson makes a sales call.

FIGURE 9.3

The CRM Account Screen Report

This account screen report shows sales data for Able Profit Machines. The sales data, including any notes from previous sales call was entered by sales representative Pat Silva, of SimNet Systems. Pat Silva has been calling on Able Profit Machines President, Bradley Able and Jack Smith. (For more information on SimNet Systems see CRM Case Study on p. 204.)

Source: Courtesy of Salesforce.com.

When bringing new prospects into the database, it is expected the salesperson will acquire this sales data and enter it into the records kept on the prospect. In most CRM systems this information goes into a shared database that allows other members of the sales team to access the information and make additions as they work with prospects. In the event a new salesperson takes over an existing prospect database, all of this information can be accessed quickly and used to plan sales strategies to work effectively with prospects.

Sales Intelligence

In addition to collecting sales data, the collection of **sales intelligence** is necessary when the sale is complex and requires a long closing cycle. Sales intelligence goes beyond data, giving salespeople access to insights into the prospect's marketplace, their firm, their competitors, even about the prospects themselves. Sales intelligence is needed today over and above sales data because prospects are looking for insights and knowledge from salespeople above and beyond the product features and benefits. In many buying situations today, prospects using advanced search engines have already learned about features and benefits. In terms of sales intelligence, prospects expect salespeople to know answers to many of the following questions. Answers to these questions create much of the value that results in successfully turning prospects into long-term customers:

Do You Know Me? You need to know more than my name and title. Do you know my role, my goals, how I am evaluated, and how long I have been with the organization? Do you know the projects I am working on, my style of doing business, and what the requirements are for me to meet my objectives? Do you know about previous dealings I have had with your company? Do I have a favorable opinion of your company and do you know my role and the role of other influencers in the decision making process?

Do You Know My Company and My Marketplace? Do you know our company mission statement, culture, and vision for the future? Do you know clearly what we are

Your OneSource for Global Business Information

OneSource delivers the most in-depth business information available, providing companies with the data needed to effectively approach targeted markets including; solutions for Sales, Marketing, M&A/Finance, Insurance, Procurement, Recruitment, Legal Compliance, Consulting, Research and more.

Global Business Information

♦Companies ♦Executives ♦Industries ♦Financials ♦Analysis Data ♦News

OneSource enables companies to:

- Access data via your web browser
- Integrate with CRM systems
- View rich company profiles
- Develop quality sales leads
- Improve pre-meeting planning
- Gain competitive intelligence
- Identify key executives
- Target new customers
- Analyze financial performance
- Research industry trends

OneSource.
Global Business Information

866-354-6936

www.onesource.com

One Source goes beyond sales data, and supplies value adding sales intelligence to salespeople involved in complex sales that have a long closing cycle. This prospect information is loaded into a customer's CRM account detail. Salespeople review this information to plan strategies for successfully moving the sale through the stages in the sales process.

doing, how we are performing in the marketplace, what issues keep us up all night, and who and what our competitors are doing? Do you know where we fit into the existing competitive landscape? Are we the leader or are we in the position of having to play catch-up to survive? Can you relate what you sell directly to what we need to accomplish our goals? Do you know who our partners are? What effect the current economy has on our business?

Do You Have Any Special Value-Add? You have a product or service you think we need, but what else can you bring to the table? Are there additional resources you can bring to bear to solve my problems or improve my internal business processes? Can you educate me on how you are truly different from the other players in your area of expertise so I can support my recommendation to work with you? Can you help me build a case for return on investment (ROI)?[35]

Answers to these questions come from many sources. CRM suppliers like Salesforce.com, InfoUSA.com, Sales-i.com, and Vecta.net have programs that supply this kind of sales intelligence to companies and salespeople. infoUSA's OneSource is one example of a supplier of sales intelligence. OneSource supplies sales intelligence to Cardinal Logistics Management, a major provider of logistics, transportation and supply-chain solutions to large retailers, manufacturers, and distribution companies. Cardinal's salespeople must know each prospect inside and out in order to sell logistics solutions effectively to their 5,000 customers. OneSource supplies 24/7, anywhere access to detailed customer profiles, executive contact data and biographies, financial statements, news trade articles, and analyst reports. A special new-alert feature keeps salespeople up-to-date on any and all developments within their customer's company and their industry, including both their customer's customer and their competitors.[36]

Most importantly, this information must be entered into the company's CRM system to get a 360-degree view of the prospect. This information will also be used to move the prospect through the steps in the sales process.

Managing the Prospect Base

High-performing salespeople today are focused on effectively managing sales activities for all prospects in their database. This means that the size and number of prospects is more carefully considered. Too few prospects in various stages of the sales cycle can quickly signal problems. Alternatively, too many customers can drain a salesperson's resources so that too little effort is focused on prospects with the best opportunities. This is a particular problem when salespeople spend too much effort on prospects that have limited potential. CRM software can help organize customer data into meaningful and easy to interpret information, as evident in Figure 9.4.

FIGURE 9.4

The Prospect Base

This CRM record presents a complete list of salesperson Pat Silva's prospects. Note this list includes information on the forecasted dollar amount of each sale, projected date of close, and what stage of the sales process the prospect is in. In CRM systems like Salesforce, clicking on any of the prospects on this list will allow the user to drill down into detailed contact information and notes supporting these projections.

Source: Courtesy of Salesforce.com.

To effectively and efficiently manage the prospect base, sales managers and salespeople often conduct an **account analysis** to estimate the sales potential for each prospect. It is a necessary step before deciding how to allocate sales calls across accounts. The portfolio model and the sales process model are two popular models salespeople use for performing account analysis and deciding how much time and effort, and what sale strategies to use with the prospects in their database.

Portfolio Models

Portfolio models involve the use of multiple factors when classifying prospects. Figure 9.5 illustrates a typical four-cell model based on two factors: overall account opportunity for the seller and the seller's competitive position, that is, the ability to capitalize on these opportunities.[37]

The portfolio model provides an excellent framework to facilitate communication between salespeople and the various sales support personnel. Teamwork at this stage in the sales cycle can develop improved strategies for working successfully with difference accounts and contacts in the prospect base. Portfolio models are most effective where salespeople must understand individual customer needs and where relationship strength is important to sales success.

Sales Process Models

Sales process models, also referred to as sales funnel models, classify prospects based on where they are in the sales process. The **sales process model** is the total set of prospects being pursued at any given time. The sales process model is illustrated in Figure 9.6. This five-step sales process model includes qualification, needs analysis, presentation/proposal, negotiations, and order. An account might be simply a qualified prospect, ready for a needs analysis, in serious negotiations with the salesperson, or ready to place an order. In sales process model reports like Figure 9.6, clicking on any part of any bar graph will drill down into and report all the supporting data on prospects in each stage of the sales process.

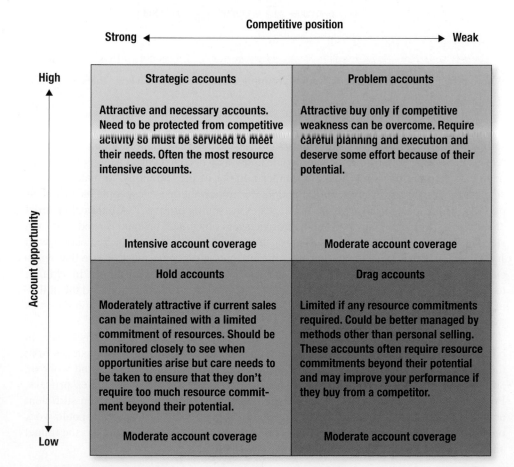

FIGURE 9.5

The Portfolio Model

This portfolio model uses account opportunity (forecasted sales) and competitive position (the ability to capitalize on the opportunity) to classify how much sales effort should be made on individual accounts in the prospect data base. Those prospects listed in the strategic accounts cell (high sales forecast and strong position for closing the sale) will receive the largest amount of sales effort, while those in the drag accounts cell will receive little, if any attention.

FIGURE 9.6

**The CRM Sales Process
(or Funnel) Model**

The sales process, or sales funnel model as it is frequently called, classifies prospects according to where they are in the sales process. It is important that salespeople balance their portfolio of prospects that are at various stages of the selling process. This enables salespeople to know how many prospects, and how much revenue is needed at each stage in the sales process to meet sales projections and budgets.

Source: Courtesy of Salesforce.com.

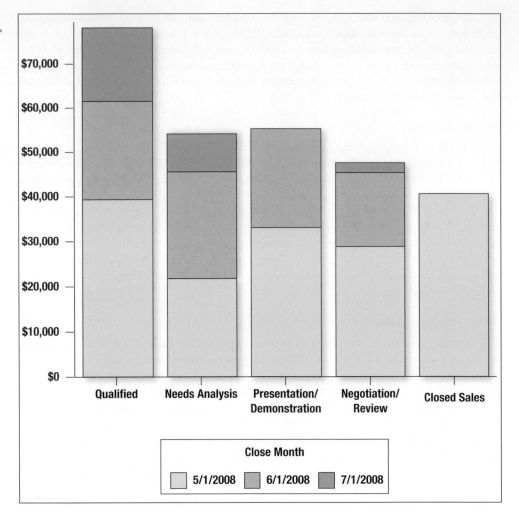

Where an account is in the sales process has implications for "if and when" the salesperson will be able to close the sale.

The sales cycle for complex technical sales such as networking installations might be several months in duration. The number of prospects in the sales process or funnel for selling networking installations may be small compared to the number for an insurance or real estate salesperson. Insurance salespeople know they need to contact a larger number of people to gain permission to make a smaller number of presentations, to make an even small number of sales. In any selling situation, it is important that salespeople balance their portfolio of prospects that are at various stages of the selling process.[38] A **balanced funnel** enables salespeople to know how many prospects and how much revenue is needed at each stage in the sales process to meet sales projections and quotas.[39] As indicated earlier with Joe Girard's "Ferris wheel" concept, this means that salespeople must ensure that sufficient prospects are regularly added to the funnel, so it does not become empty. In addition to the number of prospects, the quality of the prospects added to the funnel and the ability of the salesperson to manage the sales process will affect the number of sales opportunities that are successfully closed.

Salespeople need to ensure that they "work" the whole funnel so that it is always in balance. They should work on sales opportunities in the negotiation and close stages first; that is, close those that are near the end of the sales process. Then they should work on adding new prospects, and those that are in the earlier stages of the sales process. Prospecting is an activity that some salespeople dislike, but if it is not given sufficient attention there is a real danger that the funnel will empty. Finally, salespeople should work on those opportunities that are in the sales process, moving them along through the funnel and ensuring there is regular, predictable sales over time.[40]

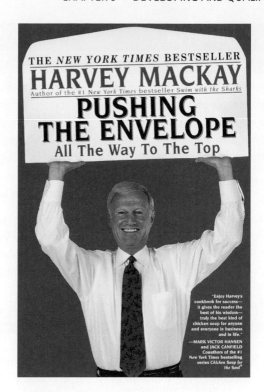

Well-known author Harvey Mackay instructs his salespeople to develop a 66-question customer profile. This information helps you know the prospects both as individuals and as business representatives.

CRM Technology for Pipeline Management

This process of managing all the prospects in the salesperson's sales funnel to ensure that sales objectives are being met is called **pipeline management**. CRM software provides an efficient and effective tool for forecasting and managing pipelines. Using sales data entered into the account detail, contact screens, notes applications, etc., sales forecasts can be continually updated as prospects move through the stages in the sales process. Prospects in the database who are no longer qualified, for whatever reason, can be quickly dropped from the sales funnel. Figure 9.7 shows part of a pipeline dashboard produced by a CRM software suite.

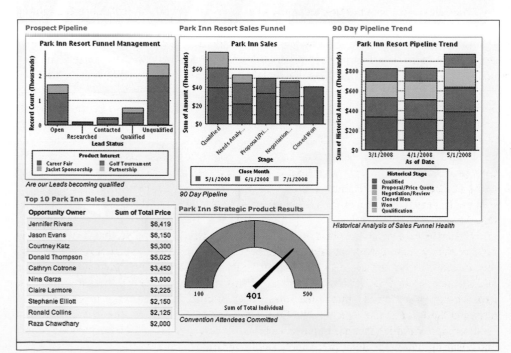

FIGURE 9.7

Pipeline Dashboards

These pipeline dashboards are at-a-glance visualizations that define, monitor, and analyze the relationships existing in the pipeline or funnel. Pipeline analytics exist in most modern CRM systems and are used to produce these important prospect movement reports. The salesperson can quickly and easily access detailed information on specific prospects, and then use this information to plan strategies for moving the prospect to the next stage of the sales process.

Source: Courtesy of Salesforce.com.

Global Business Etiquette

DOING BUSINESS IN GERMANY

Germany represents the world's third largest economy and is America's largest European trading partner. If you are a salesperson planning a business trip to Germany, keep in mind that there is greater formality in the German business community.

- Germany has been described as a "low-context" culture in which words carry most of the information. Messages tend to be explicit and direct. In this culture, negotiations (verbal or written) tend to be explicit in defining terms of the agreement. By comparison, China is a high-context culture in which exact phrasing and the verbal part of the messages tend to be less significant than your relationship with the other person.

- There is a strong emphasis on punctuality, so avoid being late for appointments. Germans tend to make appointments far in advance.

- Lunch is the most common meal for business meetings. Dining etiquette in Germany involves eating continental style—holding the fork in the left hand continually and the knife in the right hand.

- The sales presentation should include data and empirical evidence that support your proposal. Brochures and other printed information should be serious and detailed, not flashy.[d]

Pipeline analytics, defined as the ability to conduct sophisticated data analysis and modeling, are found in most CRM systems. Using pipeline analytics, new reports can be generated regarding the movement of the prospects through the sales funnel. These reports can be more clearly presented with the use of dashboards. **Pipeline dashboards** are at-a-glance visualizations that define, monitor, and analyze the relationships existing in the pipeline or sales funnel. Sales team members including the sales manager working together from a shared CRM database can collaborate to create value and enhance the sales strategies to help the salesperson move prospects through the pipeline to a successful sale. CRM pipeline dashboards allow the user to quickly and easily drill down into the reports and records supporting them. This provides for quick updates as prospects move through the sales funnel. Dashboards can also provide insight into the need to add new prospects, as existing ones are moved through the stages of the sales process.

Most salespeople use CRM software in the development of their prospecting and sales forecasting plan. This software allows the convenient preparation and management of prospect lists.

Chapter Learning Activities

Reviewing Key Concepts

Discuss the importance of developing a prospect base

Prospect identification has been called the lifeblood of selling. A continuous supply of new customers must be found to replace those lost for various reasons. *Prospecting* is the systematic process of locating potential customers. Prospecting requires careful planning.

Identify and assess important sources of prospects

Analysis of both your product and your existing customers can help to identify, locate, and profile your prospects. Important sources of new customers include *referrals* (endless chain referrals and referral letters and cards), centers of influence, friends and family members, directories, trade publications, trade shows and special events, telemarketing and e-mail, direct-response advertising and sales letters, Web sites, computer databases, cold calling, education seminars, networking, and prospecting by nonsale employees.

Describe criteria for qualifying prospects

Prospecting techniques produce a list of names that must be evaluated using criteria developed by each salesperson. The process of prospect evaluation is called *qualifying.*

The qualifying process involves finding answers to several basic questions: Does the prospect have a need for my product? Can the prospect make the buying decision? Can the prospect pay for the purchase? Does the prospect have the willingness to buy my product? An estimate of the amount of sales that could be generated from this prospect and the prospect's credit rating also should be determined.

Explain common methods of collecting and organizing prospect information

Most companies rely on Customer Relationship Management (CRM) systems to keep track of sales data. The collection of sales intelligence beyond sales data enables salespeople to impress their knowledgeable customers with insights that are above and beyond the product and/or service features and benefits.

Describe the steps in managing the prospect base

Salespeople need to allocate their resources wisely to make the most of the prospect base. They do so by conducting account analyses, using either the portfolio models or the sales funnel models.

Key Terms

Prospecting	Cold calling	Account analysis
Prospect	Networking	Sales process model
Prospect base	Social network	Balanced funnel
Referral	Qualifying	Pipeline management
Telemarketing	Sales data	Pipeline analytics
Web site	Sales intelligence	Pipeline dashboards

Review Questions

1. List and briefly explain the common causes of customer attrition.
2. During periods of economic uncertainty, the decision-making process often moves upward. What basic tips would you give a salesperson who is calling on senior executives?
3. Describe three steps progressive marketers are taking to improve the quality of the prospecting effort.

4. List the major sources of prospects.

5. Explain how the endless chain referral prospecting method works.

6. Discuss how direct-response advertising and sales letters can be used to identify prospects.

7. What is *networking*? How might a real estate salesperson use networking to identify prospects?

8. What does the term *qualifying* mean? What are the four basic questions that should be answered during the qualifying process?

9. What are the most common methods of organizing prospect information?

10. When is sales intelligence important? What are the three most important pieces of sales intelligence a salesperson needs to know?

11. Describe two popular models for performing the account analysis.

Application Exercises

1. Prior to getting involved in networking, it's a good idea to prepare an "elevator" presentation. This is a 30-second pitch that summarizes what you want people to know about you. You might think of yourself as a "product" to be sold to an employer who has a job opening. Make your presentation upbeat and brief. Who are you? What are you currently doing? What type of work are you looking for? Practice the presentation alone in front of a mirror and then present it to one or two class members.

2. You are a sales representative for Xerox Corporation. Assuming Xerox has just designed a new, less expensive, and better-quality copying machine, make a list of 15 prospects you would plan to contact. From the material in this chapter, identify the sources you would use in developing your prospect list.

3. You are in the process of interviewing for a sales position with CIGNA Insurance Company. In addition to filling out an application form and taking an aptitude test, one of the items the agency manager requests of you is to develop a list of prospects with whom you are acquainted. He informs you that this list includes the prospects you will be working with during the first few weeks of employment. The agency manager recommends that you list at least 50 names. Prepare a list of 10 acquaintances you have that would qualify as prospects.

4. Sales automation software is most commonly used in the prospecting phase of selling. New-product releases are continually being developed that provide additional features and benefits to salespeople. The software used in this book is marketed by a leader in the field. Access www.salesforce.com and research the latest version of Salesforce. Click on and examine the latest demonstration copy of this popular sales automation software.

5. Locating companies to work for is a form of prospecting. Assuming you are interested in changing careers, develop a list of 10 companies for which you would like to work. Assign each company a priority according to your interest, from the most desirable (1) to the least (10). Organize your list in six columns showing the company name, telephone number, address, person in charge of hiring, prospect information, and priority. What sources did you use to get this information?

Role-Play Exercise

For this role-play, you will assume a sales position at a Lexus dealership. You have just completed a successful sale by signing the papers for the second new Lexus this customer has purchased in the past four years. Because you know your prospect has had a very successful experience with his first Lexus, you have decided to use the referral methods described in this chapter. Review the material on referrals and plan what you will say to your customer to build your prospect base. Pair off with another student who will assume the role of your customer. Explain that satisfied customers often know other people who would consider purchasing a Lexus. You might say, "Considering the positive experience you have had as a Lexus owner, you probably know others who appreciate fine automobiles. Is there anyone who comes to mind?" If, after probing, your customer doesn't recall someone immediately, ask permission to call him later to see if anyone has come to mind. Ask this person for actual names, addresses, and other qualifying information about prospective customers whom he knows. Also, ask the customer if he would write a referral note or letter that you could use.

Case Problem

Gary Hanna, vice president of sales at Salesforce.com, says, "Once you have a relationship with a customer, maintaining that relationship is a lot more profitable than finding a new customer." A growing number of salespeople are using Salesforce.com or one of its competitors to improve service to customers. Mark Golden, sales force administrator at Ceva Logistics—the world's largest provider of logistics and freight management services—is giving Ceva's customers added value with Salesforce.com. Like most other salespeople, CEVA account managers like Darrin Marks are trying to cope with expanded duties, faster work pace, and customers with high expectations. Salesforce.com helps in the following ways:

Customer profiles. All relevant customer information is available in one centralized place. In addition to name, phone, and e-mail, he can include detailed personal information such as hobbies, interests, role in the organization, and who each contact reports to. Past activities with regard to e-mails, meetings, conference calls, and opportunities that this contact is related to can be noted for a complete 360-degree view of the contact.

Organization and planning. Darrin can plan and manage his time using the calendar management features available with Salesforce.com. By simply looking at his home page, Darrin can view all upcoming appointments and activities. Phone calls, customer meetings, and conference calls can be scheduled and recorded with reminder alerts throughout the day. When conference calls are required, managing the invitee list can be accomplished by choosing the appropriate contacts to include. Darrin can also share his calendar with fellow colleagues in order to better collaborate.

Correspondence. Salesforce.com can be used to manage all correspondence between Darrin and his customers including, e-mails, marketing brochures, and company newsletters. Darrin just needs to navigate to the customer he wants to communicate with, click the Send an E-mail button, and pick the type of correspondence he wishes to send. In addition to sending individual e-mails, features such as mass e-mail, mass stay in touch, and mass add to campaign allow Darrin to request updates from all of his contacts, or communicate about important company information with all of his contacts at once.

Questions

1. If your goal is to maintain long-term partnerships with each of your customers, what features of Salesforce.com are most helpful?

2. Let us assume you are selling copy machines in a city with a population of 100,000 people. Your territory includes the entire city. What features of Salesforce.com would you use most frequently?

3. Some salespeople who could benefit from use of Salesforce.com or a competing product continue to use a Rolodex or note cards to keep a record of the customers they call on. What are some barriers to the adoption of this type of technology?

4. Examine the Salesforce.com contact screen presented in Appendix 2.
  a. What is Bradley Able's position within the company?
  b. What is the expected close date for the Bradley Able's sales opportunity?
  c. What is the forecasted dollar amount of this potential sale?

CRM Case Study

Reviewing the Prospect Database

Becky Kemley is the sales manager in the Dallas, Texas, office of SimNet Systems, which sells network products and services. The productivity and the critical mission of Becky's customers can be considerably enhanced by selecting and using the correct LAN (local area network), WAN (wide area network), or VPN (virtual private network) system. Becky's company is called a value-added reseller (VAR) because its people help customers maximize the value of the products bought through SimNet.

Becky's sales and technical support people may spend several months in the sales process (sales cycle). Salespeople telephone and call on prospects to determine if they qualify for SimNet's attention. Time is taken to study the customer's needs (needs discovery). The expert opinion of SimNet's technical people is incorporated into a sales proposal that is presented to the prospective customer. The presentation may be made to a number of decision makers in the prospect's firm. The final decision to purchase may follow weeks of consideration within the firm and negotiations with SimNet.

Once a decision is made by a customer to buy from SimNet, Becky's people begin the process of acquiring, assembling, and installing the network system and then follow through with appropriate training, integration, and support services.

Becky's company must carefully prospect for customers. SimNet may invest a significant amount of time helping a potential customer configure the right combination of products and services. This means that only the most serious prospects should be cultivated. Further, Becky's people must ascertain that if the investment of time is made in a prospective customer, the prospect will follow through with purchases from SimNet.

Becky is responsible for assuring that prospect information is collected and used effectively. The network salespeople use Salesforce.com to manage their prospect information. The system allows salespeople to document and manage their sales efforts with each prospect.

Becky has just hired you to sell for SimNet beginning June 1. Becky has given you the files of Pat Silva, a salesperson who just has been promoted to SimNet's corporate headquarters. Becky has asked you to review the status of Pat's 20 prospect accounts. Pat's customers have been notified that Pat is leaving and that a new salesperson, you, will be contacting them. Becky wants you to review each prospect's record. You are to meet with Becky next Monday and be prepared to answer the following questions.

Refer to Appendix 2 in the back of your book for instructions on how to access and review the 20 Salesforce.com prospect records of Pat Silva. If you haven't already done so, view the Salesforce.com video demo at www.salesforce.com <http://salesforce.com>.

Questions

1. Which contact can you ignore immediately *as a prospect* for making a potential purchase?

2. Referring only to the *date close* category, which four prospects would you call immediately?

3. Referring only to the *dollar amount* of sales forecasted category, which four accounts would you call first? Does the likelihood of closing percentage category have any influence on decisions concerning which prospects to call first? Why?

4. According to information on the records, what sources did Pat Silva use most to find new prospects? Give examples.

Part 4 | **Role-Play Exercise**

DEVELOPING A CUSTOMER STRATEGY

Scenario

You are a sales representative employed by the Park Inn International hotel and convention center. One of your primary responsibilities is to identify prospects and make sales calls that result in the development of new accounts. During each of these calls, you plan to build a relationship with the customer and describe selected value-added guest services and amenities offered by the Park Inn. You also try to learn as much as possible about the customer's buying process.

Customer Profile

Shannon Fordham is the founder and chief executive officer of USA Technologies, a growing high-tech firm with over 300 employees. The company manufactures and sells security systems that can be used in residential homes, retail stores, and other commercial buildings. According to a recent article in the *Wall Street Journal*, USA Technologies is poised to grow very rapidly in the next year. The article described Shannon Fordham as a workaholic who usually puts in an 80-hour workweek. Delegation does not come easy to this personable, hard-charging entrepreneur.

Salesperson Profile

You have just completed the Park Inn sales training program and now wants to develop some new accounts. In addition to taking care of established customers, you plan to call on at least four new prospects every week.

Product

Park Inn International is a full-service hotel and convention center located in Rockport, Illinois. The hotel recently completed a $2.8 million renovation of its meeting and banquet rooms.

Instructions

For this role-play activity, you will meet with Shannon Fordham, who appears to be a good prospect. During the first sales call, plan to learn more about the prospect as an individual and acquire more information about USA Technologies. This meeting will provide you with the opportunity to begin building a long-term partnership.

During the first meeting with a prospect, you like to present a limited amount of important product information. In this case the length of the appointment is 15 minutes, so you should not try to cover too much information. To prepare for the first sales call, read Employment Memorandum 1 in Appendix 3. This memo describes the value-added guest services and amenities offered by the Park Inn. For the purpose of this role-play, Shannon Fordham should be considered a consultative process buyer. You can assume that the prospect will need help identifying and evaluating possible solutions. As you prepare for the first call, think about what may take place during future calls. Review the steps in the typical buying process (see Figure 8.3). Keep in mind that today's more demanding customers are seeking a cluster of satisfactions. Study the Product-Selling Model (Figure 7.1) prior to meeting with the prospect.

Developing a Presentation Strategy

The chapters included in Part 5 review the basic principles used in the strategic/consultative sales presentation. This information is used as you prepare presentation objectives, develop a presentation plan that adds value, and identify ways to provide outstanding service after the sale.

"To play any game well, you first have to learn the rules or principles of the game. And second, you have to forget them. That is, you have to learn to play without thinking about the rules. This is true whether the game is chess or golf or selling. Shortcuts won't work."

From Al Ries and Jack Trout's Marketing Warfare

10

Approaching the Customer with Adaptive Selling

Chapter Preview

When you finish reading this chapter, you should be able to

1

Describe the three prescriptions that are included in the presentation strategy

2

Discuss the two-part preapproach process

3

Describe team presentation strategies

4

Explain how adaptive selling builds on four broad strategic areas of personal selling

5

Describe the six main parts of the presentation plan

6

Explain how to effectively approach the customer

7

Describe seven ways to convert the prospect's attention and arouse interest

Reality Selling Today Video Series

The worldwide Hilti Corporation (www.hilti.com) specializes in providing leading-edge technology to the global construction industry. With some 20,000 employees in more than 120 countries around the world, Hilti actively pursues a value-added orientation in all of its activities.

As part of this orientation, Hilti puts its new salespeople through a rigorous training curriculum that includes one-month pretraining on Hilti products and services, a three-week intensive training in product and services sales, and a two-week training on software applications. In addition, these salespeople also ride along with experienced sales managers to get hands-on experience. Furthermore, the company offers refresher courses to keep its salespeople updated on Hilti's products and services, the construction market, and corporate strategy. Equipped with this in-depth knowledge and the value orientation that is deeply rooted in the corporate culture, salespeople like Alim Hirani, on the right in the photo above, are always well prepared to approach customers to make sales presentations, demonstrate and explain Hilti's products and services, and show the customers both the tangible and intangible benefits that Hilti can offer.

With a direct sales model, Hilti relies heavily on its salespeople to make the connection and deliver its values to its global customers. Alim is a strong believer that he and his sales team are the face of the company. His credibility is embedded in Hilti's credibility and vice versa. He always makes sure that his sales presentations are well prepared in advance. More importantly, he builds and maintains rapport with his customers from the very beginning of the business relationship because such partnership mentality motivates the customers to disclose their actual concerns. In the end, customers only value solutions that address their actual needs, and Alim as a Hilti salesperson knows that by heart.

Developing the Presentation Strategy

The presentation strategy combines elements of the relationship, product, and customer strategies. Each of the other three strategies must be developed before a salesperson can create an effective presentation strategy.

The **presentation strategy** is a well-conceived plan that includes three prescriptions: (1) establishing objectives for the sales presentation, (2) developing the presale presentation plan needed to meet these objectives, and (3) renewing one's commitment to providing outstanding customer service (Figure 10.1).

The first prescription reminds us that we need to establish one or more objectives for each sales call. High-performance salespeople like Alim Hirani understand that it is often possible to accomplish several goals during a single call. A common objective of sales calls is to collect information about the prospect's needs. Another common objective is to develop, build, or sustain a relationship with those who make the buying decision.

A carefully prepared presentation plan ensures that salespeople are well organized during the sales presentation and prepared to achieve their objectives. A six-step presentation plan is introduced later in this chapter.

Strategic/Consultative Selling Model*	
Strategic Step	**Prescription**
Develop a Personal Selling Philosophy	☑ Adopt Marketing Concept ☑ Value Personal Selling ☑ Become a Problem Solver/Partner
Develop a Relationship Strategy	☑ Adopt Win-Win Philosophy ☑ Project Professional Image ☑ Maintain High Ethical Standards
Develop a Product Strategy	☑ Become a Product Expert ☑ Sell Benefits ☑ Configure Value-Added Solutions
Develop a Customer Strategy	☑ Understand the Buying Process ☑ Understand Buyer Behavior ☑ Develop Prospect Base
Develop a Presentation Strategy	☑ Prepare Objectives ☑ Develop Presentation Plan ☑ Provide Outstanding Service

*Strategic/consultative selling evolved in response to increased competition, more complex products, increased emphasis on customer needs, and growing importance of long-term relationships.

Establishment of objectives for the sales presentation and preparation of the presentation plan must be guided by a strong desire to offer outstanding customer service. Achieving excellence is the result of careful needs analysis, correct product selection, clear presentations, informative demonstrations, win-win negotiations, and flawless service after the sale. Salespeople who are committed to doing their best in each of these areas are richly rewarded.

Presentation Strategy Adds Value

How does precall planning add value? Value is added when you position yourself as a resource—not just a vendor. You must prove that you have important ideas and advice to offer.[1] A well-planned presentation adds value when it is based on carefully developed sales call objectives and a presentation plan needed to meet these objectives. Good planning ensures that the presentation is customized and adapted to meet the needs and time constraints of the prospect. Increasingly, customers' time is very limited and they want a concise and thoughtful presentation. Careful planning is the key to delivering more value and increasing your sales productivity.[2]

Salespeople need to be aware of the changing needs of their customers or risk losing out to the competition. Some salespeople do not pay enough attention to how they conduct business with their established customers. Without a precall plan, it's easy to miss opportunities to increase your knowledge of the customer's business, sell new products, or discover ways to improve service.[3]

Planning the Preapproach

Preparation for the actual sales presentation is a two-part process. Part one is referred to as the **preapproach**. The preapproach involves preparing presale objectives and developing a presale presentation plan. Part two is called the **approach** and involves making a favorable first impression, securing the prospect's attention, and transitioning to need identification (Figure 10.2). The preapproach and approach, when handled correctly, establish a foundation for an effective sales presentation.

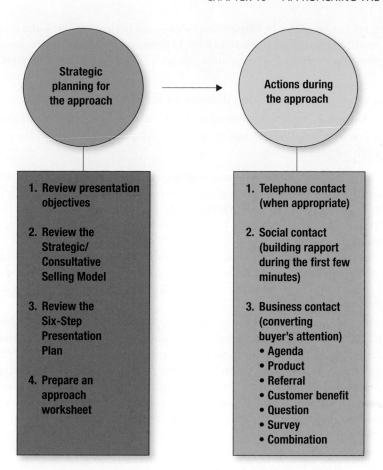

FIGURE 10.2

Preparing for the presentation involves planning for the activities that occur before meeting the prospect and for the first few minutes of actual contact with the prospect.

The preapproach should be viewed as a key step in preparing for each sales presentation. Professional salespeople complete the preapproach for every presentation whether it involves a new account or an established customer. Top salespeople often spend two or three hours planning for a 25-minute sales call. The preapproach includes the first two prescriptions for developing a presentation strategy: establishing objectives and creating a presale presentation plan.

Establishing Presentation Objectives

Preparation for a sales call is part research, part planning, and part critical thinking. Sales representatives employed by Nalco Chemical Company prepare for each sales call by filling out a 13-point precall planner. One section of this form requires the salesperson to identify the objectives of the call. Nalco is a company that emphasizes professionalism, long-term partnerships, and staying focused on customer needs.[4]

In Chapter 8, we introduced the five stages of the typical buying process (see Figure 8.3). When you are calling on a *consultative* or *strategic alliance* buyer, you will usually not cover all of these stages during a single sales call. Multicall sales presentations are especially common in complex sales. Therefore, it's best to develop presentation objectives suitable for each stage of the buying process. During the first stage—need awareness—customers may or may not be aware of their needs and problems. The need awareness stage is the "investigation" stage. To uncover and clarify needs will require the use of appropriate questions (covered in detail in Chapter 11). The following presentation objectives would be appropriate during the first call on a new prospect:

■ Establish rapport and begin building a relationship with the customer.

■ Obtain permission to ask need identification questions.

■ Obtain personal and business information to establish the customer's file.

During stage two of the buying process—evaluation of solutions—the customer is ready to consider possible problem solutions. In some cases, there may be several solutions that must be evaluated. Presentation objectives for stage two might include the following:

- Involve the customer in a product demonstration.
- Provide value justification in terms of cost reduction and increased revenues.
- Compare and contrast the features of, for example, a truck fleet lease plan with a fleet purchase plan.

Every sales call should have an **action objective**. An action objective is something that you want the customer to do during the sales presentation: provide specific financial information, schedule a visit to your manufacturing plant, agree to a trial use of your product, agree to a follow-up meeting, or place an order. An action objective brings a sharp focus to the sales presentation.[5]

Once you have an appointment with the prospect and the presentation objectives have been established, consider sending a fax or e-mail message that outlines the agenda for the meeting. This will confirm the appointment and clarify the topics to be discussed.[6]

Multicall sales presentations are common in many areas, including the retail field. The sale of expensive recreational vehicles, leased automobiles, boats, and quality sound systems for the home or business often requires more than one sales call. Some clothing stores and independent tailors make office calls to sell tailored clothing. One example is Mitchells/Richards, with stores in Westport and Greenwich, Connecticut. This progressive retailer, with a reputation for superior customer service, will make office calls upon request. Working with a customer at his office usually requires more than one sales call.[7]

Team Presentation Strategies

In today's ever-changing business environment, team selling has surfaced as a major development. Team selling is ideally suited to organizations that sell complex or customized products and services that require direct communication between customers and technical experts. Sales teams can often uncover problems, solutions, and sales opportunities that no individual salesperson could discover working alone.[8] In some situations the involvement of technical experts can shorten the selling cycle. The team approach often results in more precise need identification, improved selection of the product, and more informative sales presentations.

Team sales presentations require a more detailed precall plan than individual sales calls. Each team member must have a clear understanding of the role he or she will play during the sales call. Sales presentation objectives should be clearly stated. Team members should be given detailed information about the customer, understand the basics of a consultative sales presentation, and be prepared to add value.[9]

Companies that have moved to team sales have discovered that this approach is not easily executed. At Hickok Cole Architects in Washington, DC, team selling is the primary

Selling Is Everyone's Business

TECHNICAL STAFF ASSUME SALES ROLE

Reggie Daniel, CEO of Scientific & Engineering Solutions, says, "The company culture is to have every employee bringing in business." His three full-time salespeople and a selected group of 15 nonsales personnel get paid commissions or bonuses based on the profitability of sales they help close. Steve Newcomb, a technical staff member, helped close a sale that resulted in a $700,000 contract. He not only collected the commission on the sale, but he also received a trip to the Super Bowl. Daniel wants his technical staff to have access to the business world because sales opportunities often surface when they are involved in technical problem solving.[a]

A survey of 19,000 salespeople and sales managers found that about one-fourth of the people contacted use sales teams. A carefully conceived presentation strategy, with each participant having a clear understanding of the role and value he or she will add during the sales call, is essential.

approach used to obtain new accounts. However, the team selling process was not easily mastered by staff members. Determining who would communicate when, and determining how presentations would fall into place seamlessly, took months of practice among the company's teams, which often consisted of six or more people. Without sufficient practice, the staff at Hickok Cole discovered that team presentations were sometimes disorganized.[10]

A variation of the team approach to selling is used by some marketers. Salespeople are trained to seek the assistance of another salesperson or actually turn the customer over to another salesperson when problems surface. The other salesperson may bring to the selling situation greater ability to identify the customer's needs or select the appropriate product. Salespeople who have well-prepared presale objectives know when to seek assistance from another professional.

SELLING TO A BUYING TEAM In some cases salespeople must address and satisfy both the individual and collective concerns of each participant in a multibuyer situation. The decision makers may be members of a well-trained buying team, a buying committee assembled for a one-time purchase, or a board of directors.

As in any type of selling situation, the salesperson should attempt to determine the various buying influences. When possible, the role of each decision maker, the amount of influence he exerts, and each decision maker's needs should be determined before the presentation. Careful observation during the presentation can reveal who may use the product, who controls the finances, and who can provide the expertise necessary to make the correct buying decision.

When you make a group selling presentation, make sure all parties feel involved. Any member of the group who feels ignored could prevent you from closing the sale. Be sure to direct questions and comments to all potential decision makers in the group. As early as possible, identify the most powerful influences.

Find out if there are any silent team or committee members. A silent member is one who can influence the buying decision but does not attend the presentation. Silent members are usually senior managers who have a major influence on the buying decision. If a silent member does exist, you must find a way to communicate, directly or indirectly, with this person.[11]

The strategic planning and preparation that takes place during the preapproach can greatly enhance the adaptive selling process. This planning includes a clear understanding of the relationship, product, and customer strategies. This planning and preparation enabled Lana and her sales team to create a presentation strategy that met the relationship and product needs of Ron, one of her largest customers.

Adaptive Selling: Builds on Four Strategic Areas of Personal Selling

At the very heart of *adaptive selling* is the belief that every sales call must be tailored to the unique needs, wants, and concerns of the customer. As noted in Chapter 4, adaptive selling involves altering sales behaviors in order to improve communication with the customer. To better identify and respond to the customer's needs frequently requires complex behavioral adjustments before and during the sales call. These adjustments are based on the relationship needs and product needs of the customer. Salespeople today must develop a broader repertoire of selling strategies and apply more effective information acquisition skills.[12]

The strategic planning that takes place during the preapproach can greatly enhance the adaptive selling process. This plan includes *strategies* that you use to position yourself with the customers and *tactics* you will use when you are face-to-face with a customer. Planning the approach involves consideration of how the *relationship, product,* and *customer strategies* can enhance the sales presentation.

REVIEW THE RELATIONSHIP STRATEGY As noted in Chapter 3, salespeople need to think of everything they say or do in the context of their relationship with the customer. Customers want a quality product and a quality relationship. Building and nourishing a long-term partnership with the customer often begins with attention to many small details. Confirming the appointment with a brief e-mail message and arriving for the appointment a few minutes early sends a positive message to the customer before the first face-to-face meeting.

The first contact between a salesperson and a prospect is very important. A positive or negative first impression can be formed in a matter of seconds. The customer is receiving a variety of verbal and nonverbal messages that can either facilitate or distract from the sales call. Your behaviors and appearance create an image that others observe and remember. Identification of the customer's preferred communication style should be given a high priority during the initial contact. Once you are in the presence of the customer, absorb the many clues that will help you with style identification. Then use *style flexing* to accommodate the needs of that person.

REVIEW THE PRODUCT STRATEGY During the preapproach you will learn some new things about the potential customer. You will no doubt acquire information that did not surface during the prospecting stage. If this is the case, it pays to take another look at your product. Now it will be easier to identify features with special appeal to the person you are calling on. In addition, you can more accurately identify questions that the prospect might raise.

Product knowledge, combined with knowledge of the customer, builds confidence. Salespeople who are confident in their ability to alter the sales approach as needed are

Selling in Action

NO TECH TO HIGH TECH

 Account planning by the 70 sales representatives at Sebastiani Winery used to be a time-consuming process. Without the aid of modern technology, salespeople were forced to manually analyze two monthly reports that were inches thick. Preparing for a sales call was burdensome. Some salespeople said that they spent almost half their time analyzing reports. A major sales force automation (SFA) initiative was started in the late 1990s. The project had these four objectives:

■ Improve communication through the use of e-mail, file sharing, and intranet technology

■ Support needed development of multimedia presentations
■ Provide data analysis capabilities
■ Ease the administrative burden

Each member of the Sebastiani sales force received a laptop loaded with Windows, PowerPoint, e-mail, and Business Objects—the software needed for analyzing data. The new technology was introduced during a three-day training program. Today, salespeople have the ability to do account planning that is much more effective than in the past.[b]

much better prepared to engage in adaptive selling.[13] Customers today are eager to do business with salespeople who have developed "expert power."

REVIEW THE CUSTOMER STRATEGY Personal selling provides us with the opportunity to apply the marketing concept during every contact with the customer. All energies can be directed toward an individual who is likely to think and act differently from anyone else. Customers today have become increasingly sophisticated in their buying strategies. They have higher expectations for value-added products and long-term commitments. A customer strategy focuses on understanding the customer's needs, wants, and buying conditions. With this understanding, adaptive selling strategies are formulated to meet both the relationship and product needs of the customer.

Developing the Six-Step Presentation Plan

Once you have established objectives for the sales presentation, the next step (prescription) involves developing the presentation plan. This plan helps you achieve your objectives.

Today, with increased time constraints, fierce competition, and rising travel costs, the opportunity for a face-to-face meeting with customers may occur less frequently. The few minutes you have with your customers may be your only opportunity to win their business, so careful planning is more critical than ever.

Planning the Presentation

Once you have collected background information, you are ready to develop a "customized" presale presentation plan. Preparing a customized sales presentation can take a great deal of time and energy. Nevertheless, this attention to detail gives you added confidence and helps you avoid delivering unconvincing hit-or-miss sales talks. The plan is developed after a careful study of the **six-step presentation plan** (Figure 10.3). In most cases, the sales process includes the following activities.

1. *Approach.* Preparation for the approach involves making decisions concerning effective ways to make a favorable first impression during the initial contact, securing the prospect's attention, and developing the prospect's interest in the product. The approach should set the stage for an effective sales presentation.

2. *Presentation.* The presentation is one of the most critical parts of the selling process. If the salesperson is unable to discover the prospect's buying needs, select a product solution, and present the product in a convincing manner, the sale may be lost. Chapter 11 covers all aspects of the sales presentation.

FIGURE 10.3

The Six-Step Presentation Plan

A presale plan is a logical and an orderly outline that features a salesperson's thoughts from one step to the next in the presentation. Each step in this plan is explained in Chapters 10 to 15.

The Six-Step Presentation Plan	
Step One: Approach	☐ Review Strategic/Consultative Selling Model ☐ Initiate customer contact
Step Two: Presentation	☐ Determine prospect needs ☐ Select solution ☐ Initiate sales presentation
Step Three: Demonstration	☐ Decide what to demonstrate ☐ Select selling tools ☐ Initiate demonstration
Step Four: Negotiation	☐ Anticipate buyer concerns ☐ Plan negotiating methods ☐ Initiate win-win negotiations
Step Five: Close	☐ Plan appropriate closing methods ☐ Recognize closing clues ☐ Initiate closing methods
Step Six: Servicing the Sale	☐ Follow through ☐ Follow-up calls ☐ Expansion selling

Service, retail, wholesale, and manufacturer selling

3. *Demonstration*. An effective sales demonstration helps verify parts of the sales presentation. Demonstrations are important because they provide the customer with a better understanding of product benefits. Chapter 12 is devoted exclusively to this topic.

4. *Negotiation*. Buyer resistance is a natural part of the selling/buying process. An objection, however, does present a barrier to closing the sale. For this reason, all salespeople should become skillful at negotiating resistance. Chapter 13 covers this topic.

5. *Close*. As the sales presentation progresses, there may be several opportunities to close the sale. Salespeople must learn to spot closing clues. Chapter 14 provides suggestions on how to close sales.

6. *Servicing the sale*. The importance of developing a long-term relationship with the prospect is noted in previous chapters. This rapport is often the outgrowth of postsale service. Learning to service the sale is an important aspect of selling. Chapter 15 deals with this topic.

Adapting the Presentation Plan to the Customer's Buying Process

A truly valuable idea or concept is timeless. The six parts of the presale presentation plan checklist have been discussed in the sales training literature for many years; therefore, they might be described as fundamentals of personal selling. These steps are basic elements of most sales and frequently occur in the same sequence. However, the activities included in the six-step presentation plan must be selected with care. Prior to developing the sales call plan, the salesperson must answer one very important question: Do these activities relate to the customer's *buying process*? As noted in Chapter 8, purchasing structures and buying procedures can vary greatly from company to company. In some cases, the steps in the buying process have been clearly defined by the organization and this information is available to vendors. Selling steps are of little value *unless* they are firmly rooted in your customer's buying process.[14]

Global Business Etiquette

DOING BUSINESS IN ENGLAND

 Linda Phillips, codirector of Executive Etiquette Company, says, "First and foremost is the British attention to detail." English businesspeople also tend to be more formal in terms of dress and person-to-person communication. It's helpful to study English business customs before visiting that country.

■ Introductions in England tend to be very formal. The British look for whose name is spoken first. If you are calling on a client named Robert Timmons, the introduction of your sales manager would be, "Mr. Timmons, I would like you to meet Raymond Hill, my sales manager." In this case the client's name is first because he is the more important person. Never address someone by his or her first name unless you are invited to do so.

■ Making decisions is often a time-consuming process, so don't expect a quick close.

■ Do not use aggressive sales techniques, such as the hard sell, and avoid criticism of competing products. Focus on objective facts and evidence during the presentation.

■ It would be poor manners to discuss business after the business day in England. This is true even when you have drinks or a meal with a businessperson.[c]

The Approach

After a great deal of preparation, it is time to communicate with the prospect, either by face-to-face contact, by telephone, or some other appropriate method of communication. We refer to the initial contact with the customer as the *approach*. All the effort you have put into developing relationship, product, and customer strategies can now be applied to the presentation strategy. If the approach is effective, you may be given the opportunity to make the sales presentation. If, however, the approach is not effective, the chance to present your sales story may be lost. You can be the best prepared salesperson in the business, but without a good approach there may be little chance for a sale.

The approach has three important objectives. First, you want to build rapport with the prospect. Second, you want to capture the person's full attention. Never begin your sales story if the prospect seems preoccupied and is not paying attention. Third, you want to transition to the need discovery stage of the sales presentation.

In some selling situations the first contact with the customer is a telephone call. The call is made to schedule a meeting or in some cases conduct the sales presentation. The face-to-face sales call starts with the social contact and is followed by the business contact. The telephone contact, social contact, and business contact are discussed in this section.

Establish Your Credibility Early

Thomas A. Freese, author of *Secrets of Question-Based Selling*, says credibility is critical to your success in sales. Credibility is an impression that people often form about you very early in the sales process.[15] Sometimes little things can erode your credibility before you have a chance to prove yourself. Arriving late for an appointment, spending 45 minutes with the prospect when you said you would need only 15 minutes, or failure to send the prospect information that was promised can quickly weaken a relationship. Failure to be well prepared for the sales call will also undermine your credibility. Credibility grows when the customer realizes you are a competent sales representative who can add value throughout the sales process.

The Telephone Contact

A telephone call provides a quick and inexpensive method of scheduling an appointment. Appointments are important because many busy prospects may not meet with a salesperson who drops in unannounced. When you schedule an appointment, the prospect knows about the sales call in advance and can, therefore, make the necessary advance preparation.

Some salespeople use the telephone exclusively to establish and maintain contact with the customer. As noted in Chapter 2, inside salespeople rely almost totally on the telephone for sales. **Telesales**, not to be confused with telemarketing, include many of the same elements as traditional sales: gathering customer information, determining needs, prescribing solutions, negotiating objections, and closing sales. Telesales usually are not scripted, a practice widely used in telemarketing. In some situations, telesales are as dynamic and unpredictable as a face-to-face sales call.

In Chapter 3, we examined some of the factors that influence the meaning we attach to an oral message from another person. With the aid of this information, we can see that communication via telephone is challenging. The person who receives the call cannot see our facial expressions, gestures, or posture, and, therefore, must rely totally on the sound of our voice and the words used. The telephone caller has a definite handicap.

The telephone has some additional limitations. A salesperson accustomed to meeting prospects in person may find telephone contact impersonal. Some salespeople try to avoid using the telephone because they believe it is too easy for the prospect to say no. It should be noted that these drawbacks are more imagined than real. With proper training a salesperson can use the telephone effectively to schedule appointments. When you make an appointment by telephone, use the following practices:

Plan in advance what you will say. It helps to use a written presentation plan as a guide during the first few seconds of the conversation. What you say is determined by the objectives of the sales call. Have a calendar available to suggest and confirm a date, time, and place for the appointment. Be sure to write it down.

Politely identify yourself and the company you represent. Set yourself apart from other callers by using a friendly tone and impeccable phone manners. This approach helps you avoid being shut out by a wary gatekeeper (secretary or receptionist).

State the purpose of your call and explain how the prospect can benefit from a meeting. In some cases it is helpful to use a powerful benefits statement that gets the prospect's attention and whets the person's appetite for more information. Present only enough information to stimulate interest.

Show respect for the prospect's time by telling the person how much time the appointment may take. Once the prospect agrees to meet with you, say, "Do you have

Capturing the customer's full attention is a major objective of the approach. Attention has become a very scarce resource in today's fast-paced world.

The Definitive Authority on **Solution Selling**

KEEPING THE FUNNEL FULL

Don Thomson

"Excellent coverage of the selling process. A must read for your sales library." **Mike Leavell, Vice President (retired) Hewlett Packard Company**

In Keeping the Funnel Full, *author and award winning Hewlett Packard salesperson Don Thomson notes that "every prospect has a preferred method of communication." He states it is important to discover whether that contact method is by telephone, in person, or by e-mail. As one of HP's top-ranked sales pros, Don trail-blazed new markets in the Pacific Northwest (awarded MVP for US Western Sales Region), Western Canada (twice awarded HP Canada's Salesperson of the Year), and the Far East (doubled sales in nine countries in one year).*

your appointment calendar handy?" Be prepared to suggest a specific time: "Is Monday at 9:00 A.M. okay?"

Confirm the appointment with a brief note, e-mail message, or letter with the date, time, and place of your appointment. Enclose your business card and any printed information that can be of interest to the prospect.[16]

You should anticipate resistance from some prospects. After all, most decision makers are very busy. Be persistent and persuasive if you genuinely believe a meeting with the prospect can be mutually beneficial.

EFFECTIVE USE OF VOICE MAIL The growing popularity of voice mail presents a challenge to salespeople. What type of message sets the stage for a second call or stimulates a return call? It's important to anticipate voice mail and know exactly what to say if you reach a recording. The prospect's perception of you is based on what you say and voice quality. The following message almost guarantees that you will be ignored:

Ms. Simpson, I am Paul Watson and I am with Elliott Property Management Services. I would like to visit with you about our services. Please call me at 862-1500.[17]

Note that this message provides no compelling reason for the prospect to call back. It offers no valid item that would stimulate interest. The voice mail message should be similar to the opening statement you would make if you had a face-to-face contact with the prospect:

Miss Simpson, my name is Paul Watson and I represent Elliott Property Management Services. We specialize in working with property managers. We can help you reduce the paperwork associated with maintenance jobs and provide an easy way to track the progress of each job. I would like the opportunity to visit with you and will call back in the morning.[18]

Note that this message is brief and describes benefits that customers can receive. If Paul Watson wants a call back, then he needs to give the best time to reach him. He should give his phone number slowly and completely. It's usually best to repeat the number. If you are acting on a referral, be sure to say who referred you and why.

During the telephone contact, CRM contact screens and note windows can be important sources of information for making effective value-added calls. The calendar function is being used by this salesperson to schedule and confirm the date, time, and place for the sales call.

EFFECTIVE USE OF E-MAIL Many prospects and established customers like the convenience of e-mail correspondence and prefer it as an alternative to telephone contact. Your challenge is to make it easy for your correspondents to read and handle your e-mail. Always use a meaningful, specific subject line. People who receive large amounts of e-mail may selectively choose which ones to read by scanning the subject lines and deleting those of no interest. An e-mail with a subject line titled "Action Steps from Our 9/28 Meeting" is more likely to be read than a subject line like "Meeting Notes."[19]

The e-mail message should tell the reader what you want and then encourage a response. Identify the main point of your e-mail within the first or second paragraphs. Format the e-mail so it's easy to read. This may require the use of headings (with capitals or boldface print) to identify the main elements of the memo. Proofread all e-mails for proper grammar, punctuation, and spelling.[20] Always use the grammar and spell check tools. Messages that contain errors may misrepresent your competence. Finally, use a signature file—a small block of text that automatically follows each e-mail you send. A typical signature file includes full name, title, affiliation, phone number, and in some cases a slogan.

The Social Contact

According to many image consultants, "First impressions are lasting impressions." This statement is essentially true, and some profitable business relationships never crystallize because some trait or characteristic of the salesperson repels the prospective customer. Sales personnel have only a few minutes to create a positive first impression. Susan Bixler, author of *The New Professional Image*, describes the importance of the first impression this way:

> *Books are judged by their covers, houses are appraised by their curb appeal,*
> *and people are initially evaluated on how they choose to dress and behave. In*
> *a perfect world this is not fair, moral, or just. What's inside should count a*
> *great deal more. And eventually it usually does, but not right away. In the*
> *meantime, a lot of opportunities can be lost.*[21]

Customer Relationship Management with Technology

PLANNING PERSONAL VISITS

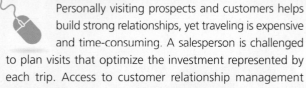

Personally visiting prospects and customers helps build strong relationships, yet traveling is expensive and time-consuming. A salesperson is challenged to plan visits that optimize the investment represented by each trip. Access to customer relationship management (CRM) prospect records helps salespeople quickly identify all the accounts in a given geographic area.

CRM empowers salespeople to rapidly review and compare an area's prospects on the basis of position in

sales cycle, potential size of account or purchase, likelihood of sale, and contribution that the visit could make to information gathering and relationship building. A well-managed CRM database provides salespeople with appropriate business and social topics to discuss when calling selected prospects for an appointment. (See the exercise "Planning Personal Visits" on p. 230 for more information.)

Building a rapport leads to credibility, which leads to trust. Once trust is established, the customer is likely to open up and share information. This information will provide clues regarding ways to create value. To be certain your first impression is appropriate, review the material in Chapter 3. The information in this chapter is timeless and can serve you well today and in the future.

DEVELOPING CONVERSATION The brief, general conversation during the social contact should hold the prospect's attention and establish a relaxed and friendly atmosphere for the

Selling in Action

THE SOCIAL CONTACT

The social contact should be viewed as effective communication on a personal basis. This brief conversation establishes the foundation for the business contact, so it should never be viewed as an insignificant part of the presentation strategy. The following guidelines can help you develop the skills needed to make a good social contact.

1. *Prepare for the social contact.* Conduct a background check on topics of interest to the person you are contacting. This includes reviewing information in the prospect database, reading industry reports, and searching the Internet. Once you arrive at the customer's office, you will discover additional information about the person's interests. Most people communicate what is important to them in the way they personalize their work environment.

2. *Initiate social contact.* The most effective opening comments should be expressed in the form of an open-ended question, such as "I understand you have just been elected president of the United Way?" You can improve the possibility of a good response to your verbal question by applying nonverbal communication skills. Appropriate eye contact, voice inflections that

communicate enthusiasm, and a warm smile will increase the customer's receptivity to your opening comments.

3. *Respond to the customer's conversations.* When the customer responds, it is imperative that you acknowledge the message both verbally and nonverbally. The verbal response might be "That is really interesting" or any other appropriate comment. Let the customer know you are listening and you want her to continue talking.

4. *Keep the social contact focused on the customer.* Because you cannot control where a conversation might go, you may be tempted to focus the conversation on topics with which you are familiar. A response such as, "Several years ago I was in charge of our company's United Way campaign and we had a difficult time meeting our goal," shifts the focus of the conversation back to you. Continue to focus the conversation on topics that are of interest to the customer. Dale Carnegie said that one of the best ways to build a relationship is to encourage others to talk about themselves.

business contact that is to follow. As mentioned in Chapter 3, there are three areas of conversation that should be considered in developing a social contact:

1. *Comments on here-and-now observations.* These comments may include general observations about an article in the *Wall Street Journal*, the victory of a local athletic team, or specific comments about awards on display in the prospect's office. Janis Taylor, sales representative with Trugreen Chemlawn, likes to start each new appointment by seeking "common ground" with her prospects. She looks for such items as a picture of the prospect's children or a trophy.[22]

2. *Compliments.* Most customers react positively to sincere compliments. Personal items in the prospect's office, achievements, or efficient operation of the prospect's business provide examples of what can be praised. A salesperson might say, "I learned recently that your company is ranked number one in customer satisfaction by J.D. Power and Associates."

3. *Search for mutual acquaintances or interests.* The discovering of mutual friends or interests can serve as the foundation for a strong social contact. Most people enjoy talking about themselves, their hobbies, and their achievements. Debra Fine, author of *The Fine Art of Small Talk*, says, "Small talk isn't stupid. It's the appetizer for all relationships."[23]

Communication on a personal basis is often the first step in discovering a common language that can improve communication between the salesperson and the prospect. How much time should be devoted to the social contact? There is no easy answer to this question. The length of the conversation depends on the type of product or service sold, how busy the prospect appears to be, and your awareness of topics of mutual interest (see Selling in Action on p. 221).

In many cases the conversation will take place over lunch or dinner. Many successful sales have been closed during or after a meal. This explains why some companies enroll their sales staff and other customer contact personnel in dining etiquette classes.

The Business Contact

Converting the prospect's attention from the social contact to the business proposal is an important part of the approach. When you convert and hold your prospect's attention, you have fulfilled an important step in the selling process. Furthermore, without this step the door has been closed on completing the remaining steps of the sale.

Some salespeople use a carefully planned opening statement or a question to convert the customer's attention to the sales presentation. A statement or question that focuses on the prospect's dominant buying motive is, of course, more likely to achieve the desired results. Buyers must like what they see and hear and must be made to feel that it is worthwhile to hear more.

Converting the Prospect's Attention and Arousing Interest

Throughout the years, salespeople have identified and used a number of effective ways to capture the prospect's attention and arouse interest in the presentation. Seven of the most common are explained in the following material:

Agenda approach

Product demonstration approach

Referral approach

Customer benefit approach

Question approach

Survey approach

Premium approach

We also discuss combining two or more of these approaches.

Agenda Approach

One of the most effective ways to move from the social contact to the business contact is to thank the customer for taking time to meet with you and then review your goals for the meeting. You might say, "Thank you for meeting with me this morning. I would like to accomplish three things during the time you have given me." This statement shows you value the person's time and you have preplanned a specific agenda. Always be open to changing the agenda based on input from the customer.[24]

Product Demonstration Approach

This straightforward method of getting the prospect's attention is used by sales representatives who sell copy machines, photographic equipment, automobiles, construction equipment, office furniture, and many other products. If the actual product cannot be demonstrated, salespeople can use appropriate audiovisual technology such as computer-generated graphics, slides, and videotapes. Trish Ormsby, a sales representative for Wells Fargo Alarm Services, uses her portable computer to create a visual image of security systems that meet the customer's security needs.[25]

Referral Approach

Research indicates that another person is far more impressed with your good points if these points are presented by a third party rather than by you. The referral approach is quite effective because a third party (a satisfied customer) believes the prospect can benefit from your product. This type of opening statement has universal appeal among salespeople from nearly every field.

When you use the referral approach, your opening statement should include a direct reference to the third party. Here is an example: "Mrs. Follett, my name is Kurt Wheeler, and I represent the Cross Printing Company. We specialize in printing all types of business forms. Mr. Ameno—buyer for Raybale Products, Incorporated—is a regular customer of ours, and he suggested I mention his name to you."

A straightforward product demonstration method for getting the grocery store meat manager's attention would be the use of this ad from Cook's (www.cookshams. com), a division of ConAgra. The salesperson can explain the value of featuring meat products that are supported by a strong media promotion and point-of-sale merchandising program.

Customer Benefit Approach

One of the most effective ways to gain a prospect's attention is to immediately point out one benefit of purchasing your product. Try to begin with the most important issue (or problem) facing the client. When using this approach, the most important buyer's benefit is included in the initial statement. For example, the salesperson selling a portable Sony projector might open with this statement:

> *The Sony VPL-CS4 lightweight projector strikes a balance between cost, size, brightness, and convenience. It's a good choice for a quick business trip or for a work-at-home presentation.*

Another example taken from the financial services field is:

> *When you meet with a Charles Schwab investment specialist, you can obtain advice on over 1,200 no-load, no-transaction-fee mutual funds.*

The key to achieving success with the customer benefit approach is advance preparation. Customers are annoyed when a salesperson cannot quickly communicate the benefits of meeting with them. Bruce Klassen, sales manager for Do All Industrial Supply, says, "Our salespeople begin the sales process by researching the prospect and the company. We need

The survey approach offers many advantages. It is generally a nonthreatening way to open a sales call. You simply ask permission to acquire information that can be used to determine the buyer's need for the product.

to be sure that our product line is going to benefit that prospect before we make even an initial sales approach."[26]

Question Approach

The question approach has two positive features. First, an appropriate question almost always triggers prospect involvement. Very few people avoid answering a direct question. Second, a question gets the prospect thinking about a problem that the salesperson may be prepared to solve.

Molly Hoover, a sales training consultant, conducts training classes for sales managers and car dealers who want to better understand the subtleties of selling to the new woman car buyers. She suggests an approach that includes a few basic questions such as:

"Is the vehicle for business or pleasure?"

"Will you be buying within the next week or so?"[27]

These opening questions are not difficult to answer, yet they get the customer mentally involved. Some of the best opening questions are carefully phrased to arouse attention. The authors of *The Sales Question Book* offer some good examples:

"Are you aware that we just added three new services to our payroll and accounting package? Could I tell you about them?"

"We are now offering all our customers a special auditing service that used to be reserved for our largest accounts. Would you be interested in hearing about it?"[28]

Once you ask the question, listen carefully to the response. If the answer is yes, proceed with an enthusiastic presentation of your product. If the answer is no, then you may have to gracefully try another approach or thank the prospect for her time and depart.

Survey Approach

Robert Hewitt, a Monterey, California, financial planner, has new clients fill out a detailed questionnaire before the first appointment. This procedure is part of his customer strategy.

He studies the completed questionnaire and other documents before making any effort to find a solution to any of the customer's financial planning needs. The survey (data collection) is an important part of the problem-solving philosophy of selling. It often is used in selling office furniture, business security systems, insurance, and other products where the need cannot be established without careful study.

The survey approach offers many advantages. It is generally a nonthreatening way to open a sales call. You simply are asking permission to acquire information that can be used to determine the buyer's need for your product. Because the survey is tailor-made for a specific business, the buyer is given individual treatment. Finally, the survey approach helps avoid an early discussion of price. Price cannot be discussed until the survey is completed.

Premium Approach

The premium approach involves giving the customer a free sample or an inexpensive item. A financial services representative might give the customer a booklet that can be used to record expenses. Sales representatives for a large U.S. textbook publisher give faculty members a monthly planner. Product samples are frequently used by persons who sell cosmetics. Creative use of premiums is an effective way to get the customer's attention.

The agenda, product, referral, customer benefit, question, survey, and premium approaches offer the salesperson a variety of ways to set the stage for the presentation strategy. With experience, salespeople learn to select the most effective approach for each selling situation. Table 10.1 provides examples of how these approaches can be applied in real-world situations.

Combination Approaches

A hallmark of adaptive selling is flexibility. Therefore, a combination of approaches sometimes provides the best avenue to need identification. Sales personnel who have adopted the consultative style, of course, use the question and survey approaches most frequently. Some selling situations, however, require that one of the other approaches be used, either

TABLE 10.1   Business Contact Worksheet

This illustrates how to prepare effective real-world approaches that capture the customer's attention.

METHOD OF APPROACH	WHAT WILL YOU SAY?
1. Agenda	1. (Office supply) "Thank you for meeting with me. During the next 45 minutes, I plan to accomplish three things."
2. Product	2a. (Retail clothing) "We have just received a shipment of new fall sweaters from Braemar International." 2b. (Business forms manufacturer) "Our plant has just purchased a $300,000 Harris Graphics composer, Mr. Reichart; I would like to show you a copy of your sales invoice with your logo printed on it."
3. Customer benefit	3. (Real estate) "Mr. and Mrs. Stuart, my company lists and sells more homes than any other company in the area where your home is located. Our past performance would lead me to believe we can sell your home within two weeks."
4. Referral	4. (Food wholesaler) "Paula Doeman, procurement manager for Mercy Medical Center, suggested that I provide you with information about our computerized 'Order It' system."
5. Question	5. (Hotel convention services) "Mrs. McClaughin, will your Annual Franchisee Meeting be held in April?"
6. Survey	6a. (Custom-designed computer software) "Mr. Vasquez, I would like the opportunity to learn about your accounts receivable and accounts payable procedures. We may be able to develop a customized program that will significantly improve your cash flow." 6b. (Retail menswear) "May I ask you a few questions about your wardrobe? The information will help me better understand your clothing needs."
7. Premium	7. (Financial services) "I would like to give you a publication entitled *Guaranteed Growth Annuity*."

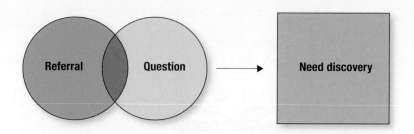

FIGURE 10.4

Combination approaches provide a smooth transition to the need discovery part of the consultative presentation.

alone or in combination with the question and survey approaches (Figure 10.4). An example of how a salesperson might use a referral and question approach combination follows:

Salesperson: Carl Hamilton at Simmons Modern Furniture suggested that I visit with you about our new line of compact furniture designed for smaller homes. He believes this line might complement the furniture you currently feature.

Customer: Yes, Carl called me yesterday and mentioned your name and company.

Salesperson: Before showing you our product lines, I would like to ask you some questions about your current product mix. First, what do you currently carry in the area of bedroom furniture?

Coping with Sales Call Reluctance

The transition from the preapproach to the approach is sometimes blocked by sales call reluctance. Fear of making the initial contact with the prospect is one of the biggest obstacles to sales success. For new salespeople, the problem can be career threatening. **Sales call reluctance** includes the thoughts, feelings, and behavioral patterns that conspire to limit what a salesperson is able to accomplish. It is an internal, often emotional, barrier to sales success. Sales call reluctance can be caused by several different thought patterns:[29]

- Fear of taking risks
- Fear of group presentations
- Lack of self-confidence
- Fear of rejection

Regardless of the reasons for sales call reluctance, you can learn to deal with it. These are some suggestions:

- *Be optimistic about the outcome of the initial contact.* It is better to anticipate success than to anticipate failure. Martin Seligman, professor of psychology at the University of Pennsylvania and author of the best-selling book *Learned Optimism*, says that success in selling requires a healthy dose of optimism.[30] The anticipation of failure is a major barrier to making the initial contact.

- *Practice your approach before making the initial contact.* A well-rehearsed effort to make the initial contact increases your self-confidence and reduces the possibility that you may handle the situation badly.

- *Recognize that it is normal to feel anxious about the initial contact.* Even the most experienced salespeople experience some degree of sales call reluctance and this reluctance can surface anywhere in the sales process.

- *Develop a deeper commitment to your goals.* Abraham Zaleznik, professor emeritus at Harvard Business School, says, "If your commitment is only in your mind, then you'll lose it when you encounter a big obstacle. If your commitment is in your heart *and* your mind, you'll create the power to break through the toughest obstacles."[31]

Selling to the Gatekeeper

Many decision makers have an assistant or secretary who manages their daily schedule. This person is often referred to as the "gatekeeper." If you want to reach the decision

In some cases, a secretary, assistant, or receptionist may screen incoming telephone calls. Be prepared to convince this person that your call is important. Always treat the gatekeeper with respect and courtesy.

Source: *Wall Street Journal*, March 10, 1999, p. A23. Reprinted by permission of Mark Litzler.

"I don't think of myself as the Jenkins Doolittle & Bloom gatekeeper. I rather prefer lead blocker."

maker, work hard to align yourself with the person who schedules this person's appointments. Rule number one is to treat the gatekeeper with respect. Learn their name and what they do. Keep in mind this person can be an important source of information. For example, the gatekeeper can tell you how the buying process works and provide information regarding new developments in the company. This person may be able to help you make a preliminary qualification before you reach the decision maker. When you treat the person as an expert by soliciting their views, you establish a relationship that can pay big dividends today and in the future.[32]

When possible, use personal referrals from someone the prospect knows. If you have met the prospect previously, describe the meeting and tell the gatekeeper why you feel a second meeting would be beneficial.

Chapter Learning Activities

Reviewing Key Concepts

Describe the three prescriptions that are included in the presentation strategy

Developing a presentation strategy involves preparing presale objectives, developing a presale presentation plan, and providing outstanding customer service. The presentation strategy combines elements of the relationship, product, and customer strategies.

Discuss the two-part preapproach process

Preparation for the sales presentation is a two-part process. Part one is referred to as the *preapproach* and involves preparing presale objectives and developing a presale presentation plan. It's best to develop presentation objectives for each stage of the buying process. Part two is called the *approach* and involves making a good first impression, securing the prospect's attention, and transitioning to need identification.

Describe team presentation strategies

In recent years, team selling has surfaced as a major development. Sales teams can often uncover problems, solutions, and sales opportunities that no individual salesperson could discover working alone. Team sales presentations require a more detailed precall plan than individual sales calls. Without careful planning and extensive practice (rehearsal), team presentations are likely to be delivered in a disorganized manner.

Explain how adaptive selling builds on four broad strategic areas of personal selling

Adaptive selling involves altering sales behaviors in order to improve communication with the customer. Sales people today are challenged to develop a broader repertoire of selling strategies. Salespeople skilled in adaptive selling consider how the relationship, product, and customer strategies can enhance the sales presentation.

Describe the six main parts of the presentation plan

After collecting background information, salespeople need to create a customized presale presentation plan. The plan is developed after careful study of the six-step presentation plan, which includes approach, presentation, demonstration, negotiation, close, and servicing the sale.

Explain how to effectively approach the customer

The approach may involve face-to-face contact, telephone contact, or some other appropriate method of communication. If the approach is effective, the salesperson will be given an opportunity to make the sales presentation. A major goal of the *social contact* is to make a good first impression, build rapport, and establish credibility. The *business contact* involves converting the prospect's attention from the social contact to the sales presentation.

Describe seven ways to convert the prospect's attention and arouse interest

Over the years, salespeople have identified several ways to convert the prospect's attention and arouse interest in the presentation. Some of the most common ways include the agenda approach, product demonstration approach, referral approach, customer benefit approach, question approach, survey approach, and premium approach.

Key Terms

Presentation strategy	Action objective	Sales call reluctance
Preapproach	Six-step presentation plan	
Approach	Telesales	

Review Questions

1. What is the purpose of the preapproach? What are the two prescriptions included in the preapproach?

2. Explain the role of objectives in developing the presale presentation plan.

3. Why should salespeople establish multiple-objective sales presentations? List four possible objectives that would be appropriate for stage one and stage two of the buying process.

4. Compare and contrast team sales presentations and individual sales calls.

5. Describe the major steps in the presentation plan. Briefly discuss the role of adaptive selling in implementing the presentation plan.

6. What are the major objectives of the approach?

7. Review the Selling in Action box on p. 221. Briefly describe the four guidelines that can help you make a good social contact.

8. What are some rules to follow when leaving a message on voice mail? E-mail?

9. What methods can the salesperson use to convert the prospect's attention to the sales presentation?

10. Discuss why combination approaches are considered an important consultative-selling practice. Provide one example of a combination approach.

Application Exercises

1. Assume that you are a salesperson who calls on retailers. For some time you have been attempting to get an appointment with one of the best retailers in the city to carry your line. You have an appointment to see the head buyer in one and one-half hours. You are sitting in your office. It will take you about 30 minutes to drive to your appointment. Outline what you should be doing between now and the time you leave to meet your prospect.

2. Tom Nelson has just graduated from Aspen College with a major in marketing. He has three years of experience in the retail grocery business and has decided he would like to go to work as a salesperson for the district office of Procter & Gamble. Tom has decided to telephone and set up an appointment for an interview. Write out exactly what Tom should *plan* to say during his telephone call.

3. Concepts from Dale Carnegie's *How to Win Friends and Influence People* can help you prepare for the social contact. Access the Dale Carnegie Training home page (www.dalecarnegie.com) and examine the courses offered. Search for the Sales Advantage Course. Read the course description and review the two main things you will learn in this program. View the online Sales Action Plan demo video at sas.infoally.com/sas/index.asp to learn how Dale Carnegie's web based coaching program enhances what is learned in the course.

Role-Play Exercise

Research the type of computer that you would like to purchase in the future or one that you have just purchased. Strategically prepare to meet a potential customer who has been referred to you by a friend and who would like to purchase a similar computer. Using Table 10.1 on p. 226, prepare four different business contact statements or questions you could use to approach your prospect. Review the material in this chapter and then pair off with another student who will assume the role of your customer. First, role-play the telephone contact and set up an appointment to get your customer into your store to meet with you and look at the computer. Second, role-play the approach you will use when the customer actually comes into the store. Review how well you made the approach.

CRM Application Exercise

Planning Personal Visits

CRM software allows trip planners to examine the status of prospects in the geographic area to be visited. Access your Salesforce/Selling Today simNet customer database at www.pearsonhighered.com/manning. Assume that you wish to visit prospects in the city of Bedford, Texas. Using Salesforce.com, find all of the prospects in Bedford, Texas. Select the Reports tab. Select the Contact by Location report. In the Generated Report section, edit the filter to include only those accounts in Bedford, Texas. Sort the resulting report by Zip code to plan your route. Sort by clicking the Zip code field. After arranging by phone to visit these people, the salesperson can print the information contained in these records and take them along. Click "Printable View" and print the report. You should now have printed information about all customers in Bedford. Salespeople today use the Internet to schedule trip transportation and lodging, and to check the weather forecast.

Reality Selling Today Video Case Problem

 The global construction industry is a lucrative market, with customer needs ranging from measuring products to sophisticated construction solutions. Hilti Corporation, the company featured at the beginning of this chapter, provides its customers around the world with leading-edge construction products and services with outstanding added value. Hilti prides itself for its direct sales model, which allows its salespeople and service teams to work directly *with* and *for* the customers.

Alim Hirani
Hilti Corporation

Alim Hirani, an account manager for Hilti, adopts the relationship marketing approach in his selling strategy. He often starts his sales calls, which have been carefully preplanned, with icebreakers such as asking about the customer's family rather than making the sales immediately. His sales presentations may take place in the client's office or even at the construction site. Consequently, he must always plan well in advance the best way to make his sales presentations for specific sales calls. At all times he must attempt to establish his own and his company's credibility by demonstrating the premium value that Hilti's products and services can offer his clients. Whenever possible, he tries to get the customer involved in product demonstration because seeing is believing. Once the customers see for themselves the benefits of Hilti's product features, moving the customers from the investigation and evaluation stages to the action stage is just a procedure.

Alim sells not only individually but also as part of a team. For major clients who require a complete package of building/construction, mechanical/electrical, telecom, and interior finishing products and services, Alim works closely with his team members to make sure the information he acquires from the customer during initial contacts is made available to other salespeople and technical personnel of the team. In the construction industry, closing the sale is—most of the time—just the beginning. Well-trained product application specialists join Alim to offer the customers after-sales services, technical support, and training. (See chapter opener on p. 208, and Reality Selling Today Role-Play 6 in Appendix 1 on p. 401 for more information.)

Questions

1. Why should Alim Hirani adopt the three prescriptions for the presentation strategy?

2. Salespeople are encouraged to establish multiple-objective sales presentations. What are some objectives Alim Hirani should consider when he calls on construction foremen at the construction site?

3. What are some special challenges Alim Hirani faces when he makes his sales presentations in a non-office setting?

4. Put yourself in the position of a construction salesperson. Can you envision a situation when you might combine different ways to convert the prospect's attention and interests into action? Explain.

CRM Case Study

Establishing Your Approach

Becky Kemley, your sales manager at SimNet Systems, has notified Pat Silva's former prospects, by letter, that you will be calling on them soon. She wants to meet with you tomorrow to discuss your preapproach to your new prospects. Please review the records in the Salesforce.com database.

Questions

1. Becky wants you to call on Robert Kelly. Describe what your call objectives would be with Mr. Kelly.

2. Describe a possible topic of your social contact with Mr. Kelly and how you would convert that to a buying contact.

3. Becky has given you a reprint of a new article about using networks for warehouse applications. Which of your prospects might have a strong interest in this kind of article? How would you use this article to make an approach to that prospect?

Partnership Selling: A Role-Play/Simulation

(see Appendix 3, p. 451)

Developing a Relationship Strategy

Read Employment Memorandum 2, which announces your promotion to account executive. In your new position, you will be assigned by your instructor to one of the two major account categories in the convention center market. You will be assigned to either the *association accounts market* or the *corporate accounts market*. The association accounts market includes customers who have the responsibility for planning meetings for their association or group. The corporate accounts market includes customers who have the responsibility for planning meetings for the company they represent. (You will remain in the account category for the rest of the role-plays.)

Note the challenges you may have in your new position. Each of these challenges is represented in the future sales memoranda you receive from your sales manager.

Read Sales Memorandum 1 for the account category you are assigned. (Note that the "A" means association and your customer is Erin Adkins, and "B" means corporate and your customer is Leigh Combs.) Follow the instructions in the sales memorandum and strategically prepare to approach your new customer. Your call objectives are to establish a relationship (social contact), share an appealing benefit, and find out if your customer is planning any future conventions (business contact).

You may be asked to assume the role of a customer in the account category to which you are not assigned as a salesperson. Your instructor will provide you with detailed instructions for correctly assuming this role.

11

Creating the Consultative Sales Presentation

Adaptive Selling Today Training Video Series

The effective use of questions is the starting point of the Consultative Sales Presentation. Questions are also used in building adaptive style selling relationships, and understanding and adapting product solutions that meet the needs of customers. Questions span the entire sales process and are also used to successfully negotiate, close, and service a sale.

Questions, Questions, Questions, the second video in our Adaptive Selling Today Training Video Series, introduces and shows how to use the four Adaptive Selling Questions described in this chapter. A top-producing, Internet telephone systems sales representative featured in the video learns one of his largest accounts may be going with another supplier.

Our salesperson's company has brought in a new sales training program on how to use questions effectively, and our salesperson is the first to learn the system. With his newly acquired knowledge and skill on the use of questions, our salesperson schedules another call to see if he can, with the use of questions, re-establish his relationship and salvage the sale.

In this follow-up call, we find out how well he has learned to adapt and use questions to discover and better understand the customer's needs, create value, and solve the customer's buying problem. Throughout the three-part video, our salesperson learns about the following questions and what these questions reveal during the sales presentation.

In the Adaptive Selling Today Training Video, Johnny, our Internet Telephone Systems salesperson, finds out he may be losing one of his top accounts. After learning about the strategic use of questions throughout the sales process, he schedules another appointment to apply what he has learned and hopefully better meet his customer's needs.

SURVEY Questions	*Reveal*	CUSTOMER PROBLEMS
PROBING Questions	*Reveal*	CUSTOMER PAIN
NEED-SATISFACTION Questions	*Reveal*	CUSTOMER PLEASURE
CONFIRMATION Questions	*Reveal*	MUTUAL UNDERSTANDING

The use of an effective questioning strategy, so important to the consultative sales process is one of the greatest challenges facing salespeople. ■

The Consultative Sales Presentation

A growing number of salespeople, like Johnny our internet telephone system salesperson, pictured above, have adopted the consultative sales presentation plan (Figure 11.1). Consultative selling, as introduced in Chapter 1, involves meeting customer needs by listening to customers, understanding—and caring about—their problems, selecting the appropriate solution, and following through after the sale. Consultative selling focuses on identification of the customer's problem and finding a solution. This approach is very different from product-oriented selling. As one author noted, "Product-oriented selling can easily lapse into product evangelism." Product-oriented selling is usually inefficient and ineffective.[2]

Transitioning from the Approach

As we note in Chapter 10, an effective approach sets the stage for the sales presentation. Once you have established rapport with the prospect and captured the prospect's full attention, you are ready to transition from the approach to need identification. There is no set formula to follow during the transition, but there are two tactics commonly used by salespeople. One is to state (or restate) the purpose of your sales call: "I want to determine whether your company might benefit from an innovative truck leasing plan we have developed." The second tactic involves getting permission to ask questions. You might

The Six-Step Presentation Plan	
Step One: Approach	☑ Review Strategic/Consultative Selling Model ☑ Initiate customer contact
Step Two: Presentation	☐ Determine prospect needs ☐ Select solution ☐ Initiate sales presentation
Step Three: Demonstration	☐ Decide what to demonstrate ☐ Select selling tools ☐ Initiate demonstration
Step Four: Negotiation	☐ Anticipate buyer concerns ☐ Plan negotiating methods ☐ Initiate win-win negotiations
Step Five: Close	☐ Plan appropriate closing methods ☐ Recognize closing clues ☐ Initiate closing methods
Step Six: Servicing the Sale	☐ Follow through ☐ Follow-up calls ☐ Expansion selling

Service, retail, wholesale, and manufacturer selling

FIGURE 11.1

Creating the Sales Presentation
A consultative sales presentation involves adding value by accurately determining the prospect's needs, selecting an appropriate product or service, and initiating an effective sales presentation.

say, "Before I describe our leasing plan, would it be all right if I ask a few questions about your current truck fleet operation?"

To be most effective, the salesperson should think of the presentation as a four-part process. The Consultative Sales Presentation Guide (Figure 11.2) features these four parts.

Part One—Need Discovery

A review of the behaviors displayed by high-performance salespeople helps us understand the importance of precise need discovery. They have learned how to skillfully diagnose and solve the customer's problems better than their competitors. This problem-solving capability translates into more repeat business and referrals and fewer order cancellations and returns.[5]

Unless the selling situation requires mere order taking (customers know exactly what they want), need discovery is a standard part of the sales presentation. It may begin during the approach, if the salesperson uses questions or a survey during the initial contact with the customer. If neither of these two methods is used during the approach, need discovery begins immediately after you transition from the approach.

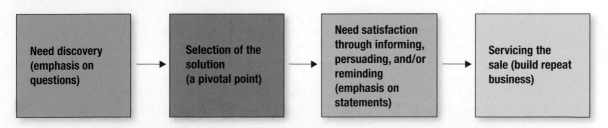

FIGURE 11.2

The Consultative Sales Presentation Guide
To be most successful, the salesperson should think of the sales presentation as a four-part process.

Pharmaceutical salespeople generally have only a short time to present their product. In some situations, the doctor may immediately indicate a willingness to prescribe. However, in other situations the salesperson may be asked to make an informative need-satisfaction presentation to several members of the practice.

The pace, scope, depth, and time allocated to inquiry depend on a variety of factors. Some of these include the sophistication of the product, the selling price, the customer's knowledge of the product, the product applications, and, of course, the time available for dialogue between the salesperson and the prospect. Each selling situation is different, so a standard set of guidelines for need discovery is not practical. Additional information on need discovery is presented later in the chapter.

Part Two—Selection of the Solution

The emphasis in sales and marketing today is on determining customer needs and then selecting or configuring custom-fitted solutions to satisfy these needs. Therefore, an important function of the salesperson is product selection and recommendation. The salesperson must choose the product or service that can provide maximum satisfaction. When making this decision, the salesperson must be aware of all product options, including those offered by the competition.

Salespeople who have the ability to conduct an effective value-added needs analysis achieve the status of trusted adviser. Mary Langston, personal shopper at Nordstrom's Michigan Avenue store in Chicago, helps customers update their wardrobes. When asked what her days are like, she says, "It starts and ends with being a good listener." She promises her customers that she will never let them walk out of the store with clothing that does not look right.[4]

Part Three—Need Satisfaction Through Informing, Persuading, or Reminding

The third part of the consultative sales presentation consists of communicating to the customer, both verbally and nonverbally, the satisfaction that the product or service can provide. The salesperson places less emphasis on the use of questions and begins making statements. These statements are organized into a presentation that informs, persuades, or reminds the customer of the most suitable product or service. Later in this chapter, and in several of the remaining chapters, we discuss specific strategies used in conjunction with the demonstration, negotiating buyer resistance, and closing the sale.

Part Four—Servicing the Sale

Servicing the sale is a major way to create value. These activities, which occur after closing the sale, ensure maximum customer satisfaction and set the stage for a long-term relationship. Service activities include expansion selling, making credit arrangements, following through on assurances and promises, and dealing effectively with complaints. This topic is covered in detail in Chapter 15.

In those cases in which a sale is normally closed during a single sales call, the salesperson should be prepared to go through all four parts of the Consultative Sales Presentation Guide. However, when a salesperson uses a multicall approach, preparation for all the parts is usually not practical. The person selling computer systems or investments, for example, almost always uses a multicall sales presentation. Need discovery (part one) is the focus of the first call.

Need Discovery Activities That Create Value

A lawyer does not give the client advice until the legal problem has been carefully studied and confirmed. A doctor does not prescribe medication until the patient's symptoms have been identified. In like manner, the salesperson should not recommend the purchase of a product without a thorough need identification. You start with the assumption that the client's problem is not known. The only way to determine and confirm the problem is to get the other person talking. You must obtain information to properly clarify the need and propose either a single solution or a range of solutions.

Customers may not realize that they actually have a problem. Even when they are aware of their need, they may not realize that an actual solution to their problem exists.

Need discovery (sometimes called *need analysis*) begins with precall preparation when the salesperson is acquiring background information on the prospect. It continues once the salesperson and the customer are engaged in a real dialogue. Through the process of need discovery, the salesperson establishes two-way communication by asking appropriate questions and listening carefully to the customer's responses. These responses usually provide clues concerning the customer's dominant buying motive (Figure 11.3).

Asking Questions

The effective use of questions to achieve need identification and need satisfaction is the single greatest challenge facing most professional salespeople. The types of questions you ask, the timing of those questions, and how you pose them greatly impact your ability to create customer value. According to research on over 35,000 salespeople by Neil Rackham, author of *SPIN Selling*, mastering the use of questions can increase one's success in sales by

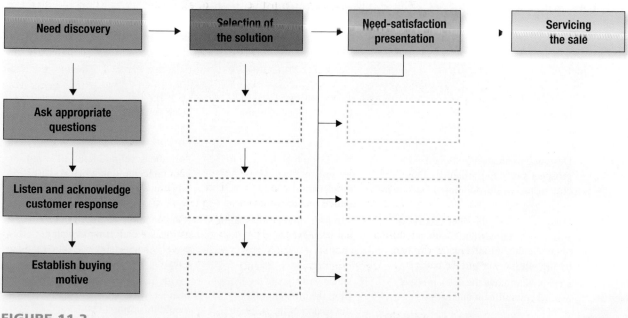

FIGURE 11.3

Three Dimensions of Need Discovery

17 percent.[5] Questions help clarify the exact dimensions of the problem, help the customer evaluate a range of solutions, and assist the customer in evaluating the potential outcome of the solution that is implemented.[6]

In every selling situation, you want the prospect to be actively thinking, sharing thoughts, and asking questions. Until the person begins to talk freely, the salesperson will have difficulty diagnosing and solving the customer's problems. A well-planned sales presentation includes a variety of preplanned questions (Table 11.1) and questions that are formulated spontaneously during the sales presentation. We describe the four most common types of questions used in the field of personal selling.

SURVEY QUESTIONS REVEAL PROBLEMS At the beginning of most sales presentations, there is a need to collect basic facts about the buyer's existing situation and problem. **Survey questions**, or *information gathering questions*, as they are sometimes called, are designed to obtain this knowledge. To accomplish this, there are two types of survey questions. **General survey questions** help the salesperson discover facts about the buyer's existing situation and are often the first step in the partnership-building process. Here is a sampling of general survey questions that can be used in selected selling fields:

> "I understand that your regional facilities don't necessarily use the same delivery carriers, is that correct?" (Shipping Service)
>
> "Tell me about the new challenges you are facing in the area of data storage." (File Server)
>
> "What is your current rate of employee turnover?" (Customer Service Training)
>
> "Can you provide me with information on the kinds of meetings and conventions you plan for your clients and employees?" (Hotel Convention Services)
>
> "Can you describe the style of home furnishings you prefer?" (Retail Home Furnishings)

In most selling situations, general survey questions are followed by specific survey questions.

Specific survey questions are designed to give prospects a chance to describe in more detail a problem, issue, or dissatisfaction from their point of view. These specific survey questions, sometimes referred to as *problem questions*, give you an opportunity to delve

TABLE 11.1   Types of Questions Used in Conjunction with Consultative Selling

A salesperson is selling fractional ownership of a jet aircraft to a well-known golf professional on the Professional Golf Association (PGA) Tour. The prospect is currently using commercial air travel.

TYPES OF QUESTION	DEFINITION	WHEN USED	EXAMPLES
Survey	Discovers basic facts about the buyer's existing situation and problem	Usually at the beginning of a sale	"Can you describe the problems you experience traveling to each of the pro golf tournaments?"
Probing	Designed to uncover and clarify the prospect's buying problem and the circumstances surrounding the problem	When you feel the need to obtain more specific information to fully understand the problem	"Are the travel problems affecting your concentration when you are preparing for the event?"
Confirmation	Used throughout the sales process to verify the accuracy and assure a mutual understanding of information exchanged by the salesperson and the buyer	After important information has been exchanged	"So you think the uncertainty associated with commercial air travel is having some effect on your game?"
Need-Satisfaction	Designed to move the sales process toward commitment and action	When you change the focus from the problem to a discussion of the solution	"With fractional ownership of your own jet, what personal benefits would this bring to your performance in the 30 tournaments you play each year?"

more deeply into the customer's buying situation. Four examples of specific survey questions are:

"Has it occurred to you that by not consolidating your shipping with one carrier, you're likely spending more than is really necessary?" (Shipping Service)

"How do you feel about installing another server to your system?" (File Server)

"To what extent is employee turnover affecting your customer service?" (Customer Service Training)

"What meal function features are most important to your guests?" (Hotel Convention Services)

"Are you looking for an entertainment center that blends in with your existing furniture?" (Retail Home Furnishings)

Survey questions, general or specific, should not be used to collect factual information that can be acquired from other sources prior to the sales call. The preapproach information gathering effort is especially important when the salesperson is involved in a large or complex sale. These buyers expect the salesperson to do their homework and not waste the buyer's time discussing basic factual information that is available from other sources.

Although survey questions are most often used at the beginning of the sales presentation, they can be used at other times. Information gathering may be necessary anytime during the sales presentation. We present the four types of questions in a sequence that has proven to be effective in most selling situations. However, it would be a mistake to view this sequence as a *rigid* plan for every sales presentation. High-performing salespeople spend time strategically preparing tentative questions before they make the sales call. Table 11.2 provides some examples. Note that both open and closed questions are listed. **Open questions** require the prospect to go beyond a simple yes/no response. **Closed questions** can be answered with a yes or no, or a brief response.

Open questions are very effective in certain selling situations because they provoke thoughtful and insightful answers. The specific survey question, "What are the biggest challenges you face in the area of plant security?" focuses the prospect's attention on problems that need solutions. Closed questions, however, can be equally effective when the sales conversation needs to be narrowed or focused on a specific issue.

TABLE 11.2   Need Discovery Worksheet

Preplanned questions (sometimes used in conjunction with company supplied forms) are often used in service, retail, wholesale, and manufacturer selling. Salespeople, such as Johnny in the P3 Questions video, who use the consultative approach frequently record answers to their questions and use this information to correctly select and recommend solutions in subsequent calls in their multicall sales situations. Open and closed questions used in the area of financial services appear in the following list.

PREPLANNED QUESTIONS TO DISCOVER BUYING MOTIVES	CUSTOMER RESPONSE
1. "Now, as I understand it, you're currently pursuing an Internet phone system to offset your high cellular costs?" (Closed/General Survey)	
2. "Are you aware that with the system you are currently using, your brokers may have to keep their laptop 'on' in order to make and receive Internet calls?" (Closed/Specific Survey)	
3. "So what happens if, say your broker is waiting for an important return call and then inadvertently logs off their laptop without a way to roll over the clients return call into a centralized system?" (Open/Probing)	
4. "Let's see if WE understand this – the brokers won't support the system you're considering because it doesn't include instant messaging? And since the brokers would be the primary users of the new system, you're concerned that the system will fail without their support, is that correct?" (Closed/Summary-Confirmation)	
5. "What if we could develop a communications system for you that included I.M. and met the SEC requirements? What positive impact could that have on your situation?" (Open/Need-Satisfaction)	
6.	
7.	
8.	

PROBING QUESTIONS REVEAL CUSTOMER'S PAIN Early in the sales process the salesperson should make every effort to fully understand the buying problem and the consequences surrounding the problem. This is especially important when the problem is difficult to describe, the solution is complex, and the potential impact of a wrong decision is enormous.[7]

Probing questions help you uncover and clarify the prospect's buying problem and the circumstances surrounding the customer's buying problem. They are used more frequently in large, complex sales. These questions often uncover the current level of customer concern, fear, or frustration related to the problem. The following probing questions, sometimes referred to as *implication* questions in Rackham's *SPIN Selling* (see Selling in Action insert on p. 242), are more focused than the survey questions presented earlier.

> "But, doesn't every incorrect label cost you to ship to an incorrect address, then cost you again to have it shipped back to you?" (Shipping Service)
>
> "What would be the consequences if you choose to do nothing about your current server situation?" (File Server)
>
> "How does senior management feel about employee turnover and the related customer service problem?" (Customer Service Training)
>
> "Is poor service at the meal function negatively affecting the number of people returning to your seminar?" (Hotel Convention Services)
>
> "Is it important that you have easy access for connecting your DVD, TIVO, and your wireless LAN network?" (Retail Home Furnishings)

Probing questions help the salesperson and customer gain a mutual understanding of *why* a problem is important. Asking effective probing questions requires extensive knowledge of your company's capabilities, much insight into your customer's buying problem, and a great deal of practice.

The best sales presentations are characterized by active dialogue. As the sales process progresses, the customer becomes more open and shares perceptions, ideas, and feelings freely. A series of appropriate probing questions stimulates the prospect to discover things that he had not considered before.

Neil Rackham conducted studies of 35,000 sales calls and from this research developed the material for his books SPIN Selling *and* The New SPIN Selling Fieldbook. *SPIN is an acronym for Situational, Problem, Implication, and Need-Payoff Questions. According to Rackham, "more than half the* Fortune *100 companies are using the SPIN Selling Model to train their sales forces."*

CONFIRMATION QUESTIONS REVEAL MUTUAL UNDERSTANDING Confirmation questions are used throughout the sales process to verify the accuracy and assure a mutual understanding of information exchanged by the salesperson and the buyer (see Table 11.1). These questions help determine whether there is mutual understanding of the problems and circumstances the customer is experiencing. Throughout the sales process there is always the potential for a breakdown in communication. Perhaps the language used by the salesperson is too technical. Maybe the customer is preoccupied and has not listened closely to what has been said. Many confirmation questions are simple and to the point.

> "If I understand you correctly, the monitoring system for data storage must be set up for both your corporate headquarters and the manufacturing operation. Is that correct?" (File Server)

> "I want to be sure I am clear that you feel there is a direct relationship between employee turnover and the problems that exist in customer service?" (Customer Service Training)

> "Did you say that your seminar attendance dropped 12 percent last year?" (Hotel Convention Services)

> "So you want a new entertainment center that blends with your current light-colored oak furniture?" (Retail Home Furnishings)

The length of the sales process can vary from a few minutes during a single call presentation to weeks in a complex multicall sales presentation. As the sales process progresses, the amount of information available to the salesperson and the customer increases. As the need discovery progresses, the customer's buying criteria or buying conditions surface. **Buying conditions** are those qualifications that must be available or fulfilled before the sale can be closed. The customer may buy only if the product is available in a certain color or can be delivered by a certain date. In some selling situations, product installation or service after the sale is considered an important buying condition by the customer. In a large, complex sale, several buying conditions may surface. The salesperson has the responsibility of clarifying and confirming each condition.

One of the best ways to clarify and confirm several buying conditions is with a **summary-confirmation question**. To illustrate, let us consider a situation in which Tammy Rodriguez, sales manager at a major hotel, has interviewed a prospect who wants to schedule a large awards banquet. After a series of survey, probing, and confirmation questions, Tammy feels confident that she has collected enough information to prepare a proposal. However, to be sure that she has all the facts and has clarified all important buying conditions, she asks the following summary-confirmation question:

> "Let me summarize the major items you have mentioned. You want all of the banquet attendees served within an eight-minute time frame after the opening speaker has finished his speech? And, you need a room that will comfortably seat 60 people banquet style and 10 of these people will be seated at the head table. Is this correct?"

Once all the buying conditions are confirmed, Tammy can prepare a proposal that reflects the specific needs of her customer. The result is a win-win situation for the customer and the salesperson. The chances of closing the sale greatly improve. In multicall sales processes, it is wise to begin subsequent calls with summary-confirmation questions that reestablish what was discussed in the previous call(s):

> "Let me begin by going over what we discussed in our last visit. Your current shipper gives you a 50 percent discount and provides their own custom label printer?" If the customer responds in the affirmative, the salesperson continues with another summary-confirmation question. "You also have to buy fairly expensive custom labels and, at around $90 a pack, you're spending over $20,000 just on labels, is that still correct?"

This enables the salesperson to verify that the previously discovered buying conditions have remained the same and not changed since the last meeting.

NEED-SATISFACTION QUESTIONS REVEAL PLEASURE The fourth type of question used in the sales process is fundamentally different from the other three. **Need-satisfaction questions** are designed to move the sales process toward commitment and action. These are helpful questions that focus on the solution. The chances of closing the sale greatly improve because need-satisfaction questions, or as they are sometimes called *solution* or *pleasure questions*, focus on specific benefits and build desire for a solution.

Survey, probing, and confirmation questions focus on understanding and clarifying the customer's problem. Need-satisfaction questions help the prospect see how your product or service provides a solution to the problem you have uncovered. The opportunity to close the sale greatly improves because you have cast the solution in a pleasurable light.

In most cases, these questions are used after the salesperson has created awareness of the seriousness of the buyer's problem. The need-satisfaction questions you ask will replace their current levels of concern, pain, or frustration with pleasurable thoughts about a solution. The following examples provide insight into the use of need-satisfaction questions:

> "And if I told you that I can offer you cost savings of at least 5 percent over your current shipping expenses, would that be meaningful?" (Shipping Service)

> "Tests on similar applications show a new file server can increase data storage by 30 to 40 percent. How much of an increase do you feel you would achieve?" (File Server)

In many selling situations a product demonstration is an essential stage in the sales process. In this case, the salesperson might use the following need-satisfaction question:

> "What benefits do you see if we provided a demonstration of one of the training modules to senior management so they can understand what you and I have discovered about reducing employee turnover?" (Customer Service Training)

Once the prospect needs are clearly identified, need-satisfaction questions can be valuable closing tools. Consider this example:

> "Considering the benefits we have summarized and agreed on, and noting the fact that our staff will deliver an outstanding meal function, would you like to sign this confirmation so we can reserve the rooms and schedule the meals that you need?" (Hotel Convention Services)

Selling in Action

SELLING IN ACTION

The use of questions to discover needs and present solutions is discussed in several popular personal selling books. For comparison purposes, the approximate equivalents to the four types of questions described in this chapter are listed.

Selling Today by Manning, Reece, and Ahearne	The SPIN Selling Fieldbook by Rackham	The New Solution Selling by Eades	The New Conceptual Selling by Heiman, Sanchez, with Tuleja	Secrets of Question Based Selling by Freese
SURVEY	SITUATION	OPEN	CONFIRMATION	STATUS
PROBING	PROBLEM	CONTROL	NEW INFORMATION	ISSUE
CONFIRMATION	IMPLICATION	CONFIRMING	ATTITUDE	IMPLICATION
NEED-SATISFACTION	NEED-PAYOFF		COMMITMENT	SOLUTION
			BASIC ISSUE	

The questions above are listed in the sequence presented by the authors. To determine the exact definition of each type of question, check the source.

SELLING A PRODUCT THAT DOESN'T EXIST

Some creative entrepreneurs start selling their product before it even exists. Greg Gianforte wanted to start an Internet software company in the late 1990s. He noted that no one seemed to be making a good product that would help companies respond to e-mail from customers. Armed with a product feature sheet, Gianforte started trying to sell a nonexistent product. He called customer-support managers at hundreds of companies. After reviewing the product features, he explained that the product would be ready in 90 days. Some of these potential customers mentioned features he had not thought of. This input helped him develop a better product. After two weeks of cold calls, he knew exactly what customers wanted and he began the development of RightNow software. It was ready for customer use in 90 days. He then hired his first three employees—all of them salespeople. Gianforte says, "Sales is really the most noble part of the business because it's the part that brings the solution together with the customer's need." Today, more than 1,200 organizations worldwide use RightNow solutions.[a]

Need-satisfaction questions such as these are very powerful because they build desire for the solution and give ownership of the solution to the prospect. When the prospect understands which parts of the problem(s) your solution can solve, you are less likely to invite objections. In some cases you may identify problems that still need to be clarified. When this happens, you can use survey, probing, or confirmation questions to obtain more information.

At this point you have received only a basic introduction to the four most common types of questions used during the selling process. (For more insight into the application of questions to the sales process, view the three videos in the "Questions, Questions, Questions" series referred to in this chapter's opening vignette. Also refer to the Video Role-Play Exercises on pp. 255–256.) We will revisit these important sales tools later in this chapter and in Chapters 12, 13, 14, and 15.

Listening and Acknowledging the Customer's Response

To fully understand the customer, we must listen closely and acknowledge every response. The authors of *First Impressions* offer these words of advice to salespeople who use questions as part of the need identification process:

> "What you do after you ask a question can reveal even more about you than the questions you ask. You reveal your true level of interest in the way you listen."[8]

Most of us are born with the ability to hear, but we have to learn how to listen. The starting point is developing a listening attitude. Always regard the customer as worthy of your respect and full attention. Once you have made a commitment to becoming a better listener, develop active listening skills.

Customer Relationship Management with Technology

REVIEWING ACCOUNT STATUS

Salespeople regularly review the status of their prospects' records in their customer relationship management (CRM) databases. In some cases, this is done on the computer screen. In other situations, a printed copy of the records can enhance the process.

Salespeople review their files to ascertain at what phase in the Consultative Sales Presentation Guide each prospect is in the sales cycle. Then they decide which action to take to help move the prospect to the next phase. Sales managers can be helpful with this process, especially for new salespeople. Managers can help salespeople evaluate the available information and suggest strategies designed to move to the next phase.

Even experienced salespeople count on their sales managers to help plan presentations. Managers can help salespeople evaluate their prospects' needs, select the best solution, and plan a presentation most likely to succeed. (See the exercise "Printing the Customer Database" on p. 256 for more information.)

DEVELOPING ACTIVE LISTENING SKILLS **Active listening** is the process of sending back to the prospect what you as a listener think the person meant, both in terms of content and in terms of feelings. Active listening requires intense involvement as you concentrate on what you are hearing, exhibit your listening attitude through your nonverbal messages (see Chapter 3), and feedback to the prospect what you think he or she meant.[9]

Developing active listening skills involves three practices that can be learned by any salesperson willing to make the commitment.

Focus Your Full Attention   This is not easy because the delivery of the messages we hear is often much slower than our capacity to listen. Thus, we have plenty of time to let our minds roam, to think ahead, and to plan what we are going to say next. Our senses are constantly feeding us new information while someone is trying to tell us something. Staying focused is often difficult and involves use of both verbal and nonverbal messages.[10] To show that you are paying attention, lean toward the prospect while saying "uh-huh," "okay," or "I understand" and nodding in agreement when appropriate. Avoid nodding rapidly or saying "uh-huh" rapidly because this will communicate impatience or a desire to turn the conversation back to yourself.[11]

Within every sales presentation there will be times when silence should be welcomed. Use silence to control the flow of information and draw out the customer. Customers are often inclined to fill silence by talking. Throughout an effective sales presentation the customer should be talking more than the salesperson.[12]

Paraphrase the Customer's Meaning   After the customer stops talking, pause for two or three seconds and then state in your own words, with a confirmation question, what you think the person meant. This technique not only helps ensure understanding but also is an effective customer relations strategy. The customer feels good knowing that not only are you listening to what has been said but you are also making an effort to ensure accuracy.

In addition to paraphrasing the content, use questions to dig for full understanding of the customer's perceptions.[13] The use of survey or probing questions is appropriate anytime you need to clarify what is being said by the prospect.

Take Notes   Although note taking is not necessary in every sales presentation, it is important in complex sales in which the information obtained from the customer is critical to the development of a buying solution. Taking accurate notes is a good way to demonstrate to the customer that you are actively listening. When you take notes, you increase your memory of what you heard. Your notes should be brief and to the point.[14] If the information you

In many selling situations, note taking will demonstrate a high level of professionalism.

receive from the customer is too technical or unfamiliar, do not hesitate to ask for clarification of information you don't understand.

Establishing Buying Motives

The primary goal of questioning, listening, and acknowledging is to uncover prospect needs and establish buying motives. Our efforts to discover prospect needs can be more effective if we focus our questioning on determining the prospect's primary reasons for buying. When a customer has a definite need, it is usually supported by specific buying motives.

The greatest time investment in personal selling is on the front end of the sales process. First you must plan the sales call and then, once you are face-to-face with the customer, you can begin the need discovery stage. It is during the early stage of the sales process that you can create the greatest value for the customer.[15]

Selecting Solutions That Add Value

The second part of the consultative sales presentation consists of selecting or creating a solution that satisfies the prospect's buying motives. After identifying the buying motives, the salesperson carefully reviews the available product options. At this point the salesperson is searching for a specific solution to satisfy the prospect's buying motives. Once the solution has been selected, the salesperson makes a recommendation to the prospect (Figure 11.4).

If the sale involves several needs and the satisfaction of multiple buying motives, selection of the solution may take several days or even weeks and may involve the preparation of

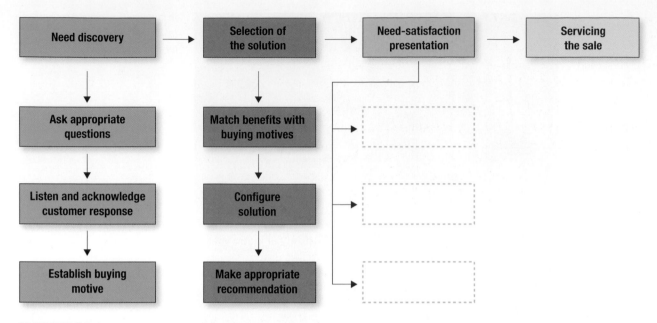

FIGURE 11.4

Three Dimensions of Product
Selection

a detailed sales proposal. A company considering the purchase of automated production equipment would likely present this type of challenge to the salesperson. The problem needs careful analysis before a solution can be identified.

Match Specific Benefits with Buying Motives

As we note in Chapter 7, products and services represent problem-solving tools. People buy products when they perceive that they fulfill a need. We also note that today's more demanding customers seek a cluster of satisfactions that arise from the product itself, from the company that makes or distributes the product, and from the salesperson who sells and services the product (see Figure 7.1). Tom Reilly, author of *Value-Added Selling*, says, "Value-added salespeople sell three things: the product, the company, and themselves. This is the three dimensional bundle of value."[16] When possible, the salesperson should focus on benefits related to each dimension of value. Of course, it is a mistake to make benefit statements that do not relate to the specific needs of the customer. High-performance salespeople present benefits that are precisely tailored to the customer's needs. Benefits that are not relevant to the customer's needs waste time and may invite objections.[17]

Configure a Solution

Most salespeople bring to the sale a variety of products or services. Salespeople who represent food distributors can offer customers a mix of several hundred items. Most pharmaceutical sales representatives can offer the medical community a wide range of products. Best Buy, a large retailer of electronics, offers customers a wide range of audio and visual entertainment options. The customer who wants to purchase an entertainment system, for example, can choose from many combinations of receivers, speakers, and so on.

Make Appropriate Recommendations

The recommendation strategies available to salespeople are similar to those used by a doctor who must recommend a solution to a patient's medical problem. In the medical field, three possibilities for providing patient satisfaction exist. In situations in which the patient easily understands the medical problem and the appropriate treatment, the doctor can make a recommendation, and the patient can proceed immediately toward a cure. If the patient does not easily understand the medical problem or solution, the doctor may need to discuss thoroughly with the patient the benefits of the recommended treatment. If the medical problem is not within his medical specialty, the doctor may recommend a specialist to provide the treatment. In consultative selling the salesperson has these same three counseling alternatives.

RECOMMEND SOLUTION—CUSTOMER BUYS IMMEDIATELY The selection and recommendation of products to meet customer needs may occur at the beginning of the sales call, such as in the product approach; during the presentation just after the need discovery; or near the end, when minor resistance has been negotiated. At any of these three times, the presentation of products that are well matched to the prospect's needs may result in an immediate purchase.

RECOMMEND SOLUTION—SALESPERSON MAKES NEED-SATISFACTION PRESENTATION
This alternative requires a presentation of product benefits including demonstrations and negotiating objections before the sale is closed. In this situation the customer may not be totally aware of a buying problem, and the solution may not be easily understood or apparent. Because of this, the salesperson needs to carefully define the problem and communicate a solution to the customer.

RECOMMEND ANOTHER SOURCE Earlier in this book we indicated that professional salespeople may recommend that a prospect buy a product or service from another source, maybe even a competitor. If, after a careful needs assessment, the salesperson concludes that the products represented do not satisfy the customer's needs, the consultative salesperson should recommend another source.

Paul Roos, a sales representative for Hewlett-Packard, once met with a customer who wanted to buy a newly introduced H-P product for an application that would not work. He explained why the application would not work and then took time to configure a competing product to meet the customer's needs. He lost that sale to a competitor, but the assistance provided confirmed his integrity and made a lasting impression on the customer. That customer later became a high-value account.[18]

Need Satisfaction—Selecting a Presentation Strategy

Decisions concerning which presentation strategy to emphasize have become more complex. This is due to several factors discussed in previous chapters: longer sales cycles, multiple buying influences, emphasis on repeat sales and referrals, greater emphasis on custom fitting of products, and building of long-term partnerships.

Selling in Action

ACTION SELLING AT CARQUEST

CARQUEST Auto Parts promises to deliver what customers need. To achieve this lofty goal, the company enrolled its 1,200 outside sales force members in *Action Selling*. A major objective of this sales training program is to help salespeople become trusted business consultants. They learned that asking—not telling—is the key to sales success. Emphasis throughout the course is placed on asking more and better questions. Duane Sparks, who developed *Action Selling*, says "The success rate of sales calls rises significantly when more than two specific customer needs are uncovered by questioning."[b]

Duane Sparks, Action Selling

Conducting business in the new economy, which is based on the assets of knowledge and information, requires that we think about ways to improve the sales presentation. This is how one author described this challenge:[19]

> *"As we move from the rutted byways of the Industrial Age to the electronic thorough-fares of the Information Age, business presentations become a measure of our ability to adapt to new surroundings. The most successful and forward-thinking companies already have assigned presentations a new, fundamental, and strategic importance."*

The need-satisfaction strategy involves assessing the customer's needs; selecting the product; and deciding whether to use an informative, persuasive, or reminder presentation (Figure 11.5).

Informative Presentation Strategy

To be informative, a message must be clearly understood by the customer. Of course, clarity is important in any presentation, but it needs special attention in a presentation whose primary purpose is to inform. The **informative presentation** emphasizes factual information often taken from technical reports, company-prepared sales literature, or written testimonials from persons who have used the product. This type of presentation is commonly used to introduce new products and services. This strategy emphasizes clarity, simplicity, and directness. Salespeople need to keep in mind the "less is more" concept. Too often the prospect is given far too much information and detail.[20]

Persuasive Presentation Strategy

Many salespeople believe that when a real need for their product exists, the stage is set for a persuasive presentation. The major goal of the **persuasive presentation** strategy is to influence the prospect's beliefs, attitudes, or behavior and to encourage buyer action. Persuasive sales presentations include a subtle transition stage where the dialogue shifts from an intellectual emphasis to an emotional appeal. Every buying decision is influenced by both reason and emotion, but the amount of weight given to each of these elements during the decision-making process can vary greatly depending on the prospect.[21]

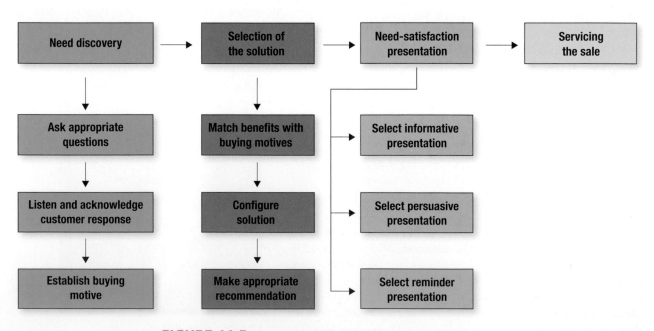

FIGURE 11.5

The Three Strategies to Use in Developing an Effective Need-Satisfaction Presentation

In the field of personal selling, persuasion is an acceptable strategy once a need has been identified and a suitable product has been selected. When it is clear that the buyer can benefit from ownership of the product or service, an enthusiastic and persuasive sales presentation is usually appropriate.

The persuasive presentation strategy requires a high level of training and experience to be effective, because a poorly planned and delivered persuasive presentation may raise the prospect's anxiety level. The persuasive presentation, when handled improperly, can trigger fear or distrust.

Reminder Presentation Strategy

Studies show that awareness of a company's products and services declines as promotion is stopped. This problem represents one of the reasons many companies employ missionary salespeople to maintain an ongoing awareness and familiarity with their product lines. Other types of salespeople also use this presentation strategy. Route salespeople rely heavily on **reminder presentations** (sometimes called *reinforcement presentations*) to maintain their market share. They know that if they do not make frequent calls and remind customers of their products, the competition is likely to capture some customers.

The reminder presentation is sometimes a dimension of service after the sale (see Chapter 15). Sales personnel working with repeat customers are in a good position to remind them of products or services offered in their own department or another department located in some other area of the business. Some products require special care and maintenance. Busy customers may need to be reminded of the maintenance services offered by your company. In some cases, the service department is a major profit generator, so reminder calls need to be given a high priority.

Some customers get used to the great quality and service you provide and begin to view your product as a commodity. Once this happens, the customer may ask for a price reduction. To keep customers focused on value rather than price, remind them (from time to time) of the value-added services you provide.[22]

Developing a Persuasive Presentation Strategy That Creates Value

There are many ways to incorporate persuasion into a sales presentation and most will create value for the customer. In this section we review a series of guidelines that should be followed during preparation of a persuasive presentation.

Place Special Emphasis on the Relationship

Throughout this book we emphasize the importance of the relationship strategy in selling. Good rapport between the salesperson and the prospect establishes a foundation for an open exchange of information. Robert Cialdini, writing in the *Harvard Business Review*, says the science of persuasion is built on the principle of liking: *People like those who like them.* Establish a bond with the customer early by uncovering areas of common interest, using praise when it's appropriate, and being completely trustworthy.[23] Don't forget to adjust your communication style to accommodate the needs of the customer (see Chapter 4).

Sell Specific Benefits and Obtain Customer Reactions

People do not buy things; they buy what the things can do for them. They do not buy an auto battery; they buy a sure start on a cold morning. Office managers do not buy laser printers; they buy better-looking letters and reports. Every product or service offers the customer certain benefits. The benefit might be greater comfort, security, feeling of confidence, or economy.

If you are selling Allstate insurance, for example, you should become familiar with the service features. One feature is well-trained employees and the convenient location of Allstate offices across the nation. The benefit to customers is greater peace of mind in knowing that they can receive good service at a nearby location. Allstate salespeople understand the importance of selling the company, the product, and themselves.

Chapter Learning Activities

Reviewing Key Concepts

Describe the characteristics of the consultative sales presentation

A well-planned and well-executed consultative sales presentation is an important key to success in personal selling. To be most effective, the presentation should be viewed as a four-part process: need discovery; selection of the solution; need satisfaction through informing, persuading, or reminding; and servicing the sale.

Discuss the use of questions to determine needs

The most effective sales presentation is characterized by two-way communication. It should be encouraged with survey, probing, confirmation, summary-confirmation, and need-satisfaction questions. Beware of assuming information about the prospect, and be sure the language of your presentation is clearly understood. Listen attentively as the prospect responds to your questions or volunteers information. Develop active listening skills.

Select solutions that match customer needs

After making a good first impression during the approach and getting the customer's full attention, the salesperson begins the presentation. The salesperson's ability is tested during this part of the sale because this is where the prospect's buying motives are established and a solution is configured.

List and describe three types of need-satisfaction presentation strategies

Once you have selected a solution that matches the customer's needs, you must decide which presentation strategy to emphasize. Need satisfaction can be achieved through informing, persuading, or reminding. The salesperson can, of course, use a combination of these presentation strategies in some cases.

Present general guidelines for creating value-added presentations

Effective presentations require a great deal of preplanning. Effective demonstrations, methods of negotiating and closing the sale, and customer service methods should be preplanned.

Key Terms

Need discovery	Probing questions	Active listening
Survey questions	Confirmation questions	Informative presentation
General survey questions	Buying conditions	Persuasive presentation
Specific survey questions	Summary-confirmation	Reminder presentations
Open questions	question	Emotional links
Closed questions	Need-satisfaction questions	

Review Questions

1. List and describe the four parts of the Consultative Sales Presentation Guide.

2. List and describe the four types of questions commonly used in the selling field.

3. Define the term *buying conditions*. What are some common buying conditions?

4. Describe the process of active listening, and explain how it can improve the listening efficiency rate.

5. Discuss the three dimensions of need discovery.

6. Distinguish between the three types of need-satisfaction presentations: informative, persuasive, and reminder.

7. What are the guidelines to be followed when developing a persuasive sales presentation?

8. What is a metaphor? Why is the use of metaphors considered a persuasive sales tool?

9. A friend of yours is planning to begin selling U.S.-made products in Japan. What tips can you give her that will improve her chances of achieving success?

Role-Play Application Exercises for "Questioning" Video Series

Most sales skill development exercises used in the classroom are product-oriented. As noted on page 234, "Product-oriented selling can easily lapse into product evangelism." This three-part video series on questioning focuses on the customer's buying process, consultative selling, and building high-quality partnerships.

The goal of this series is the identification and clarification of the customer's problem and finding a solution. The first video focuses on the appropriate use of survey and confirmation questions to identify the customer's problem. Video two introduces the use of probing and need-satisfaction questions. Probing questions examine and clarify the potential issues surrounding the customer's problem, while need-satisfaction questions focus the sales process on the appropriate solution. The third video demonstrates the use of these questions in a challenging yet typical contemporary sales setting.

The role-play exercises presented here challenge the participant to understand, apply, and integrate questioning skills presented in this chapter and in the video series. Product information needed for these exercises is found in Appendix 3 on pages 412 to 447. Customer information will be found in the B. H. Rivera Contact Report presented on page 412 (disregard any other information on this page). You will assume the role of a newly hired salesperson as described in the Position Description on page 415. Refer to the questioning material and examples presented on pages 237–242. Use a Need Discovery Worksheet like the one on page 239 for developing your questions.

After viewing the video "Questions—Discovering and Confirming Customer Problems," study the information presented in Appendix 3, pages 412 to 447. Refer to the Contact Report on page 412 (as noted, disregard any other information on this page). Assume you were assigned to this account and you are meeting B. H. Rivera to inquire about additional information regarding dates when the meeting will be held, and what audiovisual equipment might be needed. Prepare a list of general survey and specific survey questions that reveal when, during the next month, the meeting will be held and what, if any, audiovisual equipment (see page 439) might be needed. Plan to use a summary-confirmation question to verify the existing four items on the Contact Sheet. Using the questions you have created, role-play this part of the need-discovery process.

After viewing the video "Questions—Discovering Pain and Pleasure," and reviewing the information you prepared in the previous role-play, prepare three probing questions. These questions should clarify and reveal a mutual understanding of issues and consequences regarding food service, facility design, and audiovisual equipment. Also, using the information on pages 412 to 443, prepare five need-satisfaction questions that reveal how the features of your convention center provide a solution to the buying situation. Select appropriate proof devices to demonstrate these specific benefits. Using these questions, meet again with B. H. Rivera, and role-play this part of the questioning process. Prepare and use confirmation questions as the need arises.

After viewing the video "Questions Getting it Right," and using the information in the first two role-plays, prepare a need-satisfaction presentation to Cameron Rivera, a new meeting planner just hired at Graphic Forms. Cameron, a cousin of B. H., had been previously employed as a training coordinator at West College. Due to extensive growth in the company, B. H. has turned all meeting planning over to Cameron. Cameron will make the final selection of a facility for the meeting described on page 412, plus eleven more identical meetings to be scheduled in the next twelve months. You have also been informed that the Marriott and Sheraton Hotels will be making presentations (note the comparative room, parking, and transportation rates). You will travel to Graphic Forms to make your presentation. Prepare appropriate survey, probing, confirmation, and need-satisfaction questions and presentation strategies that will help secure this important account—then role-play this presentation.

CRM Application Exercise

Printing the Customer Database

Sales managers regularly help salespeople review the status of their accounts. These strategic account review meetings often involve examining all the information available on the salespeople's most promising prospects. Both the sales manager and the salesperson have a copy of all information currently available for the accounts either on their computer screens or on paper. To produce a paper record of the important useful information contained in the Salesforce.com database, click the Reports tab and select the Account Master report. Click "Printable View" and print the report.

Case Problem

When Deborah Karish wakes up in the morning, she does not have to worry about a long commute to work. Her office is in her home. As an Amgen (www.amgen.com) pharmaceutical sales representative, Deborah spends most of her day visiting hospitals, medical clinics, and doctors' offices. She spends a large part of each day serving as a consultant to doctors, head nurses, pharmacists, and others who need information and advice about the complex medical products available from her company. As might be expected, she also spends a considerable amount of time conducting informative presentations designed to achieve a variety of objectives. In some situations she is introducing a new product and in other cases she is providing up-to-date information on an existing product. Some of her presentations are given to individual health care professionals, and others are given to a group. Each of these presentations must be carefully planned.

Deborah uses informative and reminder presentations almost daily in her work. Informative presentations are given to doctors who are in a position to prescribe her products. The verbal presentation often is supplemented with audiovisual aids and printed materials. Reprints of articles from leading medical journals are often used to explain the success of her products in treating patients. These articles give added credibility to her presentations. Some of her informative presentations are designed to give customers updates on the prescription drugs she sells. Reminder presentations are frequently given to pharmacists who must maintain an inventory of her products. She has found that it is necessary to periodically remind pharmacists of product delivery procedures and policies and special services available from Amgen. She knows that without an occasional reminder, a customer can forget information that is beneficial.

In some cases a careful needs analysis is needed to determine if her products can solve a specific medical problem. Every patient is different, so generalizations concerning the use of her products can be dangerous. When doctors talk about their patients, Deborah must listen carefully and take good notes. In some cases she must get additional information from company support staff. If a customer needs immediate help with a problem, she gives the person a toll-free 800 number to call for expert advice. This line is an important part of the Amgen customer service program.

Deborah's career in pharmaceutical sales has required continuous learning. In the beginning she had to learn the meaning of dozens of medical terms and become familiar with a large number of medical problems. If a doctor asks, "What is the bioavailability of Neutogen?" she must know the meaning of the medical term and be knowledgeable about this Amgen product.

Deborah also spends time learning about the people with whom she works. She recently said, "If I get along with the people I work with it, makes my job a lot easier." When meeting someone for the first time, she takes time to assess his communication style and then adjusts her own style to meet his needs. She points out that in some cases the competition offers a similar product at a similar price. In these situations a good relationship with the customer can influence the purchase decision.

Questions

1. If you become a pharmaceutical sales representative, how important is it to adopt the three prescriptions for a presentation strategy? Explain.

2. Deborah Karish spends a great deal of time giving individual and group presentations. Why is it essential that she be well prepared for each presentation? Why would a "canned" presentation, one that is memorized and delivered almost word for word, be inappropriate in her type of selling?

3. Salespeople are encouraged to establish multiple-objective sales presentations. What are some objectives that Deborah Karish might achieve during a sales presentation to doctors who are not currently using her products?

4. What are some special challenges faced by Deborah Karish when she makes a group presentation? How might she enhance her group presentations?

5. Put yourself in the position of a pharmaceutical sales representative. Can you envision a situation when you might combine the elements of an informative, persuasive, and reminder presentation? Explain.

CRM Case Study

Planning Presentations

Becky Kemley, your sales manager at SimNet Systems, wants to meet with you this afternoon to discuss the status of your accounts. It is common for prospects to have several contacts with SimNet before ordering a network system. These multicall contacts, or sales cycle phases, usually include getting acquainted and prequalifying, need discovery, proposal presentation, closing, and account maintenance. Becky wants to know what phase each account is in and, particularly, which accounts may be ready for a presentation.

Questions

1. Which five accounts already have had a need discovery? Which two accounts are scheduled for a need discovery? Which six accounts are likely to buy but have not yet had a need discovery?

2. Which two accounts have had a need discovery and now need a product solution configured?

3. Which three accounts do not now have a network and appear to be ready for your sales presentation?

4. For those accounts listed next that are ready for your sales presentation, which strategy would you use for each: informative, persuasive, or reminder?
   a. Able Profit Machines
   b. Big Tex Auto Sales
   c. International Studios
   d. Lakeside Clinic

5. Which accounts appear to be planning to buy without a need-discovery or product configuration/proposal? What risks does this pose?

Partnership Selling: A Role-Play/Simulation

(see Appendix 3, pp. 456–457)

Understanding Your Customer's Buying Strategy

Read Sales Memorandum 2 ("A" or "B" depending on the account category you were assigned in Chapter 10). Your customer has called you back because you made such a good approach in call 1 and wants to visit with you about a convention recently assigned. In this call you are to use the information gathered in sales call 1 to reestablish a good relationship, discover your customer's convention needs, and set an appointment to return and make a presentation.

Follow the instructions carefully and prepare survey questions prior to your appointment. Keep your survey questions general and attempt to get your customer to openly share information. Use specific survey questions later during the appointment to gain more insight. Be careful about doing too much of the talking. In the need discovery, your customer should do most of the talking, with you taking notes and using them to ask confirmation and summary-confirmation questions to check the accuracy of your perceptions concerning what the customer wants. After this meeting, you will be asked to prepare a sales proposal from the information you have gathered.

Your instructor may again ask you to assume the role of a customer in the account category that you are not assigned to as a salesperson. If so, you will receive detailed customer instructions that you should follow closely. This will provide you with an opportunity to experience the strategic/consultative/partnering style of selling from a customer's perspective.

12

Creating Value with the Sales Demonstration

Chapter Preview

When you finish reading this chapter, you should be able to

1
Discuss how sales demonstrations add value

2
Explain the guidelines to be followed when planning a sales demonstration

3
Describe elements of an effective group presentation

4
Develop selling tools that add value to your sales presentation

5
Discuss the dynamic nature of adaptive selling

▶ Introduction

SimGraphics Systems (www.simgraphics.com), headquartered in North Brunswick, New Jersey, specializes in the development of visual simulation systems based on virtual reality. These systems have applications in such diverse areas as television programming, the training of medical doctors, and product design. At the University of North Carolina, for example, medical students use a virtual reality system to learn and practice eye surgery skills before working on real patients. The SimGraphics system animates virtual characters from the motion-captured performance of a human actor in real time—as the performance is taking place. Performance animation enjoys advantages in immediacy and cost-effectiveness that cannot be matched by a traditional animation system. Needless to say, it's not easy to explain this without a well-planned demonstration. SimGraphics recently opened a state-of-the-art development facility in India to tap into the huge talent pool available in that country.[1]

How the Sales Demonstration Adds Value

In today's fuzzy, complex, out-of-focus world, customers are desperately seeking help with decisions. The salesperson who can simplify things and who can communicate with clarity will be welcomed with open arms. Every effort that is made to uncomplicate the situation adds value.[2] Throughout this text, we have defined value-added selling as a series of creative improvements that enhance the customer experience. The perception of value is enhanced with a well-developed demonstration.

One of the scarcest resources today is people's attention. Some customers will be distracted and will have difficulty maintaining their concentration during the sales presentation. If the customer isn't paying attention, there is little chance of closing the sale. The increase in look-alike products and greater competition present additional challenges. The sales demonstration has become

FIGURE 12.1

Creating Value with the Sales
Demonstration

The Six-Step Presentation Plan	
Step One: Approach	☑ Review Strategic/Consultative Selling Model ☑ Initiate customer contact
Step Two: Presentation	☑ Determine prospect needs ☑ Select solution ☑ Initiate sales presentation
Step Three: Demonstration	☐ Decide what to demonstrate ☐ Select selling tools ☐ Initiate demonstration
Step Four: Negotiation	☐ Anticipate buyer concerns ☐ Plan negotiating methods ☐ Initiate win-win negotiations
Step Five: Close	☐ Plan appropriate closing methods ☐ Recognize closing clues ☐ Initiate closing methods
Step Six: Servicing the Sale	☐ Follow through ☐ Follow-up calls ☐ Expansion selling

Service, retail, wholesale, and manufacturer selling

a more important communication tool. A well-planned **demonstration** adds sensory appeal to the product (Figure 12.1). It attracts the customer's attention, stimulates interest, and creates desire. It usually is not possible to make this type of impression with words alone. The salesperson finds it easier to show what the product can do and how it can fit the customer's needs.

Strategic planning, of course, sets the stage for an effective demonstration that adds value to the sale (Figure 12.2). Some of the most important ways to create value with the demonstration are discussed next.

Documenting the Value Proposition

In Chapter 7 we defined *value proposition* as a set of key benefits and values the company promises to deliver to satisfy needs. Salespeople must be prepared to substantiate the points presented during the sales presentation. Recent research indicates that salespeople often make claims of savings and benefits to the customer but fail to back them up. Failure to demonstrate and document claims is a common barrier to closing the sale.[3]

In most business-to-business selling situations, it would be a mistake to present a value proposition that includes all of the product benefits. Some benefits may be of no interest to the target customer. Effective precall preparation and well-executed need discovery activities minimize the possibility you will spend time discussing features that provide no benefit to the customer.

In many cases the most effective value proposition is one that focuses on favorable points of difference between your product and *the next best alternative*. The salesperson recognizes that the customer can purchase the product from one or more competitors. Once the customer's requirements and preferences are clearly understood, and knowledge of the competitor's product is acquired, the salesperson can focus on key points of difference.

The most effective value proposition describes the few elements that matter most to target customers. This approach recognizes that today's buyers are extremely busy and want to

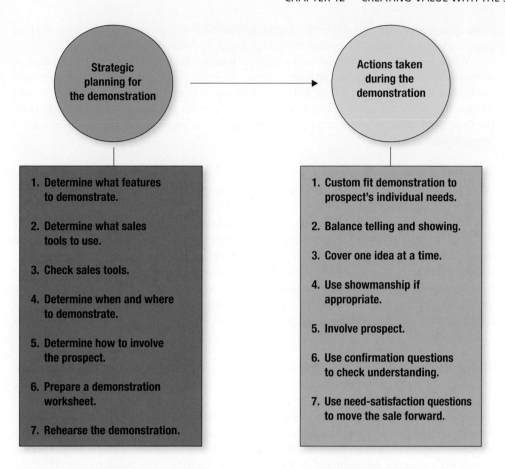

FIGURE 12.2

Poorly conducted demonstrations usually result from a lack of strategic planning and preparation.

do business with salespeople who fully grasp the critical issues in their business and are able to deliver a value proposition that is simple yet powerfully captivating. So, focus on favorable points of difference between your product and the *next best alternative.*[4]

Improved Communication and Retention

In Chapter 3, we noted the limitation of the verbal presentation; words provide only part of the meaning attached to messages that flow between the salesperson and the prospect. When we try to explain a point with words alone, people frequently do not understand our messages.

Why is communication via the spoken word alone so difficult? One major reason is that we are visually oriented from birth. We grow up surrounded by the influence of movies, television, commercial advertising, Web-based messages, and other visual stimulation. People are accustomed to learning new concepts through the sense of sight or through a combination of seeing and hearing.

Many sales representatives recognize the limitations of the spoken word. When talking to prospects about the economic benefits of delivering training programs with a satellite system, a salesperson used a table (Table 12.1) to illustrate savings. With the aid of this

TABLE 12.1   How Much Can a Satellite System Save You?

TYPE OF SYSTEM	PER PERSON COST 20 SITES	PER PERSON COST 30 SITES	PER PERSON COST 40 SITES	PER PERSON COST 50 SITES
Satellite delivery system	$7.80	$7.20	$6.60	$6.00
High-bandwidth terrestrial lines	$7.10	$7.40	$7.70	$8.00

These cost estimates are based on current satellite broadcast rates and rates for use of terrestrial lines. The per-person cost is based on an audience size of 25 trainees at each site.

table, prospects can visualize the economic benefits of the satellite delivery system compared with a competing system using high-bandwidth terrestrial lines.

When we rely on verbal messages alone to communicate, retention of information is minimal. A number of studies provide evidence to support this important point. Research conducted at Harvard and Columbia Universities found that retention increases from 14 to 38 percent when the spoken word is accompanied with effective visuals. In addition, the time needed to present a concept can be reduced by up to 40 percent with the use of appropriate visuals.[5]

Proof of Buyer Benefits

A well-planned and well-executed sales demonstration is one of the most convincing forms of proof. This is especially true if your product has dramatic points of superiority.

Salespeople representing Epson, Canon, Hewlett-Packard, and other manufacturers can offer the customer a wide range of printers. What is the real difference between a $200 basic printer and a $400 high-resolution laser printer? The laser equipment prints a neater and more attractive letter or report. The most effective way to provide proof of this buyer benefit is to show the customer material that has been printed on both printers. By letting the prospect compare the examples, the salesperson is converting product features to a buyer benefit. Be prepared to prove with tests, findings, and performance records every claim you make.

PROOF DEVICES We have noted that when trust is present, customers are more open to the sales presentation. One way to build trust is to use proof devices that enhance your credibility. **Proof devices** can take the form of a statement, a report, a testimonial, customer data, or a photograph. A salesperson selling conference services for a large hotel/conference center might use the following proof statement: "We were selected by *Training* magazine as one of the nation's top 10 conference centers." Later the salesperson shows the customer photographs of the conference facilities and guest rooms. Then the customer is given a copy of a testimonial letter from a satisfied customer. The statement, photos, and letter help build the customer's confidence in the product. Later in this chapter we will examine proof devices in more detail.

Feeling of Ownership

Many effective sales demonstrations give the prospect a temporary feeling of ownership. This pleasant feeling builds desire to own the product. Let us consider the person who

When salespeople use effective visual proof devices in their presentations, research indicates that retention increases from 14 to 38 percent; the time needed to present a concept is reduced by up to 40 percent.

The value proposition includes a mix of key benefits to meet the needs of the customer. This ad illustrates the three parts of Durkee's value proposition: support, flavor, and performance.

Courtesy of Tone Brothers, Inc.

enters a men's clothing store and tries on an Oxford suit that features the highest quality fabrics and hundreds of hand-stitched features that improve comfort and fit. The salesperson notes that there are 900 hand stitches in the collar alone. During the few minutes the customer is wearing the suit, a feeling of pride is apt to develop, and desire to own an Oxxford suit will likely build.[6]

Many firms offer prospects an opportunity to enjoy products on a trial basis. This is done to give people a chance to assess the merits of the product in their own home or business. Some firms that sell office equipment and office furniture use this sales strategy.

Guidelines for Planning Demonstrations That Add Value

A sales demonstration that adds value is the result of both planning and practice. Planning gives the salesperson a chance to review all the important details that should be considered in advance of the actual demonstration. Practice (or rehearsal) provides an opportunity for a trial run to uncover areas that need additional polish. For large, complex sales, the salesperson should plan to spend several hours preparing for the sales presentation.[7] During the planning stage, it helps to review a series of guidelines that has helped salespeople over the years to develop effective demonstrations.

Develop Creative Demonstrations

Presenting product features and buyer benefits in an interesting and appealing way requires some amount of creativity. Creativity is needed to develop a sales demonstration that can gain attention, increase desire, and add value. The ability to come up with problem-solving answers or different ways of looking at situations is greatly valued in today's fast-changing business environment. Creativity is enhanced by expertise in the field of endeavor. For salespeople, this means knowledge of the sales process, product knowledge, and an understanding of human behavior. Creativity is also enhanced by the capacity for divergent thinking and a willingness to take risks.[8]

Use Custom-Fitted Demonstrations

In adaptive selling, each presentation is custom tailored because individual client problems and priorities are unique. In other words, every aspect of the sales presentation, including the demonstration, should relate to the needs or problems mutually identified by the prospect and the salesperson.

It is possible to develop a sales demonstration so structured and so mechanical that the prospect feels like a number. We must try to avoid what some veteran marketing people refer to as the *depersonalization* of the selling/buying process. If the demonstration is overly structured, it cannot be personalized to meet specific customer wants and needs.

Bell Helicopter (www.bellhelicopter.com) sells several models with countless custom options, and each option changes its price and performance. One customer may want a helicopter for emergency medical care and another may want one for electronic news gathering. Bell's sales force, all of whom are licensed helicopter pilots, can introduce the Bell product line with a video presentation and then follow up with a demonstration flight if necessary. Sales representatives also have access to a sales configuration system that supports the customization process. Price and performance data can be quickly determined for each accessory needed by the customer. The software automatically provides answers to the numerous questions that can surface during the sales presentation.[9]

Choose the Right Setting

The location of the sales demonstration can make a difference. Some companies routinely rent space at a hotel, motel, or conference center so that the demonstration can be conducted in a controlled environment free of noise and other interruptions. Many organizations have conference rooms that can be reserved with advanced notice. In these busy times, prospects are often unwilling or unable to participate in a presentation held off premises.

Check Sales Tools

Be sure to check every item to be used in conjunction with the sales demonstration. If you are using audiovisual equipment, be certain that it is in good working condition. Always carry an extension cord and a spare bulb. If you are making a laptop presentation, be sure you can go online in front of the customer. If you plan to demonstrate a Web site, save it on a hard disk instead of going online. Be prepared for technological snags by having multiple backups. Always carry extra batteries for your laptop.[10]

Cover One Idea at a Time and Confirm Agreement

Pace the demonstration so that the customer does not become confused. Offer one idea at a time, and be sure the customer understands each point before moving on. When you neglect this practice, there is the danger that the customer's concentration may remain fixed on a previous point. Some demonstrations are ruined by a salesperson who moves too rapidly from one point to another. Consider using a confirmation question to get agreement on each key point before moving on to the next. One objective of the sales demonstration is to increase the customer's desire for a solution to their problem. Therefore, a *need-satisfaction*

IT WAS INSPIRED BY YOU. NOW IT'S RETURNING THE FAVOR.

Welcome to the incredible result of your own feedback, the most innovative high-performance helicopter in the sky: the Bell 429. Welcome to the leading edge of vertical lift.

1-800-FLY-BELL bellhelicopter.com

© 2007 Bell® Helicopter Textron Inc., all rights reserved.

Bell Helicopter sales representatives have access to a sales configurations system that supports customizing the demonstration. Sales representatives, all of whom are licensed helicopter pilots, conduct customized demonstration flights to meet their customer's unique needs.

question (see Chapter 11) can help move the sale forward. During the demonstration of an animation publishing platform, the salesperson might say, "This program can help you produce a complex animation in a very short period of time. Do you often work on projects with tight deadlines?"

Appeal to All Senses

In conducting a sales demonstration, it is a good idea to appeal to all appropriate senses. Each of the five senses—sight, hearing, smell, touch, and taste—represents an avenue by which the salesperson can attract the prospect's attention and build desire.

Although sight is considered the most powerful attention-attracting sense, it may not be the most important motivating force in every selling situation. When presenting a food product, the taste and aroma may be critical. Designers and decorators tell us that most furniture buyers still want to touch and feel the product before they buy it.

Gary Eberle, owner of Eberle Winery (www.eberle.com) located in San Luis Obispo County, California, understands the importance of reaching the prospect through as many senses as possible. He spends considerable time each year selling his wines to retailers and restaurant owners.[11] The sales presentation for a quality wine usually highlights four areas:

Consumer demand. The wine's sales potential is described in realistic terms.

Marketing strategies. Suggested ways to merchandise the wine are discussed.

Secret of Question-Based Selling *(www.qbsresearch.com), used in sales organizations around the world, focuses on asking the right questions that pique customer interest, build credibility, uncover greater needs, and solicit more accurate information.*

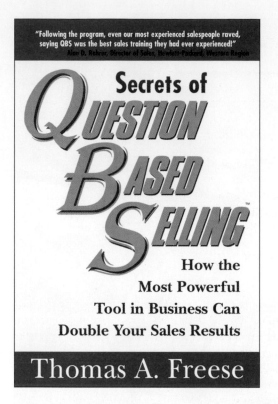

Bouquet. The distinctive fragrance of the wine is introduced.

Taste. A sample of the wine is given to the prospect in a quality wineglass.

Note that a sales presentation featuring these appeals can reach the prospect through four of the five senses. Collectively, these appeals add value. When you involve more than one sense, the sales presentation is more informative and more persuasive.

Balance Telling, Showing, and Involvement

A Chinese proverb says, "Tell me, I'll forget; show me, I may remember; but involve me and I'll understand."[12] Some of the most effective sales demonstrations combine telling, showing, and involvement of the prospect. To plan an effective demonstration, consider developing a demonstration worksheet. Simply divide a sheet of paper into four columns.

In a complex sale, it is imperative to check every part of your demonstration prior to the presentation. During the presentation, you should cover one idea at a time and secure agreement before moving on.

Demonstration Worksheet			
Feature to Be Demonstrated	Proof Device to Be Used	What I Will Say (Include Benefit)	What I or the Customer Will Do
Special computer circuit board to accelerate drawing graphics on a color monitor screen.	Monitor and software	"This monitor is large enough to display multiple windows. You can easily compare several graphics."	Have the customer bring up several windows using computer keyboard.
Meeting room setup at a hotel and conference center.	Floor plan	"This setup will provide 3 feet of elbow space for each participant. For long meetings, the added space provides more comfort."	Give the customer a tour of the room and invite her to sit in a chair at one of the conference tables.

FIGURE 12.3

The demonstration worksheet enables the salesperson to strategically plan and then rehearse demonstrations that strengthen the presentation.

Head the first column, "Feature to Be Demonstrated." Head the second column, "Proof Device to Be Used." Head the third column, "What I Will Say." Head the fourth column, "What I or the Customer Will Do." List the major features you plan to demonstrate in proper sequence in the first column. In the second column, describe the proof devices you will use. In the third column, describe what you will say about the feature, converting the feature to a customer benefit. In the fourth column, describe what you (or the customer) will do at the time this benefit is discussed. A sample demonstration worksheet appears in Figure 12.3.

When possible, try to involve the customer in the sales demonstration. The best way to highlight the style, fit, and comfort of a high-end men's suit is to have the customer try it on. The Rumination Station office chair offers rich, soft leather; cushy arms and headrest; a spacious, first-class seat; and a footrest for reclining. To fully appreciate this expensive chair the customer must try it out.

If it is not possible for the prospect to participate in the demonstration or handle the product, place sales literature, pictures, or brochures in the person's hands. After the sales call, these items remind the prospect of not only who called but also why.

Rehearse the Demonstration

While you are actually putting on the demonstration, you need to be concentrating on a variety of details. The movements you make and what you say and do should be so familiar

Many firms, like Engineered Machine Products who produce high-efficiency thermal management systems for cooling engines, have learned one of the keys to closing a large complex sale is to conduct a plant tour.

to you that each response is nearly automatic. To achieve this level of skill, you need to rehearse the demonstration.

Rehearse both what you are going to say and what you are going to do. Say the words aloud exactly as if the prospect were present. It is surprising how often a concept that seems quite clear as you think it over becomes hopelessly mixed up when you try to discuss it with a customer. Rehearsal is the best way to avoid this embarrassing situation. Whenever possible, have your presentation/demonstration videotaped before you give it.

Play it back and watch for these things:[13]

- Do you frequently use words that take away from your professional image? Examples include "you know" and "like."
- Check your pace—are you talking too rapidly or too slowly?
- Do you present information with clarity? Are you convincing?

Selling Tools for Effective Demonstrations

Nearly every sales organization provides its staff with sales tools or proof devices of one kind or another. Many of these, when used correctly, add value to the sales effort. If the company does not provide these items, the creative salesperson secures or develops sales tools independently. In addition to technology-based presentations, sales personnel can utilize a wide range of other selling tools. Creative salespeople are continually developing new types of sales tools. The following section summarizes some of the most common tools used today.

Quantifying the Solution

In Chapter 6 we explained that the process of determining whether or not a sales proposal adds value is called *quantifying the solution*. If the cost of the proposal is offset by added value, closing the sale will be much easier. In business-to-business selling, quantifying the solution is very common. Let's assume you represent a manufacturing company that sells robots—a reprogrammable machine capable of performing a variety of tasks. The two primary benefits are (1) payroll cost savings and (2) vastly improved quality. One way to quantify the solution in this case is to use a simple **cost–benefit analysis**. This involves listing the costs to the buyer and the savings to be achieved from the purchase of the robots.

Another way to quantify the solution is to calculate the net profits or savings, expressed as a percentage of the original investment. This is called **return on investment**. Using the following formula, you can determine the net profits or savings from a given investment.

$$\text{ROI} = \text{Net Profits (or Savings) Divided by Investment} \times 100$$

If the robotic system costs $16,000 but saves the firm $4,000, the ROI is 25 percent ($4000/$16,000 × 100 = 25%). Some companies set a minimum ROI for new products or cost-saving programs. Salespeople often acquire this information at the need-assessment stage and then include it in the written proposal.

Space does not permit a review of the many methods of quantifying the solution. Some of the additional ways include payback period, opportunity cost, net present value, after-tax cash flow, turnover, and contribution margin.

Product and Plant Tours

Without a doubt the best-selling aid is often the product itself. As noted previously, Bell Helicopter uses an effective video to describe various products. However, some customers do not buy without a demonstration ride. In the growing market for ergonomic office chairs, ranging in price from $700 to $1,500, furniture makers know the best way to close the sale is to provide an opportunity for the customer to sit in the chair. With growing awareness of the hazards of poor sitting posture and bad ergonomics, more people are searching for a comfortable work chair.[14]

Doug Adams was the first salesperson hired by a major manufacturer of high-quality optical equipment. Although he was not a technician or an engineer, he quickly realized that the equipment had product superiority that physicians would recognize if they saw it demonstrated. During the first year, he sold 28 machines, far surpassing the expectations of his employer.[15]

As noted in a previous chapter, plant tours provide an excellent source of product information. EMP (Engineered Machine Products) makes high-efficiency thermal management systems for cooling engines. Products are made at a state-of-the art manufacturing facility in Escanaba, Michigan. The company has learned that the key to closing many large, complex sales is a facility tour.[16]

Models

In some cases it is not practical to demonstrate the product itself because it is too big or immobile. It is easier to demonstrate a small-scale model or cross-section of the original equipment. A working model, like the actual product, can give the prospect a clear picture of how a piece of equipment operates.

With the aid of modern technology, it's possible to create a model in picture form. ClosetMaid (www.closetmaid.com), a manufacturer of ventilated wire for commercial closets and other storage products, uses desktop visualization software to create a three-dimensional presentation that allows customers to see exactly what the finished facility will look like. Sales representatives can print out a hard copy so the customer has a picture of the custom-designed model for future reference. With the aid of this visualization technology, ClosetMaid salespeople can modify closet layouts on-screen and produce a detailed bill of materials for each project.[17]

Photos, Illustrations, and Brochures

The old proverb "One picture is worth a thousand words" can be put into practical application by a creative salesperson. A great deal of valuable information can be given to the prospect with the aid of photos and illustrations. Chris Roberts, area manager for Downing Displays (www.downingretail.com), a manufacturer of trade show displays, says that the photo presentation book is the most important item he takes on a first

Salespeople can add value to their presentations with the aid of photos and illustrations. This salesperson has balanced telling, showing, and involvement by getting the sales literature into the hands of the prospect.

sales call. He says, "Because what we sell is very visual, it's important for the client to *see* the displays."[18]

Many companies develop brochures that visually reinforce specific need/benefit areas. Brochures can be effective during the initial discussion of needs when the salesperson wants to provide a brief overview of possible solutions. Someone planning to remodel a kitchen might be given a "Colors of Corian" brochure that features color photos of numerous countertop materials and kitchen design examples.[19]

Portfolio

A **portfolio** is a portable case or loose-leaf binder containing a wide variety of sales-supporting materials. The portfolio is used to add visual life to the sales message and to prove claims. A person who sells advertising might develop a portfolio including the following items:

> Successful advertisements used in conjunction with previous campaigns
>
> Selected illustrations that can be incorporated into advertisements
>
> A selection of testimonial letters
>
> One or more case histories of specific clients who have used the media with success

The portfolio has been used as a sales tool by people who sell interior design services, insurance, real estate, securities, and convention services. It is a very adaptable proof device that can be revised at any time to meet the needs of each customer.

Reprints

Leading magazines and journals sometimes feature articles that directly or indirectly support the salesperson's product. A reprint of the article can be a forceful selling tool. It is also an inexpensive selling tool. Pharmaceutical and medical sales representatives often use reprints from journals that report on research in the field of medicine. A few years ago, Closure Medical Corporation received approval to sell Dermabond (www.dermabond.com), a surgical glue used to close cuts. This innovative product received national attention when the prestigious *Journal of the American Medical Association* concluded that gluing a wound could be just as effective as sewing it shut. Salespeople representing Dermabond used the article to help educate doctors on the product's merits and applications.[20]

Global Business Etiquette

DOING BUSINESS IN ITALY

 The majority of Italian Americans have roots in Sicily or southern Italy. American businesspeople tend to think that all Italians are like the Italian Americans whom they have had contact with in America. In reality, Italy is a very varied country where you will find all types of physical characteristics—fair, dark, short, tall, and varied accents and customs.

- Italian businesspeople tend to be quite formal in terms of introductions and dress. When you introduce yourself, say your last name only and then shake hands. Wait until invited to use your first name. Personal and professional titles are used almost all the time in business dealings.

- Entertaining clients should be done at restaurants, not in the home.

- Most Italian businesspeople are not in a hurry, so be patient and do not try to rush the sale.

- The practice of gift giving will vary. A nominal gift such as a bottle of wine at Christmas is quite common.[a]

In many cases prospects are far more impressed with the good points of your product if they are presented by a third party rather than you. A reprint from a respected journal can be very persuasive.

Catalogs

A well-designed catalog shows the range and comprehensiveness of your product line. It may include specifications needed for installation and current price information. If you plan to give customers a copy of your catalog, review the important features, such as a comprehensive index or important appendix material.[21]

Graphs, Charts, and Test Results

Graphs and charts can be used to illustrate the change of some variable such as payroll expense, fuel consumption, or return on investment. For example, a bar graph might be used to illustrate the increase in fuel costs over a 10-year period.

Although graphs are usually quite descriptive, the layperson may misunderstand them. It is best to interpret the graph for the prospect. Do not move too fast because the full impact of the message may be lost.

Test results from a reliable agency often can be convincing. This is especially true when the test results are published by a respected independent agency such as J.D. Power and Associates.

Bound Paper Presentations

Although many salespeople are using some type of presentation technology in conjunction with the sales demonstration, paper is still widely used. For many sales and marketing organizations, bound paper presentations continue to be a very popular medium.[22] With the aid of computer-generated graphics, it is easy to print attractive graphs, charts, and other proof information. Product guarantees and warranties are sometimes included in a bound paper presentation. Some marketers use guarantees and warranties to differentiate their products from competing products. Customer testimonials represent another common element of bound paper presentations. A testimonial letter from a prominent satisfied customer provides persuasive evidence that the product has support in the industry. Prospects like bound paper presentations because the document is readily available for future reference.

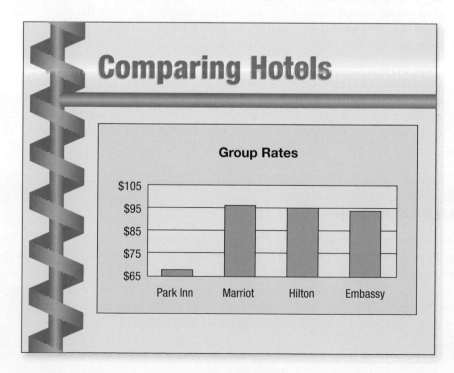

Graphs produced with Excel software can add value and be very persuasive in demonstrating key benefits of a sales presentation. This Excel graph also uses a PowerPoint background design to add more value. Go to www.pearsonhighered.com/manning and click on Caxambas PowerPoint Presentation to view a PowerPoint sales presentation.

Laptop Computers and Demonstration Software

A survey conducted by *Selling Power* magazine found that 87 percent of salespeople use laptops during their sales presentations.[23] Many salespeople will tell you that the laptop computer is the single most powerful sales tool they use. Many of the things needed during the demonstration can be stored in the computer. If the customer is interested in a specific product, pull up the appropriate brochure or videotape on your laptop screen. If the client wants a copy of printed material, you can either print the pages or send them via e-mail. If the customer raises a question regarding product availability, use your laptop to access the information. You can place an order and in some cases print an invoice.[24]

Thanks to modern computer technology, it's possible to conduct impressive multiple, simultaneous product demonstrations without leaving your office. Let's assume you are presenting a new employee disability insurance plan to members of the BMW of North America human resources staff. One key decision maker is based in Germany and the other in the United States. With the aid of Pixion PictureTalk software, or a similar product, you can use the Internet to conduct the demonstration for both persons in real time. Sales managers might use this same approach to train members of their sales team in remote offices.

Personal computers (PCs) with the support of online presentation technologies and presentation software have played an important role in increasing sales force productivity. Salespeople have instant access to customer data, so it is often easier to customize the sales presentation. Many salespeople report that PC-based presentations, using graphics software, are very effective. Today's PC can produce striking visuals and attractive printed material that can be given to the customer for future reference.

ENHANCING DEMONSTRATIONS WITH POWERPOINT The PowerPoint software program from Microsoft has been available to salespeople for 20 years. PowerPoint is so common that many prospects find the standard presentation graphics very familiar, even dull. Salespeople who want their demonstration to look unique and different can create their own corporate template, animate their logo, or put video clips of their own company information into the PowerPoint presentation. When developing a PowerPoint presentation, use bold, simple, and large fonts (such as Arial and Veranda) and put graphics on several slides. Limit the number of words to 15 or fewer per slide. Keep in mind that two quality alternatives to Power Point are Apple's Keynote and Corel's Presentations.[25]

CREATING ELECTRONIC SPREADSHEETS For many years, salespeople have been using electronic spreadsheets to prepare sales proposals. The electronic spreadsheet is an excellent tool to organize the numbers involved in preparing quotes, such as quantities, costs, and prices. The electronic spreadsheet allows the user to answer "what if " questions

Selling Is Everyone's Business

DRAWING THE CUSTOMER'S ATTENTION

Tina Cox, a technical trainer for Analytical Graphics, uses InterWrite software and its integrated wireless tablet-and-pen capabilities to teach customers how to use the company's products. Analytical Graphics produces integrated land, sea, and air analysis software. Using the approach popular among TV football commentators like John Madden, she writes on her prepared screens during the presentation. She draws on her images to show her clients the key elements of the slides. Cox believes this form of presentation technology greatly enhances her Web-based and in-person presentations.[b]

Preparing a sales presentation for a group is more demanding than one-on-one sales calls. Too much reliance on technical devices during a demonstration can affect the relationship, so important to partnering effectively with prospects.

about the effects of lowering costs or raising prices. Once the preparation work is finished, the electronic spreadsheet itself can be printed and used to serve as the proposal or to accompany the proposal.[26] The spreadsheet data can also be converted to a chart or graph that can enhance the proposal.

Many computers sold today include an electronic spreadsheet program. The leading electronic spreadsheet, Excel, is part of Microsoft's Office Suite of products. If you have access to Excel, or any other electronic spreadsheet software, you can explore the power of this tool for preparing proposals.

WEB-BASED DEMONSTRATIONS Salespeople who want to avoid long airport security lines, lengthy terminal wait times, high-priced hotels, and expensive rental care rates are turning to Web-conferencing solutions. Popular alternatives to in-person sales presentations include WebEx Communications Sales Center, Raindance Meeting Edition, Adobe's Macromedia Breeze 5, and Microsoft Office Live Meeting. Some salespeople create computerized demonstrations that are stored in a central library and accessed on demand. With a few clicks of a mouse, presenters can call up the information they wish to showcase using a Web browser. The salesperson can show PowerPoint presentations, present product features, and conduct question-and-answer sessions in real time. Prior to scheduling an online meeting, be sure to find out if the customer's firewall restricts the usage of your Web-conferencing software.[27]

Elements of an Effective Group Sales Presentation

Preparing a sales presentation for a group is more demanding than one-on-one sales calls. Meeting the diverse needs of the audience can be very challenging. Therefore, *Rule One* is to identify the titles and roles of the people who will attend. Among those attending, who is most likely to influence the buying decision? If you learn that the audience will include the prospect's CEO, your CEO should be there. Anticipate that the audience will include demanding, high-level decision makers who will likely ask some difficult questions. Be prepared![28]

Rule Two is to check out the meeting room in advance. What are the room configuration, audiovisual capabilities, seating options, lighting, and heating or air conditioning? Always arrive at the meeting room about 60 minutes before the meeting begins. Use the first 40 minutes to check and double-check presentation tools, seating arrangements, lighting, etc. Use the other 20 minutes for rapport building with attendees as they arrive.

Rule Three is to be sure your presentation is characterized by clarity and simplicity. Minimize the number of features and benefits you present. Focus on the few benefits that appeal to your prospect. Don't use jargon or technical terms that might confuse persons in attendance. If you are part of a team sales presentation (see Chapter 10), then be sure every team member understands their responsibility and the time they will be given for their presentation. Give the team time for rehearsal before the group presentation.

Rule Four is to anticipate questions you are likely to be asked and be prepared with answers that are concise and persuasive. Questions should be welcomed because they help you understand what is truly important to the customer.

Enhancing the Group Presentation with Mental Imagery

Mental imagery is the ability to visualize an object, concept, or action not actually present. A sales demonstration can be greatly enhanced with the use of auditory and visual imagery. Today there is no shortage of compact, lightweight portable presentation devices. Sony Electronics, Hitachi Software, and NEC offer sales professionals projectors that weigh only a few pounds and project a clear, bright image. These presentation tools also offer quick and easy setup.[29]

Impatica, a company that specializes in the delivery and viewing of PowerPoint presentations over the Internet and wireless networks, has developed a small, lightweight device that enables salespeople to project presentations wireless from a BlackBerry handheld. Users need only hook the ShowMate to the VGA port projector, LCD, or plasma screen and the Blackberry will deliver the PowerPoint presentation using Bluetooth technology.[30] Of course, salespeople should never rely on presentation tools to sell products. Dianne Durkin, president of consulting form Loyalty Factor, offers this advice:

> *"When a salesperson is tied to the technical device and the presentation, they miss the opportunity to build the personal relationship by asking questions and listening to the customer. A questioning and listening strategy is the secret weapon for salesperson."*[31]

Audiovisual Presentation Fundamentals

Many companies provide their salespeople with audiovisual aids such as videotapes or computer-based presentations. Unfortunately, they sometimes fail to explain how to use these tools in the most effective way. Here are some suggestions on how to use audiovisual presentations to achieve maximum impact:

1. Do not rely too heavily on "bells and whistles" to sell your products. Audiovisual technology provides support for the major points in your presentation, but it does not replace an interactive sales demonstration.

2. Be sure the prospect knows the purpose of the presentation. Preview the material and describe a few highlights. Always try to build interest in advance of the audiovisual presentation.

3. Be prepared to stop the presentation to clarify a point or to allow the prospect to ask questions. Do not permit the audiovisual presentation to become a barrier to good two-way communication.

4. At the conclusion of the audiovisual presentation, review key points and allow the prospect an opportunity to ask questions.

Plan for the Dynamic Nature of Selling

The sales presentation is a dynamic activity. From the moment the salesperson and the customer meet, the sales presentation is being altered and fine-tuned to reflect the new information available. The salesperson must be able to execute strategy instantaneously. In the movie *Top Gun*, Kelly McGillis asks Tom Cruise, "What were you thinking up there?"

His reply was, "You don't have time to think. You take time to think up there, you're dead." By that, he meant the response must be habit and reflex.[32]

During a typical presentation, the salesperson asks numerous questions, discusses several product features, and demonstrates the appropriate product benefits. The customer also is asking questions and, in many cases, voicing concerns. The successful sales presentation is a good model of two-way communication. Because of the dynamic nature of the sales presentation, the salesperson must be prepared to apply several different selling skills to meet the variety of buyer responses. Figure 12.4 illustrates how the various selling skills can be applied during all parts of the sales presentation. In creating effective presentations, the salesperson should be prepared to meet a wide range of buyer responses with effective questions, benefit statements, demonstrations, negotiating methods, and closing methods.

Consultative selling skills	Parts of the Sales Presentation			
	Need discovery	Selecting solution	Need-satisfaction presentation	Servicing the sale
Questioning skills	• As a question approach • To find needs and buying motives • To probe for buying motives • To confirm needs and buying motives	• To confirm selection	• To confirm benefits • To confirm mutual understanding • To increase desire for a solution	• To make suggestions • To confirm delivery and installation • To resolve complaints • To build goodwill • To secure credit arrangements
Presenting benefits	• As a benefit approach • To discover specific benefits	• To match up with buying motives	• To build support for the solution	• To make suggestions • To use credit as a close
Demonstrating skills	• As a product approach • To clarify need	• To clarify selection	• To strengthen product claims	• When making effective suggestions
Negotiating skills	• To overcome initial resistance to sales interview • To overcome need objection	• To overcome product objection	• To overcome source, price, and time objections	• In handling complaints • To overcome financing objection
Closing skills	• When customer has made buying decision	• When buyer immediately recognizes solutions	• Whenever buyer presents closing signals	• After suggestion • To secure repeats and referrals

FIGURE 12.4

The Selling Dynamics Matrix

A sales demonstration that creates value increases the dynamic nature of personal selling.

Audiovisual technology can provide support for the major points in your presentation. No matter how exotic the sales tool, remember you are still the central figure in the selling situation.

Why are meetings with InFocus® projectors so popular? Is it because they make it easier to share information and collaborate on team projects so meetings get finished a whole lot faster? Absolutely. To calculate the return on investment you get from InFocus projectors, visit us online at www.infocus.com/for, or call 1-888-InFocus. Great meetings begin with InFocus. The worldwide leader in digital projection.

InFocus
meeting accomplished

Chapter Learning Activities

Reviewing Key Concepts

Discuss how sales demonstrations add value

Every effort that is made to uncomplicate the sales presentation adds value. The sales demonstration will often help clarify important benefits and provide proof of product performance. The demonstration will also help the customer better understand the solution to their problem.

Explain the guidelines to be followed when planning a sales demonstration

A sales demonstration that adds value is the result of both planning and practice. During the planning stage consider the eight guidelines described in this chapter. Keep in mind people perceive impressions through the five senses.

Describe elements of an effective group presentation

Group presentations are almost always more challenging than one-on-one sales calls. Be sure you identify the titles and roles of the persons who will attend. Check out the meeting room in advance to assess audiovisual capabilities and seating options. As you prepare your presentation, take into consideration the needs of the audience. In many cases audiovisual tools can be used to enhance the group presentation.

Develop selling tools that add value to your sales presentation

Many selling tools, sometimes called *proof devices*, will help you add value to the sales effort. Be prepared to use one or more of the ten tools discussed in this chapter.

Discuss the dynamic nature of adaptive selling

From the moment the salesperson and customer meet, the sales presentation is being fine-tuned to reflect new information available. The well-prepared salesperson is able to apply a wide range of selling skills in order to move the sale forward. The salesperson should be prepared to meet a wide range of customer responses with effective questions, benefit statements, demonstrations, negotiating methods, and closing methods.

Key Terms

Demonstration	Cost–benefit analysis	Portfolio
Proof devices	Return on investment	Mental imagery

Review Questions

1. List the benefits of using a sales demonstration during the presentation of a product or service.

2. Assume the role of a sales representative for a large newspaper. What type of portfolio would you use during a sales call?

3. Discuss the advantages of using the demonstration worksheet.

4. Explain why a salesperson should organize the sales presentation so that it appeals to as many of the five senses as possible.

5. List the guidelines to follow in planning an effective demonstration.

6. Develop a list of the sales tools that the salesperson should consider when planning a sales demonstration.

7. Describe the merits of a bound paper presentation. What can be done to strengthen the persuasive power of a bound paper presentation?

8. Explain how magazine and trade journal reprints can be used to assist the salesperson in a persuasive sales presentation.

9. Describe the audiovisual presentation fundamentals.

10. What are some of the common sales functions performed by small laptop computers and demonstration software?

Application Exercises

1. In many selling situations it is difficult, if not impossible, to demonstrate the product itself. List means other than the product itself that can be used to demonstrate the product features and benefits.

2. Develop a list of sales tools you could use in a job interview situation. What tools could you use to demonstrate your skills and capabilities?

3. As noted in this chapter, demonstration software is becoming increasingly popular. Real estate salespeople are using this software to showcase homes to prospective buyers.

13

Negotiating Buyer Concerns

Reality Selling Today Video Series

Marriott International Inc. (www.marriott.com) is a world-renowned company with approximately 8,500 salespeople and 3,000 lodging properties around the world. One of its properties is the Marriott Houston Hobby, which is located within a mile of the Hobby Airport in Houston, Texas. Apart from accommodation, the hotel offers comprehensive meeting facilities complemented by expert catering and audiovisual resources.

Corporate catering manager, Heather Ramsey, in the photo above, is in charge of convention and meeting sales at the Marriott Houston Hobby Airport. She always has a ready response when customers raise concerns about prices and the tranquility of an airport hotel. She emphasizes the value to the customers by describing the state-of-the-art meeting and conference facilities offered by the hotel, its convenience to travelers, as well as other unique features not offered by the competition. Sometimes customers do not communicate openly about their needs and concerns to Heather. She must often work hard to identify their actual needs to offer them the best value and bring benefits to the hotel as well. Her negotiation process with new customers will normally involve identifying their actual needs and then listening to, clarifying, and overcoming concerns that the customers express.

Many sales professionals are very proficient in need discovery and selecting the right solution, but are weak in the area of negotiating an agreement that is favorable to the customer and the salesperson's firm. Some salespeople fail to anticipate buyer concerns and plan negotiating methods (see Figure 13.1). A recent poll reports that as many as 83 percent of sales executives from 25 industries said they generally enter negotiations with no formal strategy![1] Another common mistake is making last-minute concessions in order to close the sale.[2] In this chapter, we describe effective strategies for anticipating and negotiating buyer concerns.

The Six-Step Presentation Plan	
Step One: Approach	☑ Review Strategic/Consultative Selling Model ☑ Initiate customer contact
Step Two: Presentation	☑ Determine prospect needs ☑ Select solution ☑ Initiate sales presentation
Step Three: Demonstration	☑ Decide what to demonstrate ☑ Select selling tools ☑ Initiate demonstration
Step Four: Negotiation	☐ Anticipate buyer concerns ☐ Plan negotiating methods ☐ Initiate win-win negotiations
Step Five: Close	☐ Plan appropriate closing methods ☐ Recognize closing clues ☐ Initiate closing methods
Step Six: Servicing the Sale	☐ Follow through ☐ Follow-up calls ☐ Expansion selling

Service, retail, wholesale, and manufacturer selling

FIGURE 13.1

Negotiating Customer Concerns and Problems

We have noted previously that the heaviest time investment in value-added selling is on the front end of the sale. This is especially true for large, complex sales that require a long sales cycle. Identifying the customer's needs and developing the best solution can be very time-consuming. However, when you do these things effectively, you are creating value in the eyes of the customer. When you build value on the front end of the sale, price becomes less of an issue on the back end of the sale.[3]

Formal Integrative Negotiation—Part of the Win-Win Relationship Strategy

Frank Acuff, negotiations trainer and author of *How to Negotiate Anything with Anyone, Anywhere Around the Globe*, says, "Life is a negotiation."[4] Negotiating skills have applications almost daily in our personal and professional lives. Some traditional personal selling books discuss how to "handle" buyer objections. The message communicated to the reader is that personal selling is a "we versus they" process resulting from distributive negotiations: Somebody wins, and somebody loses. The win-win solution, where both sides win, is not offered as an option. In this chapter, we focus on integrative negotiations, which is built on joint problem solving, trust, and rapport to achieve win-win situations. Ron Willingham, author of two books on integrity selling, says:

> *When trust and rapport are strong, negotiation becomes a partnership to work through customer concerns. But when trust and rapport are weak, almost any negotiation becomes too combative.*[5]

Trust and rapport must be established on the front end of the sale and maintained throughout the sales process. High-performance salespeople, like Heather Ramsey, take time to discover the customer's needs and try to recommend the best possible solution. Always keep in mind that any agreement that leaves one party dissatisfied will come back to hurt the other party later, sometimes in ways that cannot be predicted.[6]

TABLE 13.1

Objections are often requests for more information to justify the buying decision. Objections can tell us a lot about the real source of hesitation and what type of information the customer is seeking.

OBJECTION	SOURCE OF HESITATION	REQUEST FOR . . .
"Price too high"	Perceived cost versus benefit	Value articulation
"Think about it"	Afraid to make a bad decision	Create comfort, provide proof
"Talk to boss"	Unable to justify decision	Risk reduction, benefit review
"Need more quotes"	Unsure you're their best option	Targeted solutions, value
"Set with current provider"	Doesn't see benefit of change	Differentiation
"Bad history"	Past experience is affecting current view	Offer proof of change

Adapted from "Hide-and-Seek," a table from Nancy J. Stephens, "Objections Are a 'Yes' About to Happen," *Selling*, November 1998, p. 3.

UNDERSTAND THE PROBLEM David Stiebel, author of *When Talking Makes Things Worse!*, says we need to understand the difference between a misunderstanding and a true disagreement. A *misunderstanding* is a failure to accurately understand the other person's point. For example, the salesperson believes the customer is primarily interested in price, but the customer's primary need is on-time delivery. A *disagreement*, in contrast, is a failure to agree that would persist despite the most accurate understanding.[18] Be certain that both you and the prospect are clear on the true nature of what needs to be negotiated (see Table 13.1). When the prospect begins talking, listen carefully and then listen some more. With *probing questions*, you can fine-tune your understanding of the problem.

CREATE ALTERNATIVE SOLUTIONS THAT CAN ADD VALUE When the prospect finishes talking, it is a good practice to validate the problem, using a *confirmation question*. This helps to isolate the true problem and reduce the chance of misunderstanding. The confirmation question might sound like this: "I think I understand your concern. You feel the warranty does not provide you with sufficient protection. Is this correct?" By taking time to ask this question, you accomplish two important objectives. First, you are giving personal attention to the problem, which pleases the customer. Second, you gain time to think about the best possible response.

The best possible response is very often an alternative solution. In formal negotiations, this is often referred to as **logrolling**.[19] Many of today's customers do not want to hear that there is only one way or a single solution. In the age of information, people have less time to manage their work and their lives, so they expect new levels of flexibility. There are many issues that can be introduced into the negotiations. In many cases these additional issues take the focus off price, and can actually create value for the customer and possibly for the seller. Here are additional issues that can be introduced into negotiations when a buyer is focused on price: delivery dates, financing, contract length, quality, exclusivity clauses, levels of service support, and warranties.

PERIODICALLY REVIEW ACKNOWLEDGED POINTS OF AGREEMENT Negotiating buying problems is a little like the art of diplomacy. It helps to know what points of agreement exist. This saves time and helps establish a closer bond between you and the prospect. At some point during the presentation, you might summarize by using a *summary-confirmation question*: "Let us see if I fully understand your position. You think our product is well constructed and will provide the reliability you are looking for. Also, you believe our price is fair. Am I correct on these two points?"

Once all the areas of agreement have been identified, there may be surprisingly few points of disagreement. The prospect suddenly sees that the advantages of ownership far outweigh the disadvantages. Now that the air is cleared, both the salesperson and the customer can give their full attention to any remaining points of disagreement.

The business environment is sometimes turbulent. Hence, it might be advisable in negotiations to "pack a reserve parachute." To avoid buyers' frustration when things do not go as agreed upon, lay the groundwork for the unexpected and be open about back-up plans with the buyers.[20]

DO NOT MAKE CONCESSIONS TOO QUICKLY Give away concessions methodically and reluctantly, and always try to get something in return. A concession given too freely can diminish the value of your product. Also, giving a concession too easily may send the signal you are negotiating from a position of weakness. Neil Rackham, author of several books on SPIN selling, says, "Negotiate late, negotiate little and never let negotiation become a substitute for good selling."[21]

TIMING AND THE PARETO LAW Time plays a critical role in negotiations. Most often negotiations will conclude in the final 20 percent of the time allowed. In negotiations, experience with the Pareto Law reveals that 80 percent of your results are generally agreed upon in the last 20 percent of your time. Since influence tactics are more likely to exert an effect when their target is under time pressure, negotiators should use time as a strategic weapon by buying more time to fully consider concessions or giving a deadline to speed up agreement.[22]

Know When to Walk Away

For many reasons salespeople must sometimes walk away from a potential sale. If the customer's budget doesn't allow the purchase of your product, don't press the issue. If the customer's best offer is not favorable for your company, don't continue to waste your time. If the buyer is only interested in the lowest possible price, and you represent a marketer committed to a value-added sales strategy, consider withdrawing from negotiations. If you discover that the prospect is dishonest or fails to keep their word, discontinue negotiations. Be aware of how much flexibility (your BATNA and ZOPA) you have in terms of price, specifications, delivery schedules, and so forth, and know when you have reached your "walk-away" point.[23]

Finally, when appropriate, document negotiated settlements in writing. These will be helpful when formal contracts are drawn up. Negotiation minutes will also serve as a control tool for follow-up actions.

Common Types of Buyer Concerns

Salespeople learn that patterns of buyer resistance exist and, therefore, they can anticipate that certain concerns may arise during the sales call. With this information it is possible to be better prepared for each meeting with a customer. The great majority of buyer concerns fall into five categories: need, product, source, time, and price.

Concerns Related to Need for the Product

If you have carefully completed your precall planning, then the prospect will likely have a need for your product. You still can expect, however, that the initial response may be, "I do not need your product." This might be a conditioned response that arises nearly every time the prospect meets with a sales representative. It also may be a cover-up for the real reason for not buying, which might be lack of funds, lack of time to examine your proposal carefully, or some other reason.

Sincere need resistance is one of the great challenges that face a salesperson during the early part of the sales process. Think about it for a moment. Why would any customer want to purchase a product that does not seem to provide any real benefits? Unless we can create need awareness in the prospect's mind, there is no possible way to close the sale.

If you are calling on business prospects, the best way to overcome need resistance is to prove that your product is a good investment. Every business hopes to make a profit. Therefore, you must demonstrate how your product or service can contribute to that goal. Can your product increase sales volume? Can it reduce operating expenses? If the owner of a hardware store says, "I already carry a line of high-quality tools," point out how a second line of less expensive tools can appeal to another large segment of the buying public. With the addition of the new line, the store can be in a better position to compete with other stores (discount merchandise stores and supermarkets) that sell inexpensive tools.

Concerns About the Product or Services

You will recall from Chapter 8 that consultative process buyers may lack needs awareness or need help evaluating possible solutions. Therefore, the product (solution) often becomes the focal point of buyer resistance. When this happens, try to discover specific reasons why the prospect has doubts about your product or services. Often you may find that one of the following factors has influenced the buyer's attitude:

1. *The product or service is not well established.* This is a common buyer concern if you are selling a new or relatively new product. People do not like to take risks. They need plenty of assurance that the product is dependable. Use laboratory test results, third-party testimonials from satisfied users, or an effective demonstration to create value.

2. *The present product or service is satisfactory.* Change does not come easily to many people. Purchasing a new product may mean adopting new procedures or retraining employees. In the prospect's mind the advantages may not outweigh the disadvantages, so buyer resistance surfaces. To overcome this concern, you must build a greater amount of desire in the prospect's mind. Concentrate on a value proposition that gives your product or service a major advantage over the existing one, or reconfigure the product and offer customized services to better meet the customer's needs.

Concerns Related to Source

Concerns related to source can be especially challenging when the prospect is a strategic alliance buyer. The buyer may already have well-established partnerships with other companies. If the prospect feels genuine loyalty to its current supplier, you will have to work harder to establish a relationship and begin the need discovery process.

When dealing with the loyalty problem, it is usually best to avoid direct criticism of the competing firm. Negative comments are apt to backfire because they damage your professional image. It is best to keep the sales presentation focused on the customer's problems and your solutions.

There are positive ways to cope with the loyalty objection. Some suggestions follow:

1. *Work harder to identify problems your company can solve with its products or services.* With the help of good questions, you may be able to understand the prospect's problems better than your competitors.

2. *Point out the superior benefits of your product and your company.* By doing this you hope the logic of your presentation can overcome the emotional ties that may exist between the prospect and the present supplier.

3. *Work on recruiting internal champions to build more support for your message.* Use referrals whenever possible.[24]

4. *Try to stay visible and connected.* Every contact with the prospect is one more step in building a relationship. Anthony Tringale, owner of Insurance Consulting Group in Fairfax, Virginia, says that he is involved with many potential clients in social and charitable events.[25]

Concerns Related to Time

If a prospect says, "I want time to think it over," you may be encountering concerns related to time. Resistance related to time is often referred to as the **stall**. A stall usually means the customer does not yet perceive the benefits of buying now. In most cases the stall indicates that the prospect has both positive and negative feelings about your product. Consider using *probing questions* to determine the negative feelings: "Is it my company that concerns you?" "Do you have any concerns about our warranty program?"

It is all right to be persuasive if the prospect can truly benefit from buying now. If the price may soon rise, or if the item may not be available in the future, then you should provide this information. You must, however, present this information sincerely and accurately. It is never proper to distort the truth in the hope of getting the order.

Selling in Action

YOU DON'T GET WHAT YOU DESERVE, YOU GET WHAT YOU NEGOTIATE

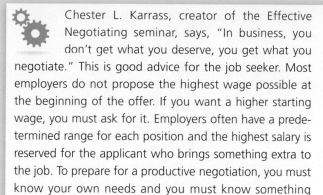

Chester L. Karrass, creator of the Effective Negotiating seminar, says, "In business, you don't get what you deserve, you get what you negotiate." This is good advice for the job seeker. Most employers do not propose the highest wage possible at the beginning of the offer. If you want a higher starting wage, you must ask for it. Employers often have a predetermined range for each position and the highest salary is reserved for the applicant who brings something extra to the job. To prepare for a productive negotiation, you must know your own needs and you must know something about the worth of the position. Many employers tell you the salary range prior to the interview. The Internet can be a good source of salary information for certain types of jobs. In terms of your needs, try to determine what you care about the most: interesting work, future promotion, or flexible work schedule. If you are willing to negotiate, you can increase your pay by hundreds or even thousands of dollars. Be prepared to sell yourself, negotiate the salary you believe is appropriate, and achieve a win-win solution in the process.[b]

Renewing a contract also calls for renegotiations. In these cases, be upfront and explain the benefits in precise terms concerning what additional values the new price will bring to the client. Sometimes it is advisable to offer a break in the payment schedule to overcome the client's adverse feelings about the price hike.[26] To enhance the relationship with long-term business partners, the seller sometimes has to look at the market to reevaluate what is really fair pricing and voluntarily renegotiate with the buyer to lower the price before the buyer asks for it.[27]

Concerns Related to Price

Price objections are one of the biggest obstacles salespeople have to conquer.[28] There are two important points to keep in mind concerning price resistance. First, it is one of the most *common* buyer concerns in the field of selling. Therefore, you must learn to negotiate skillfully in this area. Second, price objections may be nothing more than an excuse. If you are selling a product or service to a transactional buyer, price may be the primary barrier to closing the sale. When people say, "Your price is too high," they probably mean, "You have not sold me yet." In the eyes of most customers, value is more important than price. Always

The desire to buy low is quite common. However, when buyers are faced with information overload, their decisions become more difficult. When concerns surface, salespeople need to explain the benefits that add value and use skillful negotiations to gain acceptance of the selling price. If the selling price is too low, profit margins may suffer.

Fast Company, December 1998.

SELLING SAVES FACTORY JOBS

The workers at the Parker Hannifin Corporation factory in Irwin, Pennsylvania, count on Ken Sweet to save their jobs. He is the general manager. When sales at this automation-equipment plant drop, there is pressure to cut the payroll. The pressure to cut costs through layoffs builds during a recession when sales typically decline. Fortunately, Mr. Sweet has an ace up his sleeve. As general manager he is responsible for sales as well as getting the product out the door. When manufacturing operations slow down, Mr. Sweet redoubles his sales efforts. He urges his equipment-development teams to focus on potential customers that offer the best chance for big contracts. Some production workers are recruited to help with the sales effort. Jim Manion, an assembler, calls prospects that have visited the company's Web site when work is scarce at the plant. These sales efforts help save jobs.[c]

try to position your product with a convincing value proposition. Customers who perceive added value are less likely to choose a competing product simply on the basis of price. We will present specific tactics to deal with this issue shortly.

Specific Methods of Negotiating Buyer Concerns

There are eight specific methods of negotiating buyer concerns. In analyzing each buyer concern, we should try to determine which method can be most effective. In most cases we can use a combination of the following methods to negotiate buyer concerns.

Direct Denial

Direct denial involves refuting the opinion or belief of a prospect. The direct denial of a problem is considered a high-risk method of negotiating buyer concerns. Therefore, you should use it with care. People do not like to be told they are wrong. Even when the facts prove the prospect is wrong, resentment can build if we fail to handle the situation properly.

When a prospect offers buyer resistance that is not valid, we sometimes have no option other than to openly disagree. If the person is misinformed, we must provide accurate information. For example, if the customer questions the product's quality, meet the concern head-on with whatever proof seems appropriate. It is almost never proper to ignore misinformation. High-performance salespeople counter inaccurate responses from the prospect promptly and directly.

The manner in which you state the denial is of major importance. Use a win-win approach. Be firm and sincere in stating your beliefs, but do not be offensive. Above all, do not patronize the prospect. A "know-it-all" attitude can be irritating.

Indirect Denial

Sometimes the prospect's concern is completely valid or at least accurate to a large degree. This method is referred to as the **indirect denial**. The best approach is to bend a little and acknowledge that the prospect is at least partially correct. After all, if you offered a product that is objection proof, you would likely have no competitors. Every product has a shortcoming or limitation.[29] The success of this method is based in part on the need most people have to feel that their views are worthwhile. For this reason the indirect denial method is widely used. An exchange that features the use of this approach follows. The salesperson is a key account sales representative for Pacific Bell Directory.[30]

Salesperson: The total cost of placing your 6- by 8-inch ad in the yellow pages of five different Pacific Bell directories is $32,000.

Prospect: As a builder I want to reach people who are planning to build a home. I am afraid my ad will be lost among the hundreds of ads featured in your directories.

Salesperson: Yes, I agree the yellow pages in our directories do feature hundreds of ads, but the section for general contractors features fewer than 30 ads. Our design staff can prepare an ad that can be highly visible and can set your company apart from ads placed by other contractors.

Note that the salesperson used the words "Yes, I agree . . . " to reduce the impact of denial. The prospect is less likely to feel her point of view has been totally disproved. One note of caution: Avoid the "Yes . . . but" response. When you use the word *but*, it invalidates anything preceding it. A more effective response would be, "I understand your concerns, Ms. Thomas; however, there is another way to view this issue."[31]

FEEL–FELT–FOUND Successful salespeople are sensitive to clues that indicate the client feels something is wrong. One way to empathize with the client's concerns is to use the "feel–felt–found" strategy. Here is how it works. Assume the customer is concerned about the complexity of the new computer software, and says, "I do not think I will ever understand the process." Your response might be, "I understand how you *feel*, Mr. Pearson. Many of my customers *felt* the same way, until they started using the software and *found* it quite easy to master."

In their best-selling The New Conceptual Selling, *authors Heiman, Sanchez, and Tuleja recommend using the question "What are your concerns with this proposal?" They also suggest that you ask questions in a positive rather than negative manner, and that you "wait for answers."*

Outline methods for creating value in formal negotiations

We have described several specific methods for creating value in formal negotiations, but you should remember that practice in applying them is essential and that there is room for a great deal of creative imagination in developing variations or additional methods. With careful preparation and practice, negotiating buyer concerns about price should become a stimulating challenge to each salesperson's professional growth.

Work with buyers who are trained in negotiation

Buyers who are trained in negotiations resort to a number of tactics that a salesperson should be prepared for. In any case, the ultimate goal of formal integrative negotiations is to achieve win-win solutions by offering buyers the value they appreciate without compromising the sellers' benefits.

Key Terms

Negotiation	Stall	Trial offer
BATNA	Direct denial	Postpone method
ZOPA	Indirect denial	Trial close
Logrolling	Superior benefit	Unbundling

Review Questions

1. Explain why a salesperson should welcome buyer concerns.
2. List the common types of buyer resistance that might surface in a presentation.
3. How does the negotiations worksheet form help the salesperson prepare to negotiate buyer concerns?
4. Explain the value of using *probing* and *confirmation* questions when negotiating buyer concerns.
5. List eight specific strategies for negotiating buyer resistance.
6. John Ruskin says that it is unwise to pay too much when making a purchase, but it is worse to pay too little. Do you agree or disagree with this statement? Explain.
7. What is the most common reason that prospects give for not buying? How can salespeople deal effectively with this type of concern?
8. Professional buyers often learn to use specific negotiation tactics in dealing with salespeople. List and describe two tactics that are commonly used today.
9. When a customer says, "I want time to think it over," what type of resistance is the salesperson encountering? Suggest ways to overcome this type of buyer concern.
10. Discuss the merits of using need-satisfaction questions to negotiate buyer concerns.

Application Exercises

1. When conducting negotiations with a customer, take into consideration their communication style. Select two of the four communication styles (emotive, director, reflective, or supportive) and prepare guidelines for negotiating with each one. Review material in Chapter 4 before completing this exercise.
2. During an interview with a prospective employer, the interviewer raises the objection that you are not qualified for the job for which you are applying. On the basis of your observation, you do not believe the interviewer fully understands the amount of experience you have or that you really have the ability to perform the job requirements. Write how you would overcome the objection the interviewer has raised.

3. Assume you have decided to sell your own home. During an open house, a prospective buyer begins to criticize major selling points about your home.

   a. You have taken excellent care of your home, believe it to be a good home, and have done a lot of special projects to make it more enjoyable. What will be your emotional reaction to this prospect's criticisms? Should you express this emotional reaction?

   b. Underneath this surface criticism, you think this prospect is really interested in buying your home. How would you negotiate the sales resistance she is showing?

4. Acclivus Corporation (www.acclivus.com) is a leading supplier of sales training programs. As noted in this chapter, one of their most popular programs is the Acclivus Sales Negotiation course. Access the Acclivus home page on the Internet, and click the "Programs" link. Click "Negotiation" and review the information on the Acclivus Sales Negotiation course. Report your findings.

Role-Play Exercise

You work for the sales department of an apparel manufacturing company. Company XYZ, which you have met with during a recent trade fair, is going to visit your facilities next week. You understand that this company wants to "buy low" but normally places large orders. However, you want to "sell high." Your company might not be able to deliver very large orders unless you invest in new facilities. Company XYZ says it will send over a team of three people: the vice president of marketing, the purchasing manager, and a designer. They are interested in developing a collection for the next season and going over a "price exercise" with you. In addition, they are interested in placing a trial order at the price of a bulk order (i.e., large order). Delivery of the order is to be made in two weeks. Unfortunately, this trial order is well below the minimum quantity you're willing to accept, and your company normally needs one month to fill a new order.

1. How do you convey this information to the other departments within your company to prepare for this meeting? Will you invite your boss to the meeting? Why?

2. Using a negotiations worksheet, plan your responses to the following statements made by the purchasing manager: (a) We are concerned that you will not be able to meet our quality requirements, (b) Your price is too high, (c) Either take this trial order or we will look for another vendor. Decide at what point in the negotiations on price and delivery date you will decide to turn down the offer or accept the offer. Role-play your response to each of these statements.

CRM Application Exercise

Finding Keywords in a CRM Database

During sales training this week, your sales manager, Becky Kemley, led a discussion about negotiating buyer resistance and managing objections. The discussion included methods of identifying and responding to price concerns. You intend to identify those prospects that have a price objection so that you can better prepare to work with them. Using Salesforce.com, access all records containing the word "price" by going to the Reports tab and selecting "Opportunity Pipeline Report." This report lists all your opportunities. Customize this report to limit it to opportunities where price is an objection by adding the criteria "Description Contains Price." This report now contains three records in which price is an issue. This report also contains the primary contact information for these opportunities at these three companies. To find contact information for all the contacts in the Salesforce.com database for these opportunities, click the "Opportunity" link in each record.

Reality Selling Today Video Case Problem

Heather Ramsey
Marriott International Inc.

Each year public and private organizations send thousands of employees to meetings held at hotels, motels, convention centers, conference centers, and resorts. These meetings represent a multimillion-dollar business in the United States. Airport hotels such as the Marriott Houston Hobby, introduced at the beginning of this chapter, are a good example of such a destination. The Marriott Houston Hobby is located at a convenient location, only one mile from the Hobby Airport in Houston, Texas. It also has a competitive edge because it lies outside of the flight plane. In addition to convenience and tranquility, the goal of the hotel is to provide guests outstanding meeting and conferences services. The hotel offers 235 deluxe guest rooms, 52 suites, 13 soundproof meeting rooms with state-of-the-art audiovisual technology, and continuous break service that can accommodate any agenda. Lavish customized meal events from a wide variety of international cuisines are a specialty of the Marriott Houston Hobby.

In an ideal situation, Heather Ramsey, corporate catering manager at the hotel, tries to get the prospects out for a site inspection of the property. Prospects might also sample hors d'oeuvre or lunch meals during this site tour. This tour, in some ways, fulfills the function of a sales demonstration. Throughout the tour she describes special amenities and services offered by the hotel. She also uses this time to get better acquainted with the needs of the prospect. Once the tour is completed, she escorts the prospect back to her office and completes the needs assessment. Next, she prepares a detailed sales proposal or, in some cases, contracts. The proposal needs to contain accurate and complete facts because, when signed, it becomes a legally enforceable sales contract.

For big events, the sales proposal is rarely accepted without modification. Professional meeting planners are experienced negotiators and press hard for concessions. Some have completed training programs developed for professional buyers. The concessions requested may include a lower guest room rate, lower meal costs, complimentary suites, or a complimentary event such as a wine and cheese reception. It might take as long as two months to reach an agreement with sophisticated buyers.

Of course, some buyer resistance is not easily identified. Heather Ramsey says that she follows four steps in dealing with buyer concerns:

1. *Identify the actual needs of the prospects.* To achieve win-win deals, Heather spends time asking specific questions about the customer's needs such as the audience of the event, the size and timing of the event, or the customer's budget. The prospects normally focus on negotiating details of food menu choice, group rates for room rental, and audiovisual facilities.

2. *Locate the resistance.* Some prospects are reluctant to accept the offer, but the reason may be unclear. Heather has discovered in some cases that asking open-ended questions goes a long way in understanding the actual resistance. Once this perception is uncovered, Heather knows how to deal with it.

3. *Clarify the resistance.* If a prospect says, "I like your facilities, but your prices are a little high," then the salesperson must clarify the meaning of this objection. Is the prospect seeking a major price concession or a small price concession?

4. *Overcome the objection.* Heather says, "You must be prepared for negotiations by understanding both your flexibility and the customers' needs." The hotel must earn a profit or publicity, so concessions can be made only after careful consideration of the bottom line and other intangible benefits.

Heather has discovered that the best way to negotiate buyer concerns is to make sure both the prospect and the resort feel like winners once the negotiations are finalized. If either party feels like a loser, a long-term relationship will not be possible. During peak seasons, Heather might also need to negotiate the schedule of events with prospects to minimize opportunity costs for the hotel while keeping the customers happy by offering off-season concessions. Refer to the opening paragraph of this chapter for more information. (See chapter opener on p. 280, and Reality Selling Today Role-Play 7 in Appendix 1 on p. 402 for more information.)

Questions

1. If you were selling convention services for a hotel located in a large city, what types of buyer concerns would you expect from a new prospect?

2. Let us assume that you are representing the Marriott Houston Hobby Airport and you are meeting with a new prospect at the hotel for a site tour. This prospect is planning to host an important event at your hotel for 200 guests. List the questions that you might ask the prospect to identify her actual needs. In doing so, be specific about the alternatives (e.g., high-end, medium, regular packages) that you can offer the prospect and the order of presenting those to the prospects.

3. If you meet with a professional buyer who is trained in negotiation, what tactics can you expect the person to use? How would you respond to each of these tactics?

4. What subtle questions will you ask to validate that the negotiator is the decision maker without hurting her feelings? What actions will you take if you find out she is not the decision maker?

CRM Case Study

Negotiating Resistance

Becky Kemley has asked you to review Pat Silva's former prospect accounts. She wants you to look for accounts with which you might anticipate objections during a presentation.

Questions

1. Which account might voice a time objection and say, "We want to put off our decision for now," and how would you propose dealing with this objection?

2. Which account is most likely to try to get you to agree to a lower price and how would you respond?

3. Which account might say, "We want to shop around for a good solid supplier," and what would be your response?

Partnership Selling: A Role-Play/Simulation

(See Appendix 3, pp. 461 and 471)

Developing a Presentation Strategy—Negotiating

Refer to Sales Memorandum 3 and strategically plan to anticipate and negotiate any objections or concerns your customer may have to your presentation. You should prepare a negotiations worksheet to organize this part of your presentation.

The instructions for item 2e direct you to prepare negotiations for the time, price, source, and product objections. You note that your price is approximately $200 more than your customer budgeted for this meeting. You have to be very effective in negotiating a value-added strategy because your convention center is not a low-price supplier (see Chapter 2 on value-added product strategies).

During the presentation, you should use proof devices from the product strategy materials provided in Employment Memorandum 1 to negotiate concerns you anticipate. You also may want to use a calculator to negotiate any financial arrangements such as savings on parking, airport transportation, and so on. Using spreadsheet software, you may want to prepare graphs to illustrate competitive pricing. Place these materials in the front pocket of your three-ring binder (portfolio) so that you can easily access them during your presentation. You may want to secure another person to be your customer, instructing him or her to voice the objections you have anticipated, and then respond with your negotiation strategies. This experience can provide you with the opportunity to rehearse your negotiation strategies.

Adapting the Close and Confirming the Partnership

Chapter Preview

When you finish reading this chapter, you should be able to

1
Describe the proper attitude to display toward closing the sale

2
List and discuss selected guidelines for closing the sale

3
Explain how to recognize closing clues

4
Discuss specific methods of closing the sale

5
Explain what to do when the buyer says yes and what to do when the buyer says no

Adaptive Selling Today Training Video Series

Ask For the Order, or AFTO as it is also called, is the third training video in the Adaptive Selling Today Training Video Series. The video begins with a salesperson who has a fear of closing the sale. Research shows that many sales are lost because salespeople fear asking for the order, and that even when they do, it is not unusual to have to ask three or four times. Along with many successful examples of how to ask for the order, AFTO presents a three-dimensional approach to overcome any fear one may have of asking for the order.

AFTO presents many closing methods, described in this chapter, that illustrate the importance of adapting your closing questions to the customers particular buying situation. "Specific methods of asking for the order are clearly presented in dramatic sequences, representing a wide variety of selling situations.

AFTO presents a system to use throughout the sales process to gain a better understanding of your customer's needs, and ultimately help your customers make sound buying decisions. ■

Adapting the Close—An Attitude That Adds Value

Gretchen Parr-Silver, director of special event sales at Universal Studios, looks at closing from the prospect's point of view. Although the special event plan she prepared may seem perfect, she realizes that the customer may have a different point of view. A special event in her department may be a corporate reception, a wedding, a bar mitzvah, or a class reunion. She must try to see the actual event through the eyes of the customer and, from this insight, use adaptive closing questions to confirm the sale and a long-term partnership. Gretchen believes that relationship-building skills must be applied at every step of the sales process. If she is continually adding value throughout the sales presentation, closing is much easier. This is especially true in those cases in which price might be a barrier to closing.[1]

Throughout the evolution of personal selling, we have seen major changes in the way closing is perceived. Prior to the introduction of consultative selling and the partnering era, closing was often presented as the most important aspect of the sales process. The early sales training literature also presented closing methods that encouraged the manipulation of the customer. Use of any closing method that is perceived by the customer as pushy or manipulative will damage your chances of building a long-term partnership.

Closing should not be viewed as a strategy to win at the expense of the customer. The proper attitude should be "If this is the best solution for customer, I should help her make the correct decision."[2] Once the best solution is determined, *asking for the order* is the next logical step.

We take the position that in many selling situations the salesperson needs to assume responsibility for obtaining commitment from the customer. Some closing methods can move the customer from indecision to commitment. When these methods are used effectively, the prospect will not feel pressured. In some cases, we need to simply replace defense-arousing language, such as, "This is the lowest price available anywhere," with a positive *need-satisfaction question*, such as, "Wouldn't this new software help you achieve more efficient inventory control?"

Asking for the order is less difficult if the salesperson is strategically prepared for the close. Preparation for the close involves understanding customer needs, custom fitting

Closing the sale is easier if you review the value proposition effectively from the prospect's point of view.

FIGURE 14.1

Effective closing methods require careful planning.

The Six-Step Presentation Plan	
Step One: Approach	☑ Review Strategic/Consultative Selling Model ☑ Initiate customer contact
Step Two: Presentation	☑ Determine prospect needs ☑ Select solution ☑ Initiate sales presentation
Step Three: Demonstration	☑ Decide what to demonstrate ☑ Select selling tools ☑ Initiate demonstration
Step Four: Negotiation	☑ Anticipate buyer concerns ☑ Plan negotiating methods ☑ Initiate win-win negotiations
Step Five: Close	☐ Plan appropriate closing methods ☐ Recognize closing clues ☐ Initiate closing methods
Step Six: Servicing the Sale	☐ Follow through ☐ Follow-up calls ☐ Expansion selling

Service, retail, wholesale, and manufacturer selling

solutions, and planning appropriate closing methods. Throughout the sales presentation the salesperson should recognize closing clues and be prepared to use effective adaptive closing methods (Figure 14.1).

Review the Value Proposition from the Prospect's Point of View

Closing the sale is usually easier if you look at the *value proposition* from the prospect's point of view. Have you effectively summarized the mix of key benefits? Will your proposal provide a solution that solves the customer's problem? Is your proposal strong enough to win over a customer who is experiencing buying anxieties?

Gene Bedell, author of *Three Steps to Yes*, reminds us that buying often causes emotional stress, sometimes referred to as "buyer's remorse". The following buying anxieties help explain why some customers are reluctant to make a commitment to your proposal.[3]

Loss of options. If the customer agrees to purchase a $5,000 design proposal, then that money will not be available for other purchases or investments. Agreeing to purchase a product or service often means that some other purchase must be postponed. Anxiety and stress build as we think about allocating limited resources.

Fear of making a mistake. If the customer believes that agreeing with a closing request may be the wrong thing to do, he may back away just when the decision seems imminent. Fear of making a mistake can be caused by lack of trust in the salesperson.

Social or peer pressures. Some customers make buying decisions with an eye on the opinions and reactions of others. A business buyer may have to justify a purchase to her boss or employees who will actually use the product. Be prepared to deal with these anxieties as you get closer to closing the sale. Sometimes just a little gentle persuasion will help the anxious customer make a decision.

Closing the Sale—The Beginning of the Partnership

Tom Reilly, in his book *Value-Added Selling*, says " . . . you don't close sales; you build commitment to a course of action that brings value to the customer and profit to the

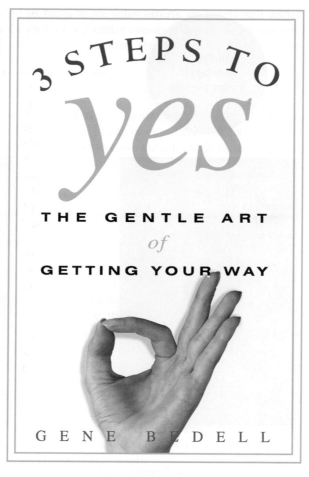

Noted author Gene Bedell reminds us that buying often causes emotional stress. A loss of options, fear of making a mistake, and/or social pressures can cause high levels of anxiety. Salespeople must be prepared to help the anxious customer make a decision.

seller."[4] There is a building process that begins with an interesting approach and need discovery. It continues with effective product selection and presentation of benefits that build desire for the product. After a well-planned demonstration and after negotiating sales resistance, it is time to obtain commitment. Closing should be thought of as the beginning of a long-term partnership.

Guidelines for Closing the Sale

A number of factors increase the odds that you will close the sale (Figure 14.2). These guidelines for closing the sale have universal application in the field of selling.

Closing should be viewed as part of the selling process—the logical outcome of a well-planned presentation strategy.

Many closing clues are quite subtle and may be missed if you are not alert. This is especially true in the case of nonverbal buying signals. If you pay careful attention—with your eyes and your ears—many prospects will signal their degree of commitment.[9] As we have noted earlier in this text, one of the most important personality traits salespeople need is empathy, the ability to sense what the other person is feeling. In this section we review some of the most common verbal and nonverbal clues.

VERBAL CLUES   Closing clues come in many forms. Spoken words (verbal clues) are usually the easiest to perceive. These clues can be divided into three categories: (1) questions, (2) recognitions, and (3) requirements.

Questions   One of the least subtle buying signals is the question. You might attempt a trial close after responding to one of the following questions:

> "Do you have a credit plan to cover this purchase?"
> "What type of warranty do you provide?"
> "How soon can our company get delivery?"

Recognitions   A recognition is any positive statement concerning your product or some factor related to the sale, such as credit terms or delivery date. Some examples follow:

> "How long will it take to get delivery?"
> "Will this plane do all the things you say it will?."
> "I have always wanted to own a boat like this."

Requirements   Sometimes, customers outline a condition that must be met before they can buy. If you are able to meet this requirement, it may be a good time to try a trial close. Some requirements that the prospect might voice are:

> "We will need shipment within two weeks."
> "Our staff will need to be trained in how to use this equipment."
> "All our equipment must be certified by the plant safety officer."

Selling Is Everyone's Business

BRAND DEVELOPMENT STARTS WITH PERSONAL SELLING

Building a brand name for a line of "unmentionables" (bras, underwear, and camisoles) can be a challenge. Alka and Mona Srivastava, sisters and business partners, readily agree that they didn't know what they were getting themselves into when they started Florentyna Intima, a lingerie company. The two economics majors knew very little about design, manufacturing, and marketing. Once they had a business plan and some money borrowed from their parents, Alka and Mona began the search for a designer and manufacturer. They needed prototypes to show to customers. Once the prototypes were completed by a firm in Bangkok, they tried to hire a sales representative to present the new line. Unfortunately, no one was willing to represent a line sold by an inexperienced manufacturer. That's when they decided to become salespeople. They hit the road, calling

Alka and Mona Srivastava.

on owners of lingerie boutiques coast to coast and visiting trade shows. Soon buyers were calling with orders. Sales have grown about 30 percent each year.[a]

In some cases, verbal buying clues do not jump out at you. Important buying signals may be interwoven into normal conversation. Listen closely whenever the prospect is talking.

NONVERBAL CLUES Nonverbal buying clues are even more difficult to detect. Once detected, this type of signal is not easy to interpret. Nevertheless, you should be alert to body movement, facial expression, and tone of voice. Some actions follow that suggest the prospect may be prepared to purchase the product.[10]

The prospect's facial expression changes. Suddenly, the person's eyes widen, and genuine interest is clear in the facial expression.

The prospect begins showing agreement by nodding.

The prospect leans forward and appears to be intent on hearing your message.

The prospect begins to examine the product or study the sales literature intently.

When you observe or sense one of these nonverbal buying clues, do not hesitate to ask for commitment. There may be several opportunities to close throughout the sales presentation. Important buying signals may surface at any time. Do not miss them.

Specific Methods for Closing the Sale

The sales presentation is a process, not a single action. Each step during the process should create another layer of trust and move the customer closer to making the purchase. Throughout the sales process you are moving closer to the close by positioning yourself as a valued resource.[11]

There is no *best* closing method. Your best bet is to preplan several closing methods and adapt the ones that seem appropriate to each customer (Figure 14.3). Given the complex nature of many sales, it is often a good idea to be prepared to use a combination of

FIGURE 14.3

Preparing for the close requires the preplanning of several closing methods. Research indicates that in many selling situations several closing attempts may be necessary.

Closing Worksheet		
Closing clue (prospect)	Closing method	Closing statement (salesperson)
"That sounds fine." (Verbal recognition)	Direct appeal close	"Good, may I get your signature on this order form?"
"What kind of financing do you offer?" (Verbal question)	Multiple options close	"We have two financing methods available: 90-day open credit or two-year long-term financing. Which of these do you prefer?"
"Well, we don't have large amounts of cash available at this time." (Verbal requirement)	Assumptive close	"Based on your cash position, I would recommend you consider our lease–purchase plan. This plan allows you to pay a very small initial amount at this time and keep the cash you now have for your everyday business expenses. I will be happy to write up your order on the lease–purchase plan."
The prospect completes a careful reading of the proposal and communicates (nonverbal clue) a look of satisfaction. (Nonverbal message)	Combination summary-of-benefits/direct appeal close	"That solution surpasses your quality requirements, meets your time deadlines, and provides your accounting department with the details it requested. Can you get your chief financial officer's signature on the order?"

closing methods. Do keep in mind that your goal is not only to close the sale but also to develop a long-term partnership.

Trial Close

A **trial close** is a closing attempt made at an opportune time during the sales presentation to encourage the customer to reveal readiness or unwillingness to buy. It is also known as the **minor point close**. When you are reasonably sure that the prospect is about to make a decision but is being held back by natural caution, the trial close may be appropriate. It is a good way to test the buyer's attitude toward the actual purchase. The trial close can also be effectively adapted to achieving incremental commitment in more complex multicall sales. A trial close often is presented in the form of a confirmation question. Here are some examples:

"We can arrange an August first shipment. Would this date be satisfactory?"

"Is the timing right to do a presentation to the executive committee?"

"Would you rather begin this plan on July first or July fifteenth?"

"Will a $2,000 down payment be possible at this time?"

Some salespeople use the trial close more than once during the sales presentation. After the salesperson presents a feature, converts that feature to a buyer benefit, and confirms the prospect's agreement that the benefit is important, it would be appropriate to use a trial close.

In broader terms, it would be appropriate to attempt a trial close after steps two, three, or four of the six-step presentation plan (Figure 14.4).

Direct Appeal Close

The **direct appeal close** has the advantages of clarity and simplicity. This close involves simply asking for the order in a straightforward manner. It is the most direct closing

FIGURE 14.4

The trial close should be attempted at an opportune time during the sales presentation. It is appropriate to initiate a trial close after steps two, three, or four of the six-step presentation plan.

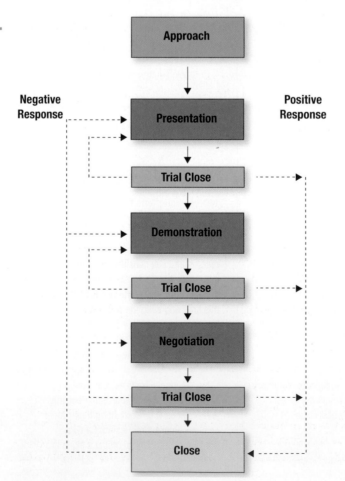

The assumptive close asks for a minor decision, assuming that the customer has decided to buy.

approach, and many buyers find it attractive. Realistically, most customers expect salespeople to ask for the sale.

The direct appeal should not, of course, come too early. It should not be used until the prospect has displayed a definite interest in the product or service. The salesperson also must gain the prospect's respect before initiating this appeal. Once you make the direct appeal, stop talking. John Livesay, West Coast ad director for *W* magazine, says being patient at the close is his "secret weapon." After asking the customer to buy, he stays silent. He avoids asking more questions or making additional statements. This approach gives the customer time to think about the proposal.[12]

A variation of the direct appeal close involves use of a question to determine how close the customer is to making a buying decision. The question might be, "How close are we to closing the sale?" This direct question calls for a direct answer. The customer is encouraged to reflect on the progress of the sale.[13]

Assumptive Close

The **assumptive close** or, as it is sometimes called, the **take-it-for-granted close**, asks for a minor decision, assuming that the customer has already decided to buy.[14] This closing approach comes near the end of the planned presentation. If you have identified a genuine need, presented your solutions in terms of buyer benefits, presented an effective sales demonstration, and negotiated buyer concerns satisfactorily, it may be natural to assume the person is ready to buy. Jeffrey Gitomer (www.gitomer.com), noted sales consultant, says the assumptive close is appropriate when the salesperson has removed perceived risks and the prospect has confidence in the salesperson.[15] The assumptive close usually takes the form of a question that focuses on a minor point. Some examples may include:

> "If you feel the Model 211 gives you the major benefits you are looking for, let's schedule delivery for next Tuesday."

> "Since our production system provides you with the order fulfillment flexibility you require, let's go ahead and place your order."

Most customers will view these statements as the natural conclusion of the events that preceded it. Assumptive closes often include a benefit with your request for action.[16]

This closing method provides a subtle way to ask for a decision when you are quite certain the customer has already decided to buy. You are only bringing the selling/buying process to a close.

close a sale in the office of a buyer for a large department store. Colleen represents a firm that manufactures a wide range of leather clothing and accessories. Near the end of her planned presentation, she senses that the prospect is quite interested in her products but seems reluctant to make a decision.

This is how Colleen handles the close: "Ms. Taylor, we have discussed several benefits that seem especially important to you. First, you agree that this line will be popular with the fashion-conscious shoppers your store caters to. Second, you indicated that the prices I quoted will allow you excellent profit margins, and third, if we process your order now, you will have the merchandise in time for the pre-holiday buying period. With this in mind, let's go ahead and process your order today." Notice that this starts with a summary of benefits and ends with an assumptive close.

Adapting to the Customer's Communication Style

In Chapter 4 we examined the concept of communication styles and achieving versatility through style flexing. We noted that people with different behavior styles will make their decisions in very distinct ways. We need to take the prospect's style into consideration when deciding how to adapt the close.[20]

DIRECTOR Most directors are goal-oriented persons who are ready to make quick decisions once they believe your solution meets their needs. They like doing business with salespeople who display confidence that they can give the customer the benefits they want. The director may reject your trial close just to test your confidence level. The highly assertive director will respect persistence and determination.

EMOTIVE The emotive needs social acceptance, so provide support for their opinions and ideas. Maintain good eye contact and be a good listener. Don't let this buyer's emotional statements throw you off balance. Spontaneous statements, spoken dramatically and impulsively, should be expected.

SUPPORTIVE You can expect the supportive customer to be slow in making the buying decision. They are more apt to worry about change or taking risks. It's important to understand their perceived risks so you can reassure them before asking for a buying decision. Curb the desire to put pressure on the supportive customer. Pressure may make this buyer more indecisive. Patience is important.

REFLECTIVE Before you ask the reflective customer for a buying decision, make sure you review important factual information. These buyers are less likely to be influenced by emotion. Ask reflectives, "Is there any other information I can provide before you make a decision?" Never pressure the reflective customer to make a quick decision.

Applying the Platinum Rule. People with different behavior styles will make their buying decisions in very distinct ways. Therefore, the prospect's communication style must be taken into consideration when deciding how to adapt the close.

Practice Closing

Your success in selling can depend in large part on learning how to make these closing methods work for you. You may not master these approaches in a few days or a few weeks, but you can speed up the learning process with preparation and practice. Role-playing is one of the best ways to experience the feelings that accompany closing and to practice the skills needed to close sales. To prepare the role-play, anticipate various closing scenarios and then prepare a written script of the drama.[21] Find someone (your sales manager, friend, or spouse) to play the role of the customer and give that person a script to act out. Practice the role-plays in front of a video recorder, and then sit back and observe your performance. The video monitor provides excellent feedback. Use the closing worksheet (see Figure 14.3) to prepare for practice sessions.

Confirming the Partnership When the Buyer Says Yes

Congratulations! You have closed the sale and have established the beginning of what you hope will be a long and satisfying partnership with the customer. Before preparing to leave, be sure that all the details related to the purchase agreement are completed. Check all particulars with the buyer, and then ask for a signature if necessary.

Once the sale has been closed, it is important to take time to reassure the customer. This is the **confirmation step** in closing the sale. Before you leave, reassure the customer by pointing out that she has made the correct decision, and describe the satisfaction that will come with ownership of the product. The reason for doing this is to resell the buyer and to prevent buyer's remorse. **Buyer's remorse** is an emotional response that can take various forms such as feelings of regret, fear, or anxiety.[22] It's common to wonder whether or not we have made the right decision. Compliment the person for making a wise decision. Once the sale is closed, the customer may be required to justify the purchase to others. Your words of reassurance can be helpful.

Before leaving, thank the customer for the order. This is very important. Everyone likes to think that a purchase is appreciated. No one should believe that a purchase is taken for granted. Even a small order deserves words of appreciation. In many cases a follow-up thank-you letter is appropriate.

In several previous chapters we note that a satisfied customer is one of the best sources of new prospects. Never hesitate to ask, "Do you know anyone else who might benefit from owning this product?" or a similar question. Some customers may even agree to write an introductory letter on your behalf.

What to Do When the Buyer Says No

High-performance salespeople learn to manage disappointment. A strong display of disappointment or resentment is likely to close the door to future sales. Losing a sale may be

Before leaving, thank the customer for the order. This is very important. Everyone likes to think that a purchase is appreciated.

painful, but it can also be a valuable learning opportunity. Doing some analysis of what went wrong can help you change the outcome of future sales. Here are some things you should do after a lost sale.[23]

1. Make sure the deal is really dead. There is always a chance that the customer's decision can be changed. You might want to mount a last-ditch effort to reopen the presentation.

2. Review the chain of events. When you experience a no-sale call, try to benefit from the experience. If you were part of a sales team, get input from each member. Soon

After the buyer says yes, be sure that all details related to the purchase agreement are completed, and then ask for a signature. A signature is required on this "Letter of Agreement."

Source: Courtesy of Beth Manning, Jody Sprock Interiors & Associates.

Beth Manning, Jody Sprock Interiors & Associates
119 19th Street, Suite 202
West Des Moines, Iowa 50265-4226
515-225-9253   Fax 515-225-9386

Letter of Agreement

Beth Manning Jody Sprock Interiors (BMJSI) is pleased to be of service to you in designing and beautifying the interior of your design project. Our design service is described in the following contract agreement.

DESIGN SERVICES: The designer may perform the following services for the client:
Schematic Design - Space Planning - Budget Estimates
Design Development - Product and Finish Specification
Procurement - Administration - Installation - Design Execution

A. DESIGN SERVICES - PURCHASING THROUGH *BMJSI* - RETAINER
Client shall pay in advance a retainer of $565.00. This is estimated to cover approximately 7 1/2 hours of design time (This includes driving time.). The $565.00 retainer will be applied to your final invoice as a credit, if procurement occurs through *BMJSI* as planned. When a minimum $2500.00 purchase is made within a three month period, the retainer will be credited to a final product invoice. If a minimum $2500.00 purchase is not made within a three month period, the retainer will be used as hourly compensation. In the event that specified products are purchased elsewhere or if a portion of the job that the designer has done research and development on is not completed, the designer will be compensated at an hourly rate ($75.00) for services/time rendered. A detailed account of the designer's hours will be charged and billed to client if the project does not proceed as planned. When a minimum sale of $2500.00 per project occurs, the hourly fee will be waived.

B. DESIGN/CONSULTATION SERVICES ONLY - NO PROCUREMENT THROUGH BMJSI
An advance retainer of $375.00 will be collected in order to begin work on the project. This covers approximately 5 hours of design research and development. Clients using design services only will be billed at an hourly rate of $75.00 (This includes driving time.). Billing will be after each appointment. Payment is due within 10 days or prior to the next appointment. *Billable design services* may include: SPACE PLANNING, DESIGN PLANNING, COLOR GUIDELINING, PHASE PLANNING, SHOPPING SERVICES, ACCESSORIZING, PROJECT MANAGEMENT, PRODUCT SPECIFICATION, BID PREPARATION.
OTHER: _____

C. TRIP CHARGE
A trip allowance will be billed for out of town job sites.

D. WARRANTIES AND WORKMANSHIP
We wish to inform you that by using a professional design firm you are guaranteed:
1. Professional coordination of fabrics and furnishings and concern for your needs first.
2. Prompt, professional follow-up if problems do arise.
3. Recommended resources that maintain the highest standards of workmanship.

BMJSI is not responsible for:
1. Work by third parties not engaged by *BMJSI.*
2. Warranties not provided by our manufacturers and resources.

CLIENT: _____   DATE: _____

DESIGNER: _____   DATE: _____

"SPECIALIZING IN LIFE STYLE DESIGN"

Global Business Etiquette

DOING BUSINESS IN SOUTH AMERICA

Although specific customs vary in the countries of South America, some generalizations can be made. For example, residents of Brazil, Argentina, and other countries have a different idea of what is appropriate personal space. They tend to stand closer to you during conversations. To step back may be viewed as being impolite. You should expect more physical contact such as pats on the back and hugs. Lunch is the main meal of the day and it's not uncommon for a business meal to last several hours. Latin Americans often arrive late for appointments. Be patient with decision makers and do not use the hard-sell approach. Be aware of language preferences. Brazilians speak Portuguese; addressing them in Spanish would be insulting. Business associates in Argentina will likely speak English and Spanish. However, your business card should be translated into Spanish.[b]

after the prospect says no, schedule a debriefing session. If you worked alone, engage in honest self-analysis. Look carefully at your performance during every aspect of the sales process; you may be able to identify weaknesses that can be corrected.

3. Interview the client. Obtaining feedback requires a delicate approach. If you probe too aggressively, you may appear argumentative. If your approach is too passive, and the client's comments are general, you will not know how to improve. The key is to couch your questions in neutral terms. Rather than asking, "Why didn't we get the order?" try this approach: "Thank you for considering our company. We hope to do business with you at some time in the future. Would you mind helping me understand any shortcomings in our sales proposal?"

Always keep the door open for future sales. Tell the prospect you would love to work with her at some time in the future. Then, put this person back on your prospect list, record any new information you have learned about the prospect, and continue to keep in touch. Marvin Gottlieb, president of The Communication Project, recalls the loss of a very large piece of business from a large IT firm. This company decided to begin doing its own training rather than outsource it to Gottlieb's company. Rather then give up hope, Gottlieb continued to maintain relationships with key people at the IT firm. After four years, he was invited to present information on a needed service. He closed a $50,000 sale in less than a month.[24]

PREPARE THE PROSPECT FOR CONTACT WITH THE COMPETITION Some prospects refuse to buy because they want to take a close look at the competing products. This response is not unusual in the field of selling. You should do everything possible to help the customer make an intelligent comparison.

It is always a good practice to review your product's strong points one more time. Give special emphasis to areas in which your product has a superior advantage over the competition. Make it easy for the person to buy your product at some future date.

Customer Relationship Management with Technology

CHANGING PROSPECT RECORDS

Prospect and customer databases are continually changing. Promotions, transfers, mergers, and many other events require constant updates to a salesperson's automated data. Most customer relationship management (CRM) software makes this an easy process and warns users against the inadvertent removal of an account. (See the exercise Changing Prospect Information on p. 320 for more information.)

Chapter Learning Activities

Reviewing Key Concepts

Describe the proper attitude to display toward closing the sale

Some of the early closing methods encouraged manipulation of the customer. Use of any closing method that is perceived by the customer as pushy or manipulative will damage your chances of building a long-term partnership. Closing should not be viewed as a strategy to win at the expense of the customer. Once the customer's need has been confirmed, salespeople should determine the most ethical and effective method to move the buyer from indecision to commitment.

List and discuss selected guidelines for closing the sale

Long sales cycles require multiple commitments. These commitments need to be obtained from the prospect throughout a multicall sales presentation. The buying motive that is of greatest interest deserves special attention at the close. Always negotiate tough points before attempting the close, display a high degree of confidence, and ask for the order more than once.

Explain how to recognize closing clues

The salesperson must be alert to *closing clues* from the prospect. These clues fall into two categories: verbal and nonverbal. Verbal clues are the easiest to recognize, but they may be subtle as well. Again, it is important to be an attentive listener. The recognition of nonverbal clues is more difficult, but careful observation helps in detecting them.

Discuss specific methods of closing the sale

Several closing methods may be necessary to get the prospect to make a buying decision; therefore, it is wise for the salesperson to preplan several closes. These closing methods should be chosen from the list provided in this chapter and then customized to fit the product and the type of buyer with whom the salesperson is dealing. In some selling situations the use of combination closes is very effective. Flexing to the customer's communication style is important.

Explain what to do when the buyer says yes and what to do when the buyer says no

The professional salesperson is not discouraged or offended if the sale is not closed. Every effort should be made to be of further assistance to the prospect—the sale might be closed on another call. Continue to keep in touch. Even if the sale is lost, the experience may be valuable if analyzed to learn from it.

Key Terms

Incremental commitment	Summary-of-benefits close (Step-by-step close)	Impending event close (Positive/negative technique)
Closing clue	Special concession close	
Trial close (Minor point close)	Multiple options close	Confirmation step
Direct appeal close	Balance sheet close	Buyer's remorse
Assumptive close (Take-it-for-granted close)		

Review Questions

1. List some aspects of the sales presentation that can make closing and confirming the sale difficult to achieve.

2. Describe three buying anxieties that sometimes serve as barriers to closing the sale.

3. What guidelines should a salesperson follow for closing the sale?

4. Why is it important to review the value proposition from the prospect's point of view?

5. Define the term *incremental commitment*. Why is it important to achieve incremental commitments throughout the sale?

6. Explain how the multiple options close might be used in the sale of men's and women's suits.

7. Is there a best method to use in closing the sale? Explain.

8. What is meant by a trial close (the minor point close)? When should a salesperson attempt a trial close?

9. Explain the summary-of-benefits close (step-by-step close).

10. What confirming steps should a salesperson follow when the customer says yes? What should be done when the customer says no?

Application Exercises

1. Which of the following statements, often made by prospects, would you interpret as buying signals?

    a. "How much would the payments be?"
    b. "Tell me about your service department."
    c. "The company already has an older model that seems good enough."
    d. "We do not have enough cash flow right now."
    e. "How much would you allow me for my old model?"
    f. "I do not need one."
    g. "How does that switch work?"
    h. "When would I have to pay for it?"

2. You are an accountant who owns and operates an accounting service. You have been contacted by the president of an advertising agency about the possibility of your auditing his business on a regular basis. The president has indicated that he investigated other accounting firms and thinks they price their services too high. With the knowledge you have about the other firms, you know you are in a strong competitive position. Also, you realize his account would be profitable for your firm. You really would like to capture this account. How will you close the deal? List and describe two closing methods you might use in this situation.

3. Zig Ziglar, Brian Tracy, and Tom Reilly are all well-known authors and speakers on the subject of closing the sale. Access each of their Web sites, www.zigziglar.com, www.briantracy.com and www.tomreillytraining.com, and research the books, courses, and videos they have available for companies and individuals to purchase, and learn more about closing the sale. Prepare a summary of what you find available. Does the material in this chapter parallel the kind of information these individuals present?

Role-Play Exercise

Examine the superior benefits of the convention center identified in Appendix 3. Specifically research the qualities of the "five-star" executive chef, award-winning renovation of the facility, the cost of parking and transportation to and from the airport, and the easy access on and off the location relative to the freeway. You should assume the role of director of sales and with this information prepare a closing worksheet on the combination summary-of-benefits/direct appeal close for a prospective customer. Also using information from the audiovisual presentation guide, prepare a special concession close, allowing free use of the laser pointer and wireless microphone (a $107.50 value) for a group presentation to the 23 people who will be staying in single rooms at the hotel. Role-play the close of a sale using these closing methods to a prospect who is also seriously considering using one of your competitors.

CRM Application Exercise

Changing Prospect Information

Adding new contacts and changing existing contact information is easy with Salesforce.com, as it is with most CRM software. Create a contact record for B. H. Rivera by selecting "Contact" from the Create drop-down list on the left side of the Salesforce.com home screen. This displays a blank record that can be completed by selecting fields with the mouse or by using the Tab key to move from field to field. In the Company field, type "Graphic Forms" and type "3195556194" (no hyphens) into the Phone field. The address is "2134 Martin Luther King"; Atlanta, GA, and 61740 are City, State, and Zip.

Most CRM software permits you to save time and avoid errors by selecting field data from menus. For example, point at the Lead Source field, and click the drop-down list. A menu of choices should appear. From this menu, select "Cold Call" as the status for the B. H. Rivera record.

You have just added a new record to Salesforce.com. Generally, most CRM applications discourage deleting records that have a customer. Deleting these records could also delete important historical information that is useful for analysis and understanding of the customer. The alternative is to make the contact inactive. This will remove them from most reports and transactions. To make a contact inactive, search for the contact record (B. H. Rivera) using the Salesforce.com Search bar. Under Action on the search results screen, press "Edit." Tab to the Inactive field and click the box. B. H. Rivera is now an inactive contact in Salesforce.com.

Case Problem

The Special Event Sales Department at Universal Studios can make your dreams come true. The staff can help you plan a wedding reception that guests will be talking about for years. (How about a Jurassic Park theme?) If you want to show appreciation to your chief executive officer who is retiring, the staff will make sure the party is truly special. The staff can also help you plan a bar mitzvah, a class reunion, or any other special event.

Gretchen Parr-Silver, director of the Special Event Sales Department, enjoys working with customers. Her customers vary greatly in terms of age, education, income, and social class. The key to working effectively with all of these people is relationship building. Once she builds rapport with clients and establishes a foundation built on trust, they are more likely to open up and discuss their needs. Event planners have at their disposal a wide range of props, facilities, and production expertise, but customer needs guide the use of these resources.

Gretchen finds that if the sales presentation is well planned and delivered, closing the sale is easier. She believes that good listening skills and careful probing can help uncover dominant buying motives. For example, the client who wants a wedding reception with a special theme may have difficulty expressing her thoughts. Gretchen must probe and listen closely in order to understand the customer's desires. She must also create value throughout the presentation in order to set the stage for the close. A special event can cost several thousand dollars, so price can be a barrier to closing.

Questions

1. What closing clues should Gretchen Parr-Silver look for?

2. What trial closes would be appropriate?

3. What tough points should be negotiated before attempting to close?

4. Can you visualize a situation in which Gretchen Parr-Silver might use a multiple options close? Explain.

5. Assume that a large corporation wants to schedule a recognition party for 40 people. This event will begin with cocktails and appetizers and end with a served meal. Special entertainment will precede the meal. What items might be included in a summary-of-benefits close?

CRM Case Study

Forecasting the Close

You are interested in discovering what your commissions may be for the next few months, just from Pat Silva's former accounts. To do this, you review the Opportunity Pipeline report. There are five fields on this report that help you forecast your performance for the next three months: Probability, Close Date, Dollar Amount, Expected Amount, and Stage. When working on these opportunities, Pat entered the information found in each of these fields. Pat maintains the Opportunity Stage field so that at any point in time this field accurately reflects where this opportunity is in the sales process. The Probability field is calculated by Salesforce.com based on this opportunity stage. In the Probability field, Pat estimated the percentage of possibility that the account might place an order. The Dollar Amount field refers to how much Pat thought the account would spend, and the month Pat believed the account would order is in the Close Date field. The expected amount field is calculated based on a formula SimNet believes is accurate. In this case it is simply the probability times the amount.

The total for each month is calculated on this report. For an estimate of your commission income, multiply each month's forecast by 10 percent.

Pat did not show that any forecasted sales were 100 percent. Pat recognized that the sales might not close, the amount anticipated (Dollar Amount) might not be achieved, and the close might not take place during the month projected. Pat knew that these prospects would not close themselves; certain steps would have to be taken to increase the possibility that the prospect would place an order. To collect your commissions, you have to discover the steps most likely to close these sales.

Questions

1. What would your commission income be for all Pat's accounts if you closed them as Pat forecasted?

2. What kind of special concession might be necessary to close the sale with Quality Builders?

3. What kind of close may be necessary to get an order from Computerized Labs?

4. What kind of close would be appropriate for the Lakeside Clinic?

Partnership Selling: A Role-Play/Simulation

(see Appendix 3, pp. 462–463, 474)

Developing a Presentation Strategy—Closing the Sale

Refer to Sales Memorandum 3 and strategically plan to close the sale with your customer. To consider the sale closed, you need to secure the signature of your customer on the sales proposal form. This guarantees your customer the accommodations listed on the form. These accommodations may change depending on the final number of people attending your customer's convention. This is an important point to keep in mind when closing the sale; however, you still must get the signature to guarantee the accommodations.

Follow the instructions carefully, and prepare a closing worksheet (see Strategic Planning Form C) listing at least four closes using the methods outlined in this chapter. Two of these methods should be the summary of benefits and the direct appeal. Remember, it is not the policy of your convention center to cut prices, so your methods should include value-added strategies.

Use proof devices to make your closes more convincing and place them in the front pocket of your three-ring binder/portfolio for easy access during your presentation. You may want to secure another person to be your customer, and practice the closing strategies you have developed.

15

Servicing the Sale and Building the Partnership

▶ Introduction

Body Glove International (www.bodyglove.com), a leading manufacturer of wetsuits for a variety of water sports, had a humble beginning. Bill and Randy Meistrell, founders of the company, were active in surfing and scuba diving in the early 1950s when good-quality wet suits were hard to find. They decided to turn this problem into an opportunity and developed their own wet suit design. The first suits were sold at a small dive shop in Redondo Beach, California. Today Body Glove International is a multimillion-dollar global company that is recognized worldwide for its quality products and outstanding **customer service**.

Sales professionals who represent the Body Glove line of products embrace the company philosophy that is based on the belief that you never sacrifice quality in any area, including service after the sale. Servicing the sale is an important element of the presentation strategy. Body Glove has invested in a modern customer service center, which is equipped with the newest technology. With the aid of modern computers, staff members can check the status of any order. The customer service staff, working with salespeople, continue to add value after the sale is closed.[1]

Servicing the sale encompasses a variety of activities that take place during and after the implementation stage of the buying process (Figure 8.3). In this chapter, we present servicing the sale as a three-part process: follow-through on assurances and promises, follow-up with ongoing communication after the sale, and expansion selling, which involves the identification of additional needs and providing solutions (Figure 15.1). Each of these strategies can add value and build the partnership. ■

Body Glove is an international company with a strong commitment to customer service. The company views customer service as a key element of partnership building.

Building Long-Term Partnerships with Customer Service

In a world of increased global competition and narrowing profit margins, customer retention through value-based initiatives can mean the difference between increasing or eroding market share. Progressive marketers are searching for ways to differentiate their service from competitors and to build emotional loyalty through value.[2]

A sales organization that can develop a reputation for servicing each sale (Figure 15.1) is sought out by customers who want a long-term partner to help them with their buying needs. Satisfied customers represent an "auxiliary" sales force—a group of people who recommend customer-driven organizations to others. If customers are pleased with the service that they receive after the sale, be assured that they will tell other people. Research shows that when someone has a good customer service experience, he tells an average of six people; when he has an outstanding experience, he tells twice as many.[3]

Achieving Successive Sales

In Chapter 1 we described *partnering* as a strategically developed, long-term relationship that solves the customer's problem. A successful partnering effort results in successive sales and referrals (Figure 1.8).

FIGURE 15.1

The Six-Step Presentation Plan

Step One:
Approach
- ✔ Review Strategic/Consultative Selling Model
- ✔ Initiate customer contact

Step Two:
Presentation
- ✔ Determine prospect needs
- ✔ Select solution
- ✔ Initiate sales presentation

Step Three:
Demonstration
- ✔ Decide what to demonstrate
- ✔ Select selling tools
- ✔ Initiate demonstration

Step Four:
Negotiation
- ✔ Anticipate buyer concerns
- ✔ Plan negotiating methods
- ✔ Initiate win-win negotiations

Step Five:
Close
- ✔ Plan appropriate closing methods
- ✔ Recognize closing clues
- ✔ Initiate closing methods

Step Six:
Servicing the Sale
- ☐ Follow through
- ☐ Follow-up calls
- ☐ Expansion selling

Service, retail, wholesale, and manufacturer selling

Servicing the sale involves three steps: follow-through, follow-up calls, and expansion selling.

Many of today's large companies want to partner with suppliers who sell and deliver quality products and services that continually improve their processes and profits. The first sale is only the beginning of the relationship—an opportunity to earn a repeat sale. Repeat sales come after the supplier demonstrates the ability to add value in various ways.[4] This value may take the form of timely delivery, superior installation, accurate invoicing, technical know-how, social contacts, or something else that is important to the customer. In business-to-business sales, the relationship should intensify as the supplier delivers extensive postsale support. Taking the customer's point of view and acting in the customer's interest, often described as *customer advocacy*, is a major factor underlying repeat business.[5]

Responding to Increased Postsale Customer Expectations

People buy expectations, not products, according to Ted Levitt, author of *The Marketing Imagination.* They buy the expectations of benefits you promised. Once the customer buys your product, expectations increase. Levitt points out that after the sale is closed, the buyer's attitude changes. The customer expects the salesperson to remember the purchase as a favor bestowed on him by the buyer.

Nitin Nohria, Harvard Business School professor and co-author of *What Really Works: The 4 + 2 Formula for Sustained Business Success*, says, "Customers are enormously punishing when companies don't meet their expectations."[6]

Increased customer expectations, after the sale is closed, require a strategic plan for servicing the sale. Certain aspects of the relationship, product, and customer strategies can have a positive influence on the customer's heightened expectations. In most business-to-business sales, the salesperson cannot service the sale alone. To properly manage the account, the salesperson will need assistance from the shipping department,

This salesperson is preparing a thank-you note that will strengthen the relationship with the customer.

technical support, engineering, and other areas. Customer service is increasingly a team effort.[7]

How do we respond to a customer who has increased expectations? First, we should be certain our customer strategy is on target. We must fully understand the needs and wants of the customer. What is the customer trying to accomplish and how can you help the person do it better?

Second, you should focus like a laser beam on follow-through and follow-up activities. Throughout every sales presentation, the salesperson will offer assurances and make some promises. The salesperson's credibility will be tarnished if any of these commitments are ignored.

Third, we should reexamine our product strategy. In some cases we can enhance customer satisfaction by suggesting related products or services. If the product is expensive, we can follow through and offer assistance in making credit arrangements. If the product is complex, we can make suggestions concerning use and maintenance. Each of these forms of assistance may add value to the sale.

Selling Is Everyone's Business

JOB SEARCHES REQUIRE WIDENING THE NET

You have a good education, but you don't have a job. This scenario is being played out in the lives of thousands of people across the nation. Before you send out another 1,000 résumés via the Internet or spend more time searching the Net for employment opportunities, consider the results of a study conducted by Drake Beam Morin (DBM) at www.dbm.com, a workplace-consulting firm. Networking is the top tactic for landing a job, outpacing other strategies such as the Internet and newspaper ads. The report indicates that 66 percent of DBM clients found new jobs via networking, whereas just 6 percent found employment through the Internet. Don't overlook the value of personal contact that gives you an opportunity to sell yourself.[a]

High Cost of Customer Attrition

Financial institutions, public utilities, airlines, retail stores, restaurants, manufacturers, and wholesalers face the problem of gaining and retaining the patronage of clients and customers. These companies realize that keeping a customer happy is a winning strategy. To regain a lost customer can be four to five times more expensive than keeping a current customer satisfied.[8]

There is no longer any doubt that poor service is the primary cause of customer attrition. A surprisingly small number of customers (12 to 15 percent) are lost due to product dissatisfaction. No more than 10 to 15 percent of lost customers leave due to price considerations. Some studies have found that from 50 to 70 percent of customer attrition is due to poor service.[9] A carefully developed strategic plan to reduce customer defection pays big dividends.

Carl Sewell, chairman of Sewell Automotive Companies with dealerships in Dallas, Fort Worth, and San Antonio, has fully embraced the customer-for-life philosophy of doing business. He lives, sleeps, eats, and breathes his obsession with customer service and the result is a family of dealerships that are the envy of almost everyone in the automobile business.[10]

Current Developments in Customer Service

Bill Gates, in his book *Business @ the Speed of Thought*, predicts that in the new millennium customer service may become the primary value-added function.[11] He recognizes that customer service is the primary method of building and extending the partnership. Customer service, in its many forms, nourishes the partnership and keeps it alive.

Salespeople are in a unique position to enhance *customer satisfaction* and *trust*, the two major contributors to relationship quality. With adequate orientation and training, members of the sales force can build long-term, profitable customer relationships. Recent research

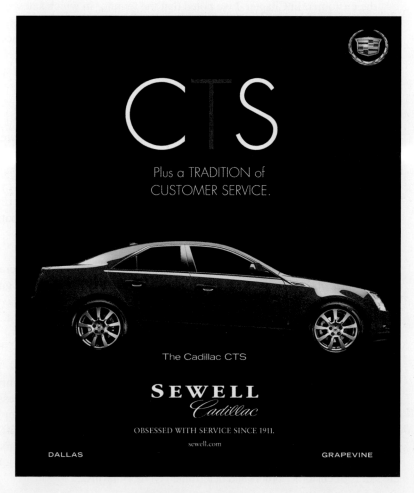

Carl Sewell, Chairman of Sewell Automotive Companies has fully embraced the customer-for-life philosophy. He lives, sleeps, eats, and breathes his obsession with customer service, and the result is a family of dealerships that are the envy of almost everyone in the automobile business.

Bill Gates, author of Business @ the Speed of Thought, *predicts that in the new economy customer service may become the primary value-added function.*

indicates that the building process involves five important service behaviors that are especially important in the context of business-to-business selling.[12]

- ■ *Diligence*   Diligence combines two types of service behaviors: responsiveness and reliability. In today's highly competitive, time-starved business environment, salespeople must provide service in a timely manner. Service behaviors that demonstrate both reliability and responsiveness include following up on commitments, returning phone calls, fulfilling customer requests, and being available when needed. There is a growing trend in which companies rely on their customers' needs, concerns, and future plans.

- ■ *Information Communication*   This service behavior involves regularly relaying product information to the customer in a clear and concise manner. Communicating information must encompass the entire sales process. Early in the sales process this may involve drawing objective comparisons between your product and competitive offerings, and continually reiterating a clear case for your product. After the sale is closed, information communication often involves providing updated information on product usage.

- ■ *Inducements*   This service behavior is aimed at personalizing the relationship with the customer. In Chapter 3 we noted that the manner in which salespeople establish, build, and maintain relationships is not an incidental aspect of personal selling. Some service behaviors provide the customer with an incentive, or an inducement, for maintaining the relationship with the salesperson. Becoming genuinely interested in the customer, talking in terms of the customer's interests, and doing special favors can strengthen the relationship with the customer.

Empathy

As the information age unfolded and the global economy heated up, we learned that it takes more than quick and accurate information communicated through advanced technology to retain customers. Empathy is one of those high-touch abilities that mark the fault line between salespeople who are highly productive and those who are average or below average in terms of productivity.[13] Salespeople who display a strong willingness to help customers and make an effort to understand them are demonstrating empathetic behavior.

Sportsmanship

This service behavior can be defined as a salesperson's willingness to tolerate setbacks and disappointments without displaying negativism. It means demonstrating good social judgment and professionalism during all customer interactions. If you have a 10:00 A.M. appointment with a customer, but you are required to wait until 10:30 A.M. for the meeting to begin, how will you handle this disappointment?

Computer-Based Systems

Customer-friendly, computer-based systems frequently are used to enhance customer service. Computers give both the salesperson and the customer ready access to information and problem-solving alternatives. Nantucket Nectars provides a good example of a company that has enhanced customer service with computer-based systems. The 150 distributors can log on to www.juiceguys.com to place and check orders. Nantucket Nectars' 85 field salespeople can log onto NectarNet, a dedicated company Web site, from their homes to check on the status of customer orders and determine inventory levels.[14]

Selling in Action

THE MOMENT OF MAGIC

 Tony Alessandra (www.alessandra.com) a well-known sales trainer and consultant, says that there are three possible outcomes when a customer does business with an organization.

The moment of truth. In these selling situations the customer's expectations were met. Nothing happened to disappoint the customer, and the salesperson did not do anything to surpass the customer's expectations. The customer is apt to have somewhat neutral feelings about her relationship with the salesperson. The moment of truth usually does not build customer loyalty.

The moment of misery. This is the outcome of a selling situation in which the customer's expectations were not met. The customer may feel a sense of disappointment or even anger. Many customers who experience the moment of misery may share their feelings with others and often make a decision to "fire" the salesperson.

The moment of magic. This is the outcome of a sale in which the customer received more than he expected. The salesperson surpassed the customer's expectations by going the extra mile and providing a level of service that added value to the customer–salesperson relationship. This extra effort is likely to establish a foundation for increased customer loyalty.[b]

Author, Sales Trainer and National Speaker, Tony Alessandra.

The sales staff at Mitchells/Richards, the highly successful clothing stores introduced in a previous chapter, uses technology to establish a more personal relationship with the customer. In a matter of seconds salespeople can review a customer's complete buying history and personal information such as their birthday and anniversary, clothing sizes, favorite colors, names of their children, and even the name of their pet. With this information salespeople are better able to bond with their customers.[15]

Customer Service Methods That Strengthen the Partnership

Customer service encompasses all activities that enhance or facilitate the sale and use of one's product or service. The skills required to service a sale are different from those required prior to the sale (Figure 15.2). High-performance sales personnel do not abdicate responsibility for delivery, installation, warranty interpretation, or other customer service responsibilities. They continue to strengthen the partnership with follow-through, follow-up, and expansion selling.

Adding Value with Follow-Through

A major key to an effective customer service strategy is follow-through on assurances and promises that were part of the sales presentation. Did your sales presentation include claims for superior performance; promises of speedy delivery; assistance with credit arrangements; and guaranteed factory assistance with installation, training, and service?

Most sales presentations are made up of claims and promises that the company can fulfill. However, fulfillment of these claims depends to a large degree on after-sale action. Postsale follow-through is the key to holding that customer you worked so hard to develop.

E-MAIL MESSAGE In many cases it is a lot quicker to send an e-mail message than to make a phone call. Salespeople report that they waste a lot of time playing "phone tag." Some customers prefer e-mail messages and may become irritated if you do not adhere to their wishes. If you know that a customer is not in the habit of checking her e-mail all that often, use the telephone as a back-up method. When in doubt, use parallel channels of communication.

LETTER OR CARD Written correspondence is an inexpensive and personal form of customer follow-up. Letters and cards can be used to thank the customer for the order and to promise continued service. Some companies encourage their salespeople to use a formal letter typed on company stationery. Other companies have designed special thank-you cards, which are signed and sent routinely after a sale is closed. The salesperson may

At Eastern Shore Seafood, value is added by giving customers the opportunity to talk directly to the customer service staff.

Sorry, We Don't Have Voice Mail.

Tired of getting automated answering systems or voice mail when you need help? At Eastern Shore Seafood, we don't just have the world's finest clam products, WE DON'T HAVE VOICE MAIL.

We staff our Customer Service Department with *real* human beings. That's because we believe that our customers deserve friendly, efficient personal service – not just a recording. So, if you would like more information on our great clam products, just give one of our "humans" a call.

EASTERN SHORE SEAFOOD
13249 Lankford Highway, Mappsville, VA 23407   1-800-446-8550   FAX: 757-824-4135

Customer Relationship Management with Technology

CONFIRMING IMMEDIATELY

Close-up and personal information sharing creates a core on which successful relationships may be built and sustained. Friends have long supplemented their personal visits with notes, letters, and telephone calls.

Contemporary technology offers new ways to save time in addition to enhancing and extending relationship-rich communications. Enlightened salespeople use the fax, phone and e-mail as fast, and thus effective, methods to give information to their customers. E-mail can be particularly useful to quickly convey temporary messages such as those that confirm, affirm, or verify. (See the exercise Corresponding with CRM on p. 342 for more information.)

enclose a business card. These thank-you cards do have one major limitation: They are mass-produced and, therefore, lack the personal touch of handwritten cards and envelopes. Personalized notes, birthday cards, and anniversary cards can make a positive impression.

CALL REPORT The **call report** is a form that serves as a communications link with people who can assist with customer service. The format varies, but generally it is a simple form with only four or five spaces. The sample call report form that appears in the text is used by a company that installs security systems at banks and other financial institutions. A form such as this is one solution to the problem of communication between the company personnel and the customer. It is a method of follow-through that triggers the desired action. It is simple, yet businesslike.

Follow-up programs can be as creative or as ingenious as you wish. Every sales organization competes on value, so you must continually think of new ways to add value. Creative use of your interpersonal communication skills can keep your messages fresh and personalized. Keep in mind that people buy both from the head and the heart. Let customers know how much you care about their business.[23] You can use these five methods independently or in combination. Your main consideration should be some

Follow-up calls allow for a two-way exchange of information. In many cases once an account is well established, you may be able to obtain repeat sales by telephone.

type of appropriate follow-up that (1) tells customers you appreciate their business and (2) determines whether they are satisfied with the purchase.

Adding Value with Expansion Selling

Personal selling is the process of identifying and filling the customer's needs. As the salesperson learns more about the customer and establishes a relationship based on trust and mutual respect, opportunities for expansion selling will arise. Expansion selling can take three forms: full-line selling, cross-selling, and upselling.

FULL-LINE SELLING **Full-line selling**, sometimes called *suggestion selling*, is the process of recommending products or services that are related to the main item sold to the customer. The recommendation is made when, in the salesperson's judgment, the product or service can provide additional satisfaction.

To illustrate, let us look at the sale of new homes by K B Home, a builder of large, planned communities. Customers who want to differentiate their home from those down the block are offered an array of options such as marble in the entryway, granite countertops, gourmet kitchen appliances, or Jacuzzi-like tubs for the bathroom. Customization has proven to be a popular value-added service to customers.[24]

Full-line selling is no less important when selling services. For example, a travel agent has many opportunities to suggest related products. Let us assume that a customer purchases a two-week vacation in Germany. The agent can offer to book hotel reservations or schedule a guided tour. Another related product would be a rental car. Sometimes a new product is simply not "right" without related merchandise. A new business suit may not look right without a new shirt and tie. An executive training program held at a fine hotel can be enhanced with a refreshment break featuring a variety of soft drinks, fresh coffee, and freshly baked pastries.

Customers may view full-line selling as a form of value-added service when it is presented correctly. There is a right way and a wrong way to make recommendations. Some guidelines to follow include:

1. *Plan for full-line selling during the preapproach step.* Before meeting with the customer, develop a general plan that includes your objectives for this important dimension of selling. Full-line selling is easier when you are prepared.

2. *Make recommendations after you have first satisfied the customer's primary need.* Although there are some exceptions to this rule, it's usually best to meet the primary need first. In the case of a new home purchase from K B Home, the customer should first select the model home and then make decisions regarding the upgrades.

3. *Make your suggestions thoughtful and positive.* "We will deliver your new copy machine on Monday. Would you like us to deliver some quality copy paper?" Avoid questions such as, "Can we ship anything else?" This question invites a negative response.

4. *When appropriate, demonstrate the suggested item or use sales tools to build interest.* If you have suggested a shirt to go with a new suit, allow the customer to see it next to the suit. If you are calling on a commercial account, show the customer a sample or at least a picture if the actual product is not available.

Full-line selling is a means of providing value-added service. When you use it correctly, customers thank you for your thoughtfulness and extra service. It is also a proven sales-building strategy.

CROSS-SELLING We have seen an increase in the use of cross-selling to grow sales volume. **Cross-selling** involves selling products that are not directly associated with products that you have sold to an established customer. A bank customer who has a home equity loan might be contacted and asked to consider purchase of a mutual fund. The customer who has purchased a town house might be a candidate for a security service. Quick & Reilly, a nationwide financial services company, has trained its 600 customer service representatives to use cross-selling when customers call concerning their current investments. Representatives from 118 offices nationwide completed cross-selling training programs. They learned how to assess the caller's financial goals and to develop a tailored proposal of products and services. Quick & Reilly achieved a 35 percent sales increase after developing the cross-selling program.[25]

A growing number of companies are using cross-selling to discover additional sources of business within established accounts. Buyers often welcome cross-selling efforts because they are searching for ways to consolidate purchases. They like the convenience of buying several items from the same source.[26] Cross-selling is most effective in those situations in which the salesperson and the customer enjoy a true partnership.

Salespeople who have a good understanding of the customer's needs and have earned the customer's respect will face less resistance when recommending a product or service. To achieve success with cross-selling, you need to use *survey questions* and *probing questions* (see Chapter 11). A general survey question such as "Can you tell me more about your expansion plans?" may uncover information needed to position your cross-selling sales strategy. However, you will likely need to use probing questions to uncover and clarify a buying problem that may open the door to a cross-selling opportunity. Keep in mind that cross-selling has to be a well-thought-out part of your strategy and process.[27]

UPSELLING The effort to sell better-quality products is known as **upselling**. It is an important selling method that often adds customer value. Mike Weber, sales manager at Young Electric Sign Company, offers us two important tips on upselling. First, you need a well-established relationship with the customer—a relationship built on trust. Second, you need to continuously qualify the prospect throughout the buying process. As customers tell you more about their needs, you may see an opportunity to upsell. Weber says his salespeople often engage in upselling at the design stage. The customer is shown a rough sketch of the desired sign and another rendition of something better. The added value of the more expensive option will often become obvious to the customer.[28] In many selling situations, such factors as durability, comfort, or economy help justify the higher-quality

Rackham and DeVincentis in their best-selling Rethinking the Sales Force *say that success no longer depends on merely communicating the value of products and services, but rather success rests on the critical ability to create value. They state that value is created by making the purchase painless, convenient, and hassle free, and that salespeople can create significant value by showing customers how to install and use the product.*

product. A professional salesperson explains to the customer why it is in his or her best interest to spend "just a little more" and get the best value for the dollar. Most customers are more concerned with making the right purchase than they are with making the least expensive purchase.[29]

Preplan Your Service Strategy

Servicing the sale is a very important dimension of personal selling, so a certain amount of pre-planning is essential. It helps to preplan your service strategy for each of the three areas we have discussed: follow-through, follow-up, and expansion selling. You cannot anticipate every aspect of the service, but you can preplan important ways to add value once the sale is implemented. Develop a servicing-the-sale worksheet, shown in Figure 15.3, prior to each sales presentation.

Partnership-Building Strategies Should Encompass All Key People

Some salespeople do a great job of communicating with the prospect but ignore other key people involved in the sale. To illustrate how serious this problem can be, let us look at the approach used by Jill Bisignano, a sales representative for a major restaurant supply firm. Jill had called on Bellino's Italian Restaurant for several years. Although she was always very friendly to Nick Bellino, she treated the other employees with nearly total indifference. One day she called on Nick and was surprised to learn that he was retiring and had decided to sell his restaurant to two longtime employees.

As you might expect, it did not take the new owners long to find another supplier. Jill lost a large account because she failed to develop a good personal relationship with other

FIGURE 15.3

Follow-through on assurances and promises, customer follow-up, and expansion selling must be carefully planned. Use of this worksheet can help you preplan ways to add value.

Servicing-the-Sale Worksheet	
Method of Adding Value	What You Will Say or Do
Follow-Through	
Set up a secured Web site or extranet so client can track the production and delivery of the custom-engineered research equipment.	Set up the secured Web site in a timely manner and then contact the customer when it is operational. Explain how to access the Web site and review the benefits of using this source of assistance.
Schedule training for persons who will be using the new technology.	Send training schedule to customer and confirm the dates with a follow-up call.
Follow-Up	
Send a thank-you letter to each member of the team that made the purchase decision.	Express sincere appreciation for the purchase and explain the steps you will take to ensure a long-term partnership.
Check to be certain that the training was effective.	Visit the customer's research facility and talk with the employees who completed the training. Answer questions and provide additional assistance as needed.
Expansion Selling	
Suggest the purchase of global positioning system (GPS) technology to enhance use of seed research equipment.	"GPS technology will enable you to track all your research and plot the findings on your computer screen."

key employees. It pays to be nice to everyone. Here is a partial list of people in your company and in the prospect's company who can influence both initial and repeat sales.

1. *Receptionist.* Some salespeople simply do not use common sense when dealing with the receptionist. This person has daily contact with your customer and may schedule most or all calls. To repeatedly forget this individual's name or display indifference in other ways may cost you dearly.

2. *Technical personnel.* Some products must be cleaned, lubricated, or adjusted on a regular basis. Take time to get acquainted with the people who perform these duties. Answer their questions, share technical information with them if necessary, and show appreciation for the work they are doing.

3. *Stock clerks or receiving clerks.* People working in the receiving room are often responsible for pricing incoming merchandise and making sure that these items are stored properly. They also may be responsible for stock rotation and processing damage claims.

4. *Management personnel.* Although you may be working closely with someone at the departmental or division level, do not forget the person who has the final authority and responsibility for this area. Spend time with management personnel occasionally and be alert to any concerns they may have.

This is not a complete list of the people you may need to depend on for support. There may well be other key people who influence sales. Always look beyond the customer to see who else might influence the sale.

Partnering with an Unhappy Customer

We have learned that unhappy customers often do not initiate a verbal or written complaint. This means that postsale problems may not come to the attention of salespeople or other personnel within the organization. We also know that unhappy customers do share their negative experiences with other people. A dissatisfied customer often tells 8 to 10 people about his problem.[30] A double loss occurs when the customer stops buying our products and takes steps to discourage other people from buying our products. When complaints do surface, we should view the problem as an opportunity to strengthen the business relationship. To achieve this goal, follow these suggestions.

1. *Give customers every opportunity to disclose their feelings.* Companies noted for outstanding customer service rely heavily on telephone systems—like toll-free "hot lines" to ensure easy access. At Federal Express, Cadillac Division of General Motors, and IBM, to name a few companies, specially trained advisors answer the calls and offer assistance. When a customer purchases a Ford vehicle, the salesperson introduces the customer to service staff who play a key role in providing postsale service. The goal is to personalize the relationship with another member of the service team. Ford has discovered that after-sale contact builds a perception of value.[31] When customers do complain, by telephone, or in person, encourage them to express all their anger and frustration. Do not interrupt. Do not become defensive. Do not make any judgments until you have heard all the facts as the customer sees them. If the customer stops talking, try to get him or her to talk some more. How you deal with anger is very important. Encourage the angry customer to vent his or her feelings. By asking questions and listening carefully to the response, you can encourage the person to discuss the cause of the anger openly. After venting feelings and discussing specific details, the angry customer will expect a response. Briefly paraphrase what seems to be the major concern and express a sincere desire to find ways to solve the problem.[32]

2. *Keep in mind that it does not really matter whether a complaint is real or perceived.* If the customer is upset, you should be polite and sympathetic. Do not yield to the temptation to say, "You do not really have a problem." Remember, problems exist when customers perceive they exist.[33]

3. *Do not alibi.* Avoid the temptation to blame the shipping department, the installation crew, or anyone else associated with your company. Never tear down the company you work

for. The problem has been placed in your hands, and you must accept responsibility for handling it. "Passing the buck" only leaves the customer with a feeling of helplessness.

4. *Politely share with the customer your point of view concerning the problem's cause.* At least explain what you think happened. The customer deserves an explanation. At this point a sincere apology is usually appropriate.

5. *Decide what action must be taken to remedy the problem.* Take action quickly and offer a value-added atonement. Don't just do what is expected, but delight the customer by exceeding his expectations. Winning customer loyalty today means going beyond making it right.[34]

The value of customer complaints can emerge in two forms. First, complaints can be a source of important information that may be difficult to obtain by other means. Second, customer complaints provide unique opportunities for companies to *prove* their commitment to service. Loyalty builds in the customer's mind if you do a good job of solving her problem.[35]

A WORD OF CAUTION When you are dealing with major or minor customer service problems and an apology is necessary, do not use e-mail. When a minor problem surfaces, call the customer personally. Do not delegate this task to someone else in your organization. If you need to apologize for a major problem that has occurred, meet with the customer in person. Schedule the meeting as soon as possible.[36]

Chapter Learning Activities

Reviewing Key Concepts

Explain how to build long-term partnerships with customer service

Servicing the sale is a major dimension of the selling process, with the objectives of providing maximum customer satisfaction and establishing a long-term partnership. Servicing the sale encompasses a variety of activities that take place during and after the buying process. In this chapter we present servicing the sale as a three-part process: follow-through on assurances and promises, follow-up with ongoing communication after the sale, and expansion selling.

Describe current developments in customer service

In the new millennium customer service has become a primary value-added function. Salespeople are in a unique position to enhance customer satisfaction and trust by displaying five important service behaviors: diligence, information communication, inducements, empathy, and sportsmanship.

List and describe the major customer service methods that strengthen the partnership

A major key to an effective customer service strategy is follow-through on assurances and promises that were part of the sales presentation. Follow-through services may involve making credit arrangements, scheduling deliveries, monitoring installation, training in the use or care of the product, and providing product updates and similar services. Salespeople can also add value with a sincere expression of appreciation. Follow-up methods include personal visits, telephone calls, e-mail messages, letters or call reports.

A salesperson depends on the support of many other people in servicing a sale. Maintaining good relationships with support staff members who help service your accounts is well worth the time and energy required.

Explain how to add value with expansion selling

As the salesperson learns more about the customer, opportunities for expansion selling will arise. Expansion selling can take three forms: full-line selling, cross-selling, and upselling.

Explain how to deal effectively with complaints

Dealing effectively with an unhappy customer should be thought of as an opportunity to strengthen the business relationship. Always give the customer every opportunity to disclose their feelings. Encourage the angry customer to vent their feelings and listen closely to what is said. Briefly summarize what seems to be the major concern and express a sincere desire to find ways to solve the problem.

Key Terms

Customer service	Call report	Cross-selling
Value reinforcement	Full-line selling	Upselling

Review Questions

1. You are currently a sales manager employed by a company that sells long-term care insurance. Tomorrow you will meet with five new sales trainees. Your major goal is to explain why it is important to service the sale. What important points will you cover?

2. Define customer service. List the three major activities associated with this phase of personal selling.

3. Explain how full-line selling fits into the definition of customer service. How does full-line selling differ from cross-selling?

4. List and describe three current developments in customer service.

5. Adding value with follow-through can involve several postsale services. List five possible services.

6. How does credit become a part of servicing the sale?

7. This chapter describes the value of the lifetime customer. Is it realistic to believe that people will become lifetime customers in our very competitive marketplace?

8. Define upselling and explain how it can add value.

9. What types of customer service problems might be prevented with the use of a call report?

10. Briefly describe the important design elements of an effective business card.

Application Exercises

1. You work as a wholesale salesperson for a plumbing supply company. One of your customers, a contractor, has an open line of credit with your company for $10,000 worth of products. He is currently at his limit; however, he is not overdue. He has just received word that he has been awarded a $40,000 plumbing contract at the local airport. The contract requires that he supply $9,000 worth of plumbing products. Your customer

does not have the cash to pay for the additional products. He tells you that unless you can provide him with some type of financing, he may lose the contract. He says that he can pay you when he finishes his next job in 60 days. Explain what you will do.

2. You have just interviewed for a job that you really would like to have. You have heard it is a good idea to follow up an interview with a thank-you note or letter and an indication of your enthusiasm for the position. Select the strategy you will use for your follow-up, and explain why you chose it.

3. Using your search engine, examine the Internet for information on customer satisfaction. Type "customer satisfaction" + selling. Are you surprised by the number of queries on this subject? Examine some of the queries related to what customers have said about a specific company's customer service program.

Role-Play Exercise

An important aspect of personal selling is the need to add value with follow-up and follow-through. Both of these account management activities can be time-consuming, especially if the salesperson is not skilled at setting up appointments that fit into a busy schedule. In this role-play, you are to set up three follow-through meetings with a customer who has just purchased convention services from the convention center you represent (see Appendix 3). First, you must contact your client three days from today to confirm the availability of the Revolving Platform Room (see p. 467) for a meeting of 300 people. Second, you must contact this same client a week from today to get approval on the number of servings of Chicken Wellington Banquet Style Dinners needed (see p. 427 and Guarantees on p. 445). And, third, because your client isn't sure about the need for a microphone (see p. 437), you need to call your client the day before the meeting (the meeting is scheduled for four weeks from today) to verify whether you or your client will supply a microphone.

Equipped with a calendar, you should establish dates and times when your client will be available to talk or meet with you. Before you meet with your client, plan to recommend at least two times of day that fit into your schedule for each of your meetings. If your client cannot meet at either of these times, ask your client to recommend a time. Do not start out by asking when your client is available because this could conflict with your busy schedule. Write the times and dates in your calendar, suggesting your client does the same, so there will be no misunderstandings. Because these dates are deadlines, suggest that your client call you back if for some reason the schedule changes. Tell your client that you will plan to be at the hotel when the client's meeting starts and that you will be available to make sure everything is properly scheduled. Tell your client to contact you (give your client your phone number and e-mail address) if there are any questions between now and the meeting date.

CRM Application Exercise

Corresponding with CRM

Waiting for a client who forgot an appointment can be very time-consuming. The client who promptly receives an e-mail reminder note is more likely to remember and honor a commitment to meet. Quickly confirming an agreement reached by telephone is easy for customer relationship management (CRM) systems such as Salesforce.com. To schedule an appointment and send a reminder e-mail, first search for the contact Ian Program. Select Ian's contact record from the Search Results screen. Then, select "New Event" from the Open Activity section. Enter "SimNet Meeting" as the subject and "Client Meeting" as the type. Click "Add to Invitees" to add Ian to the attendee list. Schedule the meeting for next Friday at 12:00 P.M. Verify that you are free at that time by checking your calendar line at the bottom. In the description field, type "I look forward to lunch with you Friday noon at Jimmy's." Click "Save" and the Send Invitation button. You have now scheduled your time for this meeting and sent Ian an immediate e-mail confirmation.

Case Problem

This chapter opens with an introduction to Body Glove International (www.body glove.com), a global company that manufactures a quality line of wetsuits for people who like water sports. Many of the consumers who are involved in water skiing, scuba diving, surfing, or jet skiing purchase Body Glove products because they represent both quality and value. The company was started in 1953 by Bill and Randy Meistrell, two people who shared a passion for surfing and diving. The first suits were custom made for customers who responded to ads placed in local publications. As sales increased, the Meistrell brothers developed a small manufacturing facility and began distributing their products through retail stores on the West Coast. Soon Body Glove became a national company and later an international company. The success of Body Glove can be traced to several factors:

- A company philosophy that is based on the belief that you never sacrifice quality. A product that is comfortable and well made attracts the customer who is willing to spend a little more to get the best product. The company used to manufacture its own products, but now it outsources all manufacturing. These companies must maintain high-quality standards established by Body Glove.

- A belief that brand management is very important. Today Body Glove International is placing more emphasis on brand management. The company wants to influence the perception of Body Glove products in the minds of customers. Company officials recognize that in a world of sensory overload caused by too much information, brands are more important than ever. Customers think about what matters to them, analyze their choices, and usually select a brand that meets their needs.

- Innovations in sales and marketing strategies that enhance product distribution and sales. Body Glove International has developed over 30 partnerships with distributors. These distributors (called *marketing intermediaries*) employ salespeople who call on retail stores. At the current time, distributors employ about 250 salespeople. The company now has a stronger global sales organization with special emphasis on South America, New Zealand, and Australia.

- Investment in a first-class customer service center. The people at Body Glove believe that excellent customer service adds value to the product. The staff makes sure that all orders are carefully processed. With the aid of modern computers, they can check on the status of any order. The staff can also process special orders quickly. The customer service employees work hard to build the strongest possible partnership with the customer.

Questions

1. The company officers have made a decision to develop partnerships with a group of distributors. These distributors will employ salespeople to call on retailers who sell Body Glove products. What steps can Body Glove take to ensure that retailers and retail customers receive excellent service?

2. How might a Body Glove salesperson add value with full-line selling? Cross-selling?

3. What types of follow-through activities and follow-up calls should Body Glove sales representatives be prepared to initiate?

4. Assume that a large order sent to one of your best customers arrived very late. The products were not available for a major weekend sale. How might you partner with this unhappy customer?

CRM Case Study

Servicing the Sale with CRM

You have taken over a number of accounts of another salesperson, Pat Silva. Most of these accounts are leads, which means that they have not yet purchased from SimNet.

Two accounts did purchase networks from Pat: Ms. Karen Murray of Murray D'Zines, and Ms. Judith Albright, owner of Piccadilly Studio. You now want to be sure that these sales are well serviced.

Questions

1. Whom should you speak with, within SimNet, before following through and contacting each of the customers? What would you need to discover?

2. What will be your follow-up strategy for each customer?

3. Does the fact that these customers initiated their orders (they were not sold the products, they bought them) influence your follow-up strategy?

4. List and describe five important service behaviors that are especially important in the context of business-to-business selling.

5. Do you see any expansion-selling opportunities with these two accounts? Which *suggestion*-selling methods should you consider?

Partnership Selling: A Role-Play/Simulation

(see Appendix 3, pp. 460–461, 472)

Developing a Presentation Strategy—Servicing the Sale

Refer to Sales Memorandum 3 and strategically plan to service the sale with your customer. After closing the sale (getting the customer's signature), there are several steps to add value and build customer confidence and satisfaction. These steps are important to providing total quality customer service and should provide for repeat sales and a list of referred customers.

Follow the instructions in item 2g of your presentation plan. You need to schedule a future appointment to telephone or personally call and confirm the number of people attending the convention and final room and menu needs (see convention center policies). Also, during this conversation, you may suggest beverages for breaks, audiovisual needs, and any other items that can make this an outstanding convention for your customer.

You should have your calendar available to suggest and write down dates and times for this future contact. Any special materials such as a calendar can be placed in the back pocket of your portfolio. You may want to secure another person to be your customer and practice the customer service strategies you have prepared.

At this point you should be strategically prepared to make the presentation outlined in Sales Memorandum 3 to your customer. Your instructor will provide you with further instructions.

Part 5 | Role-Play Exercise
DEVELOPING A PRESENTATION STRATEGY

Scenario

This role-play is a continuation of the Part 4 Role-Play Exercise. You recently met with Shannon Fordham, founder and chief executive officer of USA Technologies. The purpose of the first sales call was to begin the relationship-building process and present selected value-added guest services and amenities offered by the Park Inn. You also obtained some information regarding the customer's buying process.

Customer Profile

Prior to starting USA Technologies, Shannon Fordham spent 12 years working in sales and sales management at General Electric Corporation. Working for General Electric (GE), described by *Fortune* magazine as America's most admired company, was a great learning experience. Fordham is trying to apply the GE success formula to USA Technologies. Shannon Fordham is the classic extrovert, a person who combines high sociability and high dominance.

Salesperson Profile

Your are new to the field of selling, but you are a quick learner. The first visit with Shannon Fordham went well, and now it is time to prepare for the second sales call. Fordham is planning a large employee recognition banquet, but has not yet selected a location for this event. While working for GE, Fordham had attended more than 25 business conferences and many of these meetings were a big disappointment. Too often, according to Fordham, the meetings were held at look-alike hotels that served bland food. The food was often served by poorly trained waiters who displayed little enthusiasm for their work. Jamie took notes throughout the meeting and will address these concerns during the second sales call.

Product

The Park Inn International is a full-service hotel and convention center. After completion of a recent $2.8 million renovation, the Park Inn received the "Excellence in Renovation Design" award from the Illinois Architectural Association.

Instructions

The first sales call was basically an informative presentation. Near the end of the visit, Shannon Fordham did disclose plans for a large recognition banquet to be held on October 25. This date marks the company's second anniversary. No other information was provided, but Fordham did agree to a second meeting to be held the following week. Based on the information collected during the first call, you are now planning a persuasive presentation that will involve the first three steps of the six-step presentation plan (see Figure 15.1). Upon arrival in Shannon Fordham's office, reestablish the relationship and then initiate the agenda approach (see Chapter 10). Begin the presentation with appropriate survey, probing, and confirmation questions. These questions should be preplanned using information found in Chapter 11. As the need discovery phase of the presentation progresses, the customer's buying criteria or buying conditions should surface. Prior to the second sales call, you should also select and be prepared to demonstrate appropriate selling tools (proof devices). A variety of selling tools suitable for reproduction can be found in Appendix 3. Also, preplan feature/benefit selling statements that appeal to Shannon Fordham's needs. The importance of selling specific benefits and obtaining customer reactions cannot be overemphasized (see Chapter 11).

A major objective of the second sales call is to move the sale forward by convincing Shannon Fordham that the Park Inn offers an outstanding combination of value-added guest services and amenities, and is prepared to meet the customer's needs. The sale will not be closed during the second call, bur Jamie Julian will try to obtain a commitment to prepare a formal sales proposal that will be presented to Fordham within 48 hours. See page 449 for a sample sales proposal form.

Part

6

Management of Self and Others

Personal selling requires a great deal of self-discipline and self-direction. Chapter 16 examines the four dimensions of opportunity management. The final chapter examines the fundamentals of sales force management.

"The primary cause of success in life is the ability to set and achieve goals. That's why the people who do not have goals are doomed forever to work for those who do. You either work to achieve your own goals or you work to achieve someone else's goals."

Brian Tracy

16 Opportunity Management: The Key to Greater Sales Productivity

Chapter Preview

When you finish reading this chapter, you should be able to

1
Discuss the four dimensions of opportunity management

2
List and describe time management strategies

3
Explain factors that contribute to improved territory management

4
Identify and discuss common elements of a records management system

5
Discuss stress management practices

▶ Introduction

Julio Melara (pictured above), born to Honduran immigrant parents, made work the centerpiece of his life at an early age. Throughout high school he cut grass, worked as a busboy, delivered newspapers, and sold newspaper subscriptions. While attending college, he worked as a courier with *New Orleans City Business*, a local business newspaper. By age 23 he was top producer and head of national sales. Later he left the newspaper and went into radio advertising sales. By age 28, Melara had broken all sales records at WWL and had become the radio's first million-dollar producer. He is a self-motivated person who says that he has learned a great deal from such books as *The Power of Positive Thinking* by Norman Vincent Peale. He is also someone who believes in management of self. Goal setting is the central theme of Melara's sales philosophy (www.juliomelara.com). He believes that written goals (personal and professional) facilitate growth and success.[1]

Today Julio Melara is sharing his no-nonsense steps for achieving success with audiences throughout America. *Selling Power* magazine has named him one of America's top motivational speakers. He has shared the platform with such distinguished Americans as Zig Zigler, Secretary of State Colin Powell, Brian Tracy, and numerous business leaders.[2]

A salesperson is much like the individual who owns and operates a business. The successful sales representative, like the successful entrepreneur, depends on good self-management. Both of them must keep their own records, use self-discipline in scheduling their time, and analyze their own performance.

Opportunity Management—A Four-Dimensional Process

What makes a salesperson successful? Some people believe the most important factor is hard work. This is only partly true. Some people work hard but do not accomplish much. They lack purpose and direction. This lack of organization results in wasted time and energy. Hard work must be preceded by careful planning. Every moment spent planning, according to some experts in self-management, saves three or four moments in execution.[3]

Wasting time and energy is the key to failure in the age of information. Many salespeople are drowning in information and the flood of messages each day leaves little time to think and reflect. Sales and sales support personnel, like most other knowledge workers, are working under tighter deadlines. The response time to customer inquiries has been shortened and customers are less tolerant of delays.

As pressures build, it's easy to overlook opportunities to identify prospects, make sales, and improve service to customers. The ability to perceive opportunities and seize them is an important characteristic of high-achieving salespeople.[4] **Opportunity management** should be viewed as a four-dimensional process consisting of the following components:

1. *Time management.* There are only about 250 business days per year. Within each day there is only so much time to devote to selling. Selling hours are extremely valuable. When salespeople are asked to evaluate the major challenges they face in their work, "Not enough time" is often rated number one. Dealing with information overload and achieving balance in their life are also major challenges.

2. *Territory management.* A sales territory is a group of customers and prospective customers assigned to a single salesperson. Every territory is unique. Some territories consist of one or two counties, whereas others encompass several states. The number of accounts within each territory also varies. Today, territory management is becoming less of an art and more of a science.

3. *Records management.* Every salesperson must maintain a certain number of records. These records help to "systematize" data collection and storage. A wise salesperson never relies on memory. Some of the most common records include planning calendars, prospect forms, call reports, summary reports, and expense reports.

4. *Stress management.* A certain amount of stress comes with many selling positions. Some salespeople have learned how to take stressful situations in stride. Others allow stress to trigger anger and frustration. Learning to cope with various stressors that surface in the daily life of a salesperson is an important part of the self-management process.

Time Management

A salesperson can increase sales volume in two major ways. One is to improve selling effectiveness, and the other is to spend more time in face-to-face selling situations. The latter objective can be achieved best through improved time and territory management.

Improving the management of both time and territory is a high-priority concern in the field of selling. These two closely related functions represent major challenges for salespeople.

Let us first look closely at the area of time management. There is definitely a close relationship between sales volume and the number of customer contacts made by the salesperson. You have to make calls to get results.

Time-Consuming Activities

Some salespeople who have kept careful records of how they spend their time each day are surprised to learn how little is spent in face-to-face selling situations. A national survey of 1,500 salespeople from 13 industries found that, on average, salespeople spend 60 percent of their time on administrative duties or travel.[5] Administrative duties can include such things as completion of sales records and time spent on customer follow-through and follow-up. Salespeople need to carefully examine all of their activities and determine whether too much or too little time is spent in any area. One way to assess time use is to keep a time log. This involves recording, at the end of every hour, the activities in which

Selling Is Everyone's Business

BILL BLASS CONNECTED WITH HIS CUSTOMERS

The late Bill Blass, American fashion designer, understood the power of personal contact. He also understood that he was working for his customers, not the other way around. Growing up in Fort Wayne, Indiana, during the Depression, he often went to the movies to see Carole Lombard and other stars. He sold his first fashion drawings to New York manufacturers when he was 14. By 17, he had moved to New York and started to build relationships among the city's social elite. Although New York City became his home, he frequently traveled to places like St. Louis, Houston, and Detroit for trunk shows. Bill Blass was one of the first designers to travel with his collections and was generally regarded as the king of the trunk show. He felt it was important to connect with women who were willing to spend $3,500 for a suit. Thus, he built his global reputation one woman at a time.[a]

they were engaged during that time.[6] At the end of the week, add up the number of minutes spent on the various activities and ask yourself, "Is this the best use of my time?"

Once you have tabulated the results of your time log, it should be easy to identify the "time wasters." Pick one or two of the most wasteful areas, and then make plans to correct the problem. Set realistic goals that can be achieved. Keep in mind that wasting time is

Most people who achieve success in selling have a strong work ethic. They are "self-starters" who are committed to achieving their personal and professional goals.

To manage your time more effectively, you need to form new habits. Changing habits is hard work, but it can be done.

Reprinted by permission of *Agency Sales Magazine*, September 1997.

usually a habit. To manage your time more effectively, you need to form new habits. Changing habits is hard work, but it can be done.[7]

Time Management Methods

Sound time management methods can pave the way to greater sales productivity. The starting point is forming a new attitude toward time conservation. You must view time as a scarce resource not to be wasted.[8] The time-saving strategies presented here are not new, nor are they unique. They are being used by time-conscious people in all walks of life.

DEVELOP A SERIES OF PERSONAL GOALS According to Alan Lakein, author of *How to Get Control of Your Time and Your Life*, the most important aspect of time management is knowing what your goals are. He is referring to all goals—career goals, family goals, and life goals. People who cannot or do not sit down and write out exactly what they want from life lack direction. Brian Tracy, who developed the "Law of Direction," says, "Your ability to set clear, specific goals will do more to guarantee you higher levels of success and achievement than any other single skill or quality."[9]

The goal-setting process requires that you be clear about what you want to accomplish. If your goal is too general or vague, progress toward achieving that goal is difficult to observe. Goals such as "I want to be a success" or "I desire good health" are much too general. The major principles that encompass goal setting are outlined in Table 16.1.

TABLE 16.1 Goal-Setting Principles

The following goal-setting principles give you the power to take control of the present and the future.

1. *Reflect on the things you want to change in your life.* Then prepare written goals that are specific, measurable, and realistic.

2. *Develop a written goal-setting plan that includes the steps necessary to achieve the goal.* Review your plan daily—repetition increases the probability of success.

3. *Modify your environment by changing the stimuli around you.* This may involve finding a mentor or spending less time with persons who are negative.

4. *Monitor your behavior, and reward your progress.* Reinforcement from yourself and/or others is necessary for change.

Source: Barry L. Reece and Rhonda Brandt, *Effective Human Relations: Personal and Organizational Applications*, Boston: Houghton Mifflin Company, 2005. Reprinted by permission of the publisher.

Heather Gardner, with the investment firm of William Blair & Company, uses her BlackBerry and Microsoft Outlook calendar to record all of her planned activities.

Goals have a great deal of psychological value to people in selling. Sales goals, for example, can serve as a strong motivational force. To illustrate, let us assume that Mary Paulson, sales representative for a cosmetic manufacturer, decides to increase her sales by 15 percent over the previous year. She now has a clear goal to aim for and can begin identifying specific steps to achieve the new goal.

Mary Paulson has established a long-term goal as part of a yearly plan. Some goals require considerable time and should be part of a one-year plan. Next, Mary should set aside an hour or so at the end of each month to decide what she wants to accomplish during the coming month. Weekly planning is also important. Once a week—Friday is a good time—set goals for the next week and develop a plan for reaching them. Finally, Mary should develop a daily plan.[10]

This salesperson is using a personal digital assistant (PDA). It serves as an electronic memo pad, calendar, expense log, address book, and more. It is invaluable to salespeople who want to add value with efficient time and territory management.

PREPARE A DAILY "TO DO" LIST Sales professionals who complete the time management course offered by FranklinCovey are encouraged to engage in event control. This involves planning and prioritizing events every day.[11] Start each day by thinking about what you want to accomplish. Then write down the activities (Figure 16.1). Putting your thoughts on paper (or in your computer) forces you to clarify your thinking. Heather Gardner, a regional director with the Chicago investment firm William Blair & Company, records her daily planned activities in her BlackBerry and Microsoft Outlook calendar. On a typical day the BlackBerry will show entries for every half hour. Gardner works through her detailed to-do list by adhering to one unshakable rule: avoid nonpaying activities during working hours.[12]

Now you should prioritize your to-do list and do not let outside distractions interfere with your plan. Begin each day with the highest-priority task.

MAINTAIN A PLANNING CALENDAR Ideally, a salesperson needs a single place to record daily appointments (personal and business), deadlines, and tasks. Unfortunately, many salespeople write daily tasks on any slip of paper they can find—backs of envelopes, three-by-five cards, napkins, or Post-it notes. Hyrum W. Smith, author of *The 10 Natural Laws of Successful Time and Life Management*, calls these pieces of paper "floaters." They just float around until you either follow through on them or lose them. It's a terribly disorganized method for someone who wants to gain greater control of his or her life.[13]

The use of floaters often leads to the loss of critical information, missed appointments, and lack of focus. Select a planning calendar design (the FranklinCovey Day Planner is one option) that can bring efficiency to your daily planning efforts. You should be able to determine at a glance what is coming up in the days and weeks ahead (Figure 16.2).

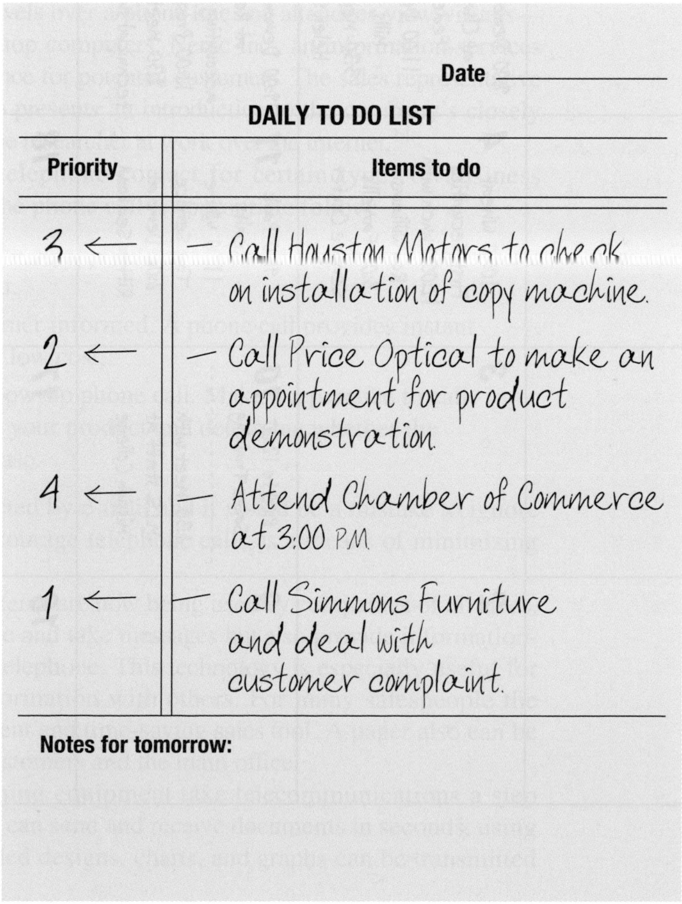

FIGURE 16.1

A daily list of activities can help us set priorities and save time. Today this list is recorded electronically in most CRM systems. The list is one of the first things salespeople see when they access the software each day.

Questions

1. Which of these elements can make the most important contribution to a career in personal selling? Explain.

2. Reflect on your own approach to accomplishing tasks and select two of Melara's elements you would find easy to adopt. Then select two elements that you would find difficult to adopt. Explain your choices.

3. How might goal setting be used in conjunction with time management?

4. How might a commitment to excellence improve the processes of territory management and records management?

5. Do you agree or disagree that the people you associate with can influence your motivation?

CRM Case Study

Managing Yourself with CRM

A key objective in managing your time is to confirm that, at any time, you are working on your highest priorities. Contacting prospective customers is the highest priority for most salespeople. The next challenge is to decide in which order prospects should be contacted. Many salespeople prioritize their accounts on the basis of their value, the amount that they are likely to spend with the sales organization.

Questions

1. On the basis of the dollar amount Pat Silva estimated that each account might spend, in what order would you contact the prospects in the Salesforce.com database?

2. If you were to rank these prospects on the basis of your sales commission, would this priority list be different from the list developed in question 1? If so, why?

3. There are several ways that this list of prospects could be prioritized, for example, by date, dollar amount, or commission. Which of these rankings is best?

17

Management of the Sales Force

🎥 Reality Selling Today Video Series

If you enter the field of personal selling and experience success, you may be given the opportunity to manage a sales force. Some salespeople are asked to accept the promotion but decline the offer. They do not want to give up a job they thoroughly enjoy. Many of the salespeople who do rise to management positions become exemplary leaders and advance to positions that offer even greater challenges.

Jaime Barauh (pictured above), district sales manager for McKesson Pharmaceutical (www.mckesson.com), started her career at this largest North American pharmaceutical distributor company as a salesperson calling on retail independent pharmacies. She attributes her success to the training she received from the company and her previous managers. In a highly competitive and ever-changing pharmaceutical industry, continuing training about new products and services is critical. McKesson adopts a multilayer training program. This includes a comprehensive online curriculum covering all products and services the company is offering, hands-on training with current managers, and frequent updates. The company also runs regional and national sales conferences where managers can network with peers and receive updated information. All new recruits also spend two weeks in the corporate distribution center working as an actual distribution staff to familiarize themselves with an extensive line of products.

An avid learner, Jaime Barauh was soon promoted to district sales manager of McKesson's distribution hub in Houston. Working under her supervision are five account managers who are responsible for some $750 million worth of business in Texas and Louisiana. As a sales manager, she makes sure that her subordinates are empowered to fulfill their responsibilities. At the same time, she sets a good example for her subordinate by her strong work ethics. She subscribes to the principle that a good leader should keep regular and open communication with followers without micro managing. Micro management is the enemy of creativity and motivation. She is also actively involved in recruiting and training new staff because she believes that such early involvement in the process will help build a strong sales team. ■

Applying Leadership Skills to Sales Management

If you enter the field of personal selling and experience success, like Jamie Barauh, you may be given the opportunity to manage a sales force. Some salespeople are asked to accept the promotion but decline the offer. They do not want to give up a job they thoroughly enjoy. Many of the salespeople who do rise to management positions become exemplary leaders and advance to positions that offer even greater challenges.

Thanks to the efforts of James Kouzes and Barry Posner, we know a great deal about the practices of exemplary leaders. Many years of research on this topic have been summarized and reported in *The Leadership Challenge*, a best-selling book written by Kouzes and Posner. The book is based on countless interviews and observations conducted around the world.

Lindsay Levin, managing director of Whites Limited, was one of many exceptional leaders cited by the authors of *The Leadership Challenge*. Whites Limited, based in London, is an auto dealership built around three departments—sales, service, and parts. Soon after assuming her new management position, she began searching for answers to one important question: "What do our customers really think of us?" She visualized Whites as a company where every customer would say, "My experience at Whites was amazing." With input from customer focus groups she was able to identify some areas that needed improvement. She then asked employees to talk about changes they would like to implement and to form small voluntary teams to work on them.

Lindsay Levin also visualized a company where everyone is treated with respect, and feels involved and valued. She took the position that a leader can never have enough communication with their people. She never hesitated to let the employees know what she was thinking and what she believed. She talked about her values often and listened attentively when employees expressed their views. Levin also recognized employee accomplishments with personal thanks and formal awards.

People who rise to the position of sales manager must understand the difference between leadership and management. Leadership is the process of inspiring, influencing,

Samuel Palmisano, CEO of IBM, began his career in sales at IBM. After achieving success in sales, he quickly rose through the ranks.

and guiding employees to participate in a common effort.[1] Stephen Covey, author of *The Eighth Habit*, says, "Leadership is communicating people's worth and potential so clearly that they come to see it in themselves."[2] Leaders are made, not born. Leadership is a series of skills that can be acquired through study and practice.

Sales management is the process of planning, implementing, and controlling the personal selling function.[3] The sales manager typically performs such management functions as planning, recruiting, training, budgeting, development of compensation plans, and assessing sales force productivity. Managing the sales force is an external management function, focused on bringing in orders and revenue from outside the company. However, it also requires coordination and cooperation with almost every internal department including marketing, finance, and distribution.[4]

The true essence of sales management has been captured by Lisa Gschwandtner, editor-in-chief of *Selling Power* magazine. She described the sales manager as a leader, coach, mentor, facilitator, goal setter, motivator, number cruncher, and communicator.[5] Figure 17.1 describes the most popular topics covered in training programs designed for sales managers. Needless to say, it's a job that requires many qualities and skills. Today's sales manager is more likely to function in a virtual office environment. Sales force automation permits salespeople to receive data on their laptops or their home computers. The use of other technology—videoconferencing, teleconferencing, e-mail, and voice mail—reduces the need for frequent face-to-face contact with members of the sales team.[6]

Sales managers can have a dramatic influence on the salespeople they supervise. Depending on the leadership qualities adopted, sales managers can have an advantageous, neutral, or even detrimental effect on the performance of sales subordinates.[7]

Effective leadership has been discussed in hundreds of books and articles. A careful review of this material indicates that most successful supervisory management personnel

Planning and Organizing Activities (total = 13 topics)	
Goal setting for salespeople	76%
Developing sales strategies	58%
Strategic sales planning	56%
Recruiting new salespeople	52%
Organizing salespeople	52%
Sales forecasting	50%
Management and Development Activities (total = 19 topics)	
Motivating salespeople	82%
Leading salespeople	66%
Training salespeople	64%
Territory management	62%
Time management	60%
Evaluation and Control Activities (total = 10 topics)	
Evaluating salespeople	64%

FIGURE 17.1

Most Popular Topics Covered in Training Programs for Sales Managers

Source: Adapted from Rolph Anderson, Rajiv Mehta, and James Strong, "An Empirical Investigation of Sales Management Training Programs for Sales Managers," *Journal of Personal Selling & Sales Management*, Summer 1997, Table 6, p. 61.

FIGURE 17.2

Basic Leadership Styles from The Ohio State Study

This matrix is similar to the Leadership Grid (formerly called the *Managerial Grid*) developed by Robert Blake and Jane Mouton. The Leadership Grid is based on two leadership style dimensions: concern for people and concern for production.

Source: Robert Kreitner, *Management*, 10th ed. (Boston: Houghton Mifflin Company, 2007), p. 449. Reprinted by permission of the publisher.

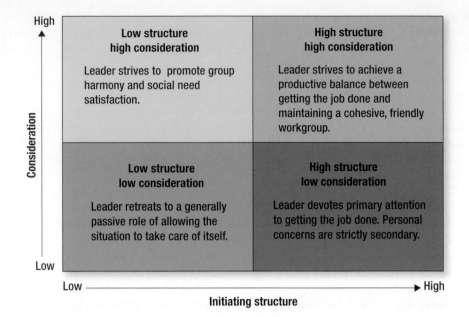

have certain behaviors in common. Two of the most important dimensions of leadership—consideration and structure—have been identified in research studies conducted by Ohio State University researchers.[8] By making a matrix out of these two independent dimensions of leadership, the researchers identified four styles of leadership (see Figure 17.2).

Structure

Sales managers who display **structure** clearly define their own duties and those of the sales staff. They assume an active role in directing their subordinates' work. Policies and procedures are clearly defined, and subordinates know what is expected of them. Salespeople also know how well they are doing because the structured supervisor evaluates their productivity and provides feedback. Structure is the set of written and unspoken policies, practices, and expectations that surround the job of the salesperson. It can include job descriptions, territory definitions, call reports, and sales process definitions.[9]

Besides supervising the sales force, sales managers often are involved in establishing sales quotas, developing long- and short-term forecasts, and seeing that goals are achieved.

The following behaviors provide evidence of structure:

1. *Planning takes place on a regular basis.* The effective sales manager thinks ahead and decides what to do in the future. Strategic planning is the process of determining the company's current position in the market, determining where you want to be and when, and making decisions on how to secure the position you want. Strategic planning gives meaning and direction to the sales force.

2. *Expectations are clearly communicated.* The law of expectations, according to Brian Tracy, states, "Whatever you expect, with confidence, becomes your own self-fulfilling prophecy."[10] There is a strong connection between what you expect to accomplish and what you actually achieve. Sales managers must effectively formulate their expectations and then communicate them with conviction to the sales force.

3. *Decisions are made promptly and firmly.* An effective sales manager is willing and able to make decisions in a timely way. An ineffective manager often postpones important decisions, hoping the problem will go away. Of course, most decisions cannot be made until all the facts are available. A good sales manager keeps the lines of communication open and involves salespeople in making the important decisions.

4. *Performance of salespeople is appraised regularly.* All employees want to know "where they stand" with the manager. An effective sales manager provides regular feedback. When a salesperson is not performing up to established standards, the sales manager takes immediate action.

Although structure is an important aspect of sales management, too much structure can create problems. In an effort to become better organized and more systematized, some sales organizations have developed detailed policies and procedures that rob salespeople of time, energy, and creativity. Filling out endless reports and forms, for example, can cause unnecessary frustration and may reduce productivity. Overcontrolling sales managers aren't just annoying; they are also inefficient.[11]

Consideration

A sales manager who displays the dimension of **consideration** is more likely to have relationships with salespeople that are characterized by mutual trust, respect for salespeople's ideas, and consideration for their feelings. A climate of good two-way communication usually exists between the manager and members of the sales team. The following behaviors provide evidence of consideration:

1. *Regular and effective communication receives a high priority.* Whenever possible the sales manager engages in face-to-face communication with salespeople. They do not rely entirely on e-mail, letters, or sales reports for information sharing but arrange face-to-face meetings. John Morrone, vice president of sales for Pitney Bowes Management Services, frequently travels with his salespeople. He says, "My claim to fame is reaching out and touching people."[12] The effective sales manager is a good listener and creates an atmosphere of cooperation and understanding.

2. *Each salesperson is treated as an individual.* The sales manager takes a personal interest in each member of the sales force. No one is treated like a "number." The interest is genuine, not artificial. The effective sales manager does not endanger effectiveness by showing favoritism to anyone.

3. *Good performance is rewarded often.* Positive reinforcement is one of the strongest morale-building factors in the work environment. Ken Blanchard, coauthor of *The One-Minute Manager*, says, "The key to developing people will always be to concentrate on catching them doing something right instead of blaming them for doing something wrong."[13] Recognition for a job well done is always appreciated.

Situational Leadership

Mastery of consideration and structure skills is an important first step toward achieving success in sales management. The next step is to match your leadership style to the

know for sure about the characteristics of motives. First, motives are individualistic. The desire for social standing (status) may be very strong for one salesperson, but not very important to another salesperson. What satisfies one person's needs may not be important to someone else. Second, motives change throughout our lives. What motivates us early in our career may not motivate us later in life.

Because people bring different interests, drives, and values to the workplace, they react differently to attempts at motivation. The owner of an incentive consulting company in Chicago rewarded one of his highly productive employees with an attractive mink coat. She thanked him sincerely, took the coat home, but never wore it. When he asked her why, she explained that she didn't wear fur.[30]

Very often intrinsic motivators (achievement, challenge, responsibility, advancement, growth, enjoyment of work itself, and involvement) have a longer-term effect on employees' attitudes and behaviors than extrinsic motivators (contests, prizes, quotas, and money). In many cases sales performance is linked directly to the appreciation the sales manager shows for a job well done. The importance of one-on-one communications cannot be overstated. Everyone likes to be treated as an individual. Taking a personal interest means learning the names of spouses and children, finding out what employees do during their leisure time, and acknowledging birthdays.[31]

Effective Use of External Rewards

Although criticisms of external rewards have a great deal of merit, the fact remains that large numbers of organizations continue to achieve positive results with carefully developed incentive programs. It is possible to design programs that have long-range benefits for both the organization and the individual employee if you follow these guidelines:

1. Design reward programs that focus on several important aspects of the salesperson's job such as developing new accounts, expanding sales of existing accounts, and improving customer service after the sale. Keep contest time frames short so more salespeople have an opportunity to win. However, don't use short-term motivation contests too often and don't use the same incentive plan over and over again.

2. Evaluate your incentive program often to determine what plan has the most impact. Is it cash bonuses? Travel? Merchandise? Bill Grassie, manager of compensation and business planning for Sprint, likes to use noncash incentives because he believes Sprint salespeople have a solid compensation package. He feels noncash incentives provide a lasting memory whereas a cash bonus is just one more way to earn money.[32] Of course, a salesperson who is not earning a lot of money in salary and commission might favor a cash incentive.

3. Avoid setting goals that are unrealistic. Some companies are under enormous pressure to meet sales and profit targets. In many cases sales targets increase while resources decline. A salesperson working for a company in Texas made the President's Club for being 220 percent above quota, and her whole team did well and was recognized as tops in the company. Her boss, the vice president for sales, immediately

Icelandic® offers a very attractive incentive program to its distribution sales representatives.

raised their overall quota by 65 percent for the next year. This was an impossible target and team morale plummeted.

Pressure to reach unrealistic sales goals can produce negative results. Employee loyalty and teamwork erode quickly and, in some cases so do business ethics. Salespeople who fear loss of their job if they do not meet established targets are more inclined to engage in unethical behavior.[33]

Should sales managers encourage their salespeople to *compete* or encourage them to *cooperate*? This is one of the dilemmas facing managers who want highly motivated salespeople, but they also want members of the sales team to share important information and become resources to each other. One answer is to develop a plan that rewards sales collaboration and the achievement of specific sales goals, whether individual goals, team goals, or both.[34]

Compensation Plans

Compensation plans for salespeople combine direct monetary payments (salary and commissions) and indirect monetary payments such as paid vacations, pensions, and insurance plans. Compensation practices vary greatly throughout the field of selling. Furthermore, sales managers are constantly searching for the "perfect" sales force compensation plan. Of course, the perfect plan does not exist. Each plan must be chosen to suit the specific type of selling job, the objectives of the firm's marketing program, and the type of customer served.

As noted in Chapter 2, the highest amount of total compensation is earned by salespeople who are involved in value-added selling. Salespeople who use this approach realize that the solution to the customer's buying problem is more important than price. They are frequently involved in team selling and in some cases they are rewarded with a team compensation plan.

A growing number of companies are abandoning compensation plans that are linked to a single target such as a sales quota. At Siebel Systems, an e-business software provider,

Customer Relationship Management with Technology

STAYING INFORMED

A key role of the sales manager is to provide a steady flow of information and advice to salespeople. Salespeople look to their managers for information about market trends, products, company policies, and assistance with their accounts. Customer relationship management (CRM) software improves and enhances the flow of information between managers and the sales force. The same features that are used to enrich communications with customers also support the sales organization's internal communications. With direct access to a shared CRM database, for example, a sales manager can review relationships with accounts in real time by examining a salesperson's notes at any time. This makes it possible for the manager to enter advice about an account directly into that account's record. (See the exercise Receiving Advice Through CRM on p. 388–389 for more information.)

40 percent of each salesperson's incentive compensation is based on the customers' reported satisfaction with service and implementation of the products they have purchased. This plan encourages continuous customer follow-up, which generates repeat business.[35]

In the field of selling there are five basic compensation plans. Here is a description of each:

- *Straight commission plan.* The only direct monetary compensation comes from sales. No sales, no income. Salespeople under this plan are very conscious of their sales. Lack of job security can be a strong inducement to produce results. However, these people also may concentrate more on immediate sales than on long-term customer development.

- *Commission plan with a draw provision or guaranteed salary.* This plan has about the same impact on salespeople as the straight commission plan. However, it gives them more financial security.

- *Commission with a draw or guaranteed salary plus a bonus.* This plan offers more direct financial security than the first two plans. Therefore, salespeople may adhere more to the company's objectives. The bonus may be based on sales or profits.

- *Fixed salary plus bonus.* Salespeople functioning under this compensation plan tend to be more company centered and to have a fairly high degree of financial security if their salary is competitive. The bonus incentive helps motivate people under this plan.

- *Straight salary.* Salespeople who work under this compensation plan are usually more company centered and have financial security.

According to the *Sales & Marketing Management* 2005 research study, most companies participating in the survey used some form of compensation plan that combined base salary and incentive.[36] The salary plus bonus and salary plus commission plans are both quite popular.

Strategic Compensation Planning

Many sales managers admit that their current compensation plan does not drive behaviors needed to achieve specific sales objectives. The purpose of strategic compensation planning is to guide salespeople in the right direction. Compensation plans can be designed to achieve a variety of sales objectives:

Specific product movement. Bonus points can be given for the sale of certain items during specified "push" selling periods.

Percentage sales increase. Sales levels can be established with points that are given only when those levels are reached.

Establish new accounts. A block of points can be awarded for opening a new account or for introducing new products through the existing outlets.

Increase sales activity. For each salesperson, points can be awarded based on the number of calls.[37]

There is no easy way to develop an effective compensation plan. There are, however, some important guidelines for your efforts to develop an effective plan. First, be sure that your

sales and marketing objectives are defined in detail. The plan should complement these objectives. If sales and marketing objectives are in conflict with the compensation plan, problems surely arise.

Second, the compensation plan should be field-tested before full implementation. Several questions should be answered: Is the new plan easy to administer? How does the proposed plan differ in terms of payout compared with the existing plan?

Third, explain the compensation plan carefully to the sales force. Misunderstanding may generate distrust of the plan. Keep in mind that some salespeople may see change as a threat.

Fourth, change the compensation plan when conditions in the marketplace warrant change. One reason for the poor showing of many plans is that firms fail to revise their plan as the business grows and market conditions change. Review the compensation plan at least annually to ensure that it's aligned with conditions in the marketplace and the company's overall marketing strategy.

Assessing Sales Force Productivity

As the cost of maintaining a sales force increases, sales managers must give more attention to measuring productivity. The goal is to analyze the profitability of each salesperson's sales volume. This task is complicated because sales territories, customers, and business conditions vary.

The problem of measuring sales force productivity is more complicated than it might appear at first glance. In most cases, sales volume alone does not tell you how much profit or loss you are making on the sales of each member of the sales force. A small manufacturer was losing money until he analyzed the profitability of sales generated by each person. He found that one salesperson created a loss on almost every order. This salesperson was concentrating on a market that had become so competitive that she had to reduce the markup to make sales.

Some sales managers view the frequency of calls as an indicator of success. This information is only helpful when compared with the profit earned on each account.

The number of calls made on an account should bear some relationship to the sales and profit potential of that account. In some cases it is possible to maintain small accounts without making frequent personal calls.

To compare a salesperson's current productivity with the past also can be misleading. Changes in products, prices, competition, and assignments can make comparisons with the past unfair—sometimes to the salesperson, sometimes to the company. It is better to measure cumulative quarterly, semiannual, or annual results in relation to established goals.

Some sales managers use performance evaluation criteria that communicate to the sales force which elements of their jobs are most important and how they are doing in each area. Evaluating salespeople involves defining the bases on which they are to be evaluated, developing performance standards to determine the acceptable level of performance desired on each base, monitoring actual performance, and giving salespeople feedback on their performance.[38] Two of the most common criteria for assessing the productivity of salespeople are quantitative criteria and qualitative criteria.

Quantitative Criteria	Qualitative Criteria
Sales volume in dollars	Attitude
Sales volume compared with previous year's sales	Product knowledge
	Communication skills
Sales volume by product or product line	Personal appearance
Number of new accounts opened	Customer goodwill generated
Amount of new account sales	Selling skills
Net profit on each account	Initiative
Number of customer calls	Team collaboration

In most cases it is best to emphasize assessment criteria that can be expressed in numbers (quantitative). The preceding quantitative items are especially significant when accompanied by target dates. For example, you might assess the number of new accounts opened during a six-month period. Of course, a sales manager should not ignore the other criteria listed here. The other items can affect a salesperson's productivity, and you do have to make judgments in these areas.

Some sales managers ask their salespeople to complete a self-evaluation as part of the overall evaluation process. Many salespeople believe that self-evaluation contributes to their personal development.[39]

Chapter Learning Activities

Reviewing Key Concepts

Describe how leadership skills can be applied to sales management

Many capable salespeople have advanced to the position of *sales manager*. This job involves such diverse duties as recruiting, selecting, training, and supervising salespeople. The sales manager is part of the management team and therefore must be a strong leader. Those who rise to the position of sales manager must understand the difference between leadership and management.

List and discuss the qualities of an effective sales manager

Effective sales managers help members of their sales force feel confident, strong, and capable of fulfilling their duties. Although the qualities of effective leaders are subject to debate, most research tells us that such people display two dimensions: *structure* and *consideration*. Sales managers who develop a leadership style that combines structure and consideration possess the skills needed to be an effective *coach*.

Discuss recruitment and selection of salespeople

Most sales managers are involved directly or indirectly in recruiting and selecting sales-people. This is an important responsibility because mistakes can be costly. A portion of the company's profit picture and the firm's image can be influenced positively or negatively by each member of the sales force. To increase the quality of new hires, many companies are placing more emphasis on personality and skills testing.

Describe effective orientation and training practices

Orientation and training salespeople are almost daily concerns of the sales manager. These duties should always be viewed as an investment in human resources. They help members of the sales force reach their fullest potential. Figure 17.3 provides a comprehensive frame-work for training salespeople.

Explain effective sales force motivation practices

We discuss the difference between *internal* and *external motivation.* In many cases intrinsic motivators (achievement, challenge, responsibility, involvement, and enjoy-ment of work itself) have a longer-term effect on employee attitudes and behavior than extrinsic motivators (contests, prizes, and money). Sales managers need to discover the individual differences between salespeople to select the most effective motivation strategies.

Develop an understanding of selected compensation plans

Compensation plans for salespeople combine direct monetary payments (salary and commissions) and indirect monetary payments such as paid vacations, pensions, and insur-ance plans. Compensation practices vary greatly throughout the field of selling. Strategic compensation planning can be used to guide salespeople in the right direction.

List and discuss criteria for evaluating sales performance

Assessing sales force productivity is a major responsibility of the sales manager. Sales managers use both quantitative and qualitative criteria. In most cases it is best to emphasize assessment criteria that can be expressed in numbers (quantitative).

Key Terms

Sales management	Coaching	Compensation plans
Structure	Internal motivation	Quantitative criteria
Consideration	External motivation	Qualitative criteria
Situational leadership		

Review Questions

1. What is the difference between leadership and management?

2. Are all sales managers' duties the same? Explain.

3. What are the two main leadership qualities displayed by most successful sales managers? Define and explain each of these qualities.

4. List and describe the four basic steps involved in coaching.

5. What is a job description? Explain the importance of job descriptions in selecting salespeople.

6. What are four sources of recruiting new salespeople?

7. What should sales managers look for in selecting new salespeople? Describe at least three important qualities.

8. List and describe three guidelines that should be followed when you design a sales motivation program based on external rewards.

9. List and describe the five basic compensation plans for salespeople.

10. What are the *best* criteria for measuring a salesperson's performance? List additional criteria that should be considered in evaluating individual performance.

Application Exercises

1. Assume that you are a manager of a wholesale electrical supply business. Sales have increased to a level where you need to hire another salesperson. What sources can you use in recruiting a good professional salesperson? What criteria can you use in selecting the person you hire?

2. Carefully analyze the following types of selling positions:

   a. A territory selling position for a national manufacturer that requires the salesperson to provide customer service to a large number of accounts plus open up several new accounts each month
   b. A retail sales position in the cosmetics department of a department store
   c. An automobile salesperson who sells and leases new and used cars
   d. A real estate salesperson who sells residential real estate

   Assuming that each of the preceding positions is full time, identify the type of compensation plan you think is best for each. Supply an explanation for each of your answers.

3. Schedule an appointment with two sales managers. Interview each of them, using the following questions as a guide:

   a. What are your functions as a sales manager?
   b. How do the functions of a sales manager differ from those of a salesperson?
   c. What criteria do you use in selecting salespeople?
   d. What kinds of training programs do you have for new salespeople?
   e. What method of compensation do you use for your salespeople?
   f. How do you evaluate the performance of your salespeople?
   g. What personal qualities are important for becoming a sales manager?

   Write the answers to these questions. Summarize the similarities and differences of the sales managers' responses.

4. The Internet lists many sources of training in the field of sales management. Using your search engine, type in " 'sales management' + training". How many queries did you find? Examine one or more of the training programs and list the topics that are covered. Compare this list of topics with the material presented in this chapter.

Role-Play Exercise

For the purpose of this role-play, assume the role of a sales manager who is currently supervising a sales team made up of 22 salespeople. Your employer manufactures and sells radio equipment for private aircraft. You plan to open a new sales territory in a western state and need a self-motivated salesperson to assume the position. You have identified a person who seems to be a qualified applicant and you have scheduled a meeting to discuss the position. Using information in this chapter, prepare a list of questions you will ask during the role-play. Use these questions to interview another class member who will assume the role of the applicant. After the role-play, review the interview process.

CRM Application Exercise

Receiving Advice Through CRM

Becky Kemley, your sales manager at SimNet Systems, regularly reviews your progress with accounts by examining your activities and notes. She recently entered a note about an account's debt problems. Find her note and the two accounts she refers to by running the "Account Update Report." Edit the filter in the Generated Report section. Create a filter to find all accounts where the description contains "Debt." Print the information contained in these records by selecting "Printable View"; then print the report.

Case Problem

One of the more interesting developments in sales force management is the use of customer feedback to improve the performance of salespeople. These programs go by a variety of names such as *360-degree feedback, customer-conscious compensation*, and *customer satisfaction rewards*. Organizations that have adopted this assessment strategy believe salespeople can benefit from feedback collected from the customers they serve. Also, the information collected can be used by the company to improve customer service.

The use of customer-driven evaluation programs is on the increase because of the rising regard for the role of sales at many companies. Tom Mott, a consultant with Hewitt Associates, says, "Salespeople who were volume pushers are now becoming the manager of their company's relationship with the customer." Mott points out that customer feedback is likely to reflect on the performance of the salesperson and the performance of the company. If problems surface in either area, customer dissatisfaction may need attention.

Data collection methodology is not uniform at this point. Some companies use telephone surveys while others use mailed questionnaires. IBM has experimented with a series of in-person meetings that bring together corporate customers, their IBM sales representatives, and the salesperson's boss.

Some salespeople have not welcomed the use of customer evaluations. Maryann Cirenza, senior account executive at Teleport Communications Group (TCG) of New York, said that she felt betrayed when she saw the questionnaire the company was sending to her customers. One of the questions asked, "Does your sales rep know your industry?" Cirenza said, "I thought the company was checking up on me." Later her anger subsided when she learned the survey was not simply a monitoring system but a trial run for a new compensation plan. After field-testing the surveys, TCG used customer feedback to set bonuses. Cirenza was actually rewarded for good customer service by earning a bonus of about 20 percent of her base pay. Greg Buseman, a Chicago-based IBM salesman, believes the shift to compensation through customer feedback has improved personal selling at his company. He now spends more time understanding the customer's business and learning to be a problem solver for his clients.[40]

Questions

1. Should the customer be given a major voice in determining how salespeople are performing? Explain.

2. Should sales force compensation be linked to customer feedback? What are the advantages and disadvantages of this approach?

3. Assume you are a sales manager preparing to develop and implement a customer feedback system. How might you gain support for this system from members of your salespeople? What data collection method would you use?

4. Research indicates that customers rank "understanding of our business" as an important criterion used to evaluate salespeople. Why is this criterion ranked so high?

Reality Selling Today Role-Play 6, Hilti Corporation

Alim Hirani
Hilti Corporation

(This mock sales call role-play scenario is created exclusively for use with the *Selling Today: Creating Customer Value* text book.)

You will be a sales representative for Hilti (see Web site at www.hilti.com), working out of the same office as Alim Hirani, featured in the Chapter 10 Reality *Selling Today* Video. The company provides the global construction industry with innovative products and services. In addition to a wide variety of high-end products such as measuring systems, drilling and demolition, installation systems, foam systems, and screw fastening systems, the company also offers its customers customized training programs and consulting services. Hilti sales representatives work directly with customers rather than through intermediary parties. (Refer back to the Chapter 10 opening vignette and case problem, and review the Chapter 10 Reality *Selling Today* Video for more information.)

Your Customer: Ellis Exhibition Inc.

You will meet with Casey Smith, procurement manager for Ellis Exhibition Inc. The company owns a 100,000-square-foot exhibition center that hosts several local and regional events in Atlanta, Georgia. Some of these events have become a must-see for the local business community. Depending on the theme and the products being showcased, Ellis Exhibition offers exhibitors outstanding display services that include floor plans, display solutions, display installation, and booth dismantlement. After an event, the installation systems are reused, while installation accessories are generally discarded. Casey Smith believes that by buying the right type of installation accessories, Ellis can save a lot of money, and therefore offer their exhibitor customers more competitive prices.

Quick Facts About the Ellis Exhibition Inc.'s Needs

- Ellis Exhibition Inc. spends about $500,000 a year on installation accessories. These accessories are galvanized, but they can also be painted to match the color theme stipulated by exhibitors.
- Ellis uses a wide variety of installation accessories, from hexagon nuts and head screws to distance holders.
- Ellis does not want to stock these accessories. Exhibitors who want to use Ellis display services are required to place their order three months in advance. Then, an Ellis accountant will calculate the necessary accessories needed for each event.
- Ellis is extremely concerned with the quality of all of its installation systems and accessories.

Your Call Objectives

In your meeting with Casey Smith, you hope to identify the specific types and the expected quantity of installation accessories. You also want to know about delivery requirements. In addition, you might be able to cross-sell other Hilti products and services, such as sprinkler systems.

Reality Selling Today Role-Play 7, Marriott International, Inc.

Heather Ramsey
Marriott International Inc.

(This mock sales call role-play scenario is created exclusively for use with the *Selling Today: Creating Customer Value* text book.)

Your Role at Marriott

You will be a sales representative for Marriott International Inc. (www.marriott.com), working out of the same hotel as Heather Ramsey, featured in the Chapter 13 Reality *Selling Today* Video. Founded in 1927 by J. Willard and Alice S. Marriott, Marriott has grown from a root beer stand to a multinational company with more than 3,000 lodging properties located in some 70 countries around the world. Apart from luxurious hotel accommodation under several well-managed brands, the company also offers outstanding services for meetings and events. From weddings to corporate meetings, Marriott's clients know that they are always in good hands. (Refer back to the Chapter 13 opening vignette and case problem, and review the Chapter 13 Reality *Selling Today* Video for more information.)

Your Customer: Hiroshi Watanabe/Chris Scott

You will meet with Chris Scott, personal secretary to Mr. Hiroshi Watanabe, owner of a high-end tailor chain stores in California. Mr. Watanabe got married to his wife twenty-five years ago in a simple wedding ceremony. The couple immigrated to the U.S. with only five dollars in their pocket. The young couple worked very hard to make ends meet, and their fate took a turn when both were hired full time for the first time by a small tailor shop, Mr. Watanabe as a one word with no comma following (deliveryman), and his wife as a helper.

With strong entrepreneurial spirit and incessant learning, they soon opened their own business using their own meager savings. Initial clients were mainly friends, but they soon found a niche in the market by combining traditional Japanese garment making with American contemporary fashion. Before they knew it, celebrities started knocking on their door, asking for custom-made evening gowns and suits. A couple of years later, they opened their first concept store under the name Watanabe, and positioned it as a high-end custom-made tailor house. They also provided customers with a full range of custom-designed accessories.

Their two sons soon joined the team, managing stores and franchisees in prime locations in Los Angeles and San Francisco, California. As their silver wedding anniversary is approaching, Mr. Watanabe asks Chris to organize something very special for his wife to make up for the hard-working years the couple has been through.

Event Planning

More information on event planning is available at www.marriott.com. You should also be able to get more information on anniversary party ideas from the internet.

Quick Facts About the Clients' Needs

- The anniversary has to be formal as many celebrities will be invited.
- The menu has to be as bountiful and sumptuous as possible.
- Costs are not a major concern. However, Chris should be shopping for the best offer.
- Chris is in charge of information gathering and screens offers from three major hotels. Chris already has an offer from a Marriott competitor.
- The goal is not only to impress the guests but also Mrs. Watanabe.
- The highlight of the anniversary is a recount of the couple's happy marriage.

Your Call Objectives

In your meeting with Chris Scott, you hope to identify Mr. Watanabe's needs. In addition, you hope to convince him that you provide the best event planning services, which your competitor cannot offer. In doing so, you should be prepared to offer Chris a number of creative ideas to make the event both formal and memorable.

Appendix 2

Use of Customer Relationship Management (CRM) Salesforce.com System

Students—A Special Opportunity

salesforce.com

Selling Today now offers you a unique opportunity to learn the reason modern software is helping to redefine sales and marketing. The software you will be using in this application is referred to as Customer Relationship Management (CRM) software. CRM systems include functions necessary to automate and support the sales force, commonly known as sales force automation (SFA) functions. There are two types of SFA software—account based and contact based. Contact-based software, such as the popular ACT! Contact Management Software, features an individual contact or customer as the method for navigating the application.

As customer accounts have become larger, with multiple buyers involved in the purchasing decision, contact-based software proved inadequate, and most sales and marketing departments have moved to an account-based software. Account-based software such as the on-line Salesforce.com application featured in this exercise, allows for capturing information on each of the buyers that influence buying within an account. (See Chapter 9 for additional types of CRM software available for managing the prospect database.)

Using the log on instructions below, you can access the Salesforce/Selling Today CRM software and Customer database. Salesforce.com is the leading Internet-hosted CRM application in the world. Internet-hosted applications are also known as SaaS, or "Software as a Service." The Salesforce/Selling Today application is easy to use and includes information about more than 20 customers. You can experience firsthand how salespeople today gain the sales advantage with this category of software.

Beginning in Chapter 1, you will find the first *Customer Relationship Management with Technology* insight. These insights, along with the *CRM Application Exercise* at the end of the chapter, are simple, easy-to-follow instructions on using Salesforce.com to store and access a wide variety of business and personal information about your customers. You will discover the convenience of using this software to stay in touch with people.

Salesforce.com includes important customer information that you will use in your *CRM Case Study* assignments for Chapters 9 through 15. You will access this information to approach, present, demonstrate, negotiate, close, and service more than $1.2 million worth of sales.

Effectively using information technology, especially Customer Relationship Management software, will give you a career advantage in today's highly competitive workplace. After mastering the exercises provided, you can report your CRM experience on your résumé.

Instructions for Using the Customer Relationship Management (CRM) Software

The software that you will be using is a demonstration version of Salesforce.com, the leading SaaS CRM software. This demonstration version is limited to only 25 accounts and 50 contacts that may be entered. The full version of Salesforce.com is more robust and can manage thousands of customers, contacts, leads, and opportunities.

Running the Software

Start your Internet browser and go to www.pearsonhighered.com/manning. Click the Using Salesforce.com link and follow the instructions for your initial log on. After logging on, the first screen that you see is your home page (see Figure A2.1).

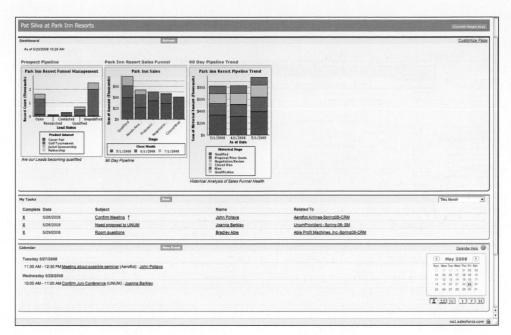

FIGURE A2.1

Sample Home Screen
The Home Screen presents dashboards that reminds one of the status of their prospecting and selling activities within their entire prospect database. It provides a quick view of progress toward achieving the sales forecast.

Source: Courtesy of Salesforce.com.

Using the Software

Salesforce.com is a browser-based program and uses standard Internet browser features. Navigation—moving around the application—is accomplished by mouse-clicking on tabs and hot links. *Hot links* are underlined fields or words on the screen. A set of *tabs* is always at the top of the Salesforce screen. Pressing one of these tabs takes you to the section of Salesforce that is the main screen for that important object or type of information, like Account, Contact, or Opportunities. When you click a hot link, the application takes you to that object (for example, a "lead") or performs that action (for example, "edit"). Therefore, when you need to do something within the application, you click a hot link or a tab.

The screen that displays the information about a customer is referred to as the Account screen. There are seven sections on the Salesforce.com Account screen. First is the Account Detail screen. This screen contains basic information about the account, such as name, address, and main phone number. If you scroll down the Account screen past the detail section, you will see the six related list sections. These sections contain additional information, or records, related to the account, such as contacts, planned activities, activity history, notes, and document attachments. There is a related list for all the sales opportunities we will be working on for this account. The first concept to master about Salesforce.com is that everything is organized around accounts: You can see that clearly from this Account screen. (See Figure A2.2.)

You can get to any of the information on the related list simply by clicking any of the hot links on that list. Clicking the first contact name on the Contact list takes you directly to all the information about that contact. Clicking "Opportunity" takes you directly to that sales opportunity. (See Figure A2.3.)

Three tools on the left side of every Salesforce.com screen make it easy and fast to use the application. First is the Search bar. Use this search capability to enter and go directly to any item in the database: Accounts, Contacts, Leads, Opportunities, Products, and so forth. Second is the Create New drop-down list. If you click this button, you will be able to create a new item for the Salesforce database. Salesforce will even help by pre-populating the new item with as much information as possible. For example, if you are looking at the Account Detail screen for Able Profit Machines and click "Create New . . . Contact,"

FIGURE A2.2

Sample Account Screen

The Account or Sales Opportunity Screen, as it is also called, provides information on each of the accounts in your prospect database. Note the tabs across the top of the screen. Pressing any of these tabs automatically takes you to that object or type of information. The first thing to master about Salesforce.com is that everything is organized around accounts.

Source: Courtesy of Salesforce.com.

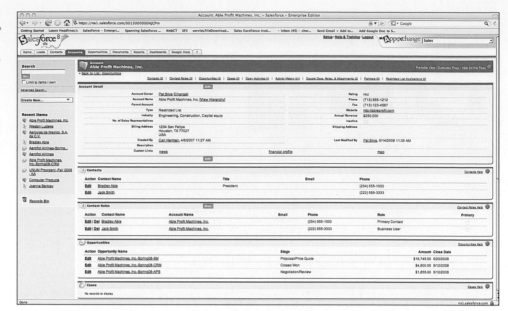

Salesforce will already have the account name, address, and phone number. The third tool is the Recent Items list. Salespeople tend to work on the same 10 or 15 items repeatedly until they have completed a major task. Salesforce always remembers the most recent 10 items and puts them on this list. Just click the hot link to take you directly to that object. You will be surprised how useful and efficient all three of these tools are.

FIGURE A2.3

Sample Contact Screen

The Contact Screen provides detailed information on each of the individuals within the account that may have influence on the sale process. Often referred to as members of the buying group, the individuals on these screens are accessed and used when strategically planning a sales call. Note the tools on the left side of the contact screen for gaining more detailed information and insight into planning effective sales strategies.

Source: Courtesy of Salesforce.com.

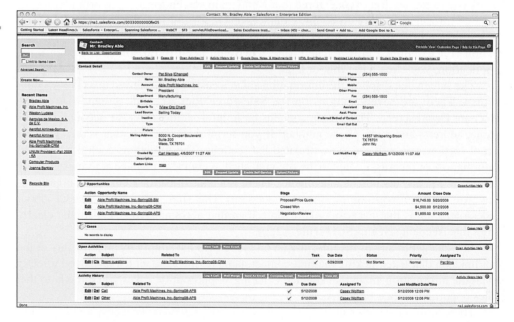

Appendix 3

**Partnership Selling: A Role-Play/Simulation
for Selling Today**

Table of Contents

A Special Note to the Student: Use of the Role-Play/Simulation Appendix

This role-play/simulation provides an opportunity to apply the principles that serve as a foundation for the four broad strategic areas of personal selling: relationship, product, customer, and presentation strategies. The activities are designed to take you from "learning about" selling to "learning to do" selling.

You will start as a convention center sales and marketing department trainee. Your sales manager will supply you with memos that will assist you in learning about your product, competition, customers, and presentations. You will be supplied many sales tools including photos, awards, schedules, menus, floor plans, references, company policies, electronic sales proposal/product configurators (see pp. 417–430) and sales planning worksheets.

The first memo on p. 412 provides background information about your product, company, industry, and competition. As a trainee your first sales and marketing assignment (see memo on p. 447) will be to create an electronic sales proposal and cover sales letter. This activity will give you an opportunity to apply information presented in Chapter 6.

After successfully communicating with your first customer and being promoted to account executive, you are instructed by your sales manager in memos on pp. 452–453 to plan and conduct your first face-to-face contact with another potential customer. The primary objective of this first contact is to establish a relationship with your customer.

The next memo from your sales manager on pp. 456–457 requests that you use your questioning skills to conduct a needs analysis involving the customer you previously contacted. Your customer, who was favorably impressed as a result of your first meeting, has called and requested a meeting to talk about an important convention being planned.

The last memo on pp. 460–461 assists you in creating and presenting a proposal that meets your customer's needs. You will create a portfolio presentation using the awards, photos, price lists, menus, references, floor plans, and schedules provided.

You can access digital images of the pictures in this simulation by clicking on the *www.pearsonhighered.com/manning* Web site. You can also access an electronic sales proposal configuration to complete the customer service/sales memorandum 1 and sales memorandum 3 assignments.

Introduction

Salespeople today are working hard to become more effective in such important areas as person-to-person communications, needs analysis, interpersonal relations, and decision making. This role-play/simulation will help you develop these critical selling skills. You will assume the role of a new sales trainee employed by the Park Inn International Convention Center.

PART I "Developing a Sales-Oriented Product Strategy" will challenge you to acquire the necessary product information needed to be an effective sales representative for the Park Inn (see Chapters 6 and 7). Your sales manager, T. J. McKee, will describe your new trainee position in an employment memorandum. Your instructions will include the study of materials featured on the following pages, viewing a video that describes the convention facilities and services provided by a competitor, and role-playing the request made in a T. J. McKee customer service/sales memorandum.

PART II "Developing a Relationship Strategy for Selling" is another major challenge in personal selling. An employment memorandum will inform you of a promotion to an account executive position. A sales memorandum will inform you of your assignment to accounts in a specific market segment. Part II also involves a role-play on the development of a relationship with a new customer in your market segment (see Chapters 3 and 10). Your call objective will be to acquire background information on your new customer, who may have a need for your services.

PART III "Understanding Your Customer's Buying Strategy" involves a needs analysis role-play (see Chapters 8 and 11). You will again meet with the customer who has indicated an interest in scheduling a business conference at your convention center. During this meeting, you will acquire information to complete Part IV, which involves preparation for the sales presentation.

PART IV "Developing a Sales Presentation Strategy" will involve preparation of a sales proposal and a *portfolio* presentation (see Chapters 11–15). This section also involves a third role-play with the customer. During the role-play, you will reestablish your relationship with the customer, present your proposal, negotiate the customer's concerns, and attempt to close and service the sale.

Throughout completion of the role-play/simulation, you will be guided by the employment and sales memoranda (from the sales manager) and instructions and additional forms provided by your instructor.

As you complete this simulation activity, note that the principles and practices you are learning to use have application in nearly all personal selling situations.

General Instructions for Role-Playing

Overview

The primary goal of a simulation in personal selling should be to strike a balance between just enough detail to focus on the process of selling and not so much as to drown in an ocean of facts. Either too much detail or too little detail can develop anxiety in role-play participants. *Partnership Selling* is designed to minimize anxiety by including only the facts needed to focus on learning the processes involved in high-performance selling.

Some anxiety will occur, however, because you are asked to perform under pressure (in terms of building relationships, securing strategic information, changing people's thinking, and getting them to take action). Learning to perform in an environment full of genuine but nonthreatening pressure affords you the opportunity to practice your selling skills so you will be prepared for real-world selling anxiety.

The following suggestions for role-playing will help you develop the ability to perform under stress.

INSTRUCTIONS FOR SALESPERSON ROLE-PLAYS

1. Be well prepared with product knowledge.
2. Read information for each role-play ahead of time.
3. Follow specific instructions carefully.
4. Attempt to sense both the context and the facts of the situation presented.
5. Conduct a mental rehearsal. See yourself successfully conducting and completing the role-play.
6. Be prepared to take notes during the role-play.
7. After the role-play, take note of your feelings and mentally put them into the context of what just occurred.
8. Be prepared to discuss your reaction to what occurred during the role-play.

INSTRUCTIONS FOR CUSTOMER ROLE-PLAYS

1. Read the instructions carefully. Be sure to note both the role-play instructions and the information you are about to share.
2. Attempt to sense both the context of the buying situation and the individual facts presented in the instructions.
3. Let the salesperson initiate greetings, conversations, and concluding actions. React appropriately.
4. Supply only the customer information presented in the background description.
5. Supply customer information in a positive manner.
6. Do not attempt to throw the salesperson off track.

Part One
Developing a Sales-Oriented Product Strategy

PARK INN
I N T E R N A T I O N A L™

EMPLOYMENT MEMORANDUM 1

To: New Convention Sales Center Trainees
From: T. J. McKee, Sales Manager
Re: Your New Sales Training Program—"Developing a Product Selling Strategy"

I am extremely happy that you accepted our offer to join the Sales and Marketing Department. Enclosed is a copy of your new position description (see p. 415). Your first assignment as a trainee will be to learn about our product and what we have recently done to provide *total quality* customer service. *To apply what you are learning, I would like you to follow up on a customer service request I recently received. (See memo p. 447.)* You will use the following product information to complete the assignment:

AN AWARD-WINNING UPDATE (See pp. 417–419)

We have recently completed a *$2.8 million investment in our convention center.* This customer service investment included renovating all guest rooms and suites, lobby and front desk area, meeting rooms, restaurant and lounge, and enclosure of the swimming pool. Enclosed is a copy of the "Regional Architect's Award" that our facility won. We are the only facility in the Metro Area to have been presented with this award.

MEETING AND BANQUET ROOMS (See pp. 433–437)

The Park Inn offers convention planners just over *8,000 square feet of award-winning meeting space* in attractive, newly renovated meeting and banquet rooms. Our Central Park East and West rooms are conveniently located on the lobby level of the hotel. Each of these rooms can accommodate 180 people in a theater-style setting or 80 in a classroom-style setting. They also have a divider wall that can be retracted and, with the combined rooms, can accommodate up to 370 people.

The Top of the Park provides a spectacular view of the city through windows that surround that ballroom. This unique room, located on the top floor, can accommodate 225 classroom style, 350 banquet style, or 450 people theater style. Also located in the Top of the Park is a revolving platform area that slowly moves, giving guests a 360-degree panoramic view of the city. The Parkview Room, which is also located on the top floor of the hotel, can accommodate 150 people theater style and 80 people classroom style.

In addition for *groups booking 40 rooms or more, we provide one luxurious suite free*. This suite features a meeting room, bedroom, wet bar with refrigerator, and jacuzzi.

Be sure your clients understand that our meeting rooms *need to be reserved*. The first organization to sign a sales proposal for a specific date has the designated rooms guaranteed.

GUEST ROOM DECOR AND RATES (See pp. 429 and 437)

Our recent renovation included complete redecoration of all 250 of our large and spacious guest rooms. This includes all new furniture, wallcoverings, drapes, bedspreads, and carpets. Our interior designer succeeded in creating a comfortable, attractive, and restful atmosphere. *Seventy of our rooms are designated nonsmoking.*

(continued)

ROOM RATES (*continued*)

	REGULAR RATES	GROUP RATES	SAVINGS
Single	$88	$78	$10
Double	$98	$88	$10
Triple	$106	$96	$10
Quad	$114	$104	$10

A comparison of competitive room, parking, and transportation rates is presented on p. 437.

BANQUET MEALS (See pp. 423–426)

Our executive chef, Ricardo Guido, recently won the *National Restaurant Association's "Outstanding Chef of the Year" Award*. His winning entry consisted of the three chicken entrees featured on the enclosed menus. Ricardo served as Executive Chef at the five-star rated Williamsburg Inn in Williamsburg, Virginia, before we convinced him to join us six months ago. He personally oversees all our food and beverage operations. Ricardo, in my opinion, is one of the outstanding chefs in the country. His expertise and commitment to total quality customer service will help develop long-term relationships with our customers.

The enclosed dinner selections are only suggestions. We will design a special menu for your clients if they wish. A 16 percent gratuity or service charge is added to all group meal functions.

HOTEL/MOTEL AND SALES TAXES

All room rates are subject to the *local hotel/motel room tax, which is an additional 8 percent. In addition, all billings must have a 4 percent sales tax added. (The sales tax is not added to the hotel/motel tax and does not apply to gratuities.)*

LOCATION, TRANSPORTATION, AND PARKING (See map on p. 421)

We are located in a dynamic growing metropolitan area of over 400,000 people. With *convenient access, just off Interstate 237 at the downtown exits*, we are within a block of the nationally recognized, climate-controlled skywalk system. This five-mile system is connected to theaters, excellent shopping, the civic center, the metropolitan convention center, and a large selection of ethnic and fast-food restaurants. Our location offers guests the privacy they deserve during their meetings, and yet is close enough to downtown to enjoy all the excitement.

Free courtesy van transportation (also known as limousine service) is provided for our overnight guests to and from the airport, as well as anywhere in the downtown area. This service saves our guests who arrive by plane from *$8.00 to $10.00 each way.*

Guests who will be driving to the hotel will find over *300 parking spaces* available to them at *no charge*. Unlike other downtown properties, our free parking saves guests up to *$6.00 per day* in parking fees. For security purposes, we have closed-circuit camera systems in the parking lot and underground parking areas.

VALUE-ADDED GUEST SERVICES AND AMENITIES

Our convention center owners have invested heavily in the facility to provide our clients with *total quality service*, unmatched by our competition. Additional value-added services and amenities include:

- A large *indoor pool, sundeck, sauna, whirlpool, and complimentary Nautilus exercise room* in an attractive tropical atmosphere (see p. 431)
- "Cafe in the Park" featuring 24-hour continental cuisine seven days a week
- "Pub in the Park" where friendly people meet, featuring *free hors d'oeuvres* Monday through Friday, 5 to 7 P.M.
- Cable television with HBO
- A.V. rental of most equipment in-house, at a nominal fee (see p. 439)
- *Free coffee and donuts or rolls* in the lobby each morning from 6 to 8 A.M.
- A team of *well-trained, dedicated, and friendly associates* providing total quality front desk, food, and guest services
- Express check in
- Electronic key entry system
- Hair dryer, iron, and ironing board in each room
- Data port capabilities for laptop computers in each room
- Desk in each room
- Video message retrieval
- Voice mail
- On-command video (choice of 50 new release movies)

SALES LITERATURE (See pp. 417–445)

Included in your product training materials are photos, references, letters, room schedules, sales proposals, and other information that you will use in your written proposals and verbal sales presentations. When you move into outside sales, you should use these tools to create effective sales portfolios.

TOTAL QUALITY COMMITMENT

Our convention center is committed to *total quality customer service. Our Partnership Style of Customer Service and Selling* is an extension of our total quality process. The Total Quality Customer Service Glossary provides definitions of terms that describe our total quality process (see p. 416).

The Hotel and Convention center industry is mature and well established. Our sales and customer service plan is to *establish strong relationships, focus on solving customer problems, provide total quality customer service, and become a long-term hotel and convention center partner with our clients*. By utilizing this type of selling and customer service, your compensation and our sales revenue will both increase substantially.

TJM:ESS

Enclosures

POSITION DESCRIPTION—CONVENTION CENTER ACCOUNT EXECUTIVE

COMPANY DESCRIPTION

The Park Inn Convention Center is a total quality, full-service equal opportunity employment convention center that has recently made large investments in the physical facility, the food and beverage department, and sales department. Company culture includes an effective and enthusiastic team approach to creating *total quality*, value-added solutions for customers in a very competitive industry. The primary sales promotion tool is *Partnership Selling* with extensive marketing support in the form of photos, reference letters, team selling, etc. The company goal is to increase revenues 20 percent in the coming year by providing outstanding customer service.

SUCCESSFUL ACCOUNT EXECUTIVE WILL

1. Acquire necessary convention center company, product, industry, and competitive information through company training program
2. Be committed to a total quality customer service process
3. Develop a list of potential prospects in the assigned target market
4. Develop long-term, total quality selling relationships that focus on solving the meeting planner's convention center needs
5. Achieve a sales volume of $700,000 to $800,000 annually

WORKING RELATIONSHIPS

Reports to: Sales Manager
Works with: Internal Support Team including Food Service, Housekeeping and Operations, Customer Service and Front Desk; External Relationships including customers, professional associations, and industry personnel

SPECIFIC REQUIREMENTS

1. Must project a positive and professional sales image
2. Must be able to establish and maintain long-term relationships
3. Must be goal oriented with a plan for self-improvement
4. Must be flexible to deal effectively with a wide range of customers
5. Must be good at asking questions and listening effectively
6. Must be accurate and creative in developing customer's solutions
7. Must be clear and persuasive in communicating and negotiating solutions
8. Must be good at closing the sale
9. Must follow through on promises and assurances
10. Must have math skills necessary for figuring sales proposals

SPECIFIC REWARDS

1. Attractive compensation package that includes base salary, a commission of 10 percent of sales, bonuses, and an attractive fringe benefit package
2. Pride in working for an organization that practices total quality management in employee relations and customer service
3. Extensive sales and educational support
4. Opportunity for growth and advancement

EOE/AA/TQM

TOTAL QUALITY CUSTOMER SERVICE GLOSSARY

DIRFT—DO IT RIGHT THE FIRST TIME means being prepared, asking the right questions, selecting the right solutions, and making effective presentations. This creates repeats and referrals.

QIP—QUALITY IMPROVEMENT PROCESS means always striving to better serve our customers resulting in high-quality, long-term relationships.

TQM—TOTAL QUALITY MANAGEMENT means the commitment to support and empower people to deliver legendary customer service.

QIT—QUALITY IMPROVEMENT TEAM means a team approach to deliver outstanding customer service.

COQ—COST OF QUALITY means the ultimate lowering of cost by providing outstanding service the first time, so as to build a list of repeat and referred customers.

PONC—PRICE OF NONCONFORMANCE means the high cost of not meeting high standards. This results in correcting problems and losing customers. PONC also causes longer sales cycles and higher sales costs.

POC—PRICE OF CONFORMANCE means the lower costs of providing outstanding customer service and achieving a list of repeat or referred customers.

WIIFM—WHAT IS IN IT FOR ME means the psychic and monetary rewards in the form of personal enjoyment, higher salaries, commissions, or bonuses caused by delivering outstanding customer service.

QES—QUALITY EDUCATION SYSTEMS means internal and external educational activities designed to improve the quality of customer service.

YOU—THE MOST IMPORTANT PART OF QUALITY means the ongoing program of self-improvement that results in outstanding customer service and personal and financial growth.

THE ALL NEW PARK INN
(With an award-winning
2.8 million dollar renovation)

➡ Use the sales information on the reverse side of this page to explain and illustrate the benefits of the totally renovated and redesigned pool, with the sauna, whirlpool, sundeck, and Nautilus fitness center.

BRIGHT, COMFORTABLE, AND STRATEGICALLY ARRANGED MEETING ROOMS

Everything you need for outstanding meetings

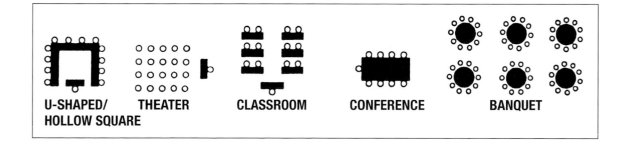

U-SHAPED/ HOLLOW SQUARE   THEATER   CLASSROOM   CONFERENCE   BANQUET

PARK INN
INTERNATIONAL™

555 West Side Street, Rockport, IL 50322
618-225-0925   Fax 618-225-9386

PARTS II to IV

PARK INN
INTERNATIONAL™

EMPLOYMENT MEMORANDUM 2

To: New Convention Center Account Executives
From: T. J. McKee, Sales Manager
Re: Your New Sales Assignment

Congratulations on successfully completing your training program and receiving your new appointment. You will find three challenges as you work with your customer's buying process.

Your *first challenge will be establishing relationships* with your customers. This will require that you do strategic planning before you can call on your client for the first time. Make sure your initial meetings focus on subjects of interest to your customer. Remember, "Customers don't care how much you know until they know how much you care."

Your *second major challenge will be to gain a complete and accurate understanding of your customer's needs*. You should prepare to ask good questions, take detailed and accurate notes, and confirm your customer's and your own understanding of their need. This process is a part of our total quality management program, which strives to provide total quality customer service. "To be an effective consultative salesperson you need to seek first to understand."

Your *third challenge as an account executive will be to make good presentations*. Our industry, as most others these days, is competitive and is characterized by many look-alike products and some price cutting. Always *organize and deliver good presentations* that focus on (1) providing solutions to immediate and long-term customer's needs, (2) negotiating win-win solutions to customer's concerns, and (3) closing sales that keep our facility full. This approach will give you a competitive edge and help you maintain high-quality, long-term profitable relationships.

Attached you will find a memorandum on an account I would like you to develop. Please follow the instructions included and provide me with appropriate feedback on your progress. I look forward to working with you on this account.

P.S. I want to compliment you on your excellent work on the B. H. Rivera account. B. H. called while you were attending a training meeting and said that your proposal and letter looked very good. Their organization was impressed with our facility, the apparent quality of our food, and your letter. Their organization will be scheduling a total of *11 more meetings* at our convention center during the next 12 months if everything works the way you describe it. Each of these sales will be reflected in your *commission checks*. Great work.

Part Two
Developing a Relationship Strategy for Selling

PARK INN
INTERNATIONAL™

SALES MEMORANDUM 1A

To: **Association Account Sales**
From: **T. J. McKee, Sales Manager**
Re: **Developing the Erin Adkins YWCA Account (Call 1, Establishing a Relationship Strategy)**

My sales assistant has called Erin Adkins, chairperson of the YWCA Physical Fitness Week program (see following contact report), and set up an appointment for you on Monday at 1:00 P.M. in Erin's office. During your first sales call with Erin, your call objectives will be to (1) establish a strong relationship, (2) share an appealing benefit of our property to create customer's interest, and (3) find out if your customer is planning any conventions in the future.

As we discussed during your training class, using Erin Adkins's prospect information presented below and the sales tools in your product strategy materials, your presentation plan should be to (see Chapters 3 and 10):

1. Use compliments, comments on observations, or search for mutual acquaintances to determine which topics Erin wants to talk about (Erin will only want to talk about three of these topics). This should set the stage for a good relationship.

2. Take notes on the topics of interest to Erin so we can add them to our customer information data bank for future calls. (Erin will share three new items of information on each topic of interest, if you acknowledge interest.)

3. Show and describe an appealing and unique benefit of our facility so we will be considered for Erin's future convention needs. (Consider using the Architect's Award, p. 419.)

4. Discuss any conventions Erin may be planning.

5. Schedule a call back appointment.

Name:	YWCA	Address:	16 Ruan Center	
Contact:	Erin Adkins	:		◄ **CONTACT**
Phone:	515-555-3740	:		**SCREEN**
Title:	Chairperson, Physical Fitness Programs	City:	Rockport	
Sec:	State:		IL	
Dear:	Erin	ZIP:	50322	

(McKee) Toni Bush, the Athletic Director of West College, supplied the following information about Erin Adkins:
1. Toni and Erin have a close relationship.
2. Erin just designed and built a new home.
3. Erin appears in local TV advertising about the YWCA.
Toni reports that in Erin's office you will observe the following:
4. An autographed picture of Tiger Woods
5. A Schwinn Air-dyne Fitness Cycle

◄ **NOTES WINDOW**

Comments, Compliments, and Questions	**Notes on New Items of Interest to Customer**
(Toni Bush suggested you mention his name.)	1. (Example) Toni Bush is my cousin
	2.
	3.
	1.
	2.
	3.
	1.
	2.
	3.

SALES MEMORANDUM 1B

To: Corporate Account Sales
From: T. J. McKee, Sales Manager
Re: Developing the Leigh Combs, Epic Design Systems Account (Call 1, Establishing a Relationship Strategy)

My sales assistant has called Epic Design Systems (see following contact report) and set up an appointment for you on Monday at 1:00 P.M. in Leigh's office. During your first sales call with Leigh, your call objectives will be to (1) establish a strong relationship, (2) share an appealing benefit of our property to create customer's interest, and (3) find out if your customer is planning any conventions in the future.

As we discussed during your training class, using Leigh Combs's prospect information presented below and the sales tools in your product strategy materials, your presentation plan should be to (see Chapters 3 and 10):

1. Use compliments, comments on observations, or search for mutual acquaintances to determine which topics Leigh wants to talk about (Leigh will only want to talk about three of these topics). This should set the stage for a good relationship.
2. Take notes on the topics of interest to Leigh so we can add them to our customer information data bank for future calls. (Leigh will share three new items of information on each topic of interest, if you verbally or nonverbally acknowledge interest.)
3. Show and describe an appealing and unique benefit of our facility so we will be considered for Leigh's future convention needs. (Consider using the Executive Chef 's Award, p. 425.)
4. Discuss any conventions Leigh may be planning.
5. Schedule a call back appointment.

Name:	Epic Design Systems	Address:	2401 West Towers	
Contact:	Leigh Combs	:	Suite 200	◄ **CONTACT**
Phone:	416–555–1000 X: CC:	:		**SCREEN**
Title:	Customer Service Manager	City:	West Rockport	
Sec:	Rhiannon	State:	IL	
Dear:	Leigh	ZIP:	50265	

(McKee) Linn Compiano, the Training Manager at Acme Supply Company, provided the following information about Leigh Combs:
1. Leigh has been on vacation.
2. Leigh is Linn Compiano's cousin.
Linn reports that in Leigh's office you will observe the following:
3. A large picture of Napoleon Bonaparte   ◄ **NOTES**
4. A degree from our state university   **WINDOW**
5. An extra-large bookcase containing many business books

Comments, Compliments, and Questions	Notes on New Items of Interest to Customer
(Linn Compiano mentioned that Leigh Combs just returned from a very enjoyable vacation.)	1. (Example) Spent one week in California 2. 3.
	1. 2. 3.
	1. 2. 3.

PORTFOLIO PRESENTATION MODEL

THREE-RING BINDER WITH POCKETS RECOMMENDED

PAGE 1 Summary of Customer's Buying Conditions 1. 2. 3. 4. 5. 6. (confirmation question)	**PAGE 2** Buying Condition 1	**PAGE 3** Proof Devices (could be more than one) (state benefits, ask confirmation question)	**PAGE 4** Buying Condition 2
PAGE 5 Proof Devices (state benefits, ask confirmation question)	**PAGE 6** Buying Condition 3	**PAGE 7** Proof Devices (state benefits, ask confirmation question)	**PAGE 8** Buying Condition 4
PAGE 9 Proof Devices (state benefits, ask confirmation question)	**PAGE 10** Buying Condition 5	**PAGE 11** Proof Devices (state benefits, ask confirmation question)	**PAGE 12** Buying Condition 6
PAGE 13 Proof Devices (state benefits, ask confirmation question)	**PAGE 14** Summary of Benefits 1. 2. 3. 4. 5. 6. (trial close)	**FRONT POCKET MATERIALS** Additional value-added pages as needed to overcome sales resistance and close the sale	**BACK POCKET MATERIALS** Additional value-added pages as needed to service the sale

PARK INN
I N T E R N A T I O N A L™

SALES PROPOSAL FORM

Customer Name: _____ Title: _____

Organization Name: _____ Telephone: _____

Address: _____

Date(s) of Meetings:_____

Kind of Meetings:_____

Buying Conditions (What the customer needs—be specific): _____

_____

_____

A. Meal Functions Needed

	Time	Description	Quantity	Price	Total
Meal 1					
Meal 2					
Other		(Beverages, setup fees, etc.)			

Total _____

Sales Tax _____

Service Charge _____

Total Meal Cost _____

B. Meeting and Banquet Rooms and Equipment Needed (describe time, date, and cost)

Total _____

Sales Tax _____

Total Meeting/Banquet Rooms and Equipment Charges _____

C. Guest Rooms Needed

Number of Rooms Needed	Description (dates, locations, special conditions)	Group Rate Per Room	Total Cost

Total _____

Room Tax _____

Sales Tax _____

Total Guest Room Charges _____

D. Total Customer Costs (from above)

A. $ _____ plus **B.** $_____ plus **C.** $_____ equals **Total Charges** $ _____

_____   _____

Authorized Signature   Date   Customer Signature   Date

_____   _____

Title   Title

Glossary

account screen The account or sales opportunity screen, as it is also called, provides information on each of the accounts in your prospect data base. Note the tabs across the top of the screen. Pressing any of these tabs automatically takes you to that object or type of information. The first thing to master about salesforce.com is that everything is organized around accounts.

active listening The process of sending back to the person what you as a listener think the individual meant, both in terms of content and in terms of feelings. It involves taking into consideration both verbal and nonverbal signals.

adaptive selling Used to describe sales training programs that encourage salespeople to adjust their communication style to accommodate the communication style of the customer.

added-value negotiating A negotiating process where both the seller and the customer search for mutual value so both feel more comfortable after a sale.

approach The first contact with the prospect, either face-to-face or by telephone. The approach has three objectives: to build rapport with the prospect, to capture the person's full attention, and to generate interest in the product you are selling.

assumptive close After the salesperson identifies a genuine need, presents solutions in terms of buyer benefits, conducts an effective sales demonstration, and negotiates buyer resistance satisfactorily, the assumption is that the prospect has already bought the product. The closing activity is based on the assumption that a buying decision has already been made.

balance sheet close A closing method that appeals to customers who are having difficulty making a decision. The salesperson draws a T on a sheet of paper and places captions on each side of the crossbar: reasons for buying now (left) and reasons for not buying now (right).

benefit A feature that provides the customer with personal advantage or gain. This usually answers the question, "How will the customer benefit from owning or using the product?"

body language A form of nonverbal communication that has been defined as "messages without words" and "silent messages."

bridge statement A transitional phrase that connects a statement of features with a statement of benefits. This method permits customers to connect the features of your product to the benefits they will receive.

business buyer behavior Refers to the organizations that buy goods and services for use in the production of other products and services that are sold, rented, or supplied to others.

business casual Clothing that allows you to feel comfortable at work but looks neat and professional.

business ethics Comprises principles and standards that guide behavior in the world of business.

buyer's remorse Feelings of regret, fear, or anxiety that a buyer may feel after placing an order.

buyer resolution theory A selling theory that recognizes a purchase will be made only after the prospect has made five buying decisions involving specific affirmative responses to the following items: need, product, source, price, and time.

buying conditions Circumstances that must be available or fulfilled before the sale can be closed.

buying motives An aroused need, drive, or desire that initiates the sequence of events that may lead to a purchase.

buying process A systematic series of actions, or a series of defined, repeatable steps intended to achieve a result.

call report A written summary that provides information on a sales call to people in the sales organization so that follow-up action will be taken when necessary.

caveat emptor A philosophy that states, "Let the buyer beware." The buyer is expected to examine the product and presentation carefully. Once the transaction is concluded, the business relationship ends for all practical purposes.

character Your personal standards of behavior, including your honesty and integrity. Your character is based on your internal values and the resulting judgments you make about what is right and what is wrong.

closed questions Questions that can be answered with a yes or no, or a brief response.

closing clue An indication, either verbal or nonverbal, that the prospect is preparing to make a buying decision.

coaching An interpersonal process between a sales manager and a salesperson in which the manager helps the salesperson improve performance in a specific area.

cold calling A method of prospecting in which the salesperson selects a group of people who may or may not be actual prospects and then calls on each one.

combination close With the combination close, the salesperson tries to use two or more closing methods at the same time.

commodity A product that is nearly identical or appears to be the same as competing products in the customer's mind.

communication style Patterns of behavior that others observe.

communication-style bias A state of mind we often experience when we have contact with another person whose communication style is different from our own.

compensation plans Pay plans for salespeople that combine direct monetary pay and indirect monetary payments such as paid vacations, pensions, and insurance plans.

complex buying decision Decisions that are characterized by a high degree of involvement by the consumer.

confirmation questions A type of question used throughout the sales presentation to find out if the message is getting through to the prospect. It checks both the prospect's level of understanding and the prospect's agreement with the presentation's claims.

confirmation step Reassuring the customer after the sale has been closed, pointing out that he has made the correct decision. This may involve describing the satisfaction of owning the product.

consideration Sales managers displaying consideration are more likely to have relationships with salespeople that are characterized by mutual trust, respect for the salesperson's ideas, and consideration for their feelings.

consultative selling An approach to personal selling that is an extension of the marketing concept. Emphasis is placed on need identification, need satisfaction, and the building of a relationship that results in repeat business.

consumer buyer behavior The buying behavior of individuals and households who buy goods and services for personal consumption.

contact screen The salesforce.com contact screen provides detailed information on each of the individuals within the account that may have influence on the sale process. Often referred to as members of the buying group, the individuals on these screens are accessed and used when strategically planning a sales call.

contract A promise or promises that the courts will enforce.

cooling-off laws The primary purpose of these laws is to give customers an opportunity to reconsider a buying decision.

cost-benefit analysis This involves listing the costs to the buyer and the savings to be achieved. A common approach to quantifying the solution.

cross selling Selling products to an established customer that are not directly related to products the customer has already bought.

culture The arts, beliefs, institutions, transmitted behavior patterns, and thoughts of a community or population.

customer relationship management (CRM) The process of building and maintaining strong customer relationships by providing customer value. A modern CRM program relies on a variety of technologies to enhance customer responsiveness.

customer service All those activities enhancing or facilitating the sale and use of a product or service, including suggestion selling, delivery and installation, assistance with warranty or service contract, securing credit arrangements, and making postsale courtesy calls.

customer service representative These people process reservations, accept orders by phone or by other means, deliver products, handle customer complaints, provide technical assistance, and assist salespeople.

customer strategy A carefully conceived plan that will result in maximum responsiveness to the customer's needs. The salesperson should develop an understanding of a customer's buying process, understand buyer behavior, and develop a prospect base.

demonstration A sales technique that adds sensory appeal to the product. It attracts the customer's attention, stimulates interest, and creates desire.

detail salesperson A salesperson representing a manufacturer, whose primary goal is to develop goodwill and stimulate demand for a product or product line. This person usually assists the customer by improving the customer's ability to sell the product.

differentiation Refers to your ability to separate yourself and your product from that of your competitors.

direct appeal close Involves simply asking for the order in a straightforward manner. It is the most direct closing approach.

direct denial Involves refuting the prospect's opinion or belief. The direct denial of a problem is considered a high-risk method of negotiating buyer resistance.

Directive style A communication style that displays the following characteristics: appears to be businesslike, displays a serious attitude, and voices strong opinions.

dominant buying motive The buying motive that has the greatest influence on a customer's buying decision.

dominance Reflects the tendency to influence or exert one's will over others in a relationship. Each of us falls somewhere on this continuum.

double win The view that "if I help you win, I win too."

electronic business Involves the use of intranets, extranets, and the Internet to conduct a company's business. Customer relation management (CRM) software is an important element of electronic business.

electronic commerce A specific form of e-business such as buying and selling activities conducted on the Internet.

emotional buying motives Motives that prompt the prospect to act as a result of an appeal to some sentiment or passion.

emotional intelligence The capacity for recognizing our own feelings and those of others, for motivating ourselves, and for managing emotions well in ourselves and in our relationships.

emotional links The connectors that link the salesperson's message to the customer's internal emotions and increase the chance of closing a sale—for example, quality improvement, on-time delivery, service, and innovation.

Emotive style A communication style that displays the following characteristics: appears to be quite active, takes the social initiative in most cases, likes to encourage informality, and expresses emotional opinions.

entry-level sales representative Anyone who is learning about the company's products, services, and policies, as well as proven sales techniques, in preparation for a sales assignment.

esteem needs The desire to feel worthy in the eyes of others, to develop a sense of personal worth and adequacy or a feeling of competence and importance.

ethics Rules of conduct used to determine what is good or bad. They are moral principles or values concerned with what ought to be done—a person's adherence to honesty and fairness.

expected product Everything that represents the customer's minimal expectations.

external motivation Action (taken by another person) that involves rewards or other forms of reinforcement that cause the worker to behave in ways to ensure receipt of the reward.

extranet A private Internet site that enables several companies to securely share information and conduct business.

feature Anything that a customer can feel, see, taste, smell, or measure to answer the question, "What is it?" Features include technical facts about such aspects as craftsmanship, durability, design, and economy of operation.

field salesperson A salesperson employed by a manufacturer who handles well-established products that require a minimum of creative selling. The position usually does not require a high degree of technical knowledge.

full-line selling This selling approach, sometimes called suggestion selling, is the process of recommending products or services that are related to the main item sold to the customer.

generic product Describes only the basic substantive product being sold.

group influences Buyer behavior is influenced by the people around us. Group influences are the forces that other people exert on buying behavior.

habitual buying decisions Decisions that usually require very little consumer involvement and brand differences are usually insignificant.

home screen The home screen presents dashboards that reminds one of the status of their prospecting and selling activities within their entire prospect data base. It provides a quick view of progress toward achieving the sales forecast.

incremental commitment When working on a large, complex sale, some form of commitment should be obtained during each step in the multicall sales presentation.

indirect denial Often used when the prospect's concern is completely valid, or at least accurate to a large degree.

The salesperson bends a little and acknowledges that the prospect is at least partially correct.

information-gathering questions Questions used to collect certain basic information from the prospect. These questions help the salesperson to acquire facts about the prospect that may reveal the person's need for the product or service.

informative presentation Emphasizes factual information that is often taken from technical reports, company-prepared sales literature, or written testimonials from people who have used the product.

inside salesperson A salesperson employed by a wholesaler who solicits orders over the telephone. In addition to extensive product knowledge, the inside salesperson must be skilled in customer relations, merchandising, and suggestion selling.

integrity Part of your character. It is what you have when your behavior is in accordance with your professed standards and personal code of moral values.

intermediate sales representative A salesperson who has broad knowledge of the company's products and services and sells in a specifically assigned territory. She maintains contact with established customers and develops new prospects.

internal motivation An intrinsic reward that occurs when a duty or task is performed.

interpersonal value Win-win relationship building with the customer that results from keeping that person's best interest always at the forefront.

management close Involving the sales manager or a senior executive to assist with the close.

marketing concept A belief that the business firm should dedicate all its policies, planning, and operation to the satisfaction of the customer; a belief that the final result of all business activity should be to earn a profit by satisfying the customer.

marketing mix The combination of elements (product, promotion, place, and price) that creates continuing customer satisfaction for a business.

modified rebuy A situation where the customer wishes to modify product specifications, change delivery schedules, or renegotiate prices.

multicall sales presentations A standard practice in some industries where products are complex and buying decisions are made by more than one person. The purpose of the first call is to collect and analyze certain basic information that is used to develop a specific proposal.

multiple options close With the multiple options close, the salesperson gives the prospect several options to consider and tries to assess the prospect's degree of interest in each.

need discovery The salesperson establishes two-way communication by asking appropriate questions and listening carefully to the customer's responses.

need-satisfaction questions Designed to move the sales process toward commitment and action. These are questions that focus on the solution.

negotiation Working to reach an agreement that is mutually satisfactory to both buyer and seller.

networking Networking is the practice of making and using contacts. It involves people meeting people and profiting from the connection.

new-task buy A first-time purchase of a product or service.

nonverbal messages "Messages without words" or "silent messages." These are messages we communicate through facial expressions, voice tone, gestures, appearance, and posture.

open questions Questions that require the prospect to go beyond a simple yes/no response.

opportunity management It should be viewed as a four-dimensional process consisting of time management, territory management, records management, and stress management.

organizational culture A collection of beliefs, behaviors, and work patterns held in common by people employed by a specific firm.

outside salesperson A salesperson, employed by a wholesaler, who must have knowledge of many products and be able to serve as a consultant to the customer on product or service applications. This position usually requires an in-depth understanding of the customer's operation.

partnering A strategically developed, high-quality relationship that focuses on solving the customer's buying problem.

patronage buying motives A motive that causes the prospect to buy a product from one particular company rather than another. Typical patronage buying motives include superior service, attractive decor, product selection, and competence of the salesperson.

perception A process whereby we receive stimuli (information) through our five senses and then assign meaning to them.

personal digital assistants These small pocket size organizers offer many features common to laptop computers.

personal selling Involves person-to-person communication with a prospect. It is a process of developing relationships; discovering customer's needs; matching appropriate products with these needs; and communicating benefits through informing, reminding, or persuading.

personal selling philosophy Involves three things: full acceptance of the marketing concept, developing an appreciation for the expanding role of personal selling in our competitive national and international markets, and assuming the role of problem solver or partner in helping customers to make complex buying decisions.

personality The thoughts, feelings, and actions that characterize someone.

persuasion The act of presenting product appeals so as to influence the prospect's beliefs, attitudes, or behavior.

persuasive presentation A sales strategy that influences the prospect's beliefs, attitudes, or behavior, and encourages buyer's action.

physiological needs Primary needs or physical needs, including the need for food, water, sleep, clothing, and shelter.

portfolio A portable case or loose-leaf binder containing a wide variety of sales-supporting materials. It is used to add visual life to the sales message and to prove claims.

positioning Refers to decisions, activities, and communication strategies that are directed toward trying to create and maintain a firm's intended product concept in the customer's mind.

postpone method When selling a complex product, it is often necessary to postpone negotiations until you can complete the needs assessment or acquire additional information regarding such things as final price or delivery dates.

potential product Refers to what may remain to be done, that is, what is possible.

preapproach Activities that precede the actual sales call and set the stage for a personalized sales approach, tailored to the specific needs of the prospect. This involves the planning necessary for the actual meeting with a prospect.

premium approach Involves giving the customer a free sample or an inexpensive item. This is an effective way to get the customer's attention.

presentation strategy A well-conceived plan that includes three prescriptions: establishing objectives for the sales presentation, preparing the presale presentation plan needed to meet these objectives, and renewing one's commitment to providing outstanding customer service.

probing questions Helps you uncover and clarify the prospects buying problem and the circumstances surrounding the problem.

product One element of the marketing mix. The term *product* should be broadly interpreted to encompass goods, services, and ideas.

product buying motives Reasons that cause the prospect to buy one particular product brand or label over another. Typical product buying motives include brand preference, quality preference, price preference, and design or engineering preference.

product configuration If the customer has complex buying needs, then the salesperson may have to bring together many different parts of the company's product mix in order to develop a custom-fitted solution. The product selection process is often referred to as product configuration.

product development Testing, modifying, and retesting an idea for a product several times before offering it to the customer.

product life cycle Stages of a product from the time it is first introduced to the market until it is taken off the market, including the stages of introduction, growth, maturity, and decline.

product strategy A well-conceived plan that emphasizes acquiring extensive product knowledge, learning to select and communicate appropriate product benefits that will appeal to the customer, and configuring value-added solutions.

promotional allowance A price reduction given to a customer who participates in an advertising or sales support program.

proof devices A proof device can take the form of a statement, a report, a testimonial, customer data, or a photograph.

prospect Someone who has three basic qualifications. First, the person must have a need for the product or service. Second, the individual must be able to afford the purchase. Third, the person must be authorized to purchase the product.

prospect base A list of current customers and potential customers.

prospecting A systematic process of identifying potential customers.

psychic income Consists of factors that provide psychological rewards; helps to satisfy these needs and motivates us to achieve higher levels of performance.

qualifying Examining the prospect list to identify the people who are most apt to buy a product.

quality control The evaluation or testing of products against established standards. This has important sales appeal when used by the salesperson to convince a prospect of a product's quality.

quantifying the solution The process of determining if a sales proposal adds value. Quantifying the solution is especially important in situations where the purchase represents a major buying decision.

quantity discount A price reduction made to encourage a larger volume purchase than would otherwise be expected.

rational buying motives Prompt the prospect to act because of an appeal to the prospect's reason or better judgment; include profit potential, quality, and availability of technical assistance. Generally these result from an objective review of available information.

reciprocity A mutual exchange of benefits, as when a firm buys products from its own customers.

reference group Two or more people who have well-established interpersonal communications and tend to influence the values, attitudes, and buying behaviors of one another. They act as a point of comparison and a source of information for a prospective buyer.

referral A prospect who has been recommended by a current customer or by someone who is familiar with the product.

Reflective style A communication style that displays the following characteristics: controls emotional expression, displays a preference for orderliness, tends to express measured opinions, and seems difficult to get to know.

relationship selling Salespeople who have adopted relationship selling work hard to build and nourish long-term partnerships. They rely on a personal, customized approach to each customer.

relationship strategy A well-thought-out plan for establishing, building, and maintaining quality relationships.

reminder presentation Sometimes called the reinforcement presentation. This assumes that the prospect has already been involved in an informative or persuasive presentation. The customer understands at least the basic product features and buyer benefits.

retail salesperson Salesperson who is employed at the retail level to help prospects solve buying problems. This person is usually involved in selling higher priced, technical, and specialty retail products.

return on investment A formula used to determine the net profits or savings from a given investment. It is a common way to quantify the solution.

role A set of characteristics and expected social behaviors based on the expectations of others. All the roles we assume may influence our buying behavior.

routing The procedure used to determine which customers and prospects will be visited during a certain period of time.

sales automation A term used to describe those technologies used to improve communications in a sales organization and improve customer responsiveness. These activities are used to improve the productivity of the sales force and the sales support personnel.

sales call plan A plan developed with information taken from the routing and scheduling plan. The primary purpose of the plan is to ensure efficient and effective account coverage.

sales call reluctance Includes the thoughts, feelings, and behavioral patterns that conspire to limit what a salesperson can accomplish.

sales engineer A person who must have detailed and precise technical knowledge and the ability to discuss the technical aspects of his products. He sometimes introduces new products that represent a breakthrough in technology.

sales forecast Outlines expected sales for a specific product or service to a specific target group over a specific period of time.

sales management The process of planning, implementing, and controlling the personal selling function.

sales territory A geographic area where prospects and customers reside.

satisfactions The positive benefits that customers seek when making a purchase. Satisfactions arise from the product itself, from the company that makes or distributes the product, and from the salesperson who sells and services the product.

seasonal discount Adjusting prices up or down during specific times to spur or acknowledge changes in demand.

security needs Needs that represent our desire to be free from danger and uncertainty.

self-actualization The need for self-fulfillment; a full tapping of one's potential to meet a goal; the need to be everything one is capable of being. This is one of the needs in Maslow's hierarchy.

self-image A set of ideas, attitudes, and feelings you have about yourself that influences the way you relate to others.

self-talk An effort to override past negative mental programming by erasing or replacing it with conscious, positive new directions. It is one way to get rid of barriers to goal achievement.

senior sales representative A salesperson at the highest nonsupervisory level of selling responsibility. She is completely familiar with the company's products, services, and policies; usually has years of experience; and is assigned to major accounts and territories.

situational leadership This leadership approach is based on the theory that the most successful leadership occurs when the leader's style matches the situation.

six-step presentation plan Preparation involving consideration of those activities that will take place during the sales presentation.

sociability Reflects the amount of control one exerts over emotional expressiveness. People who are high in sociability tend to express their feelings freely, while people who are low on this continuum tend to control their feelings.

social class A group of people who are similar in income, wealth, educational background, and occupational prestige.

social needs Needs that reflect a person's desire for affection, identification with a group, and approval from others.

solution A mutually shared answer to a recognized customer problem. In many selling situations, a solution is more encompassing than a specific product.

special concession close Offers the buyer something extra for acting immediately.

stall Resistance related to time. A stall usually means the customer does not yet perceive the benefits of buying now.

straight rebuy A routine purchase of items needed by a business-to-business customer.

strategic alliance Alliances that are achieved by teaming up with another company whose products or services fit well with your own.

strategic planning A managerial process that matches the firm's resources to its market opportunities. It takes into consideration the various functional areas of the business that must be coordinated such as financial assets, workforce, production capabilities, and marketing.

strategies The things that salespeople do as the result of pre-call planning to ensure they call on the right people, at the right time, and with the right tactics to achieve positive results.

stress The response of the body or mind to demands on it, in the form of either physiological or psychological strain.

structure Sales managers clearly defining their own duties and those of the sales staff. They assume an active role in directing their subordinates.

style flexing The deliberate attempt to adjust one's communication style to accommodate the needs of the other person.

subculture Within many cultures, the groups whose members share ideals and beliefs that differ from those held by the wider society of which they are a part.

suggestion selling The process of suggesting merchandise or services that are related to the main item being sold to the customer. This is an important form of customer service.

summary-confirmation questions Questions used to clarify and confirm buying conditions.

summary-of-benefits close Involves summarizing the most important buyer benefits, reemphasizing the benefits that will help bring about a favorable decision.

superior benefit A benefit that will, in most cases, outweigh the customer's specific concern.

Supportive style A communication style that displays the following characteristics: appears quiet and reserved, listens attentively to other people, tends to avoid the use of power, and makes decisions in a thoughtful and deliberate manner.

survey questions Questions used to collect information about the buyer's exiting situation and problem.

systems selling A form of strategic alliance that appeals to buyers who prefer to purchase a packaged solution to a problem from a single seller, thus avoiding all the separate decisions involved in a complex buying situation.

tactics Techniques, practices, or methods salespeople use during face-to-face interactions with customers.

target market A well-defined set of present and potential customers that an organization attempts to serve.

telemarketing The practice of marketing goods and services through telephone contact.

telesales The process of using the telephone to acquire information about the customer, determine needs, suggest solutions, negotiate buyer resistance, close the sale, and service the sale.

territory The geographic area where prospects and customers reside.

trade discount This discount covers the cost of services (credit, storage, or transportation) offered by channel intermediaries such as wholesalers.

transactional selling A type of selling that most effectively matches the needs of the value-conscious buyer who is primarily interested in price and convenience.

trial close A closing attempt made at an opportune time during the sales presentation to encourage the customer to reveal readiness or unwillingness to buy.

trial offer Involves giving the prospect an opportunity to try the product without making a purchase commitment.

unconscious expectations Certain views concerning appropriate dress.

upselling An effort to sell better quality products that will, in many cases, add value.

unbundling A strategy used to reduce the price by eliminating some items.

value-added product Product that exists when salespeople offer the customers more than they expect.

value-added strategies Adding value to a product with a cluster of intangibles such as better trained salespeople, increased levels of courtesy, dependable product deliveries, better service after the sale, and innovations that truly improve the product's value in the customer's eyes.

value proposition A value proposition is the set of benefits and values the company promises to deliver to customers to satisfy their needs.

value reinforcement This strategy involves getting credit for the value you create for the customer.

values Deep personal beliefs and preferences that influence your behavior.

variety-seeking buying decisions These are characterized by low customer involvement, but important perceived brand differences.

versatility Describes our ability to minimize communication style bias.

visualize To form a mental image of something you want to succeed at.

wardrobe engineering Combining the elements of psychology, fashion, sociology, and art into clothing selection.

Web site A collection of Web pages maintained by a single person or organization. It is accessible to anyone with a computer and a modem.

written proposals A specific plan of action based on the facts, assumptions, and supporting documentation included in the sales presentation. Written proposals vary in terms of format and content.

Credits

Name Index

Subject Index